MONKS AND MAGICIANS

MONKS AND MAGICIANS

Religious Biographies in Asia

Edited by

PHYLLIS GRANOFF
KOICHI SHINOHARA

MOTILAL BANARSIDASS PUBLISHERS
PRIVATE LIMITED • DELHI

First Indian Edition : Delhi, 1994

First Published : Ontario, 1988

ISBN: 81-208-1186-0

Also available at:

MOTILAL BANARSIDASS

41 U.A. Bungalow Road, Jawahar Nagar, Delhi 110 007
120 Royapettah High Road, Mylapore, Madras 600 004
16 St. Mark's Road, Bangalore 560 001
Ashok Rajpath, Patna 800 004
Chowk, Varanasi 221 001

PRINTED IN INDIA

BY JAINENDRA PRAKASH JAIN AT SHRI JAINENDRA PRESS,
A-45 NARAINA, PHASE I, NEW DELHI 110 028
AND PUBLISHED BY NARENDRA PRAKASH JAIN FOR
MOTILAL BANARSIDASS PUBLISHERS PVT. LTD,
BUNGALOW ROAD, DELHI 110 007

Table of Contents

INTRODUCTION

Every religious tradition in Asia has talked and written about certain people who somehow distinguished themselves in the service of their faith. Monks, nuns, kings, and pious lay devotees equally became objects of respect in their religious communities. Their lives and wondrous deeds were often recounted among the faithful, both as stories and songs that passed from mouth to mouth and as written texts. Lively depictions of miraculous deeds, detailed descriptions of images that suddenly appear with marvelous results, warm and humorous portrayals of daily life, all combine with careful and sober moral admonitions and intricate philosophical arguments to make these accounts as varied as their subjects themselves surely must have been.

Each major tradition in Asia preserves a vast written literature that we might well call "biographical" in the sense that it was written to recount the lives and deeds of certain individuals. Much of this material has remained largely unknown either outside its specific religious group or outside a small circle of interested scholars. It is often difficult to handle because of its sheer bulk and much of it remains untranslated into any Western language. This volume is a collection of essays on specific topics in the study of religious biographies in Asia and is meant as a first step in a long journey of understanding the particular puzzles and pleasures of this extensive literature.

The volume grew out of a grant that the three of us, Drs. Eva Dargyay, Phyllis Granoff and Koichi Shinohara, shared. We received a first grant from the Social Science and Humanities Research Council of Canada from 1984- 1986 and have since been awarded a second three-year grant to continue our study of Asian religious biographies. Each of us works on a specific tradition in Asia; Dr. Dargyay studies Tibet, Dr.Shinohara concentrates on China and Dr.Granoff on India. We decided that we would begin our investigations into religious biographies in Asia by each concentrating on the Asian tradition that we knew best and by sharing our findings with each other at conferences and in informal conversations. We found right away that although we had different backgrounds and were working on different cultural areas we definitely had common concerns and our biographies exhibited certain similar features.

We had each defined our field of inquiry by looking directly at what the tradition we were studying offers us as biographical literature. We approached our texts not as historical records but as religious texts, and our primary focus was the religious and cultural significance of the writings that we were studying. We were interested in the forms that religious biographies take in our areas and in the processes by which they might have been transmitted and preserved. Some of the questions we asked were: Who told these stories about religious figures and who wrote these biographies? Does a biography of a religious figure differ significantly from the biography of a secular leader in the same culture? On what occasions were religious biographies told or composed? How can we understand these texts in relation to other religious texts in their tradition, for example collections of miracle stories and pilgrimage tales? What possible models did a biographer have at his disposal when he wished to compose a biography? How does a biography of a religious figure differ from an autobiography, where autobiographical statements can be found in the subject's own writings? We hoped that by keeping these questions in mind we would come to an understanding of the precise nature of the stories that we found in our texts and thus to a definition of what constitutes religious biography across Asia and what its dynamics might be.

When we decided to present some of our findings as a collection of essays we asked some of our colleagues who shared our interest in religious biographies in Asia to contribute as well. We hope that in the future as we continue our research we will have many others joining us in our discussions and in later volumes that will reflect our collaborative efforts. We intend eventually to present a summary of the state of the field and a source book of translations of representative texts which at the moment must remain out of the reach of many potential investigators. If this book then is successful it will serve as an invitation to scholars from a wide range of disciplines who are already interested in Asian religious biography to join our discussions and as an enticement to others to look into this largely unexplored field for the first time.

A SURVEY OF FRENCH LITERATURE ON ANCIENT INDIAN BUDDHIST HAGIOGRAPHY

by André Couture

Except for debating over the exact nature of the final state of an *arhant* or over the possibility of laymen attaining this state, Buddhism can be said to have a rather well-established doctrine about sainthood. An *arhant* is one who already in this life has attained extinction (*nirvāṇa*). Three kinds of *arhants* are identified: first, the perfect Buddhas, who have found emancipation on their own and are ready to show others the way; then, the *arhant* properly so-called, those who have proved to be attentive auditors (*śrāvaka*) of the great Buddhas; and finally, the self-taught Buddhas known as Pratyekabuddhas. The state of *arhant* refers to the goal, the ultimate stage, but is preceded by three preparatory stages. The first is that of *srota-āpanna*, of "one who has entered the stream" leading to emancipation; the second, that of "one who returns but once" to earth (*sakṛd-āgāmin*); the third, that of "one who returns not" (*an-āgāmin*) otherwise than in a divine body.[1]

While the *Bodhisattva* ideal was not unknown to *Theravāda* sects, it was particularly developed by the Greater Vehicle. By multiplying fully awakened Buddhas, Mahāyāna Buddhism multiplied the number of those able to become Buddhas, but who have momentarily renounced Buddhahood out of compassion for those suffering in *saṃsāra*.[2] These saints practise outstanding virtues which they stretch to their ultimate limits.

This terminology with its fine distinctions, which was only gradually established, belongs above all to the *Abhidharma*. It determines categories of saints according to evaluative criteria belonging to a whole set of specific practices and doctrines. But monuments too have been erected to these saints, and biographies bear witness to these extraordinary individuals. These socio-historical testimonials confirm the vitality of the Buddhist religion; they have not yet received all the attention they deserve. This is not to say that the study of Buddhist hagiography has been totally neglected. Without at all pretending to be exhaustive, I would like to point out a number of important works produced in French which may serve as guidelines for research in this area. I shall begin by giving an account of essays on lives of the saints before examining a few important works on the one who is the elder and the preceptor of all *arhants*, the Buddha Gautama.

1. SAINTS OF ANCIENT INDIAN BUDDHISM

A. The contributions of Étienne Lamotte, André Bareau and Marcel Hofinger

Étienne Lamotte's *Histoire du bouddhisme indien* (1958) is the fullest account in French on the saints of ancient Indian Buddhism. In addition to general observations on the ideal of holiness of the monk and layman[3] and a summary of the discussions aspirations to sainthood provoked,[4] Lamotte has a lengthy section on Buddhist saints[5] and diverse observations on such saints as Ānanda and Mahākāśyapa,[6] on masters of the Vinaya such as Soṇaka, Moggaliputtatissa, Mahinda,[7] on the five Masters of Law,[8] on Piṇḍola Bhāradvāja,[9] on Gavāṃpati,[10] Kuṇḍopadhānīya,[11] *et al.* With his usual clarity, Lamotte offers an excellent introduction to this hagiography. This discussion may be supplemented by the often very abundant notes which serve as commentaries to his translations of the *Vimalakīrtinirdeśa*[12] and the *Mahāprajñāpāramitāśāstra* by Nāgārjuna.[13]

In 1959 André Bareau offered a series of brief portraits of the disciples of the Buddha. These include twenty monks, four nuns and nine laymen (including two women). Legends were spun around these characters; we even know of the previous lives of some of them. Bareau minutely summarized information from the tradition. The resulting synthesis provides us with a good idea of Buddhism's first saints. The author concludes:

> Here is a rich goldmine of documents on social structure, trades, economic and political life, customs, ideas, prejudices and even to the finest physical details of life. Now this goldmine, so valuable for

> sociologists and historians, has so far been only superficially exploited, due in good part to its very wealth, which discourages the efforts of the too few specialized researchers.[14]

Bareau intends to write a detailed article "on the relationship of the Buddha and his first disciples with their contemporaries,"[15] an outline of which has appeared in *Annuaire du Collège de France.*[16]

In these general studies on Buddhist hagiography, a rightful place must be given to the translation accomplished by Marcel Hofinger of the first part of the *Sthavirāvadāna* drawn from the *Vinaya* of the Mūlasarvāstivādins (*Bhaiṣajyavastu*). It contains thirty-six lives of saints. In addition to providing detailed notes covering incidental hagiographical references elsewhere in the ancient literature,[17] this work inquires into what the editor or compiler of all these legends intended.[18]

> In the form of stories, some better contrived than others, he has provided his readers with a moral teaching, a catechesis on the main commandments. There is nothing very scho-larly about this exposition: no scholastic subtleties, no lengthy theorizing, but Buddhist morality with its dogmatic assumptions is presented through live examples, mingled with homilies, parables and allegories.

There is no systematic teaching, but instead there are stories told to instruct.[19] Hofinger also reminds us that "most of the 'previous existences' belong with their details to Buddhist hagiography."[20] Transmigration is both the object of the teaching and a means to convey a particular ethical doctrine.[21]

B. Three particular studies of André Bareau

In discussing the youth of the Buddha in the most ancient *Sūtra-* and *Vinayapiṭakas,*[22] Bareau refers us back to the youth of the Buddhas Vipaśyin and Kāśyapa to whom were first attributed episodes later related to the historical Buddha. The lives of these Buddhas of the past are no less legendary for that, but we may see something of the process by which monks, hard pressed for edifying examples and bent on exalting their master to match the great Maurya sovereigns, managed to fill in the gaps which were evident in the opening pages of Buddha's biography. Bareau's papers can indeed help us to understand the process by which the Buddha was endowed with impressive predecessors. Two other of his essays will concern us here directly, one on ancient *stūpas*, the other on the Buddha's wife.

Bareau has in fact collected a significant amount of the information from the Chinese *Vinayapiṭakas* and certain other ancient texts on the building and veneration of *stūpas.*[23] He distinguishes between *stūpas* built over the remains of a body and those raised over the relics of a living person, notably his hair or finger-nail trimmings.[24] Burial seems to have been an ancient and customary practice, "the cremation rite being no doubt reserved, because more costly, to individuals most respectable."[25] Thus Buddhist monks were cremated, and this would seem to have been the origin of memorial *stūpas.* Reliquary *stūpas* are usually small in size: they serve to contain and protect precious relics and can be found inside memorial *stūpas. Stūpas* are built, two *Vinayas* tell us, for Tathāgata Buddhas, Pratyeka-Buddhas and Śrāvakas (as well as for *cakravartin* kings).[26] The diverse categories of Buddhist saints therefore were entitled to a cult, and texts state that reliquary *stūpas* were built for Kāśyapa,[27] Konakāmana,[28] Krakucchanda;[29] reliquary *stūpas*, memorial *stūpas* or oratories (*caitya*)[30] for the Buddha Gautama,[31] for solitary Buddhas[32] and for at least certain saints.[33]

This long article is certainly one of the most substantial studies on the veneration of saints in pre-Christian era Buddhism, during the period of the *stūpas* of Bhārhut and Sāñchī.[34] Here, in the author's own words, are some of the more important conclusions:

> Veneration rendered to *stūpas* is permeated with religious ideas foreign to the spirit of Buddhist doctrine as found in the *Sūtrapiṭakas*, and *Abhidharmapiṭakas.* The respect due to the Buddha personally or to the saints is transferred to their relics and from them to the monument containing them. [...] These ideas, from lay sources and being foreign to the spirit of Buddhism, gradually blended into Buddhist veneration of relics. The veneration is in fact inspired primarily by the marks of veneration rendered to living persons: circumambulating on the right, the head and right shoulder bared, greeting with hands folded, prostrating. Offerings are the gifts presented to important living

personalities, especially to kings [...]. In the minds of the faithful, this helps identify the Buddhas and Buddhist saints with these gods and geniuses, particularly so when death, Parinirvāṇa, has conferred upon the former the invisibility and mystery of the latter. From then on, into veneration will slip requirements of purity, inspired not only by propriety, convention and respect, but for religious reasons as well: like relics, like the saintly people they belonged to, *stūpas* are sacred.[35]

This veneration, born and bred among laymen, had become powerful enough shortly before our era to affect monks themselves, or at least some of them, and was spelled out in the canon of most of the schools. Of course we clearly see this intrusion encountering rather strong though variable opposition among monks since the Theravādins never admitted having the rules of this veneration recorded in the Pāli Canon, and the Sarvāstivādins, and to some extent the Mūlasarvāstivādins placed them in later parts of their *Vinayapiṭaka*. Monks nevertheless, just as laymen did, took part in this devotion, with rare restrictions (such as the one related to offerings of music), and adopted all its underlying ideas. Here we are far from those Abhidharma masters who denied any value in offerings presented to *stūpas*, and from those first-generation monks whom, if we are to believe the legend, the dying Buddha is said to have ordered not to be concerned about the body of the Tathāgata, since his funeral concerned only laymen. The mind-set reflected by this devotion seems

> close rather to that of the Mahāyāna, of that overflowing, encroaching devotion which enlarged the range of objects of veneration, Buddhas, Bodhisattvas, and completed the divinization of the sages, saints and heroes of ancient Buddhism.[36]

The success of the cult of the saints was no doubt rapid. Bareau, having noted that visiting holy places was a source of merit, thus summarizes the success this devotion enjoyed at a very early stage:

> These holy places spread rather rapidly, for the tumuli containing the ashes of great disciples and of monks who died and who were considered saints also became objects of veneration by the pious. Better yet, popular imagination, so fertile in India, consecrated a number of other places regarded as having been the scene of exploits of completely legendary characters, of the Bodhisattva in his previous lives or of the Buddha when he lived in a staggeringly remote past; tumuli were miraculously rediscovered underground.[37]

Bareau has also devoted a thoroughly documented essay to how mysterious a character the Buddha's wife was.[38] Relying on indications supplied by Étienne Lamotte[39] about the birth of Rāhula, he examines the main canonical texts and a few post-canonical texts capable of throwing light on the Bodhisattva's enigmatic wife. He notes only a few references to someone known merely as "Rāhula's mother" during the four centuries following the Blessed One's parinirvāṇa.[40] She it was who pointed out to her son the father who was to allow him to become a Buddhist monk and thus set foot on the Path to liberation. This allusive appellation shows the ignorance of ancient Buddhist writers: they do not seem to have known this woman's name and seemed to have "deduced her existence only from the fact that the young Rāhula, son of the Blessed One and one of his chief disciples, was a real-life character."[41] Such a character, a fleeting shadow, barely glimpsed in one single scene of three *Vinayapiṭakas*, was soon to become in the *Mahāvastu*,[42] then in the *Vinayapiṭaka* of the (late) Mūlasarvāstivādins, one of the main holy women of Buddhism. This glorious woman, bearing among other names the name of Yaśodharā, had practised striking virtues; with the Bodhisattva she formed a model couple, who had accumulated untold merits during numerous previous lives lived together.

> In the Mūlasarvāstivādin *Vinayapiṭaka*, the Bodhisattva's wife, under the name of Yaśodharā, has become the heroine of a whole series of coherent legends which exalt her and raise her to the summit of Buddhism's holy women, first as a lay person, Rāhula's mother and faithful companion of the future Buddha, then as a nun easily reaching *nirvāṇa*, for she has an absolutely flawless faith in the doctrine taught by the one who was her husband. Nevertheless she lost some of the humanness attributed to her by the tales of the *Mahāvastu* and which contributed to the charm of her personality, but this was offset by her gaining a nature on the way to divinization by the supernatural powers attributed to her.[43]

The disclosure of the account's splintering, the contradictions between the Pāli tradition and those of northern India, disagreement on this woman's name and her father's name, for example, allow one to grasp the mechanisms prevailing in the elaboration of the legend of her holiness. Bareau speculates that Rāhula's mother may have died shortly after the child's birth, which would explain the discretion of the order texts.[44]

C. The Przyluski School

To understand the timidity of French-speaking scholars of Buddhism when it comes to studying the great saints of early Buddhism, one has to stop and look back at Jean Przyluski and his disciples.

Przyluski insisted strongly on the geographical spread of Buddhism.[45] Legends and doctrines were transformed at the same time as they travelled from one region to another. To this thesis, which as such is generally agreed upon,[46] Przyluski joined a series of hypotheses deriving from his way of conceiving early Buddhism and meant to explain this religion's over-all evolution. According to Przyluski, the primitive image of the Buddha would have been "that of a sage freely talking with his disciples."[47] In reaction to the caste system and the privileges of the Brāhmaṇas, with Buddha Gautama appeared a religion founded on compassion and kindness toward all and accessible to men of every condition. This religion included a doctrine of retribution for acts (*karma*) and showed to all beyond all desires "the path to genuine contentment."[48]

> The holy man then would not be the Brāhmaṇa, but rather he who knows the truth and practises virtue. Religion must stop being formal, exterior to the individual; it is a principle of life, at once science, fervor and good will.[49]

Influences, originally Mesopotamian, would have gradually transformed this holy man in the eyes of the faithful into an universal monarch, whereas the trend among ascetics was to prefer seeing in him an Awakened One. Primitive Buddhism, fond of the happy medium, would have gradually patterned itself on brahmanical society.[50] It would have afforded more and more room to forest hermits cultivating solitary meditation (such as the ṛṣis or yogins of the brahmanical society). These Buddhist *āraṇyakas* "from all appearances, were to bring into the teaching of the Buddha the aristocratic doctrine of Arhatship.[51] The definite opposition between laymen and monks would not reflect the primitive situation, but a Buddhism modified by brahmanical concepts. Later, when Buddhism had been firmly established and the *vihāras* had spread, *āraṇyakas* "disappeared or rather joined the monastic Order."[52]

> The Order no longer included hermits, but Arhatship soon embodied the ancient ideal of the *āraṇyakas*. This haughty individualistic ideal of selfish salvation and of sterile contemplation took over more and more among the saints of the Lesser Vehicle, whereas the active and disinterested zeal of the first preachers was to persist in the school of the Greater Vehicle.[53]

Przyluski's interest in the great saints of ancient Buddhism rested upon these premises. The Brāhmaṇa convert Mahākāśyapa was the first of those to practise the ascetic precepts (*dhūtaguṇa*); he embodied holiness according to the criteria of a modified Buddhism. This *arhant* contrasted "with the Śākya *kṣatriyas* of which Buddha and Ānanda are the main representatives."[54] The following paragraph sums up well the importance the great heirs of the Buddha had for our writer:

> The truth of the matter is that Ānanda personified the ideal of primitive Buddhism, whereas Kāśyapa was the head of an already reformed Church. Ānanda might have been a saint in a Mahāsaṃgha assembly, but his popularity among the *bhikṣunīs* and laymen handicapped him among devotees of the monastic ideal. To embody this new ideal, new saints were needed: Kāśyapa, a strict observer of the *dhūtaguṇas*, Upāli, the theorist of the Vinaya. Ānanda lacked authority: the Buddha's servant, he was the friend of the humble; sensitive and compassionate, he was first of all a very great saint in a religion of love widely open to all. The monastic spirit required other virtues in the head of the Order: harshness to punish transgressions, a rough ascetic's energy.[55]

According to Przyluski, Ānanda, the intimate of the Master, ought to have been considered an accomplished saint of the primitive religion. The insinuations of which he is the object look strange; they lead one to think that the community had itself changed and had reasons to prefer Kāśyapa to him. To reach these conclusions Przyluski naturally relied on the list of primacies supplied by the *Aṅguttara-nikāya*,[56] but no doubt exaggerated the bearing of these texts. Furthermore, he laid down as a rule that the Buddhist brotherhoods of Kauśāmbī, Ujjayinī, Mathurā, etc. must have had their own saints, their own traditions, their own preferences in matters of dogma and discipline;[57] and for him, for instance, the *Aśokāvadāna* could not be understood otherwise than as "a praise of the Church of Mathurā and of its saints."[58]

In fact, Przyluski's theses on Buddhist saints are poorly supported and have often been contested. Przyluski wanted to explain Ānanda's expulsion from the Council of Rajagṛha by reference to the scapegoat myth.[59] Bareau has reviewed the history of this tradition and has shown that the expulsion of Ānanda must be considered a late addition.[60] According to

Bareau, the crucial scene is where Ānanda recites the *sūtras*. The scene in which it is discussed whether Ānanda is to be invited to the Council seems to him questionable, as well as the scene where he becomes an *arhant*. Bareau relates the trial to the public confession of the *pravāraṇā*, which must have taken place after the Council, which was carried on during the rainy season. Ānanda, not being an *arhant*, would have been the only one to have any faults to acknowledge. In his *Recherches sur la biographie du Buddha*, Bareau shows that in all likeness, the question of knowing whether Ānanda was an *arhant* or not never arose in the most ancient texts.[61] More likely, tradition raised Ānanda little by little

> from the humble rank of the Buddha's servant, almost a slave, to that of the Tathāgata's head of protocol, then finally, so much more impressive, to that of one of the wisest and holiest of the Fathers of the Buddhist Church.[62]

Przyluski also studied the figure of the holy monk Gavāṃpati, who was called to the Council of Rājagṛha and whose name means "master of the oxen," or keeper of the oxen, or first bull. But according to him, we are not to lend faith to the popular Buddhist etymology which assumed that this monk had been thus nicknamed because his feet were like a bull's and that he ruminated when he had had his fill of food.[63] He preferred to see in this bull a demon of drought and correlate his myth with other bull figures found in the ancient religion of the Asia of the monsoons, whose presence marked the passing from the dry season to the rainy season. The sacrifice of the *śūlagava* brahmanized in the *Gṛhyasūtras* would be part of the same cycle. Thus he concludes:

> In Buddhism, only the myth is kept, the sacrifice is missing. Beneath Gavāṃpati's robe can still be recognized an ancient god of Drought and Wind. The Council of Rājagṛha having taken place during the rainy season, the opening of the session naturally co-incided with the end of the dry season, that is, in mythical language, with the end of Gavāṃpati. But we cannot expect to see monks miming this event: being hostile to any bloody sac-

> rifice, Buddhism could not tolerate a rite similar to that of the *śūlagava.* This is why the Buddhist feast of entrance into the *varṣa* does not seem to have been accompanied by an extermination ceremony. Thus stripped of all ritual support, the myth may have fallen into oblivion. Actually, the Gavāṃpati episode is lacking in nearly all the Vinayas. [...] It was kept only in the *sūtras* and in the literature extending them: Commentaries and *Abhidharma.*[64]

Once again Przyluski's mythological interpretation has been criticized by Bareau in *Les premiers conciles bouddhiques.*[65] Bareau sees no reason to doubt that Gavāṃpati was a man's name, a monk's name, since there was talk of convening a council. He examines the development of this biography, notes the influence of a self-immolation motif used by the Mahāsāṅghika *Vinaya* in the story of Chou-t'i-na the bhikṣu, which preceded the account of Gavāṃpati, and shows how the normal burning and extinguishing the ritual pyre at funeral ceremonies must have become in these accounts the occasion for extraordinary wonders accomplished by the hero. Bareau also suggests that the ability to retain waters attributed to Gavāṃpati might have come from his earlier acquaintance with dike and bridge building.

> It would be good to know why Gavāṃpati, who played such a minor role in the Mahāsaṅghikas' account of the council, gained increasing importance in the post-canonical and Mahāyāna narratives. It is probably still too soon to answer these questions.[66]

Regardless of this particular case, it is clear, and Bareau often reminds us, that beneath a certain number of facts related in ancient texts are hidden legends or rites retrieved by Buddhism at a more or less ancient period. Nevertheless interpreting them will always be a delicate matter.

Tracking Przyluski's hypotheses, Dr. André Migot has produced an extensive paper on the figure of Śāriputra. His approach is lucid and has at least the merit of clearly stating the postulates it is based on. First Migot observes that it is preferable to begin the study of Buddhism with its saints, the reason being that "legends of the saints have been less reworked than those of the Buddha."[67] Each system or each school in fact tended transfer to the Buddha its own interpretation, so that the teaching ultimately attributed to the Buddha is an amalgamation of the most diverse interpretations. If it is true that behind every holy person can be detected a particular doctrinal tendency,[68] it would then be possible, thanks to hagiography, to strip the Buddha as it were of all the doctrinal coatings he has been given, and to point out precise periods in the evolution of Buddhism.[69] The saints, Migot observes, gained in popularity as the sects' ideas found an audience among the population, but the contrary is equally true: their legends faded out just as soon as their popularity.[70] "They were not deemed important enough to modify everything on their account."[71]

Migot agrees, though, that it is impossible to write an historical biography of Śāriputra: Migot proposes rather to bring out a "type" of saint, and "to look behind the 'type' for the tendency of the group he represents and the group's place in the history of Buddhist dogmas and sects."[72] Śāriputra, absent from the Parinirvāṇa-sūtras, does not seem to belong to the same traditional layer[73] as Ānanda and Mahākāśyapa. He may have been the greatest saint of the Vātsīputrīyas in the region of Kauśāmbī, and devotion to him may have been adopted by the Sthaviras. He would represent the typical unmovable arhant, which was developed under the influence of the monastic Buddhism, eventually to become the most venerated saint in the Pāli canon, model of preachers of the Good Law and author of the Abhidharma. It seems that such arhants were are not to be given more weight than the Buddhas of the past.

> What is striking [about these great Buddhist saints] is their lack of personality: each is stereotyped and represents not a live individual but an image of the Buddha conceived in the mind of a particular community, the figuration of a peculiar tendency, crystalized around an historical character who is in a way "depersonalized." The same sentences recur word for word in the mouths of divers characters, the same clichés are used indifferently for the Buddha and his disciples, depriving the characters of their vitality, transforming them into interchangeable manikins.[74]

Thus these saints are to be considered rather as "types", each embodying a peculiar form of Buddhism and not to be seen as strong personalities with their own peculiar stamp.[75] Migot's paper does not seem to have been noted by specialists. It surely merits serious attention, and no doubt, considerable refinement on the basis of further research.[76]

Another arhant on whom Przyluski has speculated is Piṇḍola Bhāradvāja. Sylvain Lévi and Édouard Chavannes[77] have shown interest in this saint, but only as a member of a group of sixteen or eighteen protectors of the Law whose veneration spread into China rather belatedly.[78] Przyluski was the first to draw attention to this personality in his own right, but this was because he believed the writers of Kauśāmbī had transformed Piṇḍola into a local saint as Mathurā writers had done with Upagupta.[79] John S. Strong has shown the weakness of such a postulate[80] and of the constructions based on it. Strong has studied the different elements of the legend and of the veneration of Piṇḍola. His study is exemplary, showing clearly both the limits of Przyluski's intuitions and the path that must be followed to disentangle Indian Buddhist hagiography.

The Przyluski school[81] has in fact displaced the stress from philosophical Buddhism to Buddhism as a religion, away from the Buddha toward the saints. Hagiography of the monks seems to allow closer contact with Buddhism as a popular religion than we may gain from the many crystallizations that accumulated around the central personality of the Buddha.

2. BUDDHIST HAGIOGRAPHY AND STUDIES ON THE BIOGRAPHY OF THE BUDDHA

The results of the above part one may be disappointing, but let us not forget that in Buddhism the Buddha is not first of all a divinity, he is the first saint (*arhant*). Even though his state of *samyaksaṃbuddha* gives his activity and teaching an unequalled prestige in our *kalpa*, he remains no less the model of all *arhants*, then of all the *bodhisattvas*. This is an old notion: "The career and nature of Buddha and of his disciples are identical, particularly of those who become Arhants."[82] It is not surprising that the Buddha's conversion, speech, deeds, etc. become clichés hagiographers love to repeat.

Buddhist hagiography then cannot be confined to conventional saints. Works on the biography of the Buddha make up a sort of first chapter able to supply a number of useful guidelines. This at least will be our perspective as we skim through the works of those three great scholars of Buddhism, Étienne Lamotte, Alfred Foucher and André Bareau, as they relate to the Buddha's biography.

A. Étienne Lamotte

Étienne Lamotte's main contribution to the biography of the Buddha is perhaps to have fully sensed and expressed the change that was going on in this type of studies. After reviewing in detail Western works on the subject, Lamotte concludes that the mythological or rationalistic methods are inadequate.

> Indeed, from the very first documents, the legend of the Buddha is set in its broad outlines, with the wondrous integral to it; nor is there anything to warrant affirming that the episodes which seem to us reasonable and normal are historically better established than the miraculous events which baffle the mind.[83]

Rather than trying to extract a core of historically likely events, it is better to look for more limited objectives thus defined: "to try, by the criticism of texts and figured monuments, to perceive the successive states of tradition and, when possible, to explain their evolution."[84] These concerns lead the author to distinguish five stages in the formation of this biography.

> Inasmuch as any chronology can be found in an endlessly repetitive literature, the disciples of Gautama became interested first in the psychological crisis which made Śākyamuni an illuminate in his final days, then in the miracles at his birth (*sūtra period*); their attention then turned to the beginnings of his public ministry and the main facts marking it. However, they did not yet try to class them chronologically (*vinaya period*). To fill the gap between the Birth and the Great Departure they contrived a kind of gospel of the infancy and youth on the matter of young Gautama's exploits and marriage (*autonomous and incomplete "Lives" period*). They then completed this biography by a summary, claiming to be chronological, of his public ministry, ending with the narrative of the Paranirvāṇa and funeral (*Mūlasarv. Vin. and related texts period*). Finally they

> reported the life of Śākyamuni according to the assumed plot of the tale of the Buddhas (*Singhalese period*).[85]

The methodological perspective is clear. The study of the Buddha's biographies (but this stands for saints too) informs us first about the biographers themselves, and the setting in which they lived. We have no direct view of the period in which the Buddha lived: "he seems to escape historical investigation."[86] In this area "the criterion of likelihood" is very hard to establish.[87] A field of autonomous discipline, the study of the legend of the Buddha is limited to discerning the "successive states of the legend of the Buddha,"[88] and allowing us to discern the causes of its development. These causes are sketched in *Histoire du bouddhisme indien*,[89] where at several points Lamotte is indebted to the analyses of Alfred Foucher.

B. Alfred Foucher

Alfred Foucher learned of Étienne Lamotte's article on "La légende du Buddha" only after the printing of the text and foreword of his *Vie du Bouddha.* On pages 349-50 he briefly explained this fact and in spite of his embarrassment rightly published a book which surely marked an important stage in Buddhist hagiography.

The holy people who accompanied the Buddha are occasionally discussed in this book. We see how Ānanda received that passionate devotion which Mahāyāna adepts thought they had invented and which was ready to overflow upon the world. Mahākāśyapa incarnated the almost superhuman type of monk, indifferent to the suffering of others and completely cut off from the world.[90] The author has chosen, however, to study the Buddha and refused to turn his book into a portrait gallery.[91]

Throughout his project, Foucher wanted to remain faithful to the historical method and tries to blaze a new trail between faith and hypercriticism,[92] between the mythological interpretation of Senart, who forgets the Buddha's humanity, and Oldenberg's euhemerism, which suppresses his divinization. Foucher accepts Buddhist reality in its wholeness. But beyond the distortions of legend, he believes he is able, up to a point, to reestablish facts. He relies for this on his first-hand experience in India and on his archaeology training. He lays out his case in a final annotation:

> [...] no European exegete quoted [by Lamotte] has, to our knowledge, begun by completing the eight great Buddhist pilgrimages, or studying on site or in Indian museums the images which popu-

> lar devotion has fed on for so long and which popular devotion so multiplied that neither time nor Moslem iconoclasts have been able to completely destroy them. The experience is within reach of everyone: whoever takes the trouble to repeat it will, we believe [...], see all the life and realism the background of rice-fields and the figuration of legendary scenes can yet today breathe into the old texts which, lost abroad, have all but dried up on the shelves of our libraries. Refreshed in the land of their birth—like the Manes in the Odyssey when they had drunk a bit of sacrificial blood—, they suddenly recover their memory and at times even the accent of truth.[93]

At the very outset of his book, Foucher stands out as an historian unwilling to disregard any aspect of the personality he is studying. He admits

> that a particle of mystery will always remain at the bottom of the crucible which no known reagent and no word in the vernacular will define. That is the secret of these unusual people, and since this secret, less perceived than felt by their contemporaries, was right away clothed in mythical accretions, it is to be feared that certain features of theirs will forever escape us.[94]

The Buddha then was an ordinary human being with his halo of more or less incommunicable experience; it is no less true that he has been transformed by the imagination of his followers. Both these faces of the Buddha are historical: texts and archaeological remains tell us about them. Now these two levels of reality held to be appreciated for what they are. Foucher goes as far as to value the psychological truth of the traditional version of the infancy and youth narratives when it is unanimous among hagiographers.

> After all, what we like to call historical truth is only too often nothing but the guess researchers in good faith have finally agreed upon: the hagiographers'

> unanimity will at least in the present case give us what might be called the traditional truth.[95]

However, to understand this biography, Foucher begins by inviting his Western reader to become familiar with elements of Buddhist doctrine which might surprise him (especially *karman* and transmigration).

> As human as it is and in many respects so close to the "lives of the saints" which we read in the *Golden Legend*, we shall understand it [the biography of the Buddha] only thanks to a kind of focusing or, if it is preferred to put it that way, a foregoing optical accommodation.[96]

This already assumes that the Buddhist hagiographers' interpretation passed through the prism of a certain vision of the world, of certain beliefs, of certain dogmas. Foucher insists that his life of the Buddha bears entirely on the historical life of the Buddha and on his search in this life for Supreme Liberation. In leaving the world to become a wandering, begging monk, the Bodhisattva

> will only be conforming to custom of those around him who right then were seeking a solution to the unsolvable problem of destiny. Whether it pleases us or not, it is according to this guiding idea that we must pursue our critical examination of Buddhist texts.[97]

Unknowingly or not, hagiographers oriented the narratives of the infancy and youth of the Buddha toward the Awakening of the Buddha. This required stressing the contrast between the kind of existence he was giving up and the one his religious vocation was urging him to embrace,[98] showing that the child was already inclined toward the highest meditations, dramatizing according to the conventions of the time his departure from the world,[99] underlining that way of outdoing oneself characteristic of the Awakened One. "The Buddha soars too high above the passions of his visitors to share any of their exploits; he is no longer an actor but a spectator of life's drama."[100] In other words, the Buddha does not live outside his Awakening: his historical truth remains imperceptible outside this experience, and for centuries the work of hagiographers consisted in preparing the narrative of this Awakening and validating it throughout the life of the Buddha. To reflect more exactly the Indian worldview, Foucher unhesitatingly wrote another book entitled *Les vies antérieures du Bouddha.*[101] For in the mind of Buddhists the present life has been preceded by a whole series of past experiences which are an integral part of the "history" of a Buddha.

Still, to penetrate the secret of this exceptional human being, Foucher needed to discover the hagiographers' processes of fabrication.[102] He notes literary clichés,[103] embellishments,[104] exaggeration to edify,[105] an editor's bewilderment, which may prove historicality,[106] conventions,[107] contradictions, apparent or not.[108] In spite of efforts to free an historical fact[109] or the initial fact,[110] he must at times give up trying to sort out the real from the fabulous.[111] He often uses the criterion of likelihood,[112] but notes its fragility:

> Historians are once again to be pitied: although deprived of any criteria of precision, they are charged with fixing the elusive uncertainty of human affairs, for likelihood and unlikelihood, the one as well as the other, especially in religious matters, can sometimes be the face of what is true, at other times the mask of what is false.[113]

Foucher's main contribution is due to his archaeology training and his care to connect the legend with Indian realities. He aimed not to reconstruct the psychological evolution of the Buddha from texts, but to understand the documents which have come down to us. Rather than ordering scenes chronologically (now unfeasible for the years throughout his preaching), he preferred allotting them geographically, which seemed to him to correspond to one of the characteristic forms of Indian mentality.[114] It is impossible "to separate the biography of the Buddha from the *geographia sacra* of Buddhism."[115] This hypothesis (which has its own limitations) allows him to build his work around the four great pilgrimages of Buddhism (Kapilavastu, Bodhgayā, Benares and Kuśinagara) and the four secondary pilgrimages (Sāṃkāsya, Śrāvastī, Rājagṛha and Vaiśālī).[116] What the master's last biographers would have arranged in the form of a continuous biography would have derived mainly from manuals used by pilgrims (*māhātmya*), which were composed to exalt the wonders of a holy place and which are attested by a pilgrim such as Hiuan-tsang.

> A law can be stated: in India, only those memories have survived, before being noted down in writing, that are related to a particular place or object, but on the other hand, these memories were apt to last as long as the material things which recalled them.[117]

From there came the notion of narrative cycles attached to a particular city, which does not mean these accounts become therefore historical. "A fiction, just because it has become localized, is not thereby historical."[118]

A final observation was made by Foucher concerning miracles which adorn the life of the Buddha (and of so many saints). Must we expect to find acts contrary to the laws of nature or healings obtained beyond all expectations? It seems not. The Buddha does not heal bodies, sickness and death are the natural lot of human beings. The Buddha does not intervene to counter the effects of acts. His birth and death are wonders equal to the multiplication of his image at Śrāvastī. The extraordinary powers he demonstrated do not exceed nature; his opponents could do as much. Nothing in these extraordinary saints which the Buddhas are can be the effect of chance.[119] Miracles, far from being the effect of a single act of supreme freedom, belong to an act's determinism. Having arrived at the end of a long series of existences, the Buddha Gautama, in the same way as his distant predecessors, had acquired the merit that allowed him to perform such feats. We must accept that "these narratives of previous births are integral parts, in the minds of Buddhists, of the history of their Master",[120] as they cannot be disassociated from the history of any saint. It is true that such wonderworks strike the imagination, attest to the Buddha's high degree of holiness and create his renown as a savior. Foucher stresses here that we must beware of preconceived ideas that we might have about miracles, whose meaning is to be specified according to each religious context. If wonderworks are only manifestations of divine powers, and if these divine powers are far below the purest spiritual experience, then of course a saint will be able to use them as needed; but we must understand too that inconsiderate and selfish exercise of these powers can only bind a person to saṁsāra and delay reaching nirvāṇa.[121]

C. André Bareau

The works of André Bareau are primarily very technical comparisons of Pāli, Sanskrit, Chinese, and sometimes Tibetan sources, for key episodes in the biography of the Buddha. Our purpose is not to summarize an unfinished endeavor already brimming with original ideas, new analyses and promising intuitions. Here we shall note only certain elements apt to throw light on Buddhist hagiography in general.

At the outset Bareau stressed that it is necessary to insist on how important it is to compare (when possible) all ancient documents available. This allows us to identify literary procedures,[122] pick out clichés,[123] stereotypes,[124] telescoping narratives,[125] interpolations,[126] doublets,[127] awkward phrases,[128] diverging versions,[129] contrasts,[130] even contradictions,[131] misinterpretations,[132] or even absurdities.[133] Comparison also allows a scholar to determine the relative antiquity of certain episodes,[134] to define stages in the evolution of a legend,[135] to show that different parts of a sermon were composed separately,[136] to discover revisions,[137] to show how a tradition relating to an historical fact wound up by being used to edify,[138] etc.

To illustrate the method Bareau uses, it would be helpful to recall his interpretation of the Benares sermon.[139] Historical investigation shows in fact that only the Vinaya texts know of this sermon; the Theravādins' Pāli *Suttas* do not mention it and the Sarvāstivādins' small *Sūtras* (as well as a small *sūtra* in the Ekottara-Āgama) give only the opening paragraph. These disturbing facts, the scholarly exegete observes, lead one to believe that the text of this first sermon as we find it in the *Vinaya* of the Theravādins, Mahīśāsakas and Dharmaguptakas "is not only apocryphal but late." He then proceeds in a way typical of his approach:

> If this is indeed so, important consequences follow regarding the history of Buddhist doctrine. For the thesis of the four holy Truths would have developed rather late and would not be, as is generally believed, the very foundation of Buddhist thought. Furthermore, the fact that an attempt was made at a certain period to make it the theme of the Buddha's first sermon while at the same time giving this sermon prime importance as is shown by his legendary name of "setting in motion the wheel of the Law" proves that at this moment there appeared and rapidly developed the tendency, soon to triumph, of making the four holy truths the core doctrine. Per-

haps the silence of our two *Sūtras*, a silence which has not been broken by later generations of disciples, is just as much resistance to this tendency as it is witness to an ancient ignorance concerning the theme of the first sermon. Besides, while both *Sūtras* are silent on the sermon on the four Truths, they shortly after minutely reproduce the sermon on the five qualities of desire. This latter and its doctrinal content then are what they wanted to foster, which is no doubt the core around which they developed because it expounds the solution provided by the Buddha to the problem they presented, and this is why their authors place it at Benares, right after the conversion of the first five disciples, the rest being added afterwards, bit by bit, to serve as an introduction. Thus we see coexisting within the same sect diverging traditions on the meaning of the Benares sermon, traditions which probably turned up in most schools, which seems to indicate for this phenomenon a very early date, prior to the great schisms of the fourth and third centuries before our era. This also shows that people were more or less vaguely aware of the artificial character of the forenamed traditions and that there would be no point in pretending that one or the other is authentic and to look for history where there is but pious discourse. If, for the reasons presented above, the tradition represented by the two *Sūtras* seems to us more ancient, it in no way follows that we must consider it as faithful to historic reality. Its only merit is to show us that in a distant past, at least some Buddhist doc-

> tor knew nothing of the theme of the first sermon or refused to consider the four holy Truths as such.[140]

Another extremely important element in Bareau's analyses is the notion of redactional milieu. This problem of course is not simple, and has given rise to all kinds of hypotheses. However, many signs tend to show that the most ancient accounts which have come down to us actually come from monastic milieus especially interested in the Awakening of the Buddha and related teachings.[141] At the same time this evidence explains the scarcity of historical details on the years before the Awakening.

> Of course no writer has felt obliged to offer his readers a complete and coordinated biographical ensemble of the Buddha or even of any part of it, and this lack of interest shown in monastic circles concerning the life of the Blessed One explains the tiny amount of historical data or seemingly such that we believe we have laid bare in the course of our investigation.[142]

In the course of his work, Bareau marks down all kinds of episodes, drawn especially from the Vinayapiṭakas, which aim at justifying rites such as ordination, but also various devotional practices. These etiological accounts may have been "borrowed from accounts of Uruvelā and Benares local guides used to justify veneration rendered in certain well specified places in the neighborhood of these two agglomerations.[143] The author clarifies a little further on that these texts would have been slowly formed "outside the circle of canonical authors, no doubt in lay circles, in those very different places of pilgrimage as were Uruvilvā, Benares and Rājagṛha, during the one or two hundred years preceding the coming of Aśoka."[144] They would have subsequently been incorporated into the different canons. Thus we can believe these portions of biography represent "the oldest witnessing of interest shown for devotional practices by monastic circles charged with compiling, editing and preserving canonical books, and especially collections of rules governing religious life."[145]

Many other aspects of these *Recherches* . . . would be worth mentioning, but what first strikes the reader of these works is that they are at the confluence of the works of Lamotte and Foucher, profiting from the intuitions of both. By delving into the problem of redactional milieus, Bareau has come to define the formational stages of the legend of the Buddha; he also endorses the notions of geographical rooting and of cycles,[146] of ties with pilgrimage centers or with archaeological documents dear to Foucher.[147] He discovers at every crossroad features of popular religion (worshipping serpents, trees, etc.) in pre-Christian Ganges Valley India. These traditional biographies thus become, less a historical document on the man himself, as so many witnesses over the five or six centuries following the death of the Buddha Gautama.

Again, let us add that ultimately what these studies forcefully bring out is how freely Buddhist writers received accounts deemed edifying.[148] A relatively simple doctrine and a few ancient memories grew little by little into a heap of often contradictory traditions of fictional episodes composed to edify.[149] Anyone claiming to solve unfailingly the enigma of historical likelihood would be shrewd indeed. It can safely be said of Buddhist hagiography in general that the teaching of the Good Doctrine outranks by far what we call attention to history; or as Bareau says, in the minds of hagiographers, the needs of preaching came before concerns over history.[150]

Conclusion

The studies gathered here indicate the importance of the publications produced so far in French to reach a better understanding of the hagiography of ancient Indian Buddhism. Great effort has been concentrated on the biography of the Buddha, and with the present state of the sources, it was no doubt methodologically right to choose this orientation. However, we believe we have shown in this survey of the literature that it was impossible to probe the life of the Buddha without touching more or less directly those saints who associated with him or were inspired by his example. Still, contrary to Chinese and Tibetan Buddhism,[151] where hagiography was a favourite path of missionary propaganda, Indian Buddhist literature in Sanskrit and Pāli developed little biography for its own sake. Despite this, it is still possible to collect very eloquent records on the great saints of early Buddhism.[152]

"I call empty the world in which there are no holy men having attained the Path." This saying placed on the lips of the Buddha about to leave the world in the *Ekottara-Āgama*[153] could rightly evoke at once the fulness of the Buddhist way and that of a world in which saints are many and abundantly venerated by devotees. It is to be hoped this area of study will stimulate the interest of researchers and that the already remarkable works on the biography of the Buddha will continue to enrich this area of study.

(Translated by Robert Jollet)

NOTES

1. André Bareau, Art. "Sainteté—Le bouddhisme", *Encyclopaedia Universalis*, Tome 14, Paris, Encyclopaedia Universalis France S.A., 1972, pp. 605-606; and Joseph Spae, "Modèles de sainteté dans le bouddhisme", *Concilium*, 149, 1979, pp. 95-105.—Louis de La Vallée Poussin has shown that Buddhist sanctity ultimately headed in other directions, which "orthodoxy" tried to reconcile. Expounding a sūtra of the Aṅguttara (III, 355), he distinguishes those who go in for ecstasy (dhyāna) and experience nirvāṇa in their body from those who adhere to doctrine and fathom it with their intelligence (prajñā). He has gone over these two tendencies pervading the history of doctrines (Louis de La Vallée Poussin, *La morale bouddhique*, Paris: Nouvelle librairie nationale, 1927, 256 p.: esp. 108-17) Musīla and Nārada (Samyutta II 115) would be fairly representative of these two types of saints (cf. Louis de La Vallée Poussin, "Musila et Narada," *Mélanges chinois et bouddhiques* (Institut belge des hautes études chinoises), 5, 1937, pp. 189-222).

2. Walpola Rahula, "Idéal du bodhisattva dans le Theravāda et le Mahāyāna", *Journal Asiatique*, 259, 1971, pp. 63-70.

3. Étienne Lamotte, *Histoire du Bouddhisme indien. T. I. Des origines à l'ère Śaka*, Louvain: Institut orientaliste, coll. "Bibliothèque du Muséon" 43, 1958 (1967 reprint), pp. 66-82.

4. *Ibid.*, cf. pp. 89-92; 300-301; 317-19.

5. *Ibid.*, pp. 765-75.

6. *Ibid.*, pp. 136-38; 317, etc.

7. *Ibid.*, pp. 223-25.

8. *Ibid.*, pp. 226-32; 363-64.

9. *Ibid.*, pp. 266-67; 354-55.

10. *Ibid.*, pp. 141, 149.

11. *Ibid.*, p. 427.

12. Étienne Lamotte, *L'Enseignement de Vimalakīrti (Vimalakīrtinirdeśa)*, traduit et annoté par Étienne Lamotte, Louvain: Institut orientaliste, coll. "Bibliothèque du Muséon" 51, 1962.

13. Étienne Lamotte, *Le Traité de la Grande Vertu de Sagesse de Nāgārjuna* (*Mahāprajñāpāramitāśāstra*). Tome 1 à 5, Louvain: Institut orientaliste, coll. "Bibliothèque du Muséon" 18 (for the two first tomes), "Publication de l'Institut Orientaliste de Louvain" 2, 12, 24 (for the three last tomes), 1949-80.—These are the references to the more important notes, with numbers referring to pages of the *Mahāprajñāpāramitāśāstra* (references, when needed, to the *Vimalakīrtinirdeśa* are abbreviated *Vim*). Ājñāta Kauṇḍinya, 102, 1426, 1576; Ānanda, 94-97, 182-83, 222-31, 1675-76; *Vim*, 182-83; Aniruddha, 167-68, 514, 651-53, 1630; *Vim.*, 167-68; Asita, 1344-45; Bakkula (ou Vakula), 1386-87, 1530, 1894; Brahmāyus, 1577-78; Cūḍapanthaka, 1543-44, 1865; Dharmaruci, 410-14; Gautamī la maigre (Kisāgotamī), 488; Gavāṃpati, 97, 1659, 1761; Godhika, 211; Hastaka Āṭavika, 562-65, 1578; Hastaka Śākyaputra, 2353-54; Losakatiṣya, 931-32, cf. 1944; Madhuvāsiṣṭha, 1659-61, 1761; Mahāgautamī, 587-88, 1403-4; Mahākāśyapa, 87-103, 190-96, 287, 615, 654, 1046-47, 1399, 1761, 2332-34; *Vim.*, 149-50; Mahākātyāyana, 2303; *Vim.*, 163-64; Maudgalyāyana, 621-40, 1530, 1576, 2331-32; *Vim.*, 145; Mère de Rāhula, 1001-8; Mṛgaśiras, 1085-88; Pūrṇa, 343-44; Rādha, 343, Revata Khadiravaniya, 548-51, 1547; Śaivala, 1546; Śāriputra, 118-21, 190-96, 287, 621-49, 701, 1630-32, 1760, 2331-32; *Vim.*, 141-42; (Saundara-)Nanda, 117-18, 286-92, 1545, 1641, 1760; Subhadra, 205-8, 1650; Subhūti, 4, 634-36; *Vim.*, 154-55; Upagupta, 572-73; Upāli, *Vim.*, 170-72; Utpalavarṇa, 634-36, 844; Vakkali, 1546; Yaśas, 1545, 385.

14. André Bareau, "Les disciples", *France-Asie* 16 fév.-juin 1959, no 153-57 (*Présence du Bouddhisme*), pp. 351-68: p. 367.

15. Cf. André Bareau, "Le Parinirvāṇa du Buddha et la naissance de la religion bouddhique", *Bulletin de l'École Française d'Extrême-Orient*, 61: 1974, p. 276, n. 1.

16. André Bareau, *Annuaire du Collège de France*, 72 (1972), pp. 460-69; *Annuaire du Collège de France*, 73 (1973), pp. 415-30.

17. Cf. Édouard Chavannes, *Cinq cents contes et apologues extraits du Tripiṭaka chinois*, 4 vol., Paris, 1910-34 (New three-volume edition, Paris, 1962); Léon Feer, *Avadāna-Çataka. Cent légendes bouddhiques.*

Amsterdam: APA-Oriental Press, 1891, 1979 reprint of the Paris 1891 edition; etc.—Léon Feer is mostly known as the translator of the hundred Buddhist legends of the Avadāna-Śataka (1891). According to him, avadāna "is an instruction which demonstrates by the facts of life the bond between an act and its inevitable consequence." (p. xiv). These examples of holy men and women whose previous lives are related bear witness both to the reality of black and mixed acts which bind to saṃsāra and all white acts which are seeds of holiness. Hagiography therefore must embrace the study of precious lives; these lives indeed could be said to show best how holiness was pictured. Feer notes elsewhere the distinct character of all those acts leading to the state of arhant: "these are tributes rendered to the Buddhas or to their monuments, to the Pratyekabuddhas or to the brotherhood, nothing else" [Léon Feer, "Comment on devient Arhat", *Journal Asiatique*, 119, 1881, pp. 460-98: p. 475). A complete bibliography of Léo Feer's works can be found in *Bibliographie bouddhique* 11, May, 1919-May 1930) (Paris: Geuthner, 1931), 1-17].

18. M. Hofinger, *Le Congrès du Lac Anavatapta*, Louvain: Institut orientaliste, 1954, p. 15.

19. *Ibid.*, cf. p. 17.

20. *Ibid.*, p. 21.

21. M. Hofinger has also published *Étude sur le Concile de Vaiśālī*. Chapter V of *Deuxième Partie* (197-212) is on the primitive hierarchy described in the source material. Here he discusses the many divergences, opposing different lists of patriarchs which have come down to us. Among other things he shows that their authority derives from a scholarly blend of seniority, science and sanctity. All references to hagiography can easily be retrieved thanks to a subject index.—Our having limited our investigation to saints of ancient Buddhism does not mean there are no important studies in French on the great figures of medieval Indian Buddhism, but Western scientific research has until now been concerned with doctrines: "we look at doctors, Sylvain Lévi used to say, "where India sees saints, supernatural human beings, wonder-workers." ("Author d'Aśvaghoṣa," *Journal Asiatique*, 215, 1929, p. 258-59. These then are studies on philosophy or Indian history rather than properly called hagiography. Amalia Pezzali's monograph (*Śāntideva: mystique bouddhique des VII*[e] *et VIII*[e] *siècles*, Firenze: Vallecchi Ediore,

1968) devoted to Śāntideva, the well-known author of *Bodhicaryāvatāra*, is to be noted. It is divided into two parts covering respectively his life and works, then Śāntideva's place as a thinker among other Mādhyamika philosophers. This work of synthesis however has been strongly criticized by J.W. de Jong ("La légende de Śāntideva," *Indo-Iranian Journal*, 16, 1974, pp. 161-83) in a very technical article which summarizes the problems to be solved relating to the legend of this saint. Cf. likewise *Hōbōgirin*, in the article "Chugan," on the Mādhyamika school, which gives the main references on Nāgārjuna, Āryadeva, etc. (fasc. 5, esp. 472-81. As for Jean Naudou's book on *Les bouddhistes kaśmiriens au Moyen Âge* (Paris: Presses Universitaires de France, 1968), this is not properly speaking a study on hagiography, but an historical work which aims at "showing with the help of Tibetan sources the productive activity, during the last centuries preceding Islamization, of Buddhists in an Indian province [...]" (p. 5). No hagiographical work covering this period however can do without this fundamental work. Furthermore, the author repeatedly stresses the difficulty in discovering the history of the grand masters of Buddhism under hagiographical amplification (cf. p. 59, on Tāranātha). On Sarvajñamitra, he observes: "It is interesting to have several versions of the legend available: this example confirms that the "biographies' (*rnam-thar*) of Indian masters, such as they appear in Tibetan sources, are the result of successive amplifications, whose initial stages, or even the first phases, were Indian". (p. 68) On paṇḍita, siddha and mahāyogin Buddhajñanapāda, "one of the chief initiators of Mantranaya and one of those whose history was not overrun by legend" (p. 74), see pages 72, 74, 75, 138, 147, 156, 157, 193; on siddha Padmasaṃbhava, see pages 91-98.

22. André Bareau, "La jeunesse du Buddha dans les Sūtrapiṭaka et les Vinayapiṭaka anciens", *Bulletin de l'École Française d'Extrême-Orient*, 61-1974, pp. 199-274.

23. André Bareau, "La construction et le culte des stūpa d'après les *Vinayapiṭaka*", *Bulletin de l'École Française d'Extrême-Orient*, 50, 1962, pp. 229-74 ["La construction"].

24. *Ibid.*, p. 230.

25. *Ibid.*

26. *Ibid.*, cf. pp. 231-32.

27. *Ibid.*, cf. pp. 232, 240, 257-61.

28. *Ibid.*, pp. 237, 261, etc.

29. *Ibid.*, p. 264.

30. A *caitya* is a "commemorative monument, empty of any relics and whose appearance is never defined in ancient texts" (cf. André Bareau, "Le Parinirvāṇa du Bouddha et la naissance de la religion bouddhique," *Bulletin de l'École Française d'Extrême-Orient,* 61, 1974, p. 290). For the difference between *caitya* and *stūpa, ibid.*, 290-91.

31. Bareau, "La construction", pp. 240-41; 261-63; etc.

32. *Ibid.*, cf. p. 240.

33. *Ibid.*, cf. p. 264.

34. Even though in principle the Hōbōgirin leaves aside "names of personalities on the human, historical or semi-historical level, especially personalities which tradition has associated with the Buddha Śākyamuni or who belong to the history of the Church: monks, princes, men of letters, etc.," this dictionary contains a certain number of elements apt to throw light on ancient Indian Buddhist hagiography, especially veneration related to it. The following articles might be mentioned: "Ban," banner (*patāka*) offered to the Buddha or the saints, fasc. 1, 49-50 (unsigned); "Buppatsu," the Buddha's hair, one of his main relics, fasc. 2, 169-71 (unsigned); "Bussokuseki," stone bearing the Buddha's footprints, fasc. 2-3, 187-90 (unsigned); "Butsuge," Buddha tooth, fasc. 3, 203-5 (unsigned); "Butsuzō," Buddha image, fasc. 3, 210-15 (unsigned); "Chōmyōtō," on the practise of offering lamps to the Buddha and holy persons, fasc. 4, 360-65 (Hubert Durt); "Chōrai," on the homage from the crown of the head, fasc., 5 esp. 375-78 (Hubert Durt); "Chū," on sticks (*śalākā*) used to count, especially the sections on "Les Bâtonnets dans la tradition historique et légendaire du bouddhisme indien" ["Sticks in the Historical and Legendary Tradition of Indian Buddhism] and "Les Bâtonnets comme bons de participation et symbole d'engagement," [Sticks as Participation Tokens and Commitment Symbols,"] fasc. 5, 443-50 (Hubert Durt); "Dabi," or cremation, fasc. 6, 573ff. (Anna Seidel).

35. Bareau, "La construction", p. 268.

36. *Ibid.*, p. 269.

37. Cf. André Bareau, "Le bouddhisme indien", pp. 1146-1215 in H.-Ch. Puech (dir.), *Histoire des religions,* Tome I. Paris, Gallimard, coll. "La Pléiade", 1970, pp. 1178-79; see also André Bareau, *Recherches sur la biographie du Buddha dans les Sutrapiṭaka et les Vinayapiṭaka anciens: II. Les derniers mois, le parinirvāṇa et les funérailles.* Tome I. Paris, École Française d'Extrême-Orient, 1970, pp. 50-53 [*Buddha dans les Sūtrapiṭaka.* Tome I].

38. André Bareau, "Un personnage bien mystérieux: l'épouse du Buddha", pp. 31-59, in L.A. Hercus, et al., *Indological and Buddhist Studies,* (Volume in Honour of Prof. J.W. de Jong), Canberra, Faculty of Asian Studies, 1982. ["L'épouse du Buddha"]

39. Étienne Lamotte, *Histoire du bouddhisme indien*, pp. 733-36.

40. "L'épouse du Buddha", p. 33.

41. *Ibid.*, p. 35.

42. 1st c.

43. "L'épouse du Buddha," p. 48.

44. Here it is worthwhile to mention that Bareau has analyzed at length the episode of Yasa (or Yasakāra), of his ordination and of his acquiring of the highest sanctity (André Bareau, *Recherches sur la biographie du Buddha dans les Sūtrapiṭaka et les Vinayapiṭaka anciens: De la quête de l'éveil à la conversion de Śāriputra et de Maudgalyāyana*, Paris, École Française d'Extrême-Orient (dist.: Adrien-Maisonneuve), 1963, pp. 202-22) [*Buddha dans les Sūtrapiṭaka*] He sees in it "a sheer novel" (p. 203) probably based on an ancient tale (cf. p. 217), using a widespread literary theme dominated in a Buddhist context by an "edifying ending which governs the whole episode and shows up everywhere in hagiographic literature: vain and fragile are the pleasures of the senses, infinitely preferable to them is the serene joy born of self-denial." Besides having a propaganda objective, this story (claiming to take place in the time of the Buddha) seems to help justify a later custom requiring the young ordained to go home and have a meal with his

family. Perhaps a "bit of complacency on the part of the community toward the upper class (haute bourgeoisie)" (p. 218).

45. Esp. Jean Przyluski, *Le concile de Rājagṛha*, Paris, Paul Geuthner, 1926-28, 307ff. [*Rājagṛha*].

46. Cf. André Bareau, *Les Sectes bouddhiques du Petit Véhicule*, Paris, École Française d'Extrême-Orient, 1955, 310 p.: pp. 47-49; Lamotte, *Histoire du Bouddhisme indien*, p. 573.

47. Jean Przyluski, *Le Bouddhisme*, Paris: Rieder, 1932, p. 24, cf. p. 10.

48. *Ibid.*, p. 14.

49. *Ibid.*, p. 8.

50. Przyluski, *Rājagṛha*, pp. 292-93.

51. *Ibid.*, p. 292.

52. *Ibid.*, p. 295.

53. *Ibid.*, pp. 295-96.

54. *Ibid.*, p. 296.

55. *Ibid.*, p. 297.

56. Cf. Jean Przyluski, *La légende de l'empereur Açoka dans les textes indiens et chinois*, Paris, P.U.F., coll. "Annales du Musée Guimet" 23 (1923), p. 48 [*L'empereur Açoka*]; voir Lamotte, *Histoire du bouddhisme indien*, pp. 765-66.

57. Przyluski, *L'empereur Açoka*, p. 2.

58. *Ibid.*, p. 8.

59. Przyluski, *Rājagṛha*, pp. 257-78.

60. Cf. André Bareau, *Les premiers conciles bouddhiques*, Paris: P.U.F., coll. "Annales du Musée Guimet," 1955, pp. 7-15. [*Conciles bouddhiques*].

61. Cf. André Bareau, *Recherches sur la biographie du Buddha dans les*

Sūtrapiṭaka et les Vinayapiṭaka anciens: II. Les derniers mois, le parinirvāṇa et les funérailles. Tome II. Paris, École Française d'Extrême-Orient, 1971, p. 56 [*Buddha dans les Sūtrapiṭaka.* Tome II].

62. *Ibid.*, p. 64.

63. Przyluski, *Rājagṛha*, p. 240.

64. *Ibid.*, pp. 255-56.

65. Bareau, *Conciles bouddhiques*, pp. 16-21.

66. *Ibid.*, p. 21.

67. André Migot, "Un grand disciple du Buddha: Śāriputra", *Bulletin de l'École Française d'Extrême-Orient*, 46, fasc. 2, 1954, pp. 405-554: p. 533 ["Śāriputra"]; cf. idem, *Le Bouddha*, Bruxelles, Éd. Complexe, coll. "Le temps et les hommes", 1983, 302 p.: p. 68.

68. Cf. idem, "Śāriputra" p. 539.

69. *Ibid.*, pp. 540-41.

70. *Ibid.*, p. 407.

71. *Ibid.*

72. *Ibid.*, p. 409.

73. *Ibid.*, p. 536.

74. *Ibid.*, p. 409.

75. *Ibid.*

76. Dr. Migot has popularized his hypotheses on the saints of Buddhism in a book entitled *Le Bouddha* (esp. p. 208ff.).

77. Sylvain Lévi, "Les seize Arhat", *Journal Asiatique*, 189, 1916, pp. 5-50; 189-304.

78. Cf. John S. Strong, "The Legend of the Lion-Roarer: A Study of the Buddhist Arhat Piṇḍola Bhāradvāja", *Numen*, 26, no 1, 1979, pp. 50-58:

pp. 54-56 ["Lion-Roarer"].

79. Cf. Przyluski, *L'emperur Açoka*, pp. 75-76.

80. Cf. Strong, "Lion-Roarer", pp. 58ff.

81. Paul Lévy has rather boldly proposed seeing in original Buddhism a mystery religion centered on an initiation rite leading to a *bodhi*. The study of ordination supplies him with a certain number of points of similarity. Going over analyses made by Przyluski concerning Ānanda, Mahākāśyapa and above all Gavāṃpati, he finds here too initiation-like themes. (cf. Paul Lévy, *Buddhism: A Mystery Religion?*, New York, Schocken Books, 1968 (1st ed., London Athlone, 1957), 111 p., esp. 82-96. For a contrary opinion, cf. Bareau, *Buddha dans les Sūtrapiṭaka*. Tome II, pp. 256-57.

82. Bareau, *Buddha dans les Sūtrapiṭaka*, p. 187; cf. p. 178.

83. Étienne Lamotte, "La légende du Buddha", *Revue de l'Histoire des Religions*, 134, 1947-48, pp. 37-71: p. 48.

84. *Ibid.*, p. 49.

85. *Ibid.*, pp. 70-71.

86. *Ibid.*, p. 49.

87. Cf. Étienne Lamotte, "Une nouvelle vie du Buddha", *Le Muséon*, 62, 1949, pp. 251-60: p. 255.

88. Lamotte, "La légende du Buddha", pp. 19ff.; republished in Idem, *Histoire du bouddhisme indien*, pp. 718-33.

89. *Ibid.*, pp. 733-56.

90. Cf. Alfred Foucher, *La Vie du Bouddha d'après les textes et les monuments de l'Inde*, Paris, Payot, 1949, p. 328.

91. *Ibid.*, p. 244.

92. *Ibid.*, p. 8.

93. *Ibid.*, pp. 349-50.

94. *Ibid.*, p. 8.

95. *Ibid.*, pp. 70-71.

96. *Ibid.*, p. 24.

97. *Ibid.*, pp. 91-92.

98. *Ibid.*, p. 71.

99. *Ibid.*, p. 95.

100. *Ibid.*, p. 244.

101. Alfred Foucher, *Les vies antérieures du Bouddha d'après les textes et les monuments de l'Inde*, Paris: P.U.F., 1955.

102. Foucher, *La vie du Bouddha*, p. 54.

103. *Ibid.*, pp. 35, 54, 77, 147, 199, 203, 256, etc.

104. *Ibid.*, p. 52, 296.

105. *Ibid.*, pp. 72-75.

106. *Ibid.*, p. 81.

107. *Ibid.*, pp. 95, 189.

108. *Ibid.*, p. 143, etc.

109. *Ibid.*, p. 35.

110. *Ibid.*, p. 236.

111. *Ibid.*, p. 185.

112. *Ibid.*, pp. 127, 221, 228, 274, etc.

113. *Ibid.*, p. 193.

114. *Ibid.*, p. 245, cf. 270.

115. *Ibid.*, p. 109.

116. In his essay, *Le Bouddhisme*, 1932, Przyluski forcefully drew attention to the role of these places of pilgrimage. "What was the binding element in monastic Buddhism? Here as in medieval Christendom the importance of the great pilgrimages cannot be overemphasized. They are of two kinds: either going to the tomb of a renowned saint to venerate his relics; or else visiting the places sanctified by the life of the Buddha, by his birth, his illumination, his first preaching and by his end. At these memorable sites where pilgrims poured in coming from throughout the Buddhist world, the devout of every sect and category, monks and laymen, Mahāsāṃghikas and Theras mingled together. These contacts bore fruit: they guaranteed a common worship for all Buddhists and fostered the spread of new ideas, beliefs and writings." (pp. 32-33).

117. Foucher, *La vie du Bouddha*, p. 18.

118. *Ibid.*, p. 109.

119. *Ibid.*, p. 10.

120. *Ibid.*, p. 27.

121. *Ibid.*, cf. pp. 270-72.

122. *Buddha dans les Sūtrapiṭaka*. Tome I, p. 28, 57.

123. Idem, *Buddha dans les Sūtrapiṭaka*. Tome I, p. 294.

124. Idem, *Buddha dans les Sūtrapiṭaka*, p. 98; *Buddha dans les Sūtrapiṭaka*. Tome I, p. 136; *Buddha dans les Sūtrapiṭaka*. Tome II, p. 5.

125. Idem, *Buddha dans les Sūtrapiṭaka*. Tome I, p. 64.

126. *Ibid.*, p. 81.

127. *Ibid.*, p. 136.

128. *Ibid.*, p. 150.

129. Idem, *Buddha dans les Sūtrapiṭaka*, pp. 144-54, 168-69.

130. *Ibid.*, pp. 148, 165-69.

131. *Ibid.*, pp. 327-28; and idem, *Buddha dans les Sūtrapiṭaka*. Tome I, p. 165.

132. Idem, *Buddha dans les Sūtrapiṭaka.* Tome II, p. 16.

133. Idem, *Buddha dans les Sūtrapiṭaka.* Tome I, p. 166.

134. Idem, *Buddha dans les Sūtrapiṭaka,* p. 49, etc.

135. *Ibid.*, pp. 141, 147-49; etc.

136. *Ibid.*, p. 180.

137. *Ibid.*, p. 181; idem, *Buddha dans les Sūtrapiṭaka.* Tome I, p. 188; etc.

138. *Ibid.*, p. 10; etc.

139. Idem, *Buddha dans les Sūtrapiṭaka,* pp. 172-82.

140. *Ibid.*, pp. 181-82.

141. *Ibid.*, p. 362; idem, *Buddha dans les Sūtrapiṭaka.* Tome I, p. 66.

142. Idem, *Buddha dans les Sūtrapiṭaka,* p. 364.

143. *Ibid.*, p. 366, cf. p. 370.

144. *Ibid.*, p. 372.

145. *Ibid.*

146. *Ibid.*, pp. 2, 170; etc.

147. *Ibid.*, cf. p. 60.

148. Cf. idem, "L'épouse du Buddha", p. 32.

149. Cf. idem, *Buddha dans les Sūtrapiṭaka.* Tome II, p. 336.

150. Idem, *Buddha dans les Sūtrapiṭaka,* p. 69.

151. Concerning these areas, may I recall a few titles. P. Demiéville, *L'oeuvre de Wang le Zélateur (Wang Fan-tche), suivi des instructions domestiques de l'aïeul (T'ai-kong kia-kiao)*, Paris: C.N.R.S. (Bibliothèque de l'Institut des hautes études chinoises, 26), 887 p.; R. Shih, *Biographies des Moines Éminents de Houei-Kiao (Traduction). Première partie: Biographies des premiers traducteurs,* Louvain: Institut Orientaliste,

1968, XIV +210 p.; J. Bacot, *Vie du poète tibétain Milarepa. Ses crimes, ses épreuves, son nirvāṇa*, Paris: Bossard, 1925; idem, *La vie de Marpa le "Traducteur"*, Paris, 1937; R.A. Stein, Vie et chants de '*Brug-pa mun-legs le Yogin*, Paris: Maisonneuve et Larose, 1972; A.M. Blondeau, "Analysis of the biographies of Padmasaṃbhava according to Tibetan tradition: classification of sources", 45-52 in *Tibetan Studies in honour of Hugh Richardson*, Warminster, 1980.

152. V.G. Migot, "Śāriputra"; Strong, "Lion-Roarer".

153. Cf. Bareau, *Buddha dans les Sūtrapiṭaka*. Tome II, p. 112.

JAIN BIOGRAPHIES OF NAGARJUNA: NOTES ON THE COMPOSING OF A BIOGRAPHY IN MEDIEVAL INDIA

Phyllis Granoff

1. INTRODUCTION

Writing biographies was a major preoccupation of medieval Jain scholars. Highly educated in literature and the science of rhetoric, these authors could as easily compose in the ornate formal style of the Sanskrit *mahakavya* as write in the breezy, more colloquial vein of story-telling known so well from the *Pancatantra* and the *Hitopadesa*, and indeed from their own vast and rich corpus of stories. The choice was often determined by the subject matter. The biographical courtly poems generally were termed *caritas*, and the *tirthamkaras* and ancient religious heroes were the usual subject for these intricate and learned compositions which kept scrupulously close to the formulas worked out by the tracts on poetics for poetry acceptable as high art.In addition, a great minister or contemporary king could also be eulogized in the style of the Sanskrit *mahakavya.* In these cases, the rich language and its associations as the medium for expressing the greatness of the *tirthamkaras* and ancient culture heroes no doubt added a further aura of dignity to the subject of the poem and his deeds. The *prabandhas*, however, closer to the vernacular language, were the normal vehicle for describing the lives of more recent figures, the many monks, kings, ministers and lay devotees, who were particularly important to the Jain community .

Sources for the various biographies of the monks and kings who played such a major role in the tradition were undoubtedly as diverse as the biographies themselves.[1] Among the biographies in the language of the Sanskrit *mahakavya*, some, like the *Kirtikaumudi* of Somesvara about the minister Vastupala, were written by the same men of the court who wrote the elaborate baroque inscriptions to which these poems bear so close a resemblance.[2] Such panegyrics written as inscriptions and these biographies may both ultimately derive from the tradition of genealogical record keeping which supplied the raw material for the many long and laudatory royal inscriptions of medieval India.[3] In contrast, the *prabandhas*, while often incorporating stray verses from the pens of the court poets in their *prasastis*,(panegyrics) or poems, seem to have drawn on different sources. These were the rich variety of legends that must have circulated widely amongst the Jains in much the same way as did the vast corpus of stories that were such an integral part of Jain religious teaching; indeed some of the didactic story collections themselves have preserved biographies, as we shall see is the case with the biography of Nagarjuna which forms the subject of this paper. There is even evidence that didactic stories in one tradition, the Digambara tradition, were retold of others in the Svetambara tradition in the *prabandhas*.[4] The exact relationship between the didactic story collections, Svetambara and Digambara, and the later biographies of the Svetambara *prabandhas* deserves careful study.

The present paper will hopefully contribute to that study. It deals with the *prabandhas* and related texts and specifically with the Jain incorporation of a Buddhist figure into their gallery of heroes. It emphasizes the connection between one type of stories,stories associated with pilgrimage sites, and medieval biographies. In so doing it highlights one particular use made of the intimate relationship between pilgrimage site and Jain saint, and between the description and praise of a holy site and the biography of a holy man that can easily be documented in medieval Jainism.[5] It is hoped that the specific process outlined in this paper will shed light on the processes of biography writing generally in religious communities in medieval India.It is also hoped that it will contribute to an understanding of the position of the Jain collections of religious biographies, the *prabandhas*, in the wider corpus of Jain story literature and thus to an appreciation of the special characteristics of these biographies.

Various Jain biographies or *prabandhas*, at least one widely known story collection and two Jain texts on pilgrimage sites, or *tirthakalpas*, relate the life of the Buddhist Nagarjuna, who is presented as a Jain saint. These biographies have received comparatively little scholarly attention.[6] Most of these texts date from a relatively late period, the thirteenth and fourteenth centuries A.D., with the earliest of them, the story collection, dating from the very end of the twelfth century A.D. They are all from the Svetambara sect in North India, specifically the Northwest, Gujarat and Saurashtra, and they all with this one exception of Nagarjuna treat famous Buddhists and other well-known non-Jain philosophers distinctly as enemies and not as Jain saints. Digambara sources do of course make repeated mention of famous Buddhists. The *Kathakosa* of Prabhacandra, for example, written around 1055 A.D., describes Dignaga as the virulent opponent of the Jain Akalankadeva, who ordered Akalanka's death when he discovered Akalanka studying Buddhism under false pretexts.[7] But beyond such numerous brief references to Buddhists, particularly philosophers with whom the Jains were regularly engaged in public debate, these Svetambara sources preserve a number of longer accounts of the Buddhist Nagarjuna, distinct from the Jain Nagarjuna known to the earlier Ardhamagadhi canon.[8] In the Svetambara Jain *prabandhas* and *tirthakalpas* and at least one story collection Nagarjuna has become a Jain and receives the reverence accorded one of their own. Because there is no outside corroborating evidence that Nagarjuna ever converted to Jainism as these biographies imply, they must be regarded as purely imaginative compositions, responses to the great popularity of Nagarjuna as a wizard and magician in medieval India, for which the many attributions of medieval alchemy texts to his pen offer other evidence.

This paper will examine these Jain lives of Nagarjuna in an effort to uncover how such a biography was structured and how such legends were combined and ultimately incorporated into a unified composition, when the goal was to write the life history of an individual. Because the biographies of Nagarjuna in these Jain sources are of a very specific type, all being biographies of a non-Jain whom it is deemed necessary to bring into the Jain fold, and because those who told them no doubt had available to them well-established legends of Nagarjuna in both Buddhist and Hindu sources, they represent in fact a special case. Any general rules for the composition of biographies that are derived from their study must be treated as wholly provisional. Nonetheless it is hoped that future research will demonstrate the wider applicability of the principles uncovered in this unusual case.

To anticipate some of these conclusions, it will be proposed that the Jain biographers of Nagarjuna utilized a core component in the well-known legends of Nagarjuna in non-Jain sources and one suggested by his name. This is Nagarjuna's connection with the snakes, and the Jains have used it to associate Nagarjuna with a related figure in their own tradition, a Jain wonder-worker and magician associated from birth with a boon from the snake Goddess. The next step was to give an air of reality to Nagarjuna's legend by localizing it, at the same time as making it believably Jain. This was done by connecting Nagarjuna with concrete and well-established holy sites in the Jain tradition, which explains in turn why Jain texts primarily devoted to extolling pilgrimage sites also relate Nagarjuna's exploits.

The process that lay behind the composition of Nagarjuna's Jain biography may be best understood as a skillful and intricate weaving together of a complex network of associations from several primary strands: the snakes, magic and alchemy. More specifically, Nagarjuna was brought firmly into the Jain gallery of wizards and magicians, famous alchemists and eccentrics, above all by making him a student of that best-known of all wizards in the Jain biographical tradition, Padaliptacarya. But he was also ushered into that elect company by several clever associations with famous places in the Jain sacred universe. To begin with Nagarjuna is usually given Mt. Dhanka as his birthplace, and in the one exception, what I shall call the variant version of his biography, he is still said to be born in a city of that name. Now Mt.Dhanka in the texts of the period is either another name for Mt.Satrunjaya, which was the outstanding pilgrimage site of the day, or it is a name for one of the holy peaks on Mt.Satrunjaya. In addition, Mt. Satrunjaya was celebrated in a variety of pilgrimage texts for its life-giving streams and wells which yielded the drink of immortality and for magical jewels and mines of silver and gold.In one story to which we shall return below, it was even associated with Nagarjuna's putative teacher Padaliptacarya, and with the snake Goddess herself as well as with a well of the drink of immortality.

For his mature career Nagarjuna is usually associated with yet another famous holy site, one which in fact is said to have received its popular name as a result of his activities there. This is Stambhana Tirtha, "The Holy Site of Solidification", where Nagarjuna finally succeeds in making his elixir of immortality by causing it to assume the necessary solid state. Here too the composers of Nagarjuna's biography have chosen very carefully and kept close to the basic system of intertwining threads. What makes Nagarjuna's association with Stambhana Tirtha possible is the sinuous snakes. Stambhana was in fact revered for being the locus of a magical image of the Tirthamkara Parsvanatha. Now biographies of Parsvanatha are unanimous in pointing out a connection between this Tirthamkara and the snake god Dharanendra. Nagarjuna is said to have brought the magical image of Parsvanatha to Stambhana on the advice of his father, the snake king, in order to make his elixir, in an act that now must seem almost natural within the associative world of these texts: the son of the snake God brings to the holy site the image of the *tirthamkara* protected by the snake deity. The holy site of Stambhana derives its sanctity from the presence of this image there and thus in turn from Nagarjuna who is responsible for having brought the Parsvanatha to Stambhana. The relationship between Nagarjuna and the site is akin to a symbiosis; Nagarjuna is made a bonafide Jain by his activities at a celebrated holy site, while the site is sanctified by his work there. In addition, this connection between Nagarjuna and Stambhana, between the magical image of Parsvanatha and the Jain holy man who was the offspring of the snake king and operated under his protection, was surely reinforced in the mind of both biography composer and hearer by the fact that the Jain tradition revered another man, Abhayadeva, as rescuer of the Stambhana image at a later date and as the recipient of a boon from the snake god Dharanendra. Even those *prabandhas* that do not connect Nagarjuna with Stambhana Tirtha when they directly tell his biography do relate the story of Abhayadeva and there note Nagarjuna's association with this holy site and this famous image of Parsvanatha. Abhayadeva's story was widely told in epigraphical sources as well as in the various biography collections, and it seems that the connection between Nagarjuna and Abhayadeva was likewise widely known. We shall return to it and to all of these points in detail as we examine some of these biographies of Nagarjuna as they appear in the *prabandhas* and the story collection and the related pilgrimage texts below.

2.THE JAIN BIOGRAPHIES OF NAGARJUNA

The medieval texts that present the life of Nagarjuna can conveniently be divided into three closely related groups, the *prabandhas* or biography collections, a story collection, and the *tirthakalpas* , or texts on pilgrimage sites(see note 5). The *prabandhas* which relate Nagarjuna's story outnumber the extant texts on pilgrimage sites which mention Nagarjuna, and it is easiest to begin our account with a summary of a typical biography of Nagarjuna from one of these sources. Although the life of Nagarjuna is told in several *prabandhas*, the *Prabandhacintamani* of Merutunga (1304 A.D.), the *Prabandhakosa* of Rajasekharasuri (1349 A.D.), the *Puratanaprabandhasamgraha* and the *Prabhavakacarita* (1277 A.D.), in fact the accounts can be grouped into two distinctive groups.[9] One account is told in the *Prabandhacintamani*, *Prabandhakosa* and the *Puratanaprabandhasamgraha*, *Nagarjunaprabandha* and *Abhayadevaprabandha*. A second account is found in the *Prabhavakacarita*, and the *Puratanaprabandhasamgraha*, *Padaliptacaryaprabandha*, which in fact belongs to a different manuscript and thus to a different text than the *Puratanaprabandhasamgraha*, *Nagarjunaprabandha* . This text, however, also contains the *Abhayadevaprabandha* and thus records both versions. In addition the version of Nagarjuna's life given in the *Padaliptacaryaprabandha* is close in some critical details to the account given in the story collection, the *Kumarapalapratibodha* of Somaprabhacarya of 1196 A.D. We shall begin our discussion with a summary of the accounts in the *Prabandhakosa* and *Prabandhacintamani*, which in many ways are the most literary and seem the most tightly constructed. From there we will continue with a summary of the variant version in the *Prabhavakacarita* and related sources, to conclude with an account from the pilgrimage texts.

Nagarjuna, according to the *Prabandhakosa*, which gives a remarkably chaste and clear account of his biography, was the son of the snake king Vasuki and a human princess Bhopala, from Mt. Dhanka. The snake king retains a paternal affection for his son throughout his life and from earliest infancy nourishes him with a variety of herbs through which Nagarjuna achieves magical powers. Nagarjuna becomes the royal preceptor of the Satavahana king in Prthivisthanapattana, and lacks little, except perhaps the ability to fly. And so he leaves his patron and travels to Palittanakapura, the city associated with the Jain wonder-worker and wizard, Padaliptacarya. Nagarjuna serves Padalipta, who is adept at flying, and one day when Padalipta has returned from one of his aerial ventures Nagarjuna seizes the opportunity to wash the tired teacher's feet. This is, however, a subterfuge. Nagarjuna really wants to know what the teacher has smeared on his feet that has enabled him to fly. He recognizes at once the formula for the magical preparation, and without Padalipta's permission he proceeds to make a batch of the unguent for his own use. Alas, because Nagarjuna has disobeyed a cardinal rule by not learning the art from a teacher, his attempt is doomed to failure. Nagarjuna lands abruptly and almost catastrophically on the edge of a deep well. Padalipta asks his injured student what the meaning of all this is; Nagarjuna truthfully replies that he has stolen the formula for flying. Satisfied by Nagarjuna's truthfulness, Padalipta instructs Nagarjuna who then successfully flies.

As the tale progresses, Nagarjuna one day hears Padalipta explain that the virtue of charity *(dana)* cannot be perfected without mastery of the science of alchemy, the test for which is successful completion of the elixir of immortality *(rasasiddhi)*. It is for this reason, and not out of any intrinsic fascination with alchemy, that Nagarjuna is said to set out to make his elixir, a twist of plot that is not entirely in keeping with Nagarjuna's reputation as someone interested in the arts of magic, but a point that ties in closely with his strong reputation for charity in the Buddhist biographies and in the Hindu story collections, and to which we shall return below.

Nagarjuna has less success with his elixir than he did with his attempts at flying. No matter what he does the elixir will not turn into the required solid state. Padalipta instructs him that two more elements are necessary, a magical image of Parsvanatha and a chaste woman to stir the potion. Nagarjuna seeks the aid of his father, the snake king Vasuki, to determine where such an image of Parsvanatha is to be found. Vasuki tells Nagarjuna of the destruction of Dvaravati, a cycle of stories found in Jainism as well as Hinduism. He then explains about the wondrous image of Parsvanatha that was submerged in the ocean at the time of the cataclysmic Dvaravati flood; much later a merchant had recovered this image on divine instruction. Nagarjuna steals the image from the merchant and sets it up on the banks of the Sedi River. There, nightly, he entices Candralekha, the wife of the Satavahana king, to assist him in the preparation of his elixir. This is in itself no small feat, and Nagarjuna must call upon the aid of some minor gods who bring the queen to him. Candralekha does Nagarjuna's bidding, but she betrays to her two sons the secret of his efforts. With a variety of subterfuges they await and ascertain the final day when the elixir stands ready. Having learned that Nagarjuna is to die only by the lash of a blade of grass, they are intent upon his death. Nagarjuna, meanwhile, hides two vessels of the elixir in a cave on Mt.Dhanka, further strengthening the earlier connection noted between Nagarjuna and this holy site. The two princes succeed in their evil machinations and Nagarjuna meets his death at their hands. To prevent the elixir from reaching mankind and thereby upsetting the balance of the universe, two gods secret it away. The two princes repent of their wicked deed, die, and go to hell. The story closes by linking Nagarjuna and his life's last work firmly to the second major Jain pilgrimage site that figures so importantly in Nagarjuna's Jain biographies. This is Stambhana Tirtha, the spot on the river Sedi where the elixir at last turned into a solid. The "Holy Place of Solidification",as the site is known after Nagarjuna's activity there, is doubly hallowed, once by its association with Nagarjuna and his elixir, and again by the presence of the magical image of Parsvanatha, which was only later moved to a city also named Stambhana.

Tirtha and saint, in this biography, cooperate in reinforcing each other's powers; Nagarjuna, linked to the holy mountain Satrunjaya by birth and by burying his elixir there, becomes one more of the numerous holy men, sages and kings, who achieved their ultimate goal on Satrunjaya. At the same time the mountain is sanctified by Nagarjuna's presence there and his activities, in much the same way as it had derived its original sanctity from the fact that it was the place where such worthies as the ancient sage Pundarika and the Jina Rsabhanatha achieved ultimate perfection. Satrunjaya is newly glorified by receiving Nagarjuna's elixir, even temporarily, much as it had been originally hallowed by the jewels and images left behind by earlier great men of the Jain tradition. The incorporation of Nagarjuna into the Jain gallery of heroes thus utilizes a well-established practice of linking holy man and holy site. Finally, holy man and holy place operate in tandem at Stambhana. Nagarjuna is responsible for the sanctity of the site in bringing the Parsvanatha there, while the site lends him its lustre in the minds of all who hear his tale and know well the prestige of Stambhana.

The account given by Merutunga in the *Prabandhacintamani* is essentially the same.Merutunga does supply some additional details; for example he relates further information about the wondrous image of Parsvanatha that Nagarjuna is compelled to steal. For Merutunga it is clearly this image and not Nagarjuna's presence there that lends sanctity to the *tirtha*, which in fact is claimed to be more potent than Nagarjuna's elixir in granting all wishes. Merutunga goes on to relate that after some time the image became submerged in the ground, only its neck remaining visible. The saint savant Abhayadevasuri, instructed by the snake king Dharanendra, uncovers the image so that it can once again be worshipped.[10] Merutunga closes his biography of Nagarjuna with a verse in praise of the Parsvanatha image, emphasizing in effect the close association of Nagarjuna with this wondrous image, which forms here an unmistakable focal point for the plot details of Nagarjuna's biography and makes comprehensible his importance in the Jain sacred universe. Nagarjuna is pulled into the tradition by linking him explicitly with this image of Parsvanatha. Primary sanctity belongs to the image, and it is by virtue of the fact that Nagarjuna helped to bring it to its present location that Nagarjuna figures as a Jain worth remembering. Even more than Rajasekharasuri, then, Merutunga seems to wish to emphasize Nagarjuna's association with Stambhana Tirtha, and his biography here seems indeed somewhere inbetween a biography and a *tirthamahatmya*, a glorification of a holy place, showing the close connection between these two genres of writing in the case of Nagarjuna's biography.

The biography of Nagarjuna is often told in summary form in tandem with the biography of his preceptor, Padaliptacarya, and there are a few details that may be mentioned there that do not occur in the sections on Nagarjuna himself. To return to Rajasekharasuri, in the section on Padaliptacarya, Rajasekharasuri gives details of Nagarjuna's theft of the image of Parsvanatha, explaining how he became friends with the merchant's sons in order to steal their statue, which he does at the very moment that they bow their heads in prayer. He also credits Nagarjuna with the rebuilding of a city in honour of his teacher and the restoration of several temples.Rajasekharasuri also makes the briefest reference to an event that is central to the second version of Nagarjuna's biography that we will discuss below. This is Nagarjuna's dedication of a temple to the Tirthamkara Neminatha.Nonetheless the version given of Nagarjuna's biography even in the section on Padalipta is in keeping with the version summarized from Rajasekharasuri's section on Nagarjuna.

Occasionally it is explicitly acknowledged in the biographies that Nagarjuna was not in fact a Jain and was only later brought into the Jain fold. Thus the *Puratanaprabandhasamgraha, Nagarjunaprabandha*, which is essentially the same biography as the *Prabandhakosa* or *Prabandhacintamani*, relates that Nagarjuna, unsuccessful at stealing the secret of flying from Padaliptacarya, is told that Padalipta cannot take him on as a bona-fide student because Nagarjuna adheres to a false faith,*mithyadrsti*. Nagarjuna converts to Jainism and is then duly taught to fly. In the second version of the biography,in the *Prabhavakacarita*, and the *Puratanaprabandhasamgraha, Padaliptacaryaprabandha*, Padalipta demands Nagarjuna's adherence to Jainism as his *gurudaksina*, his payment for instruction offered.It is perhaps best to turn now to that second version, which offers in many ways a comparable but alternative account of Nagarjuna's life.

The *Prabhavakacarita* tells of Nagarjuna in a longer section on the deeds of Padaliptacarya. Its account is exactly parallel to that given in the *Puratanaprabandhasamgraha,Padaliptacaryaprabandha*. I shall make my summary from the *Prabhavakacarita* which is the more detailed of the two texts. Unlike the accounts of the *prabandhas* reviewed thus far,in this account Nagarjuna is the son of a human being, a *ksatriya* named Samgrama who is famed for his military valour, and his human wife Suvrata. His birthplace is not Mt.Dhanka, but the city Dhanka. The couple dreams of the snake king Sesa, who announces to them the impending birth of Nagarjuna. From the very beginning Nagarjuna's behaviour is out of the ordinary.At age three he is playing with his little friends when he suddenly seizes and splits apart their toy lion, and proceeds to eat big chunks from it.His father is alarmed and tries to stop him, as the text explains because it is forbidden for a *ksatriya* to eat creatures with claws. A sage appears on the scene and instructs the father not to worry. He says that from this unusual tasting experience, Nagarjuna will succeed in reaching the highest taste.[11] Nagarjuna then prefers the company of old men , versed in various magic arts, to companions of his own age, and eventually he becomes fully accomplished in the arts of alchemy.There is no trace here of the Nagarjuna of the *Prabandhakosa* and related texts who is unable to complete his alchemical feats. Nagarjuna then begins to travel abroad, returning eventually to his home city. He camps out with his disciples on a mountain nearby and when he learns that Padaliptacarya, who is gifted with innumerable magic skills, is staying in the city he decides to make overtures to him in an effort to learn how to fly. He sends to Padaliptacarya one of his students bearing as a gift a bowl of perfectly finished alchemical elixir. Padaliptacarya disdains the gift, flinging the pot of elixir aside.But he treats the student generously, serving him a rich meal and then presents him with a gift for Nagarjuna in return: a pot of his own urine. Nagarjuna gently lifts the lid of the pot and is in no doubt as to the nature of its contents. Furious he flings the pot aside, so that it breaks into pieces and scatters its unusual contents.Now, by chance the pot makes contact with Nagarjuna's cooking fire, for as the text explains even those accomplished in alchemy must still get hungry and cook! And lo and behold at the touch of the fire Padaliptacarya's pot of urine turns into gold. The student is dumbstruck and praises Padalipta's marvelous powers. Nagarjuna too is impressed and he humbly approaches Padaliptacarya, lamenting his own miserable existence and poverty and his own meager powers compared to those of Padaliptacarya. The story from here continues in a somewhat familiar vein; Nagarjuna tries to learn by subterfuge what the unguent that Padalipta smears on his feet to give them the power of flight contains. He does divine its composition, but his attempt to fly is doomed to failure because he has not learned properly from his teacher.Nonetheless Padaliptacarya is pleased by Nagarjuna's obvious cleverness and agrees to teach him to fly. In return he asks of Nagarjuna that Nagarjuna convert to Jainism.The biography now draws to a close with an account of some of Nagarjuna's pious deeds, some of which like his founding of the city of Padaliptapura in honour of his teacher are known from the *Prabandhakosa* and related texts. One, however ,does not play a significant role in any of those texts and is important in that it connects this biography in the *Prabhavakacarita* and the *Puratanaprabandhasamgraha, Padaliptacaryaprabandha* with the story in the *Kumarapalapratibodha*. The text relates that Nagarjuna heard from his teacher the story of the Tirthamkara Neminatha and was so impressed by it that he had constructed not only a temple for Neminatha but replicas of all the major scenes in his life. The entire section on Padaliptacarya ultimately closes with a statement that Nagarjuna and Padaliptacarya die together by fasting on Mt. Satrunjaya.This last detail is also found in the *Puratanaprabandhasamgraha,Padaliptacaryaprabandha*.

It is immediately clear that this version of Nagarjuna's biography is significantly different from the first version examined above. These differences begin with the account of Nagarjuna's birth. In the *Prabandhakosa* account Nagarjuna is by birth related to the snake king; in this account he is the son of two human parents who see the snake king in a dream and learn of his birth. Nagarjuna is an accomplished alchemist in this version and does not have any connection with the holy place Stambhana and the image of Parsvanatha which are so important in the *Prabandhakosa* and related texts. Both the *Prabhavakacarita* and the *Puratanaprabandhasamgraha* text which contains this version do know of such a connection; the *Prabhavakacarita* in its account of Abhayadeva and the *Puratanaprabandhasamgraha* text in its *Abhayadevaprabandha*, but they do not mention it in these biographies and indeed tell a story which is incompatible with that account. In their story Nagarjuna is an accomplished alchemist but the story of his trials at Stambhana depends on the opposite fact, namely that he cannot make his elixir without the assistance of the magical image of Parsvanatha. In addition, in the *Prabhavakacarita* version Nagarjuna is connected with a different Tirthamkara, with Neminatha. Neminatha , it is true, is connected with Dvaravati,where Nagarjuna's magical image originated, but the *Prabhavakacarita* biography of Nagarjuna as stated before does not take any notice of the Dvaravati Parsvanatha and thus any such connection seems irrelevant to our analysis of the story. Finally, in the *Prabhavakacarita* version Nagarjuna dies a natural death for a pious Jain monk , fasting to death with his teacher on the holy mountain Satrunjaya.There is no mention of a Satavahana queen and her evil sons. In all of these points, the *Prabhavakacarita* and the *Puratanaprabandhasamgraha,Padaliptacaryaprabandha*, then , seem to record a distinct version of Nagarjuna's biography. This version,particularly in its mention of Nagarjuna's reverence for Neminatha and his making replicas of the crucial scenes in Neminatha's life, is moreover connected with the one account of Nagarjuna from Svetambara story literature.

The *Kumarapalapratibodha* account of Nagarjuna is brief and is given in the context of Kumarapala's pilgrimage.Nagarjuna is a Buddhist from Saurashtra who wishes to learn flying from Padaliptacarya.He offers Padalipta the art of transmuting worthless substances into gold in exchange for learning how to fly. Padalipta, however, is not interested in Nagarjuna's offer, for as he explains money is of no use to a monk, and anyway he already knows how to make gold! Nagarjuna then disguises himself as a pious Jain and begins faithfully to serve the teacher. He exercises the subterfuge which is common to all our sources, and with the now familiar results. Padalipta finally agrees to teach him in return for his becoming a true Jain. Nagarjuna accepts the Jain faith and begins his wanderings with his teacher. The text then says that the replicas of the famous events in Neminatha's life which Kumarapala has before him were made by Nagarjuna.

In brief, this account belongs with the *Puratanaprabandhasamgraha, Padaliptacaryaprabandha* and the *Prabhavakacarita* for several reasons. Although it gives no account of either Nagarjuna's birth or death, it knows Nagarjuna as an adept in alchemy who achieves his goal of making an elixir before he ever meets Padaliptacarya and who offers Padaliptacarya the elixir in exchange for lessons in flying, reminiscent of similar events in those two versions. It also associates Nagarjuna with faith in Neminatha and makes no mention of Stambhana Tirtha or the Parsvanatha, which as we have seen are integral to the *Prabandhakosa* and related texts.It remains now to examine the biographies of Nagarjuna in the final group of texts, the pilgrimage texts, and then to reassess the nature of Nagarjuna's biography in the Svetambara Jain tradition and the significance of these variant versions.

The story of Nagarjuna can be found in two pilgrimage texts in the Svetambara tradition , the *Vividhatirthakalpa* of Jinaprabhasuri (1333 A.D.) and the commentary of Subhasilagani to the *Satrunjayakalpa* of the mid-fifteenth century A.D. The account of Nagarjuna in both of these texts corresponds closely to the story related in the *Prabandhakosa* and summarized above, with the exception that the *Vividhatirthakalpa* omits any mention of Nagarjuna's murderers meeting their just end and the *Satrunjayakalpa* allows Nagarjuna the sanctioned death of the pious Jain, fasting on Mount Satrunjaya.

In addition , the *Satrunjayakalpa* helps us to understand Nagarjuna's associations with Mount Satrunjaya in all of these biographies.The commentary of Subhasilagani provides stories that go a long way in explaining why this particular pilgrimage site was so suitable for the biographers to select as Nagarjuna's birthplace and the place where he would hide his elixir, or the place of his death. According to one such story, Mt.Dhanka was famous for its well of the drink of immortality. The story opens as a merchant, Dhanada, and his wife Dhanavati from the town of Kuntalahvapura are introduced. They have four sons who are married to rather shrewish brides who refuse to allow their husbands to visit home. Persuaded by a friend that their behaviour is wrong, three of the sons return to their parents. The fourth goes to Mt.Dhanka and hears a Jain monk telling about a well which contains *rasa,* the drink of immortality. The person who performs religious austerities in front of a particular image of the Jina Santinatha will be vouchsafed a vision of the well. The well is also said to be situated near two lodes of gold and silver, again both associated with a *caitya* of Santinatha. It is added that when Padaliptacarya renovated the *caitya* he left more gold and jewels there. Instructions are given on how to worship properly, which includes an offering to the snake goddess Vairothya. Appeased, Vairothya will open the well of the drink of immortality at night. The fourth son then proceeds as he has heard the monk describe, obtains the drink of immortality and returns home. He becomes wealthy and spends his life faithfully and devotedly serving his parents. He erects a temple to Santinatha and makes a gold image of the Jina for his temple. The story concludes by saying that endless beings will find peace on Mt.Dhanka, which is one of the peaks of Mt.Satrunjaya.

To summarize the material on Nagarjuna from the Jain sources, then, it is clear that there are two distinct biographies preserved in a variety of texts, *prabandhas, tirthakalpas,* and at least one widely read story collection. Of these two variants it would appear that the version in the *Prabandhakosa* and related texts was the more widely known one;at least it is this version that appears in the pilgrimage texts. It is tempting to regard this version as the later, more mature version and the other version as its forerunner.It seems worth noting that by the time of the *Prabandhakosa* it is this version with the Stambhana Tirtha link that is given even in the account of Nagarjuna that finds its place within the biography of Padaliptacarya,suggesting further that it has come to replace the other version of Nagarjuna's biography, which we have seen circulated in the *Prabhavakacarita* and in the *Puratanaprabandhasamgraha* as part of the many stories associated with his teacher. A consideration of the relative chronology of the texts would tend to support such an hypothesis, with the *Kumarapalapratibodha* and the *Prabhavakacarita* being the earliest of our accounts and containing the version I have regarded as the likeliest to have been the earlier one from a consideration of its content. Nonetheless I must add that I believe that with legends of this type which no doubt had a long and rich non-written history it is risky at best to place too much emphasis on the dates of written versions. In addition it is clear that a text like that included in the *Puratanaprabandhasamgraha* knew both versions and that they both circulated at the same time.Nonetheless the *Prabandhakosa* version still seems by comparison better integrated; for example it incorporates directly into the main story line of the biography the legends of Stambhana Tirtha which we have seen in these *prabandhas* do always mention Nagarjuna specifically and which stand in contradiction to the account of Nagarjuna's life in the *Prabhavakacarita* version.It is also best to note that the *Prabandhakosa* version of Nagarjuna's biography seems more studied and careful in its very close adherence to the events of his life as told in non-Jain, specifically Buddhist sources which we shall review below.

I would like to suggest a process by which Nagarjuna's biography gradually developed in the Svetambara Jain sources, in which the story of Nagarjuna the well-known alchemist is first linked to the Jain teacher Padaliptacarya who possesses the ability to fly. Nagarjuna seeks to learn to fly from him in exchange for his alchemical secrets. His legend is localized at this point by associating him with some temples to Neminatha, whose life story he hears from Padalipta. The next step would be Nagarjuna's assimilation to the holy site of Stambhana and to the Parsvanatha image associated with Abhayadeva, that other famous Jain scholar known for his miraculous rescue of the Stambhana Parsvanátha and for his protection by the snake king. Evidence cited above in note 10 suggests that the primary association is of Abhayadeva with the Stambhana Parsvanatha and that Nagarjuna's connection is a later, secondary development not as frequently recorded in the tradition . Evidence also suggests that this association of Nagarjuna with Stambhana was first made independently of the biography of Nagarjuna, for in the *Prabhavakacarita* it is mentioned not in the section on Nagarjuna found in Padalipta's biography, but only in the section on Abhayadeva.This association would then have been assimilated into the main story of Nagarjuna and his relationship to Padalipta to give rise to the mature version of Nagarjuna's biography, that found in the *Prabandhakosa* and related sources and in the pilgrimage texts. I must add that it is true that the latest account of Nagarjuna's life, that given by Subhasilagani, combines episodes from both versions in that it allows Nagarjuna the death of the pious Jain monk as did the *Prabhavakacarita* version but not the *Prabandhakosa* version. It is necessary to conclude at this point that without further proof this outline of the process by which Nagarjuna's biography developed and changed must remain in the realm of speculation. Indeed the exact relationship of these two versions must remain somewhat of a mystery without some additional evidence. Clearer fortunately are some of the dynamics that shaped them both and the associative links that run through them both and that help us to understand how both these Jain versions developed in the context of widely known Hindu and Buddhist stories of Nagarjuna.It is perhaps best to recapitulate some of these common associative strands in the Jain biographies of Nagarjuna before passing on to a consideration of the Hindu and Buddhist sources.

From a review of the biographies of Nagarjuna in the Jain sources the following threads emerge: the biographies of Nagarjuna in these sources revolve around his associations with snakes,a magical mountain and alchemy. Nagarjuna is connected from birth with the snakes. He is in the one version the direct son of the snake king Vasuki, and in the other his birth to two mortals is presaged by a dream in which the snake king Sesa announces to the couple that Nagarjuna will be their son. Next, Nagarjuna is associated with the Jain sage Padaliptacarya, who, among other things, has a knowledge of magical herbs that enables him to fly, and who knows how to make the elixir of immortality. It is worth pausing to examine the biographies of Padaliptacarya in the same texts and to note that Padalipta is himself connected with the snakes. He is obtained by his childless parents as a boon from the snake goddess Vairothya, and his real name as given by the *Prabandhakosa* , for example,is "Nagendra", "King of the Snakes". A curious feature of the *Prabandhakosa* version of Nagarjuna's biography is that Nagarjuna is said to have become interested in making the elixir because he wished to perfect the vow of giving, something that has an alien ring to it within the context of the story as told in the *prabandhas*, and indeed within the context of Jain storytelling in general as it is exemplified by this body of texts. This point and the next one will be significant in an hypothetical reconstruction of the process by which the Jain biographies of Nagarjuna might have been composed out of the well-known Buddhist sources, and are mentioned here for that reason. This next point is that in the same version Nagarjuna's death is regarded as an unnatural death and his elixir does not reach the world. Finally, Nagarjuna is in both the versions of his biography explicitly linked with the wonderful Mt.Satrunjaya, either by birth and by deed or by his death, while in one version he is further associated with a magical image of Parsvanatha and the pilgrimage site Stambhana. The *Satrunjayakalpa*, and specifically its commentary by Subhasilagani, helps to explain the suitability of the Satrunjaya connection. Satrunjaya was famous for its magical wells and jewels and in at least one tale there is an explicit association of a well of the drink of immortality, Nagarjuna's teacher Padaliptacarya, and the snake goddess Vairothya. Here seem to join what we have earlier identified as the building strands in the weave of Nagarjuna's biography: snakes, magic and alchemy. Finally, the Stambhana association was likewise motivated by one of these primary threads, in this case again by the snakes. Nagarjuna is linked to an image of the Tirthamkara Parsvanatha who is himself tied to the snakes. This particular image would later be rescued by yet another Jain holy man protected by the snake king, the famous commentator Abhayadeva.

In these biographies Nagarjuna, then, is connected with snakes and with a famous Jain teacher who was himself connected with snakes. He is depicted as an adept of alchemy, albeit in one version motivated by charity. Nagarjuna is linked with pilgrimage sites, in both versions with Satrunjaya, and his story is told equally by texts which are essentially glorifications of holy places and by texts which assemble biographical legends. It remains now to assess the significance of these features in the light of evidence from Buddhist and Hindu stories of Nagarjuna.

3. CONCLUSIONS: APPROPRIATING THE BIOGRAPHY OF NAGARJUNA

Several detailed studies exist of the Buddhist biographies of Nagarjuna preserved in Chinese and Tibetan sources, and the stories connected with Nagarjuna in the *Kathasaritsagara* and the *Brhatkathamanjari* are well known.[12] A number of points are apparent from these texts. The first is that the Buddhists, in dealing with the origin of Nagarjuna's name, connected him with the snakes, but not necessarily by reason of birth. By birth Nagarjuna is most often regarded as human, and his association with the snakes comes later when he is given a treasury of Buddhist *sutras* by the snakes. Nagarjuna is also associated in the Buddhist texts with a holy mountain, usually Sri Parvata, and with the *tantras*, magical rites and alchemy. In addition Nagarjuna is regarded as distinguished by the virtue of *dana*, or charity, which he possessed to such an extent that some texts relate how he willingly forfeited his own life, cutting off his own head with a blade of *darbha* grass, or with a sword. Nagarjuna is also associated with a Satavahana king in Buddhist and Hindu sources, and with magical or miraculously appearing images, at least in the biography of the thirteenth century Tibetan monk Dharmasvamin.[13] To summarize, then, in the non-Jain biographies, Nagarjuna is connected with snakes, associated with alchemy, linked to a Satavahana king, meets an unusual end which is the result of his extreme devotion to the Buddhist vow of charity, and is connected with the holy mountain Sri Parvata.

The connection between the biography of Nagarjuna in these texts and in the Jain sources should be immediately apparent. In recasting the biography of Nagarjuna, the Jain authors would seem to have been concerned with maintaining a remarkable degree of fidelity to the Buddhist and Hindu accounts. Thus, they retain the connection between Nagarjuna and the snakes, suggested perhaps initially by Nagarjuna's name. They retain his association with alchemy and sacred mountains, and in one version of his biography they do not permit Nagarjuna a natural death. At the same time this same version, that of the *Prabandhakosa* and related texts, also preserves for Nagarjuna the pious attribute of his charitableness, but in these Jain biographies the statement that Nagarjuna was devoted to *dana* is oblique, the texts saying only that he begins his study of alchemy because without it he has heard that the virtue of *dana* is not possible. It does not in any way help to explain the singular nature of his death as it does in the non-Jain sources. It remained through all of this only to give Nagarjuna a distinct character and life history that would bring him firmly into the Jain tradition.

We have already seen how Nagarjuna's conversion to Jainism was easily accomplished by inserting into the basic framework of his legend, retained from the Buddhist and Hindu sources, clearly Jain details. Thus in his interest in magic and association with snakes Nagarjuna is made the pupil of Padaliptacarya, a figure well-known in Jainism both for his association with the snake goddess Vairothya and for his ability to fly and perform a variety of other similar magical feats. Next Nagarjuna's base of operations was transferred from South India and the holy mountain of Buddhism to the Jain pilgrimage center of Mt. Satrunjaya, which for the period of our texts was probably the dominant pilgrimage center in Svetambara Jainism. Nagarjuna was associated with Satrunjaya as we have seen in different ways in both versions of his Jain biography. In the *Prabandhakosa* version Nagarjuna was also linked to the famous *tirtha*, Stambhana Tirtha. All of these linkages were not at all difficult; they were motivated by specific elements in the widely known Hindu and Buddhist legends of Nagarjuna which found solid parallels in the equally celebrated Jain stories told to glorify particular teachers like Padaliptacarya and particular pilgrimage sites like Satrunjaya and Stambhana. Nagarjuna had been widely known in all the non-Jain sources as an adept at alchemy. Mt. Satrunjaya was renowned for its miraculous wells and streams containing the drink of immortality and for wondrous lodes of gold and silver. The Stambhana connection was likewise readily made with the associative link of the snakes.

Nagarjuna is brought into connection with the magical image of the Tirthamkara Parsvanatha, who in the Jain tradition was protected by the snake king. Finally, the association with Stambhana seems to have been so firm in the version of Nagarjuna's biography in which it appears that the biography came to circulate equally in pilgrimage texts that extol this sacred site as in the standard biography collections. I believe that this process implies a fundamental relationship between the growth and development of biography and pilgrimage stories, between the saint as walking locus of sanctity and the holy site as unmoving basis of his operations and likewise locus of sanctity.

In conclusion the biographies of Nagarjuna preserved in Svetambara Jain texts suggest one way in which a figure with established legends could be brought into a new context. The basic outlines of the familiar legends are retained , while concrete details, specifics of the life history, are altered to provide the new identity. It would appear that for Nagarjuna this process was well underway by the twelfth century A.D. at least, when we have the *Kumarapalapratibodha* with its summary of one version of Nagarjuna's biography. It is impossible at present to fix the earliest date of the appearance of a Jain biography of Nagarjuna, although the fact that the only Jain text attributed to Nagarjuna would appear to be a *rasa tantra* suggests that the reputation of Nagarjuna as an alchemist was well established in Jainism and indeed may have been a factor in their incorporation of Nagarjuna into their fold.[14]

A final question is less easy to answer and that is the question of the general applicability of the process suggested in this paper, where well-known stories come to coalesce around a figure through a series of associations, and concrete details of a biography are to be found rooted in links between saint and holy site. I suspect that one can only say in very general terms that if the biographies of Nagarjuna in the Svetambara texts can teach us anything about the wider process of biographical writing in medieval India and in Jainism in particular, then we should ultimately be able to document other examples of this process. We know that this was a period of active collection and writing of biographies in India, as it was of writing and gathering pilgrimage stories.The link proposed here between the two genres merits further testing. The fact that foreign pilgrims to India from China and Tibet relate the legends of Nagarjuna and other famous Buddhists and often give them a specific association with a particular pilgrimage site indeed suggests that such legends may have been frequently localized, sacred person and sacred site working in close cooperation. Again the observation that an earlier pilgrim like Hsuan-Tsang does not link Nagarjuna with the Mahabodhi temple while Dharmasvamin, who came several centuries later credits him with building a stone railing there, also seems to suggest that legend making may have been an ongoing process.[15] Indeed, it hints along the lines of the present investigation of the Jain biographies of Nagarjuna that the process of biography invention was closely tied to the institution of pilgrimage in some cases, and that biographical legend was easily expansible by localizing a saint in a desired holy place, attributing to him there various pious acts and miracles.

In addition there do exist other examples from the Jain tradition where a biography is told in both a *prabandha* collection and a *tirthakalpa*.[16] Other texts from the Digambara tradition likewise point to a close relationship between pilgrimage site and biography.One such case is that of the *pratyekabuddha* Karakanda,some of whose biographies I have studied elsewhere.[17]

Lastly there is the well-known work of Foucher on the Buddha's biography which suggests that in its very origin at least some religious biography must have been linked to pilgrimage sites, cycles of legends coalescing around specific locals.The conclusions of this study thus may not be at all irrelevant to an understanding of the wider biographical process in medieval India, and I look forward to continuing to test the hypotheses advanced here through further research.

BIBLIOGRAPHY

1.Biographies of Nagarjuna in the Jain Sources

Kumarapalapratibodha of Somaprabhacarya, edited Jina Vijaya Muni, Baroda: Gaekwad's Oriental Series, 1920, p. 179.

Prabandhacintamani of Merutunga, edited Jina Vijaya Muni, Singhi Jain Series, vol.1, Santiniketan, 1933, pp. 120-121. This is the only biography translated. Tawney, *The Prabandhacintamni or Wishing -Stone of Narratives,* Calcutta: Asiatic Society, 1901,pp. 194-197.

Prabandhakosa of Rajasekharasuri, edited Jina Vijaya Muni, Singhi Jain Series, vol.6, Santiniketan, 1935, pp. 84-86, pp. 13-

Prabhavakacarita of Prabhacandrasuri, edited Jina Vijaya Muni,Singhi Jain Series, vol. 13, Ahmedabad, 1940, pp.36-38.

Puratanaprabandhasamgraha, edited Jina Vijaya Muni,Singhi Jain Series, vol.2,Santiniketan,1936, pp. 91-86.

2.Tirthakalpas

Satrunjayakalpa of Dharmaghosa, edited Labhasagaragani, Agamodharagranthamala, 41, Ahmedabad, V.S. 2026, pp.84-86 for biography of Nagarjuna. For relevant legends about Satrunjaya, pp.. 28, 39-40.

Vividhatirthakalpa of Jinaprabhasuri, edited Jina Vijaya Muni,Singhi Jain Series, vol. 10, Santiniketan, 1934, p.104.

3.Biographies of Padaliptacarya
Prabandhakosa, pp. 11-16.
Prabhavakacarita, pp.28-40.
Puratanaprabandhasamgraha, p.93.

4. Biographies of Abhayadeva
Kharataragacchabrhadgurvavali, edited Jina Vijaya Muni, Singhi Jain Series, vol.42, Bombay, 1956, pp. 6-9.
Prabhavakacarita, pp. 161-170.
Puratanaprabandhasamgraha, p.95.

Notes

1. A summary of the texts classified as *mahakavyas* with comments on their sources can be found in Ramprasad Tripathi, *Jaina Samskrta Mahakavya Parampara aur Abhayadeva Krta Jayantavijaya*, Kanpur: Sahitya Niketan, 1984, chapter 1.The present paper is concerned with that other group of biographies which normally figured in the *prabandhas*.To date little has been done on the sources of the biographies in the *prabandhas*. This has become the central problem of my recent investigations on Jain biographies under the auspices of the grant from the Social Sciences and Humanities Research Council of Canada that has led to the publication of the present volume. I have decided to include in the present collection of essays a second paper on this question, dealing with two other biographies, those of Arya Khapatacarya and Mallavadin, and investigating the possible sources of transmission and preservation of biographical legends in medieval Jainism, particularly the role of the vast corpus of didactic story literature in this process. The present paper, then, deals with the development and transmission of the biographies of a special member of the Jain gallery of holy men, a figure whose legends were well established and carefully preserved outside the Jain tradition, while the second paper asks how the legends of holy men, whose activities were treated only in the Jain sources, were preserved and altered in the course of their history. It is my hope that these two papers will be read together, but to facilitate their appreciation by readers who might wish to read them independently, I have kept a separate introduction to each paper, despite the inevitable repetition that results.

2. On Somesvara see Bhogilal J. Sandesara, *Literary Circle of Mahamatya Vastupala and its Contribution to Sanskrit Literature*,Singhi Jain Series, volume 13, Bombay, 1953, pp. 42-52. On page 130 Sandesara notes verses that the *Kirtikaumudi*, Somesvara's poem on Vastupala, shares with that same author's *prasasti*.

3. The best source on early Indian historical writing is V.S. Pathak, *Ancient Historians of India : A Study of Historical Biographies*, London: Asia Publishing House, 1966.

4. On Jain religious literature and its abundant use of stories see A.N. Upadhye's introduction to the *Brhatkathakosa*,Singhi Jain Series, Volume 1, Bombay, 1934.On the relationship between these stories and the biographies in the *prabandhas* see my paper on Arya Khapatacarya in this volume. For the Digambara/ Svetambara connection see my paper on Haribhadra, to appear in the *Journal of Indian Philosophy*. A similar connection seems to exist between the biography of the Digamabra Samantabhadra told in the *Kathakosa* of Prabhacandra, edited A.N. Upadhye, Manikchandra Digambara Granthamala,

no.55, Delhi:Bharatiya Jnana Pitha, 1974, story number 4, and the various biographies of Siddhasena Divakara in the Svetambara *Prabandhas*. An excellent bibliography of current scholarship on Siddhasena appears in A.N. Upadhye, *Siddhasena's Nyayavatara and Other Works*, Bombay:Jaina Sahitya Vikasa Mandala,1971.Siddhasena's biography in addition shows interesting parallels to that of Nagarjuna in its close connection with pilgrimage sites. I am currently preparing a study of these biographies and related pilgrimage texts.

5. The *prabandhas*, which deal primarily with the lives of various figures important to the Jain community, and the *tirthakalpas*,which begin most often from the perspective of describing the merits of a given holy place in the style of the *puranic tirthamahatmya*,have already been recognized by scholars as closely related. In fact J. Deleu in his article, "A Note on the Jain Prabandhas", *Studien zum Jainismus und Buddhismus, Gedenkschrift fur Ludwig Alsdorf*,(ed. Klaus Bruhn and Albrecht Wezler, Stuttgart:Franz Steiner Verlag, 1981, pp. 61-73), regarded the *Vividhatirthakalpa* as a *prabandha*. The same thinking occurs in Dr. Bhogilal Sandesara's study cited above, p. 142. Jina Vijayamuni, who edited the *Vividhatirthakalpa* in the Singhi Jain Series, volume 10, 1934, drew attention to the importance of both all the known *prabandhas* and the *Vividhatirthakalpa* for a student of Jain history. At the same time as he commented upon the close affinity all these texts have for each other, however, he stopped short of explicitly calling the *tirthakalpa* a *prabandha*. The question seems to me to be an important one; to call the *Vividhatirthakalpa* a *prabandha* on the basis of occasionally shared contents seems to me to obscure a fundamental feature of biography writing in medieval Jainism which this paper attempts to describe: the close relationship between pilgrimage site and saint and between texts on pilgrimage sites and biographical writings. In fact although the distinction is not absolute, *prabandhas* do deal primarily with people, as Rajasekhara makes clear in his definition of a *prabandha* in the *Prabandhakosa*, while *tirthakalpas* set out to describe the glories of a place. The two genres do certainly overlap from time to time, with for example the *Prabandhakosa* having sections on places and the *Vividhatirthakalpa* having sections on people, but in general the distinction seems to me to be a valid and necessary one if we are to understand the dynamics of biography writing in medieval India.

In addition it would appear that the Jain tradition itself acknowledged a distinction between the terms *kalpa* and *prabandha (carita)*. To be more specific, a colophon to a manuscript of the *Samaradityakatha* of the thirteenth century, verse 23, reproduced in Jina Vijayamuni,*Jaina Pustaka Prasasti Samgraha*,Singhi Jain Series, vol.18 , 1943, p.30 describes the teachings, *sastra*, as two-fold, divided into the categories *kalpita* and *carita*. The term *carita* was widely used as synonymous with the term *prabandha* for a life history, despite Rajasekhara's efforts to keep these two terms separate by reserving *prabandha* for the life history of a recent figure and calling a *carita* anything that dealt with the deeds of the ancients. (Bhogilal Sandesara, page 144, of the volume cited earlier in this note). It thus seems to me that there is traditional evidence as well for keeping the *prabandhas* and the *tirthakalpas* distinct and regarding them as two separate types of literature.

6. K. Sacchidananda Murty in his study of the various accounts of Nagarjuna's life notes only the existence of a biography of Nagarjuna in the *Prabandhacintamani* (K. Sacchidananda Murty, *Nagarjuna*, Delhi:National Book Trust, 1971, p.30). More recently, Deleu in the article cited above, p. 69, treated the Jain biographies of Nagarjuna from the *prabandhas* and the *Vividhatirthakalpa* and briefly noted their mutual similarities and differences.In addition he affirms that the *Prabandhakosa* account is a translation into Sanskrit from the Prakrit of the *Vividhatirthakalpa*, while suggesting that the *Vividhatirthakalpa* was itself based on the Sanskrit account of Merutunga. This last piece of information was also given by Jina Vijayamuni in his Hindi introduction to the *Prabandhakosa*, Singhi Jain Series, vol. 6, 1935, in the paragraph in which he discusses the relationship between the *Prabandhakosa* and the *Vividhatirthakalpa*.

7. *Kathakosa*, edited by Dr. A.N. Upadhye, Manikchandra Digambara Jain Granthamala, no.55, Varanasi: Bharatiya Jnanapitha, 1974, pp.3-8. Virtually the same story is told in the Svetambara sources of the monk Haribhadra.I have studied these legends in a paper on the biographies of Haribhadra soon to appear in the *Journal of Indian Philosophy*.

8. This Nagarjuna, disciple of Himavant, is mentioned in verses 35-36 of the *Nandisutta*. The dictionary of Prakrit proper names gives other references, most of which I have been unable to trace because of the problems of locating Jain texts in North American libraries. See Dr. Mohan Lal Mehta and Dr.K. Rishabh Chandra, *Prakrit Proper Names*,L.D. Institute Series, number 28, Ahmedabad: L.D. Institute, 1970, pp. 316-317.

9. The accounts of Nagarjuna in the collections published under the single title *Puratanaprabandhasamgraha* are impossible at the moment to date. For the reasons I shall give in the discussion below I believe that they represent an earlier stratum of the legend, although this is purely conjectural. For some speculation on the dates of these versions see the Hindi introduction to the text by Jina Vijaya, who would hesitantly date them in fact considerably later than either the *Prabandhakosa* or the *Prabandhacintamani*.

10. It is worth noting that the authoritative sectarian biography of Abhayadeva in the *Kharataragacchabrhadgurvavali* (Singhi Jain Series, vol.42, 1956), does not at all connect the Stambhana Tirtha image with Nagarjuna. This may in fact suggest that the original association was indeed between Abhayadeva and the Parsvanatha and that Nagarjuna's connection with the image was only secondary. Likewise a *prasasti* or colophon to a manuscript of the *Mahaviracarita* by Nemicandrasuri mentions Abhayadeva in connection with the image of Stambhana and makes no mention of Nagarjuna *(Jaina Pustaka Prasasti Samgraha*, colophon number 6, page 9). Inscriptional evidence concerning the Kharataragaccha in which Abhayadeva is mentioned leads to the same conclusion, namely that the primary connection is between Abhayadeva and the Parsvanatha. (*Epigraphia Indica*, vol.1, pp. 313-324; vol.2, pp.34-86).

11. The text here and in the verses that follow describing Nagarjuna's alchemical training is definitely corrupt(verses 254-259). Nonetheless the overall sense seems clear.

12. An exhaustive study of this material is Murty's study mentioned in note 5 and that by N. Walleser in *Asia Minor*, vol.1, 1923, pp.421-455, "The Life of Nagarjuna from Tibetan and Chinese Sources".

13. Translated by G. Roerich, Patna: K.P. Jayaswal Research Institute, 1959, p. 94.

14. Jyoti Prasad Jain, "Jain Authors and Their Works", *Jaina Antiquary*, vol.33, no.1, July 1980, p. 27.

15. Roerich, *op.cit.*, page 65. See also the other late Tibetan Buddhist sources on Indian Buddhism, cited by Siglinde Dietz, *Der Buddhistische Briefliteratur Indiens*, Asiatische Forschungen, Band 84, Wiesbaden: Otto Harrassowitz, 1984, p. 24.

16. For some instances see Deleu's article cited above in note 5.

17. See my article, " The Miracle of a Hagiography Without Miracles: Some Comments on the Jain Lives of the Pratyekabuddha Karakanda", *Journal of Indian Philosophy*, vol.14, 1986, pp.389-403.

18. See Andre Couture's article in this volume for details.

THE BIOGRAPHIES OF ARYA KHAPATACARYA: A PRELIMINARY INVESTIGATION INTO THE TRANSMISSION AND ADAPTATION OF BIOGRAPHICAL LEGENDS

Phyllis Granoff

The Svetambara Jain tradition has preserved and recorded portraits of its famous monks in a variety of sources. Best known of these are the collections which assemble short accounts of different monks which were each designated by the term *prabandha*.[1] Extant Jain *prabandhas* stem from Gujarat and Rajasthan and are to be found in collections that were made from the thirteenth and fourteenth centuries A.D. Many of the *prabandhas* are written in a jaunty colloquial style and in a Sanskrit that is replete with vernacular expressions. All of the collections were written by monks and several explicitly state that they were composed at the request of a king or minister or someone else close to secular authority.[2] All of these texts are as rich in content as they are in linguistic interest.

These Jain *prabandhas* are of particular importance to a scholar exploring the larger topic of religious biography in India for a number of reasons, among which is their comparatively late date. Although Jainism from an early period recorded the lives of the Tirthamkaras, the founders of Jainism, the idea of collecting stories that tell the deeds of the eminent monks seems to have been a relative late-comer in the history of Svetambara Jain literature. Scholars consider either Hemacandra's *Parisistaparvan* in Sanskrit (dated 1170-1172 A.D.) or Bhadresvara's Prakrit *Kahavali*, dated to the twelfth century A.D., as the first example of a collection of biographies of gifted Svetambara monks.[3]

The late appearance of such biographies written about monks who lived often hundreds of years before these texts were composed raises several interesting questions. What prompted the recording and compilation of these biographies at this particular point in history? When the Svetambara monks decided to record the lives of eminent monks did they have before them a rich and reliable oral and/or written tradition? What are the sources for these lives and how did the lives circulate before they were ever written down in these collections? I have explored some of these questions before in my discussions of the Jain biographies of Nagarjuna and Haribhadra.[4] I should like to return to these questions here, particularly to the question of how the biographies might have circulated and been kept alive in the tradition, through an examination of the biographies of Arya Khapatacarya.

I shall attempt to show that a case like the biographies of Arya Khapatacarya suggests that possibly a select few of the *prabandhas* are not as novel within the Svetambara tradition as at first might appear, but in fact belong solidly within the tradition of didactic story telling for which the Jains, both Svetambaras and Digambaras are so famous. At the same time, I hope to be able to indicate that these biographies were nonetheless carefully adapted to their new context, as indeed were all stories in the tradition, and that subtle changes in fact can be observed in the biographies of Arya Khapatacarya as they moved from one type of text to another. In addition, I shall bring in a discussion of the biographies of another Jain monk, Mallavadin, that likewise occur in the didactic story collections and the *prabandhas*, to point out that the case of Arya Khapatacarya's biographies must be treated as only one of many possible patterns in the relationship between the didactic story collections and the *prabandhas*.

To some extent the supposition that there is a link between the didactic story collections and later biographies of Jain monks is not an entirely new discovery. In his work on the *Parisistaparvan* of Hemacandra, Hermann Jacobi, relying on the scholarship of Ernst Leumann, correctly pointed out that Hemacandra drew his materials from the story -telling tradition that begins with the commentaries to the various *sutras*, particularly the *Avasyaka* and its commentaries. He also noted, however, that the reliance was a close one and that often Hemacandra makes few alterations in the older material.[5] *Prabandha* collectors like Prabhacandra, the author of the *Prabhavakacarita*, in their turn explicitly state that they relied in part on Hemacandra, and thus the *prabandhas* might be assumed under Jacobi's theory to have intimate links, even indirectly through Hemacandra, with the rich corpus of stories on which Hemacandra himself had drawn.[6] One of the tasks of this paper will be to show that such an inference is only partially justified.

In fact Jacobi did not directly address the issue of the *prabandhas* and their position in Svetambara literature. In addition, when Jacobi was writing there were few texts of a later period available from the large corpus of Svetambara story literature. Stories from the various commentaries were eventually collected into *Kathakosas* , "Treasure Houses of Stories", in much the same way *prabandhas* were assembled in a text like the *Prabandhakosa*,

"Treasure House of *Prabandhas*".[7] With more of this material available we are now in a better position to assess the role of these didactic stories in the transmission and preservation of at least some of the biographical material that eventually found its way into the various *prabandha* collections, and thus to assess the nature of these *prabandhas* themselves and their position in Svetambara Jain literature. We are also in a better position to explore the significance of the differences between the accounts in the *prabandhas* and those in the didactic story collections and at least begin to ask how the *prabandhas* adapted didactic stories to their own needs. It seems thus worthwhile to return to the question of sources of biographies and the relationship between biographies and didactic stories.

For such a study the legends of Arya Khapata offer a particularly suitable example in that they can be found prior to their appearance in the *prabandhas* in the *Avasyaka* commentaries and in eleventh and twelfth century collections of didactic tales, and roughly contemporary with their incorporation in the *prabandhas* in a commentary to a famous hymn.The biography of Arya Khapatacarya thus affords ample opportunity to study the contexts in which some biographical legends might have been disseminated amongst the Jain public.

What emerges from the study is a picture of a remarkably stable core of legend that was put to various uses by the religious tradition. Such stability in the basic story material is a common feature of both the didactic stories of the Jain tradition and the biographical collections. This stability may be reflected in the fact that contexts change but the basic story remains constant as does its cast of characters.A more familiar scenario, however,is where the basic plot of the story is solidly unchanged but the protagonists may differ. The Hindu tradition offers a close parallel in its use of its own myths, which the tradition normally also designates as stories, "*katha*", where famous myths, for example the story of the appearance of the *linga*, the *lingodbhava*, or the story of Siva losing his *linga* in the Daruvana after he has maddened the wives of the sages with lust, are told again and again in richly different contexts, migrating from *tirtha* to *tirtha*, but with the story remarkably stable.[8] The biographies of Arya Khapata fall somewhere inbetween these two models, with the basic story remaining for the most part unchanged except in minor details, but an occasional important character taking a different name or different religious affiliation. The final result is in each type of text a distinct image of Arya Khapata consistent with the particular context given the biography and its purpose in that text. Thus the *Avasyaka* tradition knows him as a wonder-worker, the didactic story tradition as a promoter of the faith whose zeal in spreading Jainism should serve as an example to all, the *prabandhas* as wonder-worker, promoter of the faith and along with his followers as an ardent anti-Buddhist, and thus in its own terms as a paradigmatic Jain, and finally the commentary to the hymn knows Arya Khapata as a vehicle through which the hymn may work its magic. We turn now to a brief examination of the biographies of Arya Khapatacarya, beginning with the *prabandhas*, and thence to a consideration of the didactic story tradition and the commentary to the hymn.

I.Sources for the Life of Arya Khapatacarya

Arya Khapatacarya was known in the Svetambara tradition for his prodigious and often humorous feats of magic. He belongs to a small but select group of wizards and wonder-workers, amongst whom may be included Padaliptacarya,Nagarjuna and Arya Khapata's disciple Mahendra. Arya Khapata's biography is told in a number of sources. It occurs in two of the major *prabandha* collections, the *Prabandhakosa* and the *Prabhavakacarita*. In addition we find Arya Khapata's story told in a virtually identical manner in two earlier works which are not in fact concerned primarily with biographies or with the deeds of celebrated monks. They are didactic story collections and belong to the vast story literature of the Svetambara Jains. The first of these is Acarya Pradyumnasuri's *Mulasuddhiprakarana* with Devacandrasuri's commentary.[9] The date of Devacandrasuri's commentary, written in Prakrit, is 1089-1090 A.D., which places this account of Arya Khapatacarya several hundred years before his biography in an actual biography collection, either that in the *Prabandhakosa* of 1349 A.D. or that in the *Prabhavakacarita* of 1277 A.D. The story also occurs in another Prakrit text which is very similar to the *Mulasuddhiprakarana*. This is the *Akhyanakamanikosa* of Srinemicandrasuri (1073-1083 A.D.) and its commentary of Amradevasuri, 1134 A.D., again considerably earlier than either of the *prabandha* collections. The present edition of the *Mulasuddhiprakarana* does not include any information about the composition of the text, but we do know from the *prasasti* to the *Akhyanakamanikosa* that the commentary which is rich in stories was composed in the home of a wealthy merchant at the request of the author's teacher and for the sake of a devoted lay disciple.[10] Both of these story collections with their commentaries belong to Gujarat, and it is perhaps worth noting at the outset that Arya Khapatacarya is not unique in having his biography figure in such texts. There are other monks in the Svetambara tradition whose biographies are included in the didactic collections, and this paper will deal with one of them , Mallavadin, when it comes to assessing how widely applicable are the conclusions drawn from a consideration of Arya Khapatacarya's biographies. In addition, even within the Digambara tradition the biography of the famous monk Akalanka occurs first in a text of similar nature, the *Kathakosa* of Prabhacandra as I have noted elsewhere, and the biography of the monk Samantabhadra appears in the same text. Both of these biographies also seem to have influenced later Svetambara biographies of other monks which appear in the *prabandhas*.[11] Arya Khapata's story is likewise told in the *Kumaralapalapratibodha* of Somaprabhacarya, a text composed in 1195 A.D. at the request of two wealthy lay devotees.[12] Finally the biography of Arya Khapatacarya occurs in a commentary to a famous hymn, the commentary of Sri Gunakarasuri to the *Bhaktamarastotra* of Manatunga, which is dated 1370 A.D. and thus falls squarely within the time frame of the composition of the *prabandha* collections.[13] Arya Khapata's story seems to have been relatively stable as it was transmitted over the centuries in these diverse types of texts. It is also amongst the oldest of the biographical stories we have in the *prabandhas*, figuring briefly in the *Avasyaka* and its commentaries.[14] We turn now to a consideration of our texts.

II. Arya Khapatacarya in the *Prabandha* Collections.

As is often the case it is easiest to begin from the *Prabandhakosa* of Rajasekharasuri which offers us a clear account of Arya Khapata's deeds. The account begins somewhat unusually, for instead of naming precisely the particular lineage to which Arya Khapata belongs (his *gaccha)*, Rajasekhara states merely that Arya Khapata appeared in some lineage or other, he does not say which. He had a student named Bhuvana, who was also his nephew and who plays a major role in the events to follow. Arya Khapata goes to Bhrgukaccha, where reigns the King Balamitra, a devoted Buddhist. The Buddhists, he goes on to state, were very gifted at logic, but more important they are at this moment overweeningly arrogant at having gotten themselves such a powerful protector.[15] But to Rajasekhara this seems but natural, for here he interjects a bit of proverbial wisdom, which might be freely rendered thus, " To begin with a she monkey acts crazy, but what will she not do when bitten by a scorpion?" The Buddhists go so far as to offer a challenge to the Svetambara Jains in a particularly insulting fashion. They throw grass into the Svetambara temple, a gesture which Rajaskehara explains is meant to imply that their Svetambara rivals are no better than animals. But Arya Khapata is not at all angered; after all he is a great religious leader, and again a bit of folk wisdom elaborates: does the great ocean, lord of the waves, get agitated by the stirrings of tiny fish in its midst? Bhuvana, Arya Khapata's disciple and nephew, however , becomes outraged and hurls a challenge back at the Buddhists. King Balamitra now intervenes and demands to know of Bhuvana what he has said. He replies that the king's teachers, the Buddhists, like dogs that bark noisily inside the house but cower once outside the gate, are abusing the Svetambara Jains. And so Bhuvana has come to test their mettle in debate at the king's court. The king agrees and summons the Buddhists, who are struck dumb with the blows of his logic which are like blows of a lion's paws to a jackal. The king awards victory to the Jains , whence great joy reigns in their temples. But the Buddhists are like lotus gardens withered by the frost. And here the plot thickens, for a Buddhist teacher from Gudasastrapura, hearing of the Buddhist defeat and humiliation, the great logician Vrddhakara, arrives on the scene. The king tries to warn him of Bhuvana's great prowess, but nothing will stop the Buddhist, and he who was never before defeated in debate is now defeated by Bhuvana. Here again Rajasekhara interjects, the King of Death never has his fill of mortal creatures, and the wretched Buddhist master starves himself to death and becomes a demi-god *(yaksa)*in Gudasastrapura. Because of his previous hatred of the Svetambara Jains he now torments them by causing them to fall ill,terrifying them and stealing their money. The community at Gudasastra sends word to Arya Khapata who comes at once. He enters the temple of the *yaksa* and proceeds to place his shoes on the ears of the image of the *yaksa* and his feet on its chest. People gather, and even the king appears on the scene. As soon as he sees the king, Arya Khapata covers himself with his white robe and lies still. Wherever the king pulls back the robe, he is treated to the sight of the teacher's buttocks. Furious at the insult, the king orders him beaten. But lo and behold the blows levelled on Arya Khapatacarya fall on the limbs of the king's wives,which are tenderer than the softest flower blossoms.A hue and cry rises from the harem and the king is struck with wonder at Arya Khapata's magic prowess.[16] He falls at his feet. Even the *yaksa* image humbly comes forward to massage Arya Khapata's feet. The crowd presses forward as Arya Khapata thunders at the *yaksa*, "You lowest of the low, you dare to torment my followers? Go ahead, torment them if you dare!" The *yaksa* replies by pledging always to protect the Jain religious community, and the king and all the bystanders amazed at the goings on become loyal followers of Arya Khapata.When Arya Khapata leaves the temple, the stone image of the *yaksa* follows him. Two large stones and two large stone pots and many minor deities also accompany him. Arya Khapata dismisses them all when he reaches the city gates and they return to the temple. The two pots he stations at the town gate so that all should know what took place there. The king, now a faithful Jain, returns to his palace. The people call Arya Khapata "Prabhavananartikirangacarya"," The Dancing Master of the Dancer, Spreading the Faith".We shall see in our investigation of Arya Khapata in the story collections that the title fits in well with his role in the didactic tales, where his story is told as an example of spreading the faith.

The story now moves on to another event. Two monks come from Bhrgupura with some bad news for Arya Khapata after his victory. They tell him that a certain monk has secretly read a book that Arya Khapata had with him and from it learned the magic secret of making objects come to him *(akrstilabdhi)*. With this magic power he gathers to himself all the delicious dishes prepared in the homes of the wealthy merchants. Although his fellow monks have told him to stop, he is such a slave to his palate that he would not heed their admonitions. And so the monks have had no recourse but to expel him. And now furious at his expulsion this monk has become a Buddhist. In fact the Buddhists have virtually elevated him to the position of chief monk. In return he sends their begging bowls flying through the air to the homes of the faithful and returns them filled, flying through the sky , to the Buddhist monastery.Seeing this great marvel all the common folk are converting to Buddhism. The two Jains then beg

Arya Khapata to do something to stop this. After giving the matter some thought Arya Khapata journeys back to Bhgrupura, where he stays incognito. Suddenly the Buddhists' begging bowls are struck in mid-flight by a magically created stone and fall shattered to the ground, dropping rice and sweet meats on everyone's heads. The miserable monk who was the cause of all this trouble to begin with realizes that Arya Khapata has won and he beats a hasty retreat. Arya Khapata then proceeds to the Buddhist monastery. The image of the Buddha rises to greet him and sings his praises. And once again the Jain faith is spread among the people. Arya Khapata retires from the scene of his victory and with this really Rajasekhara closes his account of Arya Khapata's deeds. What follows is an act of his disciple, Mahendra, and I summarize it briefly below.

In the city Pataliputra the King Dahada is a devotee of the Brahmins and causes the Jain monks much misery. He orders them to bow down to the Brahmins and when they refuse, saying that it is not fitting that a monk should bow down to a householder, the king then threatens that if they do not bow down to the Brahmins he will cut off their heads. The Jain monks ask for seven days grace. It just so happens that Arya Khapata's disciple, Mahendra, chances to pass by Pataliputra at that moment. The monks tell him of their plight and he takes two branches, one red and one white, and goes before King Dahada. It is now the morning of the eighth day and the king orders that the Jain Svetambara monks be brought forward and made to bow to the Brahmins. Mahendra raises the red staff and waving it he asks the king, "Shall they bow from this direction or from that?" Instantly the heads of the Brahmins fall off and roll to the ground. Terrified, the king begs for forgiveness and promises never to mistreat the Jain monks. Mahendra raises the white staff, waves it and the Brahmins now have their heads back.[17] The king is taught the true doctrine and becomes a Jain, as do all the Brahmins. And so the faith was spread. One manuscript here adds that even Bhuvana returns to the faith, implying that it was Bhuvana, Arya Khapata's nephew, who had deserted the Jains and become a Buddhist, carrying out the magical feat of filling their begging bowls and transporting them through the sky. In all the other accounts of Arya Khapata that we will study here it is indeed Bhuvana who is the culprit, but it is worth noting that this would be the only mention of his name in this episode in the *Prabandhakosa* and that the majority of manuscripts do not add this remark. All other manuscripts simply end the story now with the statement that Arya Khapata installed his nephew Bhuvana in his position and died by voluntary starvation. There is no indication that Bhuvana had wavered from the faith and only later became a great Jain monk.

I have summarized the account of Arya Khapata in the *Prabandhakosa* in some detail in order to have a frame of reference as we consider the other stories. Passing now to the *Prabhavakacarita*, chapter 5, the biography of Padaliptacarya, in which Arya Khapata's biography is also told, we find some interesting differences, although the basic story remains the same. Prabhacandra first gives us the setting for the story, and he tells us that King Balamitra of Bhrgukaccha is the nephew of the famous Kalakacarya, a Jain monk whose biography was often told. Arya Khapata is then introduced as is his nephew Bhuvana,who, it is said has the power of grasping whatever he hears, even if he hears it only once (vs. 147). It is also said that Bhuvana had defeated the Buddhists and wrested from them a Jain holy place, here unnamed, as the sun defeats the darkness (vs 148). A Buddhist teacher Vaddakara comes from Gudasastrapura to defeat the Jains. The story proceeds as in the *Prabandhakosa;* Vaddakara is defeated by Bhuvana, here simply called " the disciple of the Jain master" (verse 151) and dies in fury and becomes a *yaksa* who torments the Jains. This is reported by two monks to Arya Khapata. Arya Khapata then gives a book to Bhuvana, telling him never to open it, and proceeds to Gudasastrapura(vs.155). The account again is very much like the one we have just reviewed; Arya Khapata enters the *yaksa* temple and puts his shoes on the ears of the *yaksa* (vs.156).The temple priest comes in and sees this and reports to the king, who removes Arya Khapata's robe with the same results as in the *Prabandhakosa* account, and orders him beaten,again with the same results. Here Arya Khapata, propitiated by the king, gets up and does a dance, ordering the *yaksa* to follow him.He leaves the temple, accompanied by the *yaksa* and minor Gods(164-165).He also causes two large stone pots which need a thousand men to move them to follow him, and seeing all these wonders the king and all the subjects become followers of Jainism (vs.166-167).The king requests him to return the *yaksa* to the temple, which he does, but he leaves the pots where they are (vs. 168).

There follows the story of the flying begging bowls, and it is absolutely clear that Bhuvana, Arya Khapata's nephew, is the culprit. Two monks come from Bhrgukaccha, sent to Arya Khapata by the community of monks, and tell him that Bhuvana has disobeyed his orders and opened the book (vs.169-170).All is as in the *Prabandhakosa* account, Arya Khapata breaking the flying bowls with an invisible stone,and the culprit absconding.Arya Khapata enters the Buddhist temple and demands that the Buddha bow down to him; the image comes forward and falls at his feet.At the door of the temple is a Buddhist stupa (*buddhanda*, vs.180) which he also orders to bow at his feet. When the teacher tells the stupa to rise it does so only half-way, and it has remained in this position since that time, known by all the people as *"nirgranthanamita"* ," the one that was made to bow down by the Jain"(vs 182).

The account then continues with the same story of Mahendra that Rajasekhara has included.Here King Dahada, however, is not a follower of any one faith but torments all religious people equally, making the Buddhist monks go naked and Saiva ascetics give up their matted locks; he forces the Vaisnavas to abandon worship of Visnu and those who follow the Kaula path to sport braids; he makes unbelievers profess religion and wants Jain monks to bow down to Brahmins, and finally he forces the Brahmins to drink alcohol (vs. 183-187).The

Jain community in this account sends for Mahendra and Mahendra asks the astrologers to set a suitable moment for the Jains to bow down to the Brahmins. There is no mention of the seven days period of grace. Mahendra appears along with the Jains, carrying his two magic staffs, and the account proceeds as summarized from Rajasekhara, except that Mahendra does not take personal credit for the miracle. Mahendra tells those assembled that this was an act of the deities who protect Jainism.The king begs him to propitiate the Jain Gods, which he does(vs. 211-217). A divine voice is heard, proclaiming that the only recourse for the now headless Brahmins is to become Jain monks (vs.218). Mahendra then waves his magic stick and the Brahmins return to life. He tells the king that he wishes his teacher Arya Khapata to initiate the Brahmins, and when the king insists that no one could be greater in spreading the faith than Mahendra, Mahendra says that he is nothing compared to Arya Khapata who had freed the holy place Asvavabodha in Bhrgukaccha from the Buddhists, with the skill of one rescuing a dish of milk from a cat(vs. 224).The text then concludes with the statement that in this way Arya Khapata spread the faith (vs 228) and Mahendra achieved renown. Many other great men who propagated Jainism followed Arya Khapata; their lineage is still alive in Asvavabodhatirtha (vs.229).

The account in the *Prabhavakacarita* differs from that in the *Prabandhakosa* on several points.First it is made perfectly clear that the bad Jain monk who becomes a Buddhist is indeed Arya Khapata's nephew, and there is no effort made to redeem him in the eyes of the community. Mahendra is the only disciple of Arya Khapata mentioned; there is no indication that Arya Khapata installed his nephew in his position before he died. King Dahada, Mahendra's adversary is not a devout Hindu in this version,and the miracle is not Mahendra's but belongs to the protecting deities of Jainism. The Brahmins are made Jain monks as the condition for their restitution to life, and Arya Khapata is directly connected with Mahendra's miracle here in that it is he who performs their consecration ceremony. Finally Arya Khapata is said to have rescued the holy place in Bhrgukaccha known as Asvavabodhatirtha, "the holy place where the horse was enlightened", from the Buddhists. This seems to be an isolated reference to Arya Khapata's connection with this pilgrimage site. Although this holy site is known to the *Vividhatirthakalpa* of Jinaprabhasuri, 1333 A.D., the standard Svetambara account of pilgrimage sites, Arya Khapata is not mentioned there at all, nor is it said that the site was ever under the control of the Buddhists.[18] The *Prabhavakacarita* does give an account of the origin of this holy site in the biography of Vijayasimhasuri, chapter 6, but again without connecting the site with Arya Khapata. Bhrgupura is certainly known in early Buddhist literature, and in one account it is said to have been founded by a Buddhist monk, although in Hsuan Tsang's accounts of his travels in India it is not considered to be a Buddhist center by any means.[19] Perhaps further research will throw more light on this reference and help elucidate its significance. For now let us turn to a consideration of Arya Khapata in the didactic story collections so that we can better assess his treatment in these *prabandhas* and understand their place in the larger body of literature that includes his biography.

III. Arya Khapatacarya in the Tradition of the Didactic Story

It seems best to begin our investigation with a consideration of the story of Arya Khapatacarya in the *Avasyaka* and its commentaries which stand in many ways at the source of the vast story literature of the Svetambaras. Unfortunately the only commentaries to the *Avasyaka* that are available to me are the commentary of Jnanasagaramuni and the Sanskrit *Avasyaka Katha* cited in the *Abhidhana Rajendrakosa*.[20] While a more detailed study of Arya Khapatacarya in the *Avasyaka* must therefore await a later date, at the present state of my knowledge I can say that Arya Khapata in the two texts I have examined is regarded simply as a wonder-worker and not as a propagator of the faith. Arya Khapata is mentioned in the *Avasyaka*, verse 932, as an example of someone who is *vijjasiddho*, "accomplished in the arts of magic". The brief account of his life in the commentary mentions that in Gudasastrapura there was a *parivrajaka*, a monk, defeated by *sadhus* in debate. He became extremely angry, and on his death became a demi-god, a *vyantara*, who tormented the *sadhus*. He was awakened to the true faith by Arya Khapatacarya. Next is given a brief account of Bhuvana's transgressions. Bhuvana, the nephew of Arya Khapata, has become a Buddhist (*bauddhamilita*) and with his magic power he brings them food. Arya Khapata arrives on the scene and the delinquent Bhuvana vanishes. Arya Khapata then causes a Buddhist temple (*bauddhaprasada)* to bow down to him. This is all that Jnanasagaramuni tells us of Arya Khapata but it contains at least two very significant points for our discussion. Jnanasagaramuni tells us unambiguously that the demi-god who torments the Jain monks is not a Buddhist as he is in both the *prabandha* accounts, and that the monk who converts to Buddhism and satisfies his gluttony with magic is Bhuvana, Arya Khapata's nephew. The *Avasyakakatha* is similar; the opponent is not a Buddhist and the rest of the story is otherwise identical to that in the *Mulasuddhiprakarana* that we will review in some detail below with the exception that Arya Khapata is not praised as a spreader of the faith, but rather as one accomplished in magic powers. Arya Khapata's story is also said to be found in the *Brhatkalpabhasya* and *Curni* and the *Nisitha*, however, I have been unable to locate the story although I do find Arya Khapata mentioned in one text as one skilled in magic.[21]

If we turn to the *Mulasuddhiprakarana* and its commentary, the earliest of our didactic story collections, we find the story of Arya Khapata given as an example of spreading the faith. It is the second story in the text and Arya Khapata is introduced as someone who is "*vidyasiddha*", "accomplished in the arts of magic", exactly as we find him designated in the *Avasyaka*.[22] The story begins with the setting, Bhrgukaccha, where Arya Khapata has arrived in the course of his normal wanderings. Two Jain monks from Gudasastrapura then come to him to tell him that an ascetic, a *parivvayago* who denied the doctrine of karmic retribution *(akiriyavai)*, had come there. Next then follows a brief summary in verse of his doctrines which resemble those of the materialist or Carvaka. He did not believe in *dharma*, he did not believe in merit or sin, he did not believe in supernatural beings and in the hereafter and he did not believe that there is any soul beyond the collocation of physical elements. It is then said that he was defeated in debate and died of despondency, only to be reborn as a demi-god *(vantara)* .Hideous in appearance, cruel, exceedingly fierce, remembering his previous humiliation, he now appears in the sky and shouts out, " O all of you evil ones, you vile heretics, outside the Vedic faith, devoid of shame! If you do not defeat me in debate at once I shall kill all the Jains by all sorts of terrible torments! Whether you enter the netherworld or flee to the heavens, wherever you go, you will never be freed from the evil effects of your own bad deeds!" Thus this wicked demi-god torments the Jain monastic community. On hearing this Arya Khapata leaves the whole community of monks and his nephew behind and through his magic powers in an instant travels to Gudapura.He enters the temple of the *vyantara* and does as we have read in the other accounts, he puts his shoes on the ears of the demi-god. The temple priest comes and sees this outrage and summons the king. The story then continues exactly as in the *Prabhavakacarita*, with the robe pulled back to reveal the teacher's posterior and the blows to Arya Khapata falling on the king's wives in the harem. Finally, when the king begs Arya Khapata for forgiveness, Arya Khapata rises. The *vyantara* follows him as do other minor gods.The two stone pots at the entrance of the temple also follow Arya Khapata.A crowd assembles and begs Arya Khapata to leave the gods in the temple. Arya Khapata agrees, but he adds that only someone as great as he is can make the stone pots go back.The author of the text states that they still stand today where Arya Khapata left them! The *vyantara* becomes a faithful protector of Jainism and the people who witnessed the events become Jains.

The story then switches back to Bhrgupura, where it is said Arya Khapata's nephew, greedy for good food, has become a Buddhist.With his magical powers he causes their begging bowls to fly through the sky to the homes of the faithful. Arya Khapata breaks them with his magic stone and Bhuvana flees. Arya Khapata enters the temple and when the Buddhist monks tell him to bow down to them he tells the Buddha to bow down him. The image falls at his feet as does a Buddhist stupa at the door that he also orders to do him homage. As in the *Prabhavakacarita* this Buddhist stupa is called "the one that was made to bow down by the Jain","*niyanthonamiyanamo*". The people are all astonished and realize the greatness of the Jain teachings at the feet of whose monk even stone images prostrate themselves. This concludes the account.There is no mention of Mahendra or King Dahada.

The story of Arya Khapata in the *Akhyanikamanikosa* is virtually the same as that in the *Mulasuddhiprakarana* commentary we have just summarized. It is given as an example of furthering the cause of Jainism and spreading the faith.The only significant point of difference is perhaps the direct mention of Camunda among the gods in the *vyantara* temple who submit to Arya Khapata and follow him out, for we shall see that Arya Khapata defeats Camunda in the commentary to the *Bhaktamarastotra*, to which we shall turn below after some brief remarks on Arya Khapata's story in the *Kumarapalapratibodha*.

The *Kumarapalapratibodha* reproduces the story of Arya Khapata as it appears in the *Mulasuddhiprakarana* with one very telling addition, which may be seen to illustrate neatly the basic stability of the biography as it appeared in a variety of texts designed for slightly different purposes and at the same time its inherent flexibility to make subtle changes to match its changing environments. The *Kumarapalapratibodha* adds a few details. It names the king in Gudasastrapura, who is called "Venivaccharau", or Venivatsaraja, when the story of Arya Khapata and the *vyantara* is related, only to pick up this detail at the end and say that when the king witnessed the great powers of Arya Khapata he converted to Jainism, and where there had been a temple to the Buddhist Goddess Tara he had built a temple to the Jain Goddess, Siddhaiya or Siddhayika, the patron Goddess of Mahavira.Finally the text relates that this temple came under the control of the Digambaras for some time but that now Kumarapala has had a temple to Ajitanatha made there by one of the members of his court, Abhaya, son of Yasadeva. In a text that is mostly concerned with the conversion of a king and with the relationship of the faith to the state and state patronage, it seems fitting that Arya Khapata's story should ultimately conclude by stressing the conversion of a king and the dedication of that king to the faith; that kings must and do continue to protect the faith is then further emphasized by continuing the history of this particular place: from Vatsraja to Kumarapala, who has also had a temple erected at the site. In contrast , then , to the other biographies of Arya Khapatacarya in the didactic story collections which had emphasized his role in spreading the faith, this recitation of Arya Khapata's deeds seems to emphasize not only his wondrous powers and his ability to spread Jainism, but also the deeds of the king he converts and of Kumarapala as well. In a text that sets out to tell the story of the conversion of Kumarapala, such an addition seems fitting indeed.

In summary of the presentation of Arya Khapata in the didactic story collections, it seems that the most important divergences from the biographies in the *prabandhas* are as follows. The demi-god who torments the Jains was never a Buddhist, but an atheist. The deserter to Buddhism is Arya Khapata's nephew Bhuvana, and there is no mention in any of the accounts available to me to date of Mahendra and the Brahmins. Both of these points are consistent with the accounts given in the *Avasyaka*, which must have served as the source of the biography for the didactic collections. Finally, it might be added that the story of Arya Khapatacarya is included in the *Mulasuddhiprakarana* and the *Akhyanikamanikosa* as an example of propagating the Jain faith and in keeping with this fact tends to emphasize Arya Khapata's magical powers less for themselves than for the higher goal which they served.

IV. Arya Khapata and the *Bhaktamarastotra*.

The *Bhaktamarastotra* of Manatunga was greatly reverenced by both Svetambara and Digambara Jains. Arya Khapata's story is told in a fourteenth century commentary to the hymn which gives for each verse a brief story of a miracle performed through the greatness of that particular verse. Arya Khapatacarya figures in two of these stories, those associated with the hymn verses 22 and 23. In verse 22 is told a version of the *yaksa* story, closer to that in the *prabandhas* than in the Prakrit didactic story collections. The commentary , written in Sanskrit, is contemporary with the *prabandhas* and illustrates an alternate adaptation of Arya Khapata's biographical legends. The story runs as follows. In Gudasastrapura a Buddhist teacher named Vrddhakara was defeated by the Jain monk Bhuvana. Dying of humilation at this defeat, Vrddhakara became a *yaksa* and tormented the Jain monks. The monastic community approached the elderly Arya Khapata who had discovered the means to combat the *yaksa* through his constant repetition of verse twenty-two of the *Bhaktamarastotra* and brought him to Gudasastrapura. He enters the temple and puts his shoes on the *yaksa's* ears and his feet on its chest and covering himself with his robe falls asleep. The priest finds him and orders him out and in the morning the king and citizens come to say their prayers. The king orders Arya Khapata beaten; the blows land on his queens in the harem. The king begs his forgiveness and takes his feet. Arya Khapata rises and the *yaksa* follows him. Arya Khapata rebukes the *yaksa* and then makes him the guardian of the faith. They all leave the temple, followed by other gods as well. Even the two stone pots move. The gods are dismissed at the city gate and return to the temple but the pots can still be seen there at the gate. The king and all the people become Jains.

It is immediately apparent that this is the same story as can be found in the *Prabandhakosa*. The only significant difference is that here Arya Khapata's powers come directly from the hymn. He is no longer the *vidyasiddha*, the wizard skilled in magic, but a vehicle through which the power of the hymn may act. The same is true in the commentary to verse 23 in which it is said that Arya Khapata through reciting the twenty-third verse of the hymn received a boon from Sarvanubhuticakra. This boon enabled him to subdue evil demi-gods *(vyantara)* and with it he proceeded to Ujjaiyini where he stayed in the temple of Candi. Now Candi was hostile to those who spent the night in her temple, particularly when they were Svetambaras. And so she approached Arya Khapata, ugly, red-faced as if flushed with drink. Arya Khapata sat still in meditation._The Goddess grew angrier and angrier. He scratched her neck, sorely wounding her. Crying she offered him a boon. He made her give up accepting blood sacrifices and ordered her to stop tormenting people. In the morning she followed Arya Khapata out of the temple and at the city gate took her leave of him, bowing at this feet. His nail marks still can be seen on her neck.The townspeople, witness to the event, realized the greatness of Jainism.

This story seems to be a variant of Arya Khapata's defeat of the *yaksa*.We have see in the *Akhyanakamanikosa* that Camunda was among the deities who bowed to Arya Khapata at Gudasastrapura.Here the scene is switched to the famous temple of Candi in Ujjaiyini, where other famous Jains were credited in the later tradition with the defeat of popular Hindu goddesses.[23] It seems safe to conclude that the *Bhaktamara* commentary continues the venerable tradition of using a familiar story of a famous monk to illustrate a religious point. It alters the story to make that point, attributing Arya Khapata's widely acknowledged magic powers to the powers of the hymn.[24] It remains now to review our evidence and consider some more general conclusions.

V.Review of the Biographies of Arya Khapatacarya

It is difficult to make broad general conclusions on the basis of an investigation of one biography. For this reason I shall confine myself here to a discussion of what the evidence suggests about the transmission and adaptations of Arya Khapatacarya's stories, namely that at least for Arya Khapata the legends in the *prabandhas* would seem to be faithful and subtle adaptations of legends preserved in the *Avasyaka* tradition and in the didactic story collections. As a warning, however, against assuming with Jacobi that therefore the biographies of the monks go back to the didactic stories which were their sources and vehicle of transmission, I should like at the conclusion of this section to introduce some evidence from the biographies of another famous Jain, the scholar and logician Mallavadin. There are in fact two distinct biographies of Mallavadin. The one, appearing in the didactic story collection , the *Akhyanakamanikosa,* and the closely related *Kahavali* of Bhadresvara, appears in only one *prabandha*, the *Prabhavakacarita* of Prabhacandra. The biography of Mallavadin in the *Prabandhacintamani* and the *Prabandhakosa* is in fact a totally different biography with only the faintest resemblances to that in the story collections. Its sources are at the moment a matter of speculation, but a consideration of the legends of Mallavadin is nonetheless essential in putting into perspective any conclusions that may be drawn here about Arya Khapata's biographies and their relation to the story collections. Let us begin, then, with a consideration of just what this investigation of Arya Khapata's biographies in these different texts reveals about their possible sources and transmission.

Arya Khapata's deeds are related in a variety of texts which can be grouped under two general headings: the *prabandhas* and didactic story collections, with a third lone and distinctive text, a commentary to the *Bhaktamarastotra*. Jacobi in his study of the *Parisistaparvan* of Hemacandra which many have considered as the forerunner of the *prabandhas* identified the *Avasyaka* and its commentaries and the rich story literature of the Svetambaras as the source for Hemacandra's stories. There is one obvious limitation to extending this hypothesis to the *prabandhas* themselves: for the majority of the *prabandhas* no earlier written account survives even amongst the vast repertoire of stories known to date.Nonetheless the evidence does suggest that in the case of Arya Khapatacarya, where versions exist in the story literature prior to the *prabandhas*, the stories exhibit a remarkable stability with a few telling changes. In the case of Arya Khapatacarya the *prabandhas* do introduce new material not present in the story collections examined to date. The new material stresses Jain - Buddhist hostility by converting the materialist opponent into a Buddhist, brings Arya Khapata into association with an important local pilgrimage site, Asvavabodhatirtha in Bhrgukaccha, and attaches a story about his disciple Mahendra. In addition in the *Prabandhakosa*, Bhuvana ,his nephew and disciple, is either not made into a culprit who converts to Buddhism out of greed for food, or is exonerated and made Arya Khapata's successor. In the hymn to the *Bhaktamara* a further change is made in that Arya Khapata's powers are made to derive from the magical powers of the hymn.A second story associating him with the well-known defeat of Camunda at Ujjaiyini is also added.

In each of these cases it seems possible to recognize a specific adaptation for specific needs. Most obviously the commentary to the hymn collects stories to show the greatness of the hymn: the locus of power is thus switched from holy man to holy word. In the case of the *prabandhas* we are on more speculative ground in trying to fathom the reasons for the changes.Perhaps the *Prabandhakosa* is heir to a *gurvavali* or an account of monastic lineage in which Bhuvana succeeded Arya Khapata and not Mahendra.It would then seem understandable that the text should in such a case either not make Bhuvana the culprit at all or go to pains to exonerate him as it does. The emphasis on Jain-Buddhist hostility which is apparent from making the materialist into a Buddhist is in fact not unique to this story and I have dealt with it elsewhere at some length.[25] I tried to show that given the fact that the *prabandhas* were collected for those in positions of secular authority it seems reasonable to assume that they sought to present Jainism in a favorable light to secular leaders. One way of doing so might have been by distinguishing it carefully from Buddhism which was anathema to secular leaders elsewhere in the country.Perhaps it is possible to regard the change from atheist opponent to Buddhist opponent as reflecting this tendency, but such a supposition is merely that and awaits adequate proof. Finally, the connection of a religious figure with a pilgrimage site is also not unique to the case of Arya Khapata and is a process I have dealt with in a paper on Jain biographies of Nagarjuna.[26] The connection of Arya Khapata and

Bhrgukaccha, which is where in the stories the Jains defeat the Buddhists, is thereby made concrete. Worshippers at the holy place who might easily forget about the debate between the Buddhists and Jains are not allowed to forget Arya Khapata, hearing his story told at the pilgrimage site and connected not with an abstract philosophical argument at the king's court but with saving their sacred site.

We seem to have come a considerable distance from the initial discussion on the transmission of biographical legends and the sources of the *prabandhas*. It would seem possible to conclude that indeed stories about Arya Khapata the wizard, the *vidyasiddha*, circulated in the *Avasyaka* tradition. These stories were elaborated on in didactic collections to show how Arya Khapata furthered the faith and in these stories his conversion of the non-believers is emphasized. In the *prabandhas* the stories are given further elaborations, retaining an emphasis on his furthering the faith and praising his spreading the doctrine, but also stressing Jain- Buddhist hostility, giving Arya Khapata a holy place to save and adding a story about his disciple. In addition, the story was differently elaborated in a commentary to the *Bhaktamarastotra*, thus expanding the rich process of embellishment and adaptation of story material for religious purposes. The *prabandhas* of Arya Khapatacarya thus have a recognizable context within Svetambara literature and they do indeed belong somewhere in the tradition of story telling for religious purposes.This would imply,of course, that they are no more reliable history than are the stories in the *Bhaktamara* commentary and the various didactic story collections; they are themselves stories adapted and fitted into a specific context. That the Svetambaras were addicted to telling stories they humorously admit. In the *Prabhavakacarita* account of the great debate between the Digambara Kumudacandra and the Svetambara Vadidevasuri the Digambara taunts the Svetambaras that they are good at story telling which is their life-blood, while he is beyond such tales and searches for facts by which people can know the truth (page 176, verses 144-145).Scholars continue to attempt to confound the two and to search for the truth in the stories themselves.I shall beg that question, for my search is at the moment for those sinuous paths by which the stories grew and changed.And as part of that search I now take a slight detour to consider the biographies of Mallavadin, for they place definite limits on any attempt to draw even those *prabandhas* with known antecedents in the didactic story collections totally into the world of the didactic story collections by indicating that even when a biography was told in the didactic story collections the *prabandhas* could and did have totally different biographies from other to date unknown sources.

VI. The Biographies of Mallavadin

The biography of Mallavadin occurs in all the major *prabandhas*, the *Prabandhakosa, Prabandhacintamani* (1305 A.D.), and the *Prabhavakacarita*, with a brief summary given in the appendix to the *Puratanapraband-*

hasamgraha.[27] In addition the biography of Mallavadin is also told in the *Kahavali* of Bhadresvara and in the *Akhyanakamanikosa.*[28] In fact there are actually two distinct biographies of Mallavadin, the one that appears in the *Kahavali, Akhyanakamanikosa* and *Prabhavakacarita*, and the one that appears in the later *prabandhas*. There is very little in common between these two biographies beyond the stories that Mallavadin wrote the *Dvadasaranayacakra* after an encounter with the Goddess of Knowledge and that he defeated the Buddhists. A brief summary of the two biographies may help in making this clear.

In the didactic story collection, the *Akhyanakamanikosa,* and the closely related *Kahavali* and in the *Prabhavakacarita* Mallavadin is one of three sons of Durlabhadevi, who is herself the sister of the Jain monk Jinananda. His story is essentially the same in these three texts; my summary is made directly from the *Akhyanakamanikosa.* Along with his mother, who becomes a Jain nun, and his brothers, Ajitayasa and Yaksa, Malla becomes a monk. Jinananda agrees to a debate with a Buddhist Buddhananda in the city Bhrgukaccha, and the condition is set that the loser and all his coreligionists must leave the famous city. As fate would have it, Jinananda loses . He leaves Bhrgukaccha and makes his way to the city of Vallabhi. There his three nephews pursue their study of Jainism under his tutelage and all become learned, especially Malla. But Jinananda withholds from them the sacred knowledge of the book , the *Dvadasaranayacakra*, which it is explained forms part of the ancient lore that must be studied with great precaution and reverence: before reciting the text and at its conclusion one must worship the Jinas with deep devotion. To fail in that worship brings disastrous consequences for the entire monastic community. One day, Jinananda, as chance has it, leaves his library under the care of his sister and proceeds on his monastic wanderings. Durlabhadevi explicitly warns Malla against reading the *Dvadasaranayacakra*, but chance again intervenes. She leaves him alone for a few moments and overcome by curiosity, Malla disobeys her wishes and opens the book. He recites its first verse. The goddess whose duty it is to protect the teaching and indeed to convey and safeguard wisdom realizes at once his transgression and snatches the book away. Malla is overcome by despondency when the book suddenly vanishes. He tells his mother what he has done and she shares the unfortunate news with the other members of the monastic community who become equally demoralized. Malla makes a vow that he will eat only rough grain *(valla)* until he gets the book back. The other monks worry that he will become ill if he does not eat substances like ghee which cause beneficial effects on digestion, and he eventually agrees to eat his coarse fare with brown sugar and ghee. Malla takes refuge in a cave near the city and begins his penance. One day the Goddess of wisdom decides to test his cleverness and asks him, "What are sweet?" (*Ke mittha*) He replies, "Coarse grains" (*valla).* Six months later she asks again, "With what?" (Kena) and he quickly responds, "With ghee and brown sugar" (*ghayagudena).* The goddess is pleased with his replies (the *Prabhavakacarita* specifically states that she is pleased with his power to remember things, vs.31).She grants him a boon and he asks her for the book, the *Dvadasaranayacakra*, that she had earlier taken from him. She gives him the first verse, telling him that it is all he will need to write down the rest of the text himself.Empowered by this boon from the goddess, he then does write his work and with great ceremony he is welcomed back into the city of Vallàbhi by the monastic community.

The scene then shifts to Bhrgupura, and to Malla's defeat of the Buddhists, the only incident that his two biographies hold in common. Malla recalls how his teacher, Jinananda,had been defeated and humiliated by the Buddhists in Bhrgupura and hastens to the city of their defeat.He is at first treated with contempt by his Buddhist opponent, in part because of his young age, and in part because his own teacher had already met his match in the Buddhist. Eventually the debate begins. Malla speaks first, setting forth his arguments with lengthy and complicated logical support in a performance that lasts six days. At the end of that time he orders the Buddhist to repeat his position and attack it. The Buddhist returns to his own lodgings, but he dies in despondency when he finds he cannot even reproduce Malla's complicated arguments let alone defeat them. The king wishes to expel all the Buddhists in keeping with the original condition of the debate, but Malla is moved by compassion and prevents him from banishing his opponents.The *Akhyanakamanikosa* concludes by saying that after spreading the doctrine and bringing its message to many souls Malla died and went to heaven.

There are some differing details in the *Kahavali* account and in the *Prabhavakacarita*. For example in the *Kahavali* his compassion is emphasized and in the *Prabhavakacarita* additional information about the writings of his brothers is provided.On the whole, however, these three texts agree with each other very closely and without the evidence from the *Prabandhakosa* and the *Prabandhacintamani* one might be led to the false conclusion that Mallavadin's biographies in the later tradition were directly descended from stories about him that circulated in the didactic collections, exactly as we have seen is the case for Arya Khapatacarya.The biography of Mallavadin in the *Prabandhakosa*, *Prabandhacintamani* and the brief notice in the appendix to the *Puratanaprabandhasamgraha* must come as a surprise to someone already familiar with Mallavadin in the didactic story collections and related accounts and makes us reconsider such an hypothesis of the direct linear transmission of even a few of the biographical legends from the story collections into the *prabandhas* with only subtle modifications.It also forces us to consider other alternatives to the didactic story collections as means of transmission and preservation of biographical legends in medieval Jainism.

The accounts of Mallavadin in the later *prabandhas* show as intimate a connection with each other as did his biographies in the group of texts that have just been reviewed above. I make my summary here from the *Prabandhakosa*.

The *Prabandhakosa* account of Mallavadin stands out from the other *prabandhas* in the same collection in that it is the only biography written in verse and it seems for all intents and purposes to have been taken over directly from another, unfortunately, unnamed source. Mallavadin's story is here associated with the legends of King Siladitya of Vallabhi. The story opens by introducing the Brahmin Devaditya in the town of Kheta in Gujarat.He has a daughter Subhaga, a child-widow, who has somehow come into the possession of a magic formula, a *mantra*, with which she can summon the sun. Drawn to her side by the power of the *mantra*, the sun God makes love to her and she finds herself pregnant.Her father in time notices the typical signs of pregnancy appearing on Subhaga: her face grows pale, her limbs languid. He rebukes her for her unchaste behaviour, at which she protests, saying that the sun had taken her by force one day when she had summoned him through her *mantra*. The father finds this an unlikely explanation, and sorrowful though he is, he sends her with a servant to Vallabhi.She gives birth to a son and a daughter and remains in Vallabhi, living on an allowance that her father provides for her.

In time her two children grow up, both sharing in the splendour of the sun. When they turn eight Subhaga sends them both to school, but the boy is mocked by his companions because he has no father. He asks his mother why the children say that he has no father, but his mother dismisses him with a curt warning not to pester her. The boy resolves to kill himself, when the sun appears before him and tells him that he is his father. He vows to kill anyone who troubles the child.He then gives to his son a small pebble and advises him that if he should strike any foe with the pebble, the opponent will die instantly.The child kills all his schoolmates who tease him and eventually is called to account for his behaviour before the king. Hardly repentant, he shouts that he can kill kings as well as children and with that he strikes the king with his magic pebble and the king falls dead.He becomes king in his stead, known now as Siladitya, perhaps best rendered as "the one with the sun and the magic stone on his side".He also gets a magic horse from the sun.

His first act as king is to marry off his twin sister to the king of Bhrguksetra.She gives birth to a child with divine markings that foretell his future supernatural greatness.Siladitya also repairs the Jain temples at Satrunjaya, bringing himself into that elect company of such virtuous laymen as King Srenika who did so much for the Jain faith.

It is at this point that the Buddhists arrive on the scene.They boldly proclaim to King Siladitya that should the Svetambaras defeat them in debate then peace be with them;should the Buddhists win, then the Svetambaras must be forced out of the king's realm. Fate turns against the Jains and they are defeated. They leave Siladitya's kingdom and the king begins to honour the Buddhists. Even worse perhaps, the Buddhists gain control of the Jain holy site at Satrunjaya and worship the Tirthamkara Rsabha as the Buddha.

In the meantime King Siladitya's sister has become a widow, and disgusted with worldly existence she has taken Jain vows under the monk Susthitacarya. She also has the monk ordain her eight-year-old son. One day he chances to ask his mother yet another fateful question.This time he seeks to know why there are so few Jains and if they had always been so few in number. His mother tells him that once in fact the Svetambaras had been numerous in every city in the kingdom. And then because they had no gifted teacher to promote their faith, her brother, King Siladitya, had been won over by the Buddhists.She goes on to tell him how the famous holy site,Satrunjaya, which grants release, has been captured by the Buddhists as if by a host of ghouls.

The young boy, hearing this account, is suddenly filled with rage at the Buddhists. He makes a vow that he must extirpate all the Buddhists, as a river flood uproots trees in its way. The young Malla, and here his name is given for the first time, takes leave of his mother, and burning inside like the cosmic fire of destruction that puts an end to the universe, he goes to practice religious austerities on some mountain.Nothing is said about the nature of his austerities or the kind of food he takes, only that he breaks his fast with food he begs from a neighboring village. In a few days the Guardian Goddess of the Faith speaks to him from the heavens. She asks the question we have seen in the other accounts, "What is sweet?" and he gives her the same answer, "Coarse grain." The question and its answer are equally surprising and without context here in the *Prabandhakosa*, because the text has never mentioned that Malla is subsisting on *valla*. When six months later the Goddess returns to ask, "With what?" and Malla answers, "With ghee and brown sugar", the exchange is again without any obvious context.In the accounts that I have grouped together above as a distinct biography of Mallavadin the fact that he is going to eat only *valla* is distinctly mentioned and becomes an issue between the young monk and the rest of the monks, who eventually persuade him to take ghee and brown sugar as well.All these foods are directly named in the *Kahavali* and the *Akhyanika-manikosa* and they are at least alluded to in the *Prabhavakacarita*. Thus the exchange between the Goddess and Malla is given a context in the biography discussed above, while it is not really comprehensible in the *Prabandhakosa* and related accounts. The Goddess is nonetheless pleased with Malla's ability to remember these fragments of conversation and appears before him.She gives him the book *Nayacakra*, but he mistakenly commits the transgression of placing it on the ground. Angered by this lack of respect the Goddess denies him the power to see her in full manifest physical form.

Armed with the book, Mallavadin hastens to Vallabhi.He announces himself to his uncle King Siladitya with these words, "In vain have the Buddhists swallowed up the world. I, Mallavadin, your nephew, heedful, have arisen, their equal in battle." Mallavadin defeats the Buddhist master, here unnamed, in debate after six months. The Buddhist dies of grief and the king banishes all Buddhists from his realm. King Siladitya also rescues the holy place Satrunjaya from their hands and gives it back to the Svetambaras. He then organizes a pilgrimage to Satrunjaya, with which event the biography of Mallavadin is briefly interrupted. What intervenes is a description of the sack of Vallabhi by the Muslims, with the Jain images magically flying through the air to safety, propelled by their superintending deities.[30] Mallavadin learns of all this and with his followers settles in Pancasarapura. The text finally concludes his biography by saying that he became the spiritual leader at many of the holy sites under the control of the Nagendragaccha and that his followers took over the holy site of Stambhana.[31]

The account of Mallavadin in the *Prabandhacintamani* is essentially the same as that given here from the *Prabandhakosa*. Among the differences may be mentioned that the *Prabandhacintamani* does not indicate that Mallavadin in any way angered the Goddess, and that it connects him with only one holy site, Stambhana. The brief notice in the *Puratanaprabandhasamgraha* appendix adds that Mallavadin studied in disguise as a Buddhist. It was while he was with the Buddhists that one night the Goddess of Learning spoke to him , asking him, "What are sweet"? to which he replied, "Coarse grains". Six months later on another nocturnal visit she asks, "With what?" and he answers,"With ghee and brown sugar." Here the exchange between Malla and the Goddess is totally divorced from the fast, for there is no mention of Malla's undertaking any religious austerities whatsoever. The story goes on to say that pleased with him the Goddess defeated the Buddhists and that the King Siladitya then banished them from his realm.

To summarize the salient features of Mallavadin's biography in the *Prabandhakosa* and related sources, the most obvious feature of these accounts seems to me to be their clearly militant tone and hostile stance against the Buddhists. In these texts Malla, true to his name which means "warrior", is just that: a spiritual warrior whose main act is to secure divine aid in extirpating his enemy, the Buddhists. Malla, in keeping with his martial mission, is a descendant of the sun, who must be regarded as his maternal grandfather, and the nephew of the famous King Siladitya, likewise renown for his military victories and in this account as the son of the sun God. There is no question of mercy for the Buddhists here: this is above all the story of Mallavadin's courageous revenge of a Buddhist defeat and the subsequent rescue of a stolen holy site. In addition, there is no hint in these texts of the young Jain monk who was so eager for knowledge that he violates his teacher's explicit warning and opens a forbidden text. Such was the portrait of Mallavadin in the other group of texts, which devoted their attention primarily to Mallavadin's pious training, his transgression and repentance, and even in his debate against the Buddhists stressed not his anger and fury, his prowess and boldness, but his compassion. Here Malla seeks wisdom to carry out his act of revenge.

If, then, the tone of the two biographies is totally at variance, so are many of their details. We have already noted that in the didactic story collection and related accounts the encounter with the Goddess is part of Mallavadin's penance which he performs in order to regain the lost *Dvadasaranayacakra;* there is no question yet of any intention to defeat the Buddhists. By contrast in the *Prabandhakosa* Malla is consistently motivated by a desire to conquer the Buddhists; where he performs religious austerities it is solely with that goal in mind. It is worth pausing to consider further Malla's austerities in the two biographies, for their differing treatment of this event suggests a theory for their conceivable interrelationship at least in this one episode.

It was noted above that the *Prabandhakosa* and related accounts make less sense in their description of Malla's encounter with the Goddess than did the biography in the *Akhyanakamanikosa* and related texts. The two facts,however, that both biographies have the Goddess pose the same question and receive the same answers and that the questions and answers seem to be unusual at best and possibly unique to Mallavadin's biographies point to one episode's being derived from the other, if not both being derived from a common source. Given the observation that the exchange between Malla and the Goddess only makes sense in the *Akhyanakamanikosa* and similar accounts, it is tempting to conclude that for this episode it is that version that is original, with the *prabandhas* then offering a later, adapted version of the episode.

A second point the two biographies have in common is Mallavadin's defeat of the Buddhists. If we assume that here too the *prabandhas* are enlarging upon the *Akhyanakamanikosa* and related sources, then the direction of the shift is in increasing the picture of Jain/ Buddhist hostility. Indeed this was the direction of the shift between didactic story collection and *prabandhas* that was pointed out for the biographies of Arya Khapatacarya. But here the picture clouds. For if we can relate the two biographies to each other in these two episodes and posit a course of development from didactic story collection to *prabandhas* in the case of these two episodes, we are still left with the uncomfortable reality that the biographies are otherwise totally at variance, in tone and in detail. It becomes then necessary to ask, where does the story of Mallavadin as Siladitya's nephew and grandson of the sun God come from? What is the significance of the emphasis on holy sites and rescuing holy sites in the *Prabandhakosa* and related versions where the *Akhyanakamanikosa* tradition is totally silent about Mallavadin and any holy site? It would seem undeniable that if the *Prabandhakosa* and related accounts do in two episodes show a resemblance to the account in the *Akhyanakamanikosa* they are also heir to another tradition, no hint of which is found in the biography of Mallavadin in the didactic story collection.

There are in the *prabandha* versions of Mallavadin's biography two possible clues to the nature of alternate pathways of creation,transmission and preservation of those of Mallavadin's biographical legends not to be found in the didactic story collections. The first is the connection with a famous king about whom a variety of stories circulated, Siladitya. It seems possible to assume that cycles of heroic legends concerning kings and told in bardic circles could have provided one occasion for the circulation of stories about religious heroes as well; the religious figure was simply made the associate of the king and his stories were then told by the same groups that preserved the cycles of stories about that king.[32] In addition, that Mallavadin's story in the *Prabandhakosa* and *Prabandhacintamani* is linked with several specific sites through his own actions and with Satrunjaya through the actions of Siladitya whom he returns to the Jain fold, suggests that perhaps some of the legends about him that are foreign to the didactic story collections might have been developed and circulated at pilgrimage sites.If these two hypotheses are valid, then the final analysis would suggest that there were many possible sources of the legends about Jain monks that eventually were included in the thirteenth and fourteenth century *prabandha* collections. Didactic story collections would be only one of these sources. Finally the case of Mallavadin, the relationship of his biographies in the *prabandhas* to the biography in the didactic story collections, would resemble the case of Arya Khapatacarya only to the extent that two episodes in the biography would be attributable to stories preserved in the didactic story literature, although here the *prabandhas* would be making a radical and not subtle change in content, in overall tone from repentance to revenge, and in the characterization of their hero from merciful magnanimous debater to angry warrior. Furthermore the case of Mallavadin would have shown that even where a biography was preserved in the didactic literature, there might exist divergent traditions, totally distinct legends, perhaps preserved at pilgrimage sites, and perhaps incorporated in the cycles told of kings and preserved by local bards, which became part of the *prabandha* biographies. As much as Mallavadin's story in the *Prabandhakosa* belongs to the didactic story collections, then, it also belongs to other traditions and courses of transmission and preservation of legends.

VII. Final Conclusions

This paper has traced the biographies of two Jain monks from the didactic story collections into the *prabandhas*, primarily of Arya Khapatacarya and secondarily of Mallavadin. In the case of Arya Khapatacarya it suggested that it would seem indeed that the Jain biography collections, late though they are, are heir to a continuous tradition that is part of the Svetambara story literature. It was nonetheless stressed that the *prabandhas* have subtly altered their stories of Arya Khapatacarya, particularly increasing the anti-Buddhist tone of his biography. It was also mentioned that the process of adaptation of stories occurred also outside the *prabandhas*, with Arya Khapatacarya's story also figuring slightly changed in a commentary to a hymn.

As a counterbalance to the natural tendency to generalize too widely from specific cases, the paper then presented the case of the biographies of Mallavadin. Mallavadin's biography also occurs in didactic story collections before it appears in the *prabandhas*. In this case, however, it is impossible to conclude that the *prabandhas* are simply making use of earlier material that was transmitted in the didactic story collections. Here the biography in the *Akhyanakamanikosa* and related texts and that in the majority of the *prabandhas* differ too greatly in tone and in detail. One is led to the inevitable conclusion that even where a biography was available in the story collections it was not always that biography that the authors of the *prabandhas* incorporated. It was then also speculated that the references to Mallavadin's associations with specific pilgrimage sites and a famous king with his own legends might offer a clue to the possible manner in which these other legends were preserved, if we are to assume that they are not in fact new with the *prabandha* authors, which seemed less likely given the fact that all the *prabandha* authors describe themselves as adhering to an older tradition. For Mallavadin, then, the *prabandha* biography would have been only partially kept alive in the didactic story collection and further reworked, elaborated and preserved among those pilgrimage sites where the texts tell us he established firmly the authority of his own group and in bardic circles that sang the exploits of the king with whom he was linked. The *prabandhas*, in short, preserve their variety even in their history, a history that must have been as complex and rich as the *prabandha* stories themselves.

Notes

1. For a discussion of the exact frame of reference of the term *prabandha* the reader is referred to my paper , "Jain Biographies of Nagarjuna: Notes on the Writing of a Biography in Medieval India", included in this volume.

2. The *Parisistaparvan* of Hemacandra was written at the request of King Kumarapala of Gujarat. The *Prabandhavali* of Jinabhadra was composed at the instruction of the famous minister Vastupala for the education of his son Jaitrasimha. (Dr.Bhogilal J. Sandesara, *Literary Circle of Mahatmya Vastupala*, Singhi Jain Series, vol.3, Bombay:Bharatiya Vidya Bhavan, 1953, p. 144).The *Prabandhakosa* of Rajasekharasuri in its colophon states that Rajasekharasuri composed the text in Delhi at the residence of Mahanasinha at his request. Rajasekharasuri takes pains to glorify the lineage of his patron who was close to the circles of royal power.(*Prasasti* to *Prabandhakosa*,edited Jina Vijaya, Singhi Jain Series, volume 6, Santiniketan: Singhi Jaina Pitha, 1935, page 131.)

3. There is some speculation about the date of Bhadresvara's *Kahavali* which is yet to be published. See Dalsukh Malvania, "On Bhadresvara's *Kahavali*", *Indologica Taurinensia*, vol.XIII, 1983,pp.77-95 . My date for the *Parisistaparvan* comes from Dr.Gulabchandra Chaudhari, *Jaina Sahitya Ka Brhad Itihasa*, volume 6, *Kavya Sahitya*, Varanasi: Parsvanatha Vidyasrama Sodha Samsthana, Parsvanatha Vidyasrama Granthamala,volume 20,1973, p.76.In addition the *Kahavali* should probably itself be regarded as somewhat inbetween a "biography collection" like the later *prabandhas* and a didactic story collection, as an examination of its contents given by Malvania indicates. It is also worth noting that it calls itself a collection of *kaha* and not *prabandhas*.

4. See my paper on Nagarjuna and my "Jain Lives of Haribhadra: An Inquiry into the Sources and Logic of the Legends", forthcoming in *Journal of Indian Philosophy*.

5. Hermann Jacobi, *Sthaviravali or Parisistaparvan*, Calcutta: Asiatic Society of Bengal, 1932, introduction, pp. i-x.

6. See the *prastavika* to the *Prabhavakacarita*, lines 11-15.

7. For a history of story literature in Jainism and a general discussion of the development of *kathakosas* see A.N. Upadhye's introduction to the *Brhatkathakosa*, published in the Singhi Jain Series, vol.1, Bombay, 1944. See also the introduction to the *Akhyanikamanikosa* of Acarya Nemicandra, Prakrit Text Society Series no.5, Varanasi: Prakrit Text Society, 1962.

8. Examples abound in the *Puranas*. The *Skanda Purana, Prabhasa Khanda*, for example tells the story of Sumbha and Nisumbha in *adhyaya* 24 , the *lingodbhavamurti* in chapter 34, the *mahisasuramardini* in chapter 36, the Daruvana episode in chapter 39, and the burning of Kama in chapter 41. See also Hermann Kulke, *The Cidambaramahatmya*, Wiesbaden: Otto Harrassowitz, 1970, pp. 76 ff. for the use of the Daruvana episode in the *Cidambaramahatmya*. In these cases the stable story changes location; the myth is said to have taken place at different holy spots. The Jain tradition will similarly alter a famous story, attaching it now to one holy man, now to another. A good example of this is the conversion of the poet Dhanapala. It is attributed to Vardhamanasuri, the founder of the Kharataragaccha line, in the *Prabandhacintamani*, pp. 36-42 , edited Jina Vijaya Muni, Singhi Jain Series, vol. 1, Santiniketan: Singhi Jain Pitha, 1933, while in the *Prabhavakacarita* of Prabhacandra it is Mahendra who converts Dhanapala (edited, Jina Vijaya Muni, Singhi Jain Series, vol 13, Bombay: Bharatiya Vidya Pitha, 1931,pp. 138-151.) The event is ultimately associated with the Kharatara teacher Jinesvarasuri in Somatilaka's *Samyaktvasaptatikavrtti*, summarized by Jina Vijaya Muni in his Hindi introduction to the *Kathakosaprakarana* of Jinesvarasuri, Singhi Jain Series, volume 11, Benaras: Bharatiya Vidya Bhavan, 1949 in a detailed study of the biographies of Jinesvarasuri.Finally, when we come to the later tradition, the story of Dhanapala's conversion remains the same but the monk who converts him is different again. See the *Bhojacaritra* of Sri Rajavallabha, edited by Dr. B.Ch. Chhabra and S. Sankaranarayanan, Jnanapitha Murtidevi Jain Granthamala Sanskrit Grantha no.29, Calcutta: Bharatiya Jnana Pitha,1964,chapter 1, verses 261 ff, pp. 24-30.Further examples are given by J.Deleu, " A Note on the Jain Prabandhas", in K. Bruhn and A.Wezler,*Studien zum Jainismus und Buddhismus*, Stuttgart: Franz Steiner Verlag, 1981, pp. 63-73. This article also has a brief comparison of the *Prabandhacintamani* and *Prabandhakosa* accounts of Arya Khapata on p. 64.

9. Edited by Amritlal Mohanlal Bhojak, Prakrit Text Series, vol.15, Ahmedabad:Prakrit Text Society, vol.2, 1971, pp. 13-14.

10. The story of Arya Khapatacarya is on pages 174 and 175 and the *prasasti* is page 370.

11. See my paper on Haribhadra cited above.The story of Samantabhadra is story number 4, pages 10-14 in A.N.Upadhye's edition of the *Kathakosa* of Prabhacandra, Manikchandra Digambara Granthamala, no.55, Delhi: Bharatiya Jnana Pitha, 1974. Samantabhadra's biography seems to have influenced the biography of Siddhasena Divakara in the Svetambara tradition, a biography I hope to study at a later date.An excellent review of current scholarship on

Siddhasena may be found in Dr.A.N.Upadhye's *Siddhasena's Nyayavatara and Other Works*, Bombay: Jain Sahitya Vikasa Mandala,1971.

12. The text is edited by Muniraja Jinavijaya in the Gaekwad's Oriental Series, Baroda, 1920. See page iii of the introduction for further details of its author and the occasion of its composition.Arya Khapata's story is on pages 440-443.

13. Edited by Professor Hiralal Rasikdas Kapadia, Sheth Devchand Lalbhai Jain Pustakoddhar Fund Series, no.79, Bombay, 1932.The date is given in the *Jinaratnakosa* of Hari Damodar Velankar, Poona: Bhandarkar Oriental Research Institute, 1944, p. 287.

14. *Srimadavasyakaniryukter Avacurni* of Jnanasagaramuni, Devchandra Lalbhai Jaina Pustakoddhara Grantha 108, Bombay 1965 on vs.932, p.399.While it is true that this particular commentary is dated 1384 A.D. and thus was not written before the *prabandha* collections were made, nonetheless it is closely based on the eighth century commentary of Haribhadra and I am assuming that it accurately transmits the legends of Arya Khapatacarya as they were handed down in the *Avasyaka* tradition.I might add here that the whole subject of the *Avasyaka* and its commentaries and story literature has not been adequately studied to date. The best source of information on the *Avasyaka* and its commentaries is a thesis by Dr.Nalini Balbir, *Etudes D'Exegese Jaina Les Avasyaka* completed in 1986. I thank Dr. Balbir for making available to me a copy of her monumental study.

15. The Jain *prabandhas* frequently mention the Buddhists' skill in logic.Haribhadra's nephews go to study Buddhist logic (see my paper referred to above) and in the biography of Santisuri in the *Prabhavakacarita*,chapter 16, pp. 133-137, vs 73, the Jain students are studying Buddhism which they find very difficult to master. Encounters with the Buddhists also fill these biographies; as one example I cite Mallavadin who defeated the Buddhists at this very town of Bhrgukaccha (see *Prabhavakacarita*, page 78, vs. 41-61.)

16. There is an interesting and close parallel to the story of Arya Khapata's humiliation and defeat of the *yaksa* in the *Puratanaprabandhasamgraha* which does not record the story of Arya Khapata. In its section on King Vikrama is given a brief account of the Jain monk Siddhasena Divakara. It is said that Siddhasena was massaging the feet of his teacher one day and chanced to ask his permission to translate the Jain texts into Sanskrit.The teacher finds this an audacious desire and expels him as unworthy from the monastic community. Siddhasena begs for a penance and the teacher tells him to spread the Jain faith amongst nonbelievers. Siddhasena then assumes the guise of a Saiva ascetic and departs. He wanders for seven years, after which he finds himself in Malwa where he stops

to rest in the temple called "Gudhamahakala", "The Temple of the Hidden Mahakala".He shows his disrespect for the Saiva faith by sleeping with his feet facing the image of Siva. Although told not to do this he persists. The king then sends his men who beat him, but at that very moment the kings harem catches on fire. The king comes running and asks him why he does not worship the image.He replies that the image would not survive his prayer, but the king tells him to worship it anyway.The image splits open and an image of the Jain Tirthamkara Parsvanatha is revealed.

This account of Siddhasena is distinctly different from all the other accounts, none of which has him insult the image by placing his feet near it, or impress the king by causing his harem harm when the king has him beaten. It seems clearly to have borrowed the famous story of Arya Khapata here.For other biographies of Siddhasena see the following: *Prabandhacintamani*,edited Jina Vijaya Muni, Singhi Jain Series, vol.1, Santiniketan: Singhi Jain Jnanapitha, 1933, pp. 7-8; *Prabandhakosa*, pp.15-21; *Akhyanikamanikosa*, pp .171-172; *Kumarapalacaritrasamgraha*, edited Jina Vijaya Muni, Singhi Jain Series, vol.41,Bombay: Bharatiya Vidya Bhavan, 1956, pp. 5, 13, 47 and *Prabhavakacarita*, pp. 54-61.

The miracle of transferring blows to an oppressor's harem is told also of an image, the image of Vira in Satyapura. The Muslim lord of Gajjani (Ghazni) in V.S. 1081 comes to Satyapura and sees the magnificent image of Vira. He attempts to carry off the image, which refuses to be moved. Eventually his followers beat the image, but the blows fall on the ladies in their harem. See Jinaprabhasuri's *Vividhatirthakalpa*, edited Jina Vijaya Muni, Singhi Jain Series, vol.10, Santiniketan: Singhi Jaina Jnanapitha,1934, *Satyapuratirthakalpa*, no.17, p.29.

17. This story of Mahendra and his two magic sticks raises the interesting question of the relationship between the biographies in the *prabandhas* and the folk literature we commonly call fairy tales. There is a well-known fairy tale in which a princess is kept prisoner by *raksasas*, or demons, who have two sticks, one of gold and one of silver.With the golden stick they cause her to sleep the sleep of the dead while they are out. With the silver stick they bring her back to life when they return. The fairy tale has been retold by Lalbihari De and appears in a recent collection, *Satavarser Rupakatha*, Calcutta: Book Trust,1983, pp. 12-27, "Candracuda Rajaputra", or "The Prince with the Moon on his Head". The same motif occurs in other Bengali fairy tales which were published by G.H.Damant in the *Indian Antiquary*, volume 1, 1872, pages 115-120, "Bengali Folklore: A Legend from Dinajpur," and p. 219. Here it is the gold wand that revives the woman and the silver wand that returns her to death. In any consideration of the possible sources of the biographies of the *prabandhas* and any discussion of their possible paths of transmission and their development, it is necessary to keep in mind the rich store of folk literature that exists from these regions and which has been inadequately published and studied to date.

18. *Vividhatirthakalpa*, edited Jina Vijaya, Singhi Jain Series, vol.10, Santiniketan: Singhi Jain Pitha, 1934, page 20, section 10.

19. See Waters, *On Yuan Chwangs Travels in China*, Delhi: Munshiram Manoharlal, 1961 and references therein.See also Bimal Churn Law, *Geographical Essays Relating to Ancient Geography of India*, Delhi: Bharatiya Publishing House, 1976, p.47. Some further information is given by Charlotte Krause, *Ancient Jaina Hymns*, Scindia Oriental Series, Number 2, Ujjain: Scindia Oriental Institute, 1952, in her discussion of a hymn to Muni Suvrata, the Tirthamkara to whom the site was devoted.See pages 1-22.

20. Volume VI, pages 1145-1146, Delhi: B.R. Publishing Corporation, reprinted 1985.

21. For the reference to the *Nisitha* see the introduction to the *Akhyanikamanikosa*, edited Sri Punyavijayaji, Prakrit Text Society, vol. 5, Ahmedabad:Prakrit Text Society, 1962, page 5.The introduction is by Umakant P.Shah.Arya Khapata is mentioned in two places in the *Nisitha* and its commentaries according to the index in the edition edited by Acarya Pravar Sri Jindas Mahattar, Agama Sahitya Ratnamala , book 3, Delhi: Bharatiya Vidya Prakashan, 1982, in four volumes.

22. The story is pages 13 and 14 of the text, edited Amritlal Mohanlal Bhojak, Prakrit Text Society, no.15, Ahmedabad: Prakrit Text Society, 1971.

23. The *Kharataragacchabrhadgurvavali*, edited Jina Vijaya Muni, Singhi Jain Series vol.42, Bombay: Bharatiya Vidya Bhavan, 1956, page 19 attributes this to Jinadattasuri and many vernacular poems associate Jinavallabha with the defeat of Camunda. See the Sanskrit introduction to the book *Apabhramsakavyatrayi*, edited Lalchandra Bhagawandas Gandhi, G.O.S. vol.37, Baroda, reprinted 1967, especially page 32.

24. There is a striking parallel in the Hindu tradition that comes from the *Padmapurana*. The *Uttarakhanda* has a section called the *Gitamahatmya* which tells a miracle story associated with each chapter of the *Gita*, chapters 171-188. Chapter 176 tells the story of Raikva and King Janasruti known from the *Chandogya Upanisad*, 4.1-4.3 .The only substantial change is that in this story Raikva's powers are due to his recitation of chapter five of the *Gita*, exactly as Arya Khapatacarya's powers in the *Bhaktamara* commentary are due to his recitation of a specific verse of the hymn. The relationship between these texts deserves a careful study. The *Padmapurana* is replete with stories glorifying particular ritual observances and holy places as well as sections on the glories of the *Gita* and the *Bhagavata*. It would be instructive to analyze these various

stories in the *Padmapurana* to determine the possible relationships between these tales and their Jain counterparts.

25. See my paper on Haribhadra cited above.

26. The essay appears in this volume.

27. The *Prabandhacintamani* has been edited in the Singhi Jain Series, volume I, by Jinavijaya Muni, Santiniketan, 1933. The story of Mallavadin is on page 107. In the *Prabhavakacarita* Mallavadin appears in chapter 10, pp. 77-79 and in the *Prabandhakosa*, chapter 7, pp. 21-23. The summary given in the *Puratanaprabandhasamgraha* appendix is number 311 and reads very much as if it was made from the *Prabandhacintamani* account, although it does have a different story of Malla's encounter with the Goddess and defeat of the Buddhists.

This Mallavadin was definitely a Svetambara, as is clear from his own remarks in the *Dvadasaranayacakra*, cited by Muni Jambuvijaya in the Sanskrit introduction to the text, Atmananda Jain Granthamala, vol.92, Bhavnagar, 1966, p.ll. Asim Kumar Chatterjee, *A Comprehensive History of Jainism up to 1000 A.D.*, Calcutta: Firma KLM Private, Limited, 1978, p. 330 wrongly identifies him with a Mallavadin mentioned in a Surat copper plate inscription of a King Karka. That Mallavadin was a Digambara Jain belonging to the Sena *gaccha* of the Mula Samgha. See the inscription itself and the Gujarati discussion of the inscription in Acharya Girjashankar Vallabhaji, *Historical Inscriptions of Gujarat (From Ancient Times to the End of the Vaghela Dynasty)*, part 3, Shree Forbes Gujarati Series, no 15, Bombay: Forbes Gujarati Sabha, 1942, inscription 125 b, pp.120-142.

Mallavadin also figures in the biography of Vastupala as it is recorded in the *Prabandhakosa*, pp. 109-112. This Mallavadin, leader of the Jain community at Stambhatirtha, is a composer of extemporaneous verse and an admirer of the minister. At first shunned by Vastupala when he utters the first half of a verse in his praise, and misunderstood to be reciting erotic poetry, Mallavadin eventually wins the minister over, again by clever use of poetry. Such encounters between monks and those in political power, often conducted through the medium of clever verses of flattery, are common in the *prabandhas*. The incident tells us little about the formation of Mallavadin's biography and so I have confined mention of it to this note. It does, however, point to the way in which these biographies might grow. The monk Mallavadin, associated with the holy place of Stambhana, reappears in a biography of the celebrated minister Vastupala when the minister visits that pilgrimage place. The holy site serves as a central depot of stories which then may branch out in a variety of directions and become intertwined through a variety of associations.

28. Although the text of the *Kahavali* has never been published we are fortunate in having the biography of Mallavadin from the *Kahavali* published in the introduction to his *Dvadasaranayacakra*, edited by Muni Jambuvijaya, and cited in the immediately preceding note. Muni Jambuvijaya also states in his Sanskrit introduction to the *Dvadasaranayacakra* that the biography of Mallavadin appears in the *Samyaktvasaptativrtti* of Samghatilakacarya (note 2, page 11).Unfortunately this text is not available to me. The biography in the *Akhyanikamanikosa* is on pages 172-174 of the Prakrit Text Society edition cited earlier in this paper.

29. In the *Prabhavakacarita* version Malla is said to decide to eat *nispava*, "rough grain" vs.26, and the ghee and brown sugar are also not directly named. Nonetheless the text does say that the monks persuaded him to take *vikrti*, or substances like ghee, (vs 28) and so the fast and the questions that the goddess proposes are indeed linked.

30. This is not the only possible consequence for Jain images and temples in the event of a Muslim conquest. The *Vividhatirthakalpa* of Jinaprabhasuri (1335 A.D), published in the Singhi Jain Series. volume 10, edited Jina Vijaya, Santiniketan, 1934, also tells of images broken when the powers of the superintending Gods failed and later restored. I am preparing a study of Jain and Hindu reactions to Muslim destruction of their sacred sites based on the *Vividhatirthakalpa* and texts like the *Ekalingamahatmya* which has been edited and published by Dr. Premalata Sarma, Delhi:Motilal Banarsidas,1976.

31. On Stambhana and its place in other Jain biographies in the *prabandhas* see my paper on Nagarjuna in this volume.

32. The biography of Siddhasena seems to reinforce this hypothesis that cycles of stories told of kings were important in the development and transmission of the *prabandha* biographies. As it appears in the *Akhyanikamanikosa* the biography of Siddhasena makes no mention of any specific king, but in all the versions in the various *prabandhas(Prabandhakosa,Prabandhacintamani, Prabhavakacarita*, and *Puratanaprabandhasamgraha)* Siddhasena's biography is linked closely with the cycle of stories told in Jain circles of the legendary King Vikramaditya. In addition the stories that are told of Siddhasena in the *prabandhas* with the exception of the three stories that are also present in his biography in the *Akhyanikamanikosa*, namely the accounts of his conversion and debate with Vrddhavadin, his desire to rewrite the Jain canon into Sanskrit and his penance and miraculous manifestation of an image of Parsvanatha in a Saiva temple, are mostly concerned with the relationship of Siddhasena to either Vikramaditya or to other kings, suggesting that they might well have circulated as part and parcel of the heroic legends told of those kings. It must also be noted

that the story of Siddhasena and the miracle at the Mahakala temple is part of the Jain recension of the *Vikramadevacarita*, and that Siddhasena's association with this king was firm enough to lead to the erroneous attribution of the *Vikramadevacarita* to Siddhasena. See Edgerton's introduction to his edition and translation in the Harvard Oriental Series, volume 26, Cambridge: Harvard University Press, 1926, pp. xxxix and lviii in particular.

The relationship between stories of monks and stories of important secular leaders which were the property of local bards requires careful study. A good place to begin, I suspect , is with the biographies of the Kharataragaccha monks which are mirrored in some of the clan histories of Rajasthan told by the traditional bards. The Jain tradition preserves the biographies of the Kharataragaccha monks in a number of texts, see for example the *Kharataragacchabrhadgurvavali*, edited by Jina Vijaya Muni in the Singhi Jain Series,volume 42, Bombay, 1956. Some of the bardic stories on the origin of the various Jain families have been given by Agar Chand Nahta and Bhanwarlal Nahta in *Kharataragaccha Pratibodhita Gotra Aur Jatiyam*, Calcutta: Sri Jinadattasuri Sevasamgraha, Samvat 2030. Finally, an analysis of the biographies of Siddhasena in the *Akhyanikamanikosa* and the various *prabandhas* akin to that done here for Mallavadin would no doubt lead to further speculation about the means in which these legends were developed and preserved. The biographies of Siddhasena are in fact extremely complex and show resonances to other biographies of monks, particulary Arya Khapatacarya (see note 16, above), Haribhadra and Hemacandra. Haribhadra, it is told, planted the magic books that Siddhasena is said to find (*Prabandhakosa,* page 24 where Haribhadra gets the books and places them in the magic pillar and page 17 where Siddhasena recovers them). Siddhasena's manifestation of the image of Parsvanatha comes to resemble closely Hemacandra's miracle at Somesvara.Siddhasena's biography, then, starting from the didactic story collection is expanded greatly with stories of the monk's intimate relationship to kings and with a number of legends that associate him with other great monks and with pilgrimage sites.

SRONG-BTSAN SGAM-PO OF TIBET: BODHISATTVA AND KING

Eva K. Dargyay

I

Tibetans have sometimes been called the most religious people in the world, and it is true that religion has permeated all aspects of Tibetan civilization. As a consequence, Tibetan literature is of a distinctively religious character, while secular literature is for the most part conspicuously absent. This is also true with regard to biographical literature. The Tibetan word for biography illustrates this very well: *rnam thar* means "features of liberation". A Tibetan *rnam thar* records a person's way to liberation,or nirvana, and therefore secular events are of subordinate importance. This characteristic of Tibetan biographical, or better hagiographical, literature becomes evident in the texts telling the life story of eminent political leaders.

While in Chinese and Mongolian literature, political leaders were portrayed as the embodiment of virtue, heroism, and political shrewdness, the Tibetan texts depict them as divine beings who are only concerned with guiding their subjects toward the lofty goal of Buddhism, supreme enlightenment and buddhahood. For this reason the Tibetan biographies of kings may be considered to be much closer in spirit to Indian royal biographies, which transfigure the mundane into a celestial realm even at the cost of neglecting factual history, than to Chinese biographies.[1] Tibetans recorded historical facts in their archives and annals, but they considered them as not distinctive enough to be incorporated in the sacred biographies. Obviously, the Tibetans felt that the very nature of a ruler's personality did not come forth in his political deeds but in his spiritual aspirations. Thus, visions, dreams, miraculous occurrences, prophecies, recollections of past events, religious pledges and vows dominate the biographical accounts. Western scholarship was quick to condemn this literary genre as "historically useless", although it speaks vividly about how Tibetans wanted to see their past. The Tibetan biographies may not yield many historical facts and concrete details, but they do let us gaze with amazement into the depth of the soul of the Tibetan people.

The biography of King Srong-btsan sgam-po (ca. 600-649) illustrates this better than any other Tibetan work because of the unique historical importance of Srong-btsan sgam-po and because of the crucial role ascribed to him in the propagation of Buddhism. The issues which in other biographies are sometimes blurred come into focus here: the irrelevance of political and temporal acts compared with the manifestation of the divine, and the dominance of sacred reality over the temporal sphere.

To appreciate the idiosyncrasies of Srong-btsan sgam-po's biography, we first have to gain an understanding of the historical situation in which he lived, and which he helped to create. In short, Srong-btsan sgam-po was instrumental in Tibet's making the transition from a tribal culture to a civilization of higher sophistication. Some of the important events associated with his reign characterize this transition. The king built a formidable empire challenging his mighty neighbors, China, India, Nepal, and the Arabs. He introduced his people to Indian scholarship and Chinese administrative skills, but above all he is praised for introducing Buddhism to Tibet. This claim is made throughout the historiographic literature of Tibet, although it is not always accepted by Western scholars.[2] In any case, in traditional accounts the king embodies Tibet's departure from her tribal and mythic past and her entry into the new phase of Buddhist civilization.

At this point one might speculate that the king's biography should be an attempt to amalgamate the two worlds of tribal mythology and the new Buddhist religion. Careful research into the biography reveals, however, that this is not in fact the case.

The king's biography documents his religious role not only as sovereign of Tibet, but as saviour of the Tibetans. The text is not a biography in the usual sense, and it hardly records any facts associated with the king's life; rather it is a declaration of his divine identity.[3] Avalokitesvara, the bodhisattva of universal compassion, becomes manifest as king Srong-btsan sgam-po who gives humane laws to the people of Tibet so that they may proceed on their way toward *nirvana*. About ninety percent of the text records events located in a divine, supramundane realm *(buddhaksetra)*. All the deeds performed by the king or one of his earlier embodiments are enactments of the bodhisattva's resolution to lead all sentient beings to buddhahood. History becomes the medium through which Buddha's compassion materializes, and Tibetan history in particular is an illustration of a universal scheme of salvation. Due to this situation the biography dwells extensively on describing the divine nature of the king, but pays very little attention to his mundane performances. Vostrikov rejected the text for this reason as a valid historical source.[4]

In the discussion below I am going to examine the following problems: When was the idea that Srong-btsan sgam-po is the bodhisattva Avalokitesvara first documented? Did the author of the king's biography use another Buddhist text as a model for his work? And if so, what are the implications of this fact for our understanding of the king's biography and the Tibetan concept of sacred kingship in general?

II

The conception of divine kingship was developed in Tibet during the 7th/9th centuries, at a time when crucial transformations of Tibetan civilization were in progress. Tibetan historians call this period the time of the kings of religion, while Western scholarship prefers to label it "the time of the ancient monarchy", or "the time of the early kings". Furthermore, Western scholars consider the assertion, found in Tibetan historiographic works, that King Srong-btsan sgam-po (ca. 600-649 A.D.) was an embodiment of Avalokitesvara, the bodhisattva of compassion, to be a much later pious fabrication, and not a concept created during the era of the kings of religion.[5]

Scholars, such as Giuseppe Tucci, have further speculated that the legend was created when Tibet rid herself of Mongolian dominance and celebrated her re-gained cultural and political independence (these events took place in the 13th century).[6] The assumption is that the account about Srong-btsan sgam-po as King of Religion and an embodiment of Avalokitesvara at once authenticates secular rulership and lends to it the authority to control the Buddhist institutions by declaring the ruler to be a perfect exponent of the religion.[7]

Sources from the time of the kings of religion speak a language which,at least for the taste of our time,is not precise enough. There are many references to religion, but which religion?, to accepting the doctrine, but which doctrine?, to subordination, but to whom? In a Tun-huang document edited and studied by Hugh Richardson[8] it is said:

> This is the dharma which descended from the heavens: The lords over men, the sons of god(s), the best kings, Srong-btsan sgam-po, the king divinely manifested, and the mighty *(btsan po)* Khri-srong lde-btsan, they learned the dharma of the Perfection of Wisdom, the one [taught] by the Sugata,...and worked the weal of all beings living in this world, in Tibet the land of men.

This excerpt from the longer edict may be understood as pointing to Srong-btsan sgam-po as an embodiment of Avalokitesvara, but need not necessarily be so interpreted. The Tibetan word *'phrul gyi rgyal po,* which I translated as "divinely manifested king", can be understood as referring to the heavenly origin of the Tibetan kings. Thus, scholars have been led in the past to conclude that these edicts and proclamations with their ambiguous wording were purposely interpreted by later Tibetan historians in order to convince the contemporary world that the new religion, Buddhism, had been introduced to Tibet by Srong-btsan sgam-po, one of the most celebrated kings of the past, and that therefore any opposition to it was pointless.[9]

But there is another document which gives indisputable testimony to the fact that King Srong-btsan sgam-po was considered an incarnation of Avalokitesvara already during the era of the early monarchy. It is a letter written by the Indian Buddhist master Buddhaguhya to King Khri-srong-lde-btsan, who ruled roughly a hundred years after Srong-btsan sgam-po's death. The discussion of this letter shall be a major focus in what follows.

Buddhaguhya, the author of this letter, was a famous tantric master. An eclectic account of his life is given by Khetsun Sangpo.[10] But there is also older material available. In the *Blue Annals*[11] Buddhaguhya is mentioned as one of the early propagators of *rdzogs chen* in Tibet, which makes him a contemporary of Buddhajnana, Vimalamitra the Elder (who was his direct disciple), and king Khri-srong lde-btsan. Taranatha[12] portrays Buddhaguhya as an ecstatic visionary who conversed with the bodhisattva Manjusri as if he were human. Driven by admonitions given to him during these visions, he went, together with Buddhasanti, to Mt. Potala to "see Avalokitesvara" where they encountered Tara and Bhrkuti preaching the *buddhadharma* to various non-human creatures at the foot and lower reaches of the mountain. When they arrived at the summit, Buddhaguhya and his companion found only a stone image of Avalokitesvara there. Buddhaguhya was unable to see the spiritual reality behind this image, subject as he was to a delusion created by his senses which were clouded by ignorance. He was then approached by an old woman who told him to go to Mt. Kailash, or Tise as the Tibetans call it, where he would obtain supranormal powers (*siddhi*). There an invitation by Khri-srong lde-btsan, the Tibetan king, reached him. According to Taranatha he did not follow this call because of the advice of Manjusri, who guided Buddhaguhya as his personal deity. Instead Buddhaguhya taught the Tibetans the *kriya yoga* in three sections.[13]

The letter of Buddhaguhya consists of an introduction in which Buddhaguhya praises the addressee, King Khri-srong lde-btsan, as the heir of a family of bodhisattvas, and his forefather Srong-btsan sgam-po, as an embodiment of Avalokitesvara. There follow four sections with spiritual advice for the king, the ministers, the practitioners of meditation (*sgom chen*), and for the common clergy (*spyi' i bande*). At the end of the introductory part Buddhaguhya says that instead of following the king's invitation he will send an instruction which is a representation of yoga (*man ngag yo ga a ba ta ra*). It may well be that Taranatha refers to this letter in his *History of Buddhism in India* when he said, "At that time, the Tibetan king Khri-srong lde-btsan sent Manjusri of dBus and others to invite him (Buddhaguhya). But he did not go there, because permission for this was refused by (the god) Manjusri. So he preached to them (the Tibetans) the three *kriya yoga*" The fact that the letter is organized in four sections, while Taranatha mentions only three, must not be seen as ruling out such a theory, for two of the sections in the letter address the clergy, and thus could have been counted as one.

An even older source mentioning Buddhaguhya is the *sBa bzhed*, the nucleus of which goes back to the time of King Khri-srong lde-btsan.[14] This text was written by gSal-snang of the sBa clan in order to record the events associated with the spread of the *buddhadharma* during the reign of King Khri-srong-lde btsan (8th century A.D.). This source starts its report with Khri-ide gtsug-btsan reading the will of his forefather, King Srong-btsan sgam-po. Minister 'Gar had written down the king's will on copperplates, which now are discovered by Khri-ide gtsug-btsan in the royal archives of mChims-phu (mChing-phu). In this will, Srong-btsan sgam-po predicts a rapid growth of Buddhism in the future, with lavish royal patronage, and that many will join the *sangha* and don the yellow robes. Khri-ide gtsug-btsan thinks that now the time has come to realize his forefather's will.

Khri-ide gtsug-btsan sends two envoys to India, Branka mu-le ko-sha and gNyags Jnanakumara, in search of the *buddhadharma*. They learn about Buddhaguhya and Buddhasanti who meditate at Mt. Tise. The Tibetans want to invite them to Tibet, but they reject the invitation. Instead, being experts in the *Las rnam par 'byed pa* (Toh. 338) and the *gSer 'od* (Toh. 556), they recommend that these two texts be "invited" to Tibet. The Tibetans apparently obtained copies of the texts, and offered them to the king who had five temples built to house these sacred texts.[15] But the *sBa bzhed* does not report that Buddhaguhya had written a letter to the king. Khetsun Sangpo reports these circumstances, but supplements them with information derived from the *Padma bka' than:* Buddhaguhya sent his letter to the king when he was invited to bSam-yas and acted as pandit in translating several Buddhist texts from Sanskrit into Tibetan. This claim is supported by evidence from the Tibetan Tanjur which lists 22 works in whose translation he had participated.[16]

The evidence supplied by all the above sources demands a more comprehensive assessment of Buddhaguhya and his letter to King Khri-srong lde-btsan. First, Buddhaguhya's character needs to be examined. According to Taranatha's *History of Buddhism in India*, Buddhaguhya was an ecstatic visionary whose entire religious life gravitated toward parapsychological experiences. When he arrived with Buddhasanti at the summit of Mt. Potala and when both could only discover a stone image of Avalokitesvara, he failed to cope with the situation in the same way as Buddhasanti did, who immediately reinterpreted what he had seen by taking into account his own ignorant mind. On their way down, when Buddhaguhya asked his companion what kind of *siddhi* he had obtained, he reacted jealously when he learned that the other had acquired higher powers than he did. Was this such a traumatic experience for Buddhaguhya that he wished to make up for his failure at a later opportunity? If so, did Buddhaguhya see the messenger sent by Khri-srong lde-btsan as a spiritual rather than earthly envoy who provided another opportunity for him to realize his spiritual goal, to internalize the visualization of Avalokitesvara? If the surmise is correct that the Mt. Potala pilgrimage was such a crucial experience in Buddhaguhya's spiritual life then it may be an understandable reaction that he was prepared to see Avalokitesvara embodied in the ancestor of the present Tibetan king, who had sent an envoy with the name Manjusri to Buddhaguhya. This last fact must have deeply impressed him, because Manjusri was his personal deity with whom he conversed as one would with a human companion.

Perhaps, then, it would have been natural for Buddhaguhya to have interpreted the situation in the following way: when a man named Manjusri, which was also the name of Buddhaguhya's protective deity, brought an invitation for him to see a king living beyond the snowcapped mountains of the Himalayas, to assist the king in proliferating the *buddhadharma,* Buddhaguhya saw this as intimately related to his pilgrimage to Mt. Potala. But now he was determined not to fail as he did the first time. Thus, despite the remoteness of this king, yet unknown to Buddhaguhya, despite other differences, Buddhaguhya wanted to see the sacred reality within the profane. The king's ancestry becomes a lineage of bodhisattvas, the most important forefather is seen as an embodiment of Avalokitesvara, the bodhisattva still veiled in distance, but nearer to Buddhaguhya now than at Mt. Potala where he could see only a stone image. The two tantric deities Buddhaguhya had seen at the foot and on the shoulder of Mt. Potala, Tara and Bhrkuti, become the bodhisattva-king's queens.

In other words, I propose that we consider that Buddhaguhya interpreted an historical situation in the light of his unsuccessful mystical experience and that we entertain the theory that his initial failure to visualize Avalokitesvara predestined him to see the historical situation in such a way. In such an understanding we can assume that he strove to remedy his lack of faith, obvious in his pilgrimage to Mt. Potala, by putting all his faith into a situation which at best was mysterious to him. We can never verify such an hypothesis, but the letter at least suggests that Buddhaguhya saw historical facts, the Tibetan dynasty of the 8th century, as the ephemeral side of an essentially sacred reality, the reality of the bodhisattva's compassionate guidance of all living beings toward buddhahood.

Such an understanding of political or temporal events was common in India during the middle ages. Other religious figures are well known for their penchant to see a sacred reality in and behind conventional reality. Caitanya, for instance, the late Vaisnava mystic, is said to have perceived every river as the Yamuna, and every grove as Vrndavana,the famous places where Krsna exhibited his divine feats.[17] Thus to suggest that Buddhaguhya transformed in a similar way the factual reality of the era of King Khri-srong lde-btsan into a sacred reality known to him through ecstasy and visions is not unreasonable.

What are the means Buddhaguhya applied to achieve this transformation in his letter? In the first line of the initial verse Buddhaguhya addresses the king of Tibet as lord of all Black Heads (a common name at that time for the Tibetans) whose first lord was sPur-rgyal of Bod. This was common knowledge to every Tibetan at that era and thereby established an undeniable base for further communication: The Tibetan text may be understood so that the first line ("Lord of all Black Heads, sPu-rgyal of the Bod") is in apposition to the following line, which introduces the addressee of the letter as "Khri-srong lde-btsan, son of Ag-tshom-mes". In other words, Buddhaguhya sees Khri-srong lde-btsan as representative of the mythic first king and primordial ancestor of the Tibetan royal house. The first two lines are a vocative phrase which can be translated as follows:

> "O Khri-srong lde-btsan, son of Ag-tshom-mes, [and heir to]
> sPu-rgyal of the Bod, lord over all Black Heads!"[18]

The following three lines declare the bodhisattva lineage as uninterrupted; this means that the entire dynasty is considered as a lineage of bodhisattvas.[19] This claim is supported by two further assertions of Srong-btsan sgam-po as an embodiment of Avalokitesvara, and rLung-nam 'phrul-gyi rgyal-po (i.e. King 'Dus-srong) as lord. Thus in the second part of this verse, Buddhaguhya says that because of the rule of 'Dus-srong and because Srong-btsan sgam-po embodied Avalokitesvara this lineage of bodhisattvas is uninterrupted. Its rightful heir and present king is Khri-srong lde-btsan:

> "Because of rLung-nam 'phrul-gyi rgyal-po, the Lord, and
> Srong-btsan sgam-po, the embodiment of Avalokitesvara, the
> lineage of bodhisattvas is uninterrupted."[20]

The question that most obviously arises is whether Buddhaguhya could have drawn on Buddhist sources when he saw the Tibetan king as bodhisattva Avalokitesvara. Its answer involves the search for a model which Buddhaguhya might have applied to the Tibetan kings.

In Buddhist literature we find many references to universal monarchs *(cakravartin)* who were bodhisattvas at the same time. For instance, in the *Large Sutra on Perfect Wisdom* we read:

> There are Bodhisattvas who, coursing in the six perfections, have become Universal Monarchs. Having taken the perfection of giving for their guide they will provide all beings with everything that brings ease--food to the hungry, drink to the thirsty. They will provide perfumes, garlands, ointments, medicinal powders, incense, beds, seats, asylum, homes, money, grain, jewels, pearls, gold, silver, coral, ornaments, and the means of life--until, having established beings in the ten ways of wholesome action, they are reborn among the gods of Brahma's group...and know full enlightenment in the various Buddha-fields.[21]

The *Prajnaparamita sutras* were the core of the Mahayana scriptures, and thus every Buddhist was well acquainted with their content. If we take into consideration the idiosyncrasy of Buddhaguhya, his predisposition towards mystical experiences, and the sudden invitation from the Land of Snow, then it becomes plausible that he understood the situation not only in the light of his previous unsuccessful attempt to visualize Avalokitesvara, but also in the light of this passage from the *Prajnaparamita sutra*.

The next question is how the Tibetans might have responded to Buddhaguhya's vision of the Tibetan kings as bodhisattvas in general, and Srong-btsan sgam-po as Avalokitesvara in particular. There are not too many documents expressing opinions about religious belief which stem from the time of the early dynasty and which may be treated with any amount of credibility. Nonetheless, the vagueness in Tibetan sources when they refer to Srong-btsan sgam-po can be explained as quite natural. At this time the Tibetans were not yet fully familiar with the Buddhist allegoric pantheon; thus they felt more comfortable likening the king to the limitless space of the heavens, the abode of gods and ancestors. This is what they did, for example, in the above mentioned edict, originally inscribed on a stone pillar and a copy of which was discovered among the Tun Huang documents. The edict was most probably composed a few years after Buddhaguhya had written his letter, and it refers to Srong-btsan sgam-po as "Lord of men, son of gods" who has been divinely manifested.[22]

Buddhaguhya's letter testifies that by the second half of the 8th century the idea of King Srong-btsan sgam-po as Avalokitesvara existed. In the light of these new findings, the ornate story in the *Mani bka' 'bum* must be regarded as nothing but the Tibetan elaboration of an idea first expressed by Buddhaguhya, the Buddhist master from India. Because of these circumstances, we should regard the Tibetan references to Srong-btsan sgam-po as Avalokitesvara as echoes of Indian ideas, and for a further study of these ideas we should ask whether the Tibetans accepted this suggestion of a bodhisattva-king, and if so, how they dealt with this *sujet* in their own literature. This brings me to the hagiography in the *Gab pa mngon byung*.

III

There is no question that the Tibetans, more precisely the aristocratic and Buddhist elite at the Tibetan court, eagerly embraced the idea of a bodhisattva-king. Later historiographic sources bear witness to this enthusiasm, and there is no need to dwell on this subject any longer.

The second part of my contribution will deal with the way by which the Tibetans adopted and modified the idea of the bodhisattva-king. In other words, I want to explore the literary work which preserves Srong-btsan sgam-po's hagiography.[23]

The text starts with Avalokitesvara's well-known mantra, *Om mani padme hum*, before outlining the religious parameters within which we have to understand the entire text: Buddha Amitabha is the ultimate reality *(dharmakaya)*, while Avalokitesvara manifests the first level of revelation where he and the disciples communally rejoice in teaching and listening to the dharma *(sambhogakaya)*. On the next lower level of revelation, king Srong-btsan sgam-po embodies the ultimate truth on earth as *nirmanakaya*. Within this framework the hagiography unfolds like a divine play divided into five parts:

1. Avalokitesvara in Amitabha's Pure Field *(buddhaksetra)*: Avalokitesvara is born from light emitted from Buddha Amitabha's right eye. The text also records a second birth of Avalokitesvara which happens at the same place, Amitabha's Pure Land (Sukhavati). In that second instance, Avalokitesvara is born as a son of a king living in the Pure Land, and after Buddha sees the young prince for the first time he predicts that he will become the epitome of all the Buddhas' charismatic deeds. When the young prince learns about the endless suffering inflicted upon all sentient beings he pledges to generate *bodhicitta* so that they will eventually be liberated. But soon he is frustrated because of his overwhelming task, and violates his pledge. As a result his head disintegrates into several pieces. This in turn leads Avalokitesvara to realize that despite all the difficulties he must accomplish the task he has accepted for himself. He reinforces his pledge and promises that the thousand arms which have now grown on him will become a thousand *cakravartins*, or universal monarchs, to assist him in liberating all sentient beings.

2. The second chapter connects the events taking place in Amitabha's Pure Land with those occurring shortly before Buddha Sakyamuni enters *parinirvana*. Avalokitesvara asks of Sakyamuni what Ananda forgot to ask, namely that Sakyamuni should not enter *nirvana*, because there are still creatures who need his guidance; they live in the Land of Snow (Tibet). Sakyamuni. however, replies to Avalokitesvara that it will be his task to liberate them. This prophecy will direct the further fate of Avalokitesvara in his various incarnations: as monkey ancestor of the Tibetan race; as cultural hero giving to his people the skill of working the soil, and the knowledge of ethics; and finally as the great king Srong-btsan sgam-po who entrenches the *buddhadharma* firmly in the hearts of the Tibetans.

3. The third chapter tells the story of three statues made during the lifetime of Buddha Sakyamuni and which portrayed him at the age of eight, twelve, and twenty-five. This story is relevant in so far as two of these statues show up in the dowry of two of King Srong-btsan sgam-po's queens.

4. The fourth chapter records Avalokitesvara's first earthly embodiment in the Land of Snow. From light radiating from Avalokitesvara's left hand a mythic monkey is born. He prefers to live as a celibate yogi but a female rock-demon persuades him to marry her "for the benefit of sentient beings", as she puts it. Their off-spring represent the six clans which constituted the Tibetan people initially. The monkey-ancestor introduces his hungry off-spring to agriculture, and through the cultivation and consumption of grain the monkey youngsters gradually acquire human shape.

The second step in the humanization of the semi-human monkeys is to teach them the basics of Buddhist ethics. Avalokitesvara does this, but not in the shape of the monkey-ancestor, but as a tiny boy. I have the impression that here the text wants to present Avalokitesvara in the role of a first monarch introducing law and order to the Tibetans. This is not explicitly stated in the text, and the hesitation to do so is quite understandable, as the overwhelming majority of all written sources confirm that the Tibetans' first ruler was gNya'-khri btsan-po and not the child Avalokitesvara. Nonetheless, my guess is supported to some extent by the text's statement that this introduction of Buddhist ethics is the "disciplining through the *buddhadharma*", a deed otherwise associated with Srong-btsan sgam-po's first legislation, which is undoubtedly based upon the ten moral precepts of Buddhist ethics. In a way, then, the miraculous boy teaching the semi-monkeys in Buddhist ethics foreshadows the later historical king's issuing the first written code of laws in Tibetan history.

5. The fifth part deals specifically with the establishment of the Tibetan monarchy. The initial state of the human race in Tibet was one of social chaos, or as the text puts it, "At this time the differentiation of ruler and ruled did not exist in Tibet". For this reason the first ruler of Tibet had to come from Abroad, in this case, from India. Here the text tells for the second time,at least in my opinion, the story of the first Tibetan ruler, but now in its commonly accepted form. For our present case, this is of no interest.

After a brief reference to some of the most prominent members of the protohistorical part of the Tibetan dynasty the text records the miraculous birth of Srong-btsan sgam-po. The queen conceives when light from Avalokitesvara's right eye emerges and assumes the shape of a small boy (the text says he was one foot tall). This event is marked with a thousandfold outburst of cascades of light showering the entire universe. All Buddhas recognize that now the time has come to liberate the sentient beings of the Land of Snow, that its most sublime king, Srong-btsan sgam-po, is about to be born.

The young prince starts out to realize his main objectives while he is still an infant. He appoints the most gifted young man, Thon-mi Sambhota, to go to India to obtain proper education in the art of writing, grammar, poetry, and similar disciplines. The next important event, second only to the prince's birth, is his inauguration as fully endowed king. The young prince asks his parents to transfer the entire royal power to him:

> Because I have previously promised Buddha Amitabha to discipline the land of Tibet by means of the dharma you ought to endow me now with the true power.[24]

At this moment when Avalokitesvara's strategy for liberating the sentient beings of the land of Snow is about to fulfill itself, the divine potential of the universe erupts in the form of a light which reveals all the levels of evolution: Buddhas and bodhisattvas shower limitless light over the earth and each ray unfolds into a *buddhaksetra*. In the centre of all these individual *ksetras* the primordial

Buddha rNam-par snang-mdzad Gangs-can-mtsho (Vairocana Haimavata ?)[25] appears emitting limitless light. The forms and numbers of emanations multiply and the entire universe abounds with the light of reality. More than any other paragraph this one illustrates the religious role attributed to king Srong-btsan sgam-po in this hagiography. One might be tempted to call him a messianic figure in this context, although otherwise Buddhism rules out such a concept.

The king's first act is to promulgate a legal code, but unlike that existing previously, it is based upon the dharma and therefore will establish the subjects in happiness. The understanding is that by enforcing religiously grounded laws the ruler enables the subjects to live a moral life, which eventually will make them happier, as it brings them closer to the realization of enlightenment. In some sense, he duplicates here what a previous incarnation of Avalokitesvara has done, when the tiny boy appeared in the world to teach the semi-human monkeys Buddhist ethics.

Another prominent deed of the king is the making of a statue of his personal *istadevata (yidam)*, Avalokitesvara. This story leads us again to India and Ceylon (Singhala) but I shall not further elaborate on it; it might suffice for the present purpose to say that the chosen statue represented Avalokitesvara as Kha-sar-pa-ni (Khasarpana).[26] When a monk from Singhala had brought the statue of Khasarpana to Tibet, the king was tremendously pleased and venerated the statue together with all the other sacred objects.

The third exceptional deed of the king was his marriage with a Chinese and a Nepalese princess. As in previous cases the actual deed starts in the realm of Avalokitesvara. Light emanates from his heart; one beam travels to Nepal, the other to China, thus predefining the suitable queens for the king. The Nepalese princess is called Bhrkuti, the name of a goddess closely associated with Avalokitesvara Khasarpana (and who was visualized by Buddhaguhya during his approach to Mt. Potala), while the Chinese princess is an embodiment of Tara, who had been the consort of the monkey/Avalokitesvara when mankind was about to appear on earth. With this episode the hagiography comes to an abrupt end.

IV

Srong-btsan sgam-po's hagiography depicts a grand Buddhist empire as the epitome of a Buddhist version of *historia sacra* in which the spiritual goal of humanity, a universal realization of *nirvana*, will be achieved. Thus the conception of the ruler blends with that of the bodhisattva. Royal law and Buddha law converge, resulting in the happiness of the people.

In examining the details of Srong-btsan sgam-po's hagiography I noticed certain similarities with the *Inquiry of Vimalaprabha (Vimalaprabha-pariprccha sutra)*, an apocryphal sutra which is contained in the sutra collection of the Tibetan canon.[27] The text is already listed in the *lDan-dkar-ma*, the oldest extant Tibetan catalogue listing the canonical texts translated prior to the beginning of the 9th century.[28] This demonstrates that it was readily available to Tibetan scholars from the 8th century onwards, thus making it possible that they had used the text as a kind of model for their own compositions. Its antiquity is further documented through a manuscript discovered in the Tun Huang caves. Tun Huang contained a multilingual and voluminous monastic library. To protect the collection from the looting bands of the Tangut the entrance to the library was walled up in 1035 and remained untouched till the beginning of the 20th century, when European scholars discovered the treasure and transported parts of the collection to Paris and London.[29] The Tun Huang manuscript of the *Inquiries of Vimalaprabha* was edited and translated by F. W. Thomas.[30] According to Thomas the work was presumably composed in Sanskrit, but certainly not in Tibetan. In the entire text, references to the north-western territories of the Indian subcontinent and the Western Himalayas abound, which reveal innumerable historiographical, local and social particulars.

The central figure of this text is Vimalaprabha, a female bodhisattva who pledges to further and promote the Buddhist doctrine at all costs. She is reborn as two historical figures: King Ajatasatru's daughter and later as the Rab-nges, the daughter of the defeated king of Skar-rdo.

The story is told in three segments each representing a different time-frame. (1) The first one is located in a *buddhaksetra* where Vimalaprabha pledges to protect Khotan and its thriving Buddhist civilization. She receives all kinds of *mantras* and *dharanis* to enable her to carry out this task. (2) The second segment records an episode taking place at the court of king Ajatasatru, who ruled over ancient Magadha during the beginning of the 5th century B.C. where he has met with the historical Buddha on several occasions.[31] Vimala-prabha is reborn as Ajatasatru's daughter. She, along with some of her close relatives, like her brother, Kumara Vajrasena, will play important roles in the third episode. (3) The third episode tells the story of the Tibetans' assault on Khotan, the country's defeat and subsequent resurrection. During this episode Vimalaprabha is reborn as Rab-nges, daughter of Isvara-varman I, the defeated king of Skar-rdo, and wife of the king of the Gold Race. She performs extraordinary deeds to protect Khotan from the onslaught of the Tibetan barbarians, and to restore her Buddhist culture.

In what follows I shall compare the *Inquiry of Vimalaprabha* with Srong-btsan sgam-po's hagiography. To begin, the first part of each text recounts events which happened in a certain *buddhaksetra*. In both cases, the candidates for extraordinary deeds on earth, Vimalaprabha/Rab-nges and Avalokitesvara/Srong-btsan sgam-po, are prepared for carrying out their tasks. The "Hagiography" continues this account into the second chapter.

The second part of the "Inquiry" corresponds with the fourth chapter of the "Hagiography". In both cases the divine beings, Vimalaprabha and Avalokitesvara, let appear their appropriate manifestations on earth. Vimala-prabha is reborn as King Ajatasatru's daughter, and Avalokitesvara lets appear a youthful teacher, who instructs the semi-human ancestors in ethics, which transforms them into humans. In the case of the Vimalaprabha the events are associated with the most sacred era of Buddhist history, that is when Sakyamuni wandered over this earth. In the case of the "Hagiography" the events are related to the very beginning of the Tibetan race, which stands here for mankind in general.

The third episode in the "Inquiry" is related to the fifth chapter of the "Hagiography". In the first case, Vimalaprabha is reborn as Rab-nges, daughter of the ill-fated king of Skar-rdo; in the second one, Avalokitesvara lets emerge King Srong-btsan sgam-po as the sole truly divine ruler of the Land of Snow. Both characters are mostly concerned with establishing the *buddhadharma* in their countries, and entrenching Buddhist morality deeply into the hearts of their subjects. Salvation for an entire nation is in both cases the objective realized through the incarnations of a bodhisattva who fulfills through this act an ancient prophecy. Both figures function as prime protectors of their countries. In the case of the "Inquiry" such is stated clearly in the text itself; and regarding Avalokitesvara's involvement with Tibet, it is well known that he has become the main patron of this country, with the Dalai Lamas as his chief embodiment.

History, and in both cases we deal with unquestionable historical events (the Tibetan conquest of Khotan, and the rule of Srong-btsan sgam-po), is seen as the outflow of a divine plan carefully crafted in a *buddhaksetra*, eons before mankind emerged on this planet. Both texts paint a scenario which may justify our talking here of a Buddhist teleology. The instruction of sentient beings in the *buddhadharma* does not happen due to their *karma*, but due to a resolution adopted eons ago by Buddhas and bodhisattvas. Historical events are neither random happenings nor the fruits of previous acts *(karma)*, but mirror a divine plan of salvation which was drafted in the past.

The ideology underlying such thought contrasts to some extent with common Buddhist concepts, self-responsibility, freedom of choice, inevitability of karma, etc., but it might well have catered to the latent anxiety of those who perceived themselves to be lost in a meaningless universe evolving through ages without destination. We also have to keep in mind that this era, the 7th/8th centuries saw such powerful and impressive monarchs as Lalitaditya of Kashmir, Harsa, the Palas of Bengal, and the T'ang emperors of China. The frequent warfare imposed by these rulers upon their subjects may have led to the rise of "millenarian" expectations on the side of the common people, while the glory of historical rulers provided a suitable symbol for concretizing the essence of religious saviours, such as the bodhisattvas.

V

One may argue against my hypothesis that Srong-btsan sgam-po's hagiography was to some extent inspired by the "Inquiry of Vimalaprabha" because the "Inquiry" portrays the Tibetans as barbarians attacking a Buddhist civilization, while the "Hagiography" describes a Tibetan king as the epitome of the Buddhist ruler. Furthermore, both events ,the rule of the pious Buddhist bodhisattva-king and the Tibetan infidels' attack on Khotan , happened roughly at the same time.

My hypothesis is that the idea of Srong-btsan sgam-po as bodhisattva-king originated among the Buddhist missionaries who had come from India to Tibet in the 8th century. Most likely, Buddhaguhya was the one who put this idea into writing, as we have learned from his letter. Perhaps he was the only Indian master who felt this way, but because of his pastoral epistle sent to King Khri-srong lde-btsan, the idea gained official status. It must have appealed tremendously to the king, who saw himself as carrying out the will of Srong-btsan sgam-po, his ancestor (as we learned from the *sBa bzhed*).[32]The awareness of his mission was heightened when Buddhaguhya stated that the royal family of Tibet was a lineage of bodhisattvas, thus making Khri-srong lde-btsan into the stewart of Srong-btsan sgam-po, that is, Avalokitesvara.

Although the king and part of the nobility had enthusiastically embraced the *buddhadharma*, the population at large, including the army, adhered still to their pre-Buddhist beliefs. Thus, the king had to word his divine nature so that it was acceptable to the masses, whenever he made official proclamations, as in the stone pillar edicts. This accounts for the vagueness in these statements when it comes to declaring the king's bodhisattva nature. At the same time, because there were no visible signs of the Buddhist faith among the Tibetan soldiers, when they attacked Khotan, the Khotanese saw the attacking Tibetan army as infidels destroying Buddhism. The resulting feelings were expressed in the *Inquiry of Vimalaprabha*. A copy of this text may have fallen into the hands of the victorious Tibetan soldiers who handed it over to their superiors as part of the booty. Thus the book ended up in the royal library at the Tibetan court, as documented by the *lDan dkar ma* catalogue. At some time later, perhaps still during the dynastic period, the Tibetan ruler (either Khri-srong lde btsan or one of his successors) wanted a complete description of the divine descent of his house. He commissioned a knowledgeable monk, most likely one who belonged to the court clergy, to put into words what had long been known to the ruler's family. While searching for "sources" the monk may have been inspired by the *Inquiry of Vimalaprabha*, despite the fact that it portrayed the Tibetans in a way which was diametrically opposed to the intentions found in the "Hagiography". The monk would have been inspired, then by the larger framework of ideas in the sutra. The monk's endeavour resulted in a work, perhaps in verses, which contained the vital elements of what is preserved in Srong-btsan sgam-po's hagiography as it exists today.

The assumption of an original hagiography in verses would also help to explain the stability of the narrative, the verses providing the essential structure of the whole. It would also account for the fact that each version contains verses which are almost word-for-word identical.

In conclusion, my studies have shown that the king's hagiography is a complex work which draws its main idea, that the king is an embodiment of Avalokitesvara, from an Indian visionary who conveyed this opinion to the contemporary Tibetan ruler. Later, and we do not know when, the idea would have been expanded into a full-fledged narrative about the origin of the Tibetan people and their bodhisattva-kings. The result of this development is exemplified by Srong-btsan sgam-po's hagiography as preserved in the *Mani bka' 'bum*.

NOTES

1. For a study of *puranic* mythology and the Indian royal biography see Phyllis Granoff, "Holy Warriors: A Preliminary Study of Some Biographies of Saints and Kings in the Classical Indian Tradition", *Journal of Indian Philosophy*, 12, 1984, pp. 291-303.

2. For example, R. A. Stein, *La Civilization Tibétaine*, Second Enlarged Edition, Paris: LeSycomore, n.d. [1962], p. 38; G. Tucci, *The Religion of Tibet*, translated by G. Samuel, Berkeley/Los Angels, University of California Press, 1980, p. 1f.

3. Srong-btsan sgam-po's hagiography is preserved in a number of versions. The most popular are found in the *Mani bka' 'bum* and the *Gab-pa mngon byung*.

4. A.I. Vostrikov, *Tibetan Historical Literature*, Soviet Indology Series 4, Calcutta: Indian Studies Past and Present, 1970, p. 55.

5. R. A. Stein reaffirms this position in the revised edition of *La civilisation Tibetaine op.cit.*, p. 17, where he says that the myth as recorded in the *Mani bka' 'bum* may go back to the 12th century. See also A. MacDonald who assumes that the *Mani bka' 'bum*, in which the king's biography is contained, received its final revision in the last third of the 12th century (Ariane MacDonald, "Une lecture des Pelliot Tibetain 1286, 1287, 1038, 1047, et 1290", in *Etudes Tibetaines dediees a la memoire de Marcelle Lalou*, Paris: Librairie d'Amerique et d'Orient, 1971, p. 203).

6. G. Tucci elaborates on the background in his *opus magnum Tibetan Painted Scrolls*, vol. 1, Rome: La libreria dello stato, 1949, pp. 17f., 110.

7. *Ibid.*, p. 4.

8. "The Dharma that Came from Heaven", *Buddhist Thought and Asian Civilization*, ed. by L. S. Kawamura and K. Scott, Emeryville, California: Dharma Publishing, 1977, pp. 219-29.

9. G. Tucci, *Religions of Tibet*, Berkeley: University of California Press, 1980, pp. 1-3.

10. *Biographical Dictionary of Tibetan and Tibetan Buddhism*, vol. 1, "The Arhats, Siddhas, and Panditas of India", Dharamsala, India: Library of Tibetan Works and Archives, 1973, pp. 542-46.

11. Tr. by N. Roerich, 1949. Rpr. Delhi: Motilal Banarsidass, 1976, pp. 170, 191.

12. A. Schiefner (tr.), *Taranatha's Geschichte des Buddhismus in Indien*, St. Petersburg: Imperial Academy of Sciences, 1869, pp. 222-25; Lama Chimpa and Alaka Chattopadhyaya (trs.), *Taranantha's History of Buddhism in India*, Simla, India: Indian Institute of Advanced Study, 1970, pp. 280-83; Lama Chimpa and Alaka Chattopadhyaya, trs. *Taranatha's History of Buddhism in India*, Simla, India: Indian Institute of Advanced Study, 1970, pp. 280-283.

13. Buddhaguhya is mentioned in the Tibetan sources together with two Tibetan kings, Khri-lde gstug-brtan, also spelled Khri-lde Gtsug-btsan, (r. 704-755), and his son Khri-srong lde-btsan (r. 755-797). The discovery of Srong-btsan sgam-po's will is always associated with Khri-lde gtsug-brtan (Khtesun Sangpo, *op.cit.*, p. 543.15; *Deb t'er dmar po gsar ma, Tibetan Chronicles by bSod nams grags pa*, ed. by G. Tucci (Serie Orientale Roma, 24), Rome: Instituto Italiano per il Medio ed Estremo Oriente, 1971, fol.22.4 and fol. 23a.4, translation, p. 149 and 151; *Blue Annals*, tr. by Roerich, p. 40, and *Une chronique ancienne de bSam-yas: sBa-bzed*, ed. by R.A. Stein, Paris: Adrien Maisonneuve, 1961, table 1). But the *Deb ther dmar po gsar ma* alleges that the prophecy pointed at Khri-srong lde-btsan which his father, Khri-lde gtsug-brtan wrongly understood as pointing at himself as the fulfiller of Srong-btsan sgam-po's legacy. The *sBa bzed* has Khri-lde gtsug-brtan sending the two Tibetan envoys to Buddhaguhya and Buddhasanti, while Taranatha (tr. by Chattopadhyaya, p. 282) lets Khri-srong lde-btsan send them. The addressee of Buddhaguhya's letter is beyond any doubt Khri-srong lde-btsan (see Dietz, *op.cit.*). Bu-ston mentions Buddhaguhya only as a translator working together with other Indians and the seven Tibetans first ordained as monks (*History of Buddhism (chos-hbyung)*, tr. by E. Obermiller, Heidelberg: Otto Harrassowitz, 1931, pt.2, p. 190). The prophecy is not explicitly referred to by Bu-ston, but he does record that when Khri-srong lde-btsan ascended the throne the minister familiarized the young king with the "biography of his father and grandfather", which inspired the monarch with great faith (Bu-ston, p. 187).

14. R. A. Stein, *Une chronique ancienne de bSam-yas: sBa-bzed*, Paris: Adrien Maisonneuve, 1961, table 1.

15. Bu-ston confirms this information, *op.cit.*, p. 186.

16. S. Dietz, *Die Buddhistische Briefliteratur*, vol. 1, Asiatische Forschungen, Band 84, Wiesbaden: Otto Harrassowitz, 1984, pp. 112-13.

17. E. C. Dimock, *The place of the Hidden Moon: Erotic Mysticism in the Vaisnava Sahajiya Cult of Bengal*, Chicago and London: University of Chicago Press, 1966, p. 165 ff. talks about the transformation of an essentially divine world into the phenomenal world which common people perceive. References to this event in Caitanya's biographies are given by Deb, Narayan, A., *The Life and Times of Srikrisna Caitanya*, Calcutta: Firma KLM Private, 1984, p. 88.

18. *bod kyi spur rgyal mgo nag yongs kyi rje / khri srong lde'u btsan ag tshom mes kyi sras /* (S. Dietz, *op.cit.*, vol. 2, p. 184).

19. This statement is in disagreement with the common Tibetan tradition which distinguishes between the *chos rgyal* part of the dynasty, which begins with Srong-btsan sgam-po, who is considered to be the first *chos rgyal*, but the 33rd in the dynasty, and the earlier non-Buddhist part comprising the 32 kings prior to Srong-btsan sgam-po.

20. *rlung nam 'phrul gyi rgyal po'i dpon po yis / srong btsan sgam po spyan ras gzigs kyi sku / byang chub sems dpa'i sku rgyud gdung ma chad / (S. Dietz, op.cit.*, vol. 2, p. 184).

21. E. Conze, *The Large Sutra on Perfect Wisdom*, Berkeley: University of California Press, 1975, p. 71.

22. H.E. Richardson, *op.cit.*, pp. 219ff.

23. *Chos skyong ba'i rgyal po Srong-btsan sgam-po'i rnam thar mdor bsdus nyer mkho gsal ba'i me long zhes bya ba 'gro kun ma rig mun sel bzhugs so in Gab pa mngon byung*, pp. 455-510. This work will be referred to below as "hagiography".

24. *Gab pa mngon byung*, p. 494.2.

25. This "ur-Buddha" is mentioned also in some of the Buddhist Donor Chronicles (*chab brjod*) of Zanskar; a publication describing these documents is forthcoming.

26. Khasarpana images played a vital role in the propagation of early Buddhism in mNga'-rise (Ladakh) where some beautiful examples may still be seen. Furthermore, several Khasarpana *sadhanas* were incorporated into the *Sadhanamala* (Benoytosh Bhattacharyya, *The Indian Buddhist Iconography*, Calcutta: Mukhopadhyay, 1958, pp. 128ff.).

27. This text is contained in one or two volumes (depending upon the edition) of the Kanjur (vol. Pa of the Narthang edition) together with other texts which constitute also "inquiries". In the Derge edition it is contained in vol. Ba fol. 211-259 (Toh. 168).

28. G. Gronbold, *Der buddhistische Kanon. Eine Bibliographie*, Wiesbaden: Otto Harrassowitz, 1984, p. 31.

29. A. Macdonald and Y. Imaeda (eds.), *Choix de documents tibetains conserves a la Bibilotheque nationale*, Paris: Bibliotheque Nationale, 1978, vol. 1, p. 10.

30. F. W. Thomas (ed. and tr.), *Tibetan Literary Texts and Documents Concerning Chinese Turkestan*, London: The Royal Asiatic Society, 1935, pt. 1, pp. 137-258.

31. E. Lamotte, *Histoire du Bouddhism*, Leuven: Institut Orientaliste, 1958, rpt. 1967, pp. 100ff.

32. Despite the fact that the document with Srong-btsan sgam-po's will is discovered by Khri-lde gstug-brtan, Bu-ston (*op.cit.*, p. 187) as well as bSod-nams grags-pa (*op.cit.*, p. 151) indicate that the prophecy was meant for Khri-srong lde-btsan.

Two sources of Chinese Buddhist biographies: *stupa* inscriptions and miracle stories

Koichi Shinohara

1. Introduction

Aside from the mythological life of the Buddha and other highly legendary materials, Buddhist tradition in India appears to have produced only a limited amount of biographical writings. Chinese Buddhism in contrast produced a very large body of biographical writings. In fact, the extensive Buddhist historical writings produced in China largely consist of biographies. In the case of Ch'an Buddhism, its extensive literature presenting diverse theoretical viewpoints is frequently organized in the form of biographical writings. Students of Chinese Buddhist biographies need to face the very basic question of why Chinese Buddhism produced such a large body of biographical literature in any serious attempt to come to terms with their subject matter.

One strategy for exploring this large question is to examine the nature of the sources that lie behind these biographies, asking how the information concerning monks was first recorded, preserved, and then used by compilers of the biographical collections. The emphasis in such an exploration should first be on identifying the types of sources that were used frequently in the compilation of monks' biographies. Once identified, it should then be possible to focus on each of these types and attempt to understand what these sources can tell us about why the Chinese Buddhist community felt it important to write, preserve, and collect biographical records of important monks. This analysis should also show what forces were at work in drawing biographical sketches in these sources. By comparing these source materials with the corresponding biographies in the later collections, it should then be possible to examine the manner in which compilers of biographical collections used their sources. Such a study should help us understand how Chinese Buddhist biographies came to have their present form.

In this paper I shall examine two types of sources in some detail. I will first point to the importance of *stupa* inscriptions as a source for Chinese Buddhist biographies. The reason for the unprecedented quantity of such biographies must lie at least in part in the fact that Chinese Buddhism adopted the well-established Chinese convention of writing biographies as tomb inscriptions, a convention which produced the remarkably large body of secular biographies in China. The practice of erecting *stupa* inscriptions for deceased monks similarly resulted in the accumulation of a great deal of written biographical materials in Chinese Buddhism.

But the issue is a complex one. For one thing, though a majority of the biographies of Chinese Buddhist monks preserved in the extant large collections may have been based at least in part on *stupa* inscriptions,[1] a considerable number of biographies in these same collections appear to have come from different sources.[2] I will attempt to throw some light on this complex issue through examining one other type of source for Chinese Buddhist biographies, namely, stories of miracles. A discussion of miracle stories and their relationship to *stupa* inscriptions will hopefully enable us to gain further insight into the nature of the very extensive biographical literature in Chinese Buddhism. While compilers of Chinese Buddhist biographies also no doubt used sources other than *stupa* inscriptions and miracle stories, a detailed discussion of those other sources must be postponed for a future occasion.[3]

A few more words on the general orientation of this investigation may be helpful.

(1) I consider biography to be an important form of religious literature in China and my aim is to investigate how the biographies of Buddhist monks were typically composed, revised, and preserved in China. In the final analysis the process of compilation, revision, and preservation must have varied from case to case, and the range of variation may have been considerable. Nevertheless, there appears to have been a pattern, a set of conventions that governed the composition of *stupa* inscriptions, for example, and a certain consistency in the manner in which compilers of large collections collected and used the sources available to them. I am interested in identifying this pattern and describing the process "ideal-typically". This is a difficult task, especially given the volume of existing Chinese Buddhist biographies and the paucity of the data on their sources. Here I must confine myself to offering a few general observations based on an analysis of isolated examples. These observations, it is hoped, will throw some light on certain specific but limited aspects of the process in question.[4]

(2) I shall limit my task to the examination of the biographies contained in the three most important collections of Chinese Buddhist biographies: Hui-chiao's (497-554) "Biographies of Eminent Monks" (*Kao-seng chuan*, around

531),[5] Tao-hsüan's (596-667) "Further Biographies of Eminent monks" *(Hsü kao-seng chuan,* 645 according to the compiler's preface but expanded later),[6] and Tsan-ning's (919-1001) "Sung Biographies of Eminent Monks" *(Sung kao-seng chuan,* 988). I shall examine the use of *stupa* inscriptions and miracle stories in these collections.

(3) This paper is organized in the following manner. I will begin with a general and hypothetical discussion of Chinese *stupa* inscriptions, emphasizing the relationship of *stupa* inscriptions to the Chinese conventions of tomb inscriptions, and explore some possible ways in which it might have affected the nature of Chinese Buddhist biographies. In this context, I will contrast the secular or lay orientation of the composers of *stupa* inscriptions with the monastic orientation of the compilers of the large biography collections. I will compare a small number of surviving *stupa* inscriptions used by the compiler of the Sung collection with the corresponding biographies in the collection to show how Tsan-ning (and most probably his predecessors) used *stupa* inscriptions. I will then make a systematic examination of explicit references to *stupa* inscriptions in the three collections. This examination will reveal, among other things, that the three compilers relied heavily but by no means exclusively on *stupa* inscriptions for their source material.

My discussion of miracle stories begins with a detailed comparison of preserved fragments from the miracle story collection *Ming hsiang chi* and Hui-chiao's biographies that are at least partly based on this source. This comparison suggests that the relationship between miracle stories and the biographical format based primarily on *stupa* inscriptions was a very complex one. This will be followed by a more detailed analysis of two examples in which the role of miracle stories in the development of biographies may be traced concretely.

2. Hypothesis concerning *stupa* inscriptions

Traditional Chinese biographies[7] were composed in two contexts: as a part of the funeral rites which served the interest of the family and as a component of official dynastic histories. The two contexts were closely interrelated, and we have evidence indicating clearly that by the T'ang period (618-907), except in the cases of the highest ranking officials, the official biographies prepared for inclusion in dynastic histories were based directly on funerary documents.[8] After the death of an important personage, a document recording relevant facts in the life of the deceased ("Account of Conduct", *hsing chuang*) was produced.[9] The family of the deceased then requested one of the more well-known literary figures, generally occupying important government positions, to write the texts for the tomb inscriptions (generally called *mu chih ming* and *shen-tao pei*). The texts, often in the calligraphy of another well-known figure(s), were then carved and placed in the appropriate places around the tomb. In addition a copy of the Account of Conducts along with other funeral documents was sent to an office of the central government as material for the future compilation of the dynastic history.

Chinese Buddhist monks adopted the same steps with some modification in producing *stupa* inscriptions. Relevant facts about the deceased monk were collected and the Account of Conduct was composed by his disciples, since the monk had renounced the householder's life and did not have a family of his own. Interestingly, in most cases it was still an eminent secular literary figure with a high government position who was asked to write the *stupa* inscription *(t'a pei ming)* and the practice of requesting another such figure to produce the calligraphy was also often followed. A very small number of biographies of Buddhist monks found their way into dynastic histories, but the normative collections of these biographies were compiled by the monks Hui-chiao, Tao-hsüan, and Tsan-ning as "Biographies of Eminent Monks", "Further Biographies of Eminent Monks", and "Sung Biographies of Eminent Monks". These collections were eventually included in the imperially sanctioned Buddhist canon.[10]

The nature of Chinese Buddhist biographies must have been deeply affected by the process through which they came into being. Limiting our discussion to the biographies that came from *stupa* inscriptions for the time being, this question may be explored hypothetically as follows. We noted that the *stupa* inscriptions in most cases were written by secular men of letters. These secular authors of biographies of monks must in most cases have been sympathetic to Buddhism, and perhaps represent the lay Buddhist religiosity of the community. Nevertheless, these secular writers who admired these monks from a distance as lay followers must also have interpreted the lives of these religious men very differently from the way those committed to follow the path themselves as monks interpreted them. For example, many of the biographies in the three "Biographies of Eminent Monks" collections place considerable emphasis on the relationship between these monks and the court. This emphasis is more understandable if we keep in mind that the authors of the inscriptions on which these biographies were based and perhaps a large part of their intended readership, those who visited the *stupa* of the deceased monks, were themselves high officials or aspirants to high government offices. At the stage of *stupa* inscriptions, the basic orientation of these biographies of monks was not simply "religious" but "secular" in important ways.

The compilers of the "Biographies of Eminent Monks" collections were all seriously committed monks. They collected biographies recorded in *stupa* inscriptions and other biographical sources and organized the large number of biographies they collected within a framework of ten categories of activities in which monks could attain eminence.[11] The underlying viewpoint behind these works was monastic and highly orthodox.[12] Thus, there was a significant gap between the basic orientation of the compilers of biographical collections and the original orientation of the materials they used for their collections: the biographies in *stupa* inscriptions were compiled by secular authors and reflect their basic orientation; these same biographies in slightly modified forms were made to serve different purposes in the biography collections. The Chinese Buddhist biographical tradition was, to the extent that its sources were *stupa* inscriptions, a product of this complex relationship and reflected the inherent tensions in it.

3. Examples of *stupa* inscriptions

A number of the texts of *stupa* inscriptions and in some cases the stones on which they are carved[13] are still preserved. I have compared the existing texts of *stupa* inscriptions[14] with biographies in the "Biographies of Eminent Monks" collections, and have so far identified 21 cases, all from Tsan-ning's Sung collection, where the texts of the inscriptions on which the biographies are based are still preserved.[15] In 13 of these 21 cases, the biographies in the Sung collection mention the existing inscriptions explicitly. In the other eight cases,[16] the comparison of the texts shows the dependence of the biography on the *stupa* inscription beyond any doubt.

Other types of inscriptions and similar materials were also used by Tsan-ning as virtually equivalent to *stupa* inscriptions in preparing his *Sung kao-seng chuan* biographies. In some cases these inscriptions were composed in a manner that is virtually indistinguishable from *stupa* inscriptions. Some of these materials are also preserved: I have so far identified four such examples. Two inscriptions (called *pei* or *pei ming* in their titles) ostensibly prepared for temple buildings were used by Tsan-ning as sources for his biographies. In one case (the *Fa-hua-ssu chieh-t'an-yüan pei* [Inscription for the Ordination Hall of the Temple of the Lotus Flower], ie., an inscription for a building in which the monk Hsüan-yen lived for decades) Tsan-ning mentions the inscription in the biography, indicating that he had in fact treated this inscription as a *stupa* inscription. In another (the *Hsi-ching hsing-shan-ssu ch'uan-fa-t'ang pei-ming* [Inscription for the Transmission of the Teaching Hall of the Temple for Promoting the Teaching in the Western Capital] associated with the monk Wei-k'uan[17]) Tsan-ning does not mention the inscription, but the comparison of the inscription and the biography makes the dependence clear. The inscription primarily describes the life of the monk, and the building is only mentioned briefly as the place where the monk transmitted the teaching. I believe that these inscriptions were understood both by their authors and contemporary readers as the equivalents of *stupa* inscriptions. The only difference is that they were probably not actual tomb inscriptions, but must originally have been placed at the sites of the temple buildings with which the subjects had been closely associated. Here, then, we have an example of biographical inscriptions, themselves not *stupa* inscriptions proper, which were nevertheless written in the manner of *stupa* inscriptions.

Another example (*Sung-yüeh kuei-ch'an-shih ying-t'ang-chi* [Record of the Image Hall of the meditation master Kuei of the Sung-shan mountain]) describes a miracle, but again the story of the miracle centers around the monk Yüan-kuei, and the life of this monk is described in a manner similar to that of *stupa* inscriptions.[18]

The fourth example is a text entitled "a biography" (*chuan*). The *T'ang hu-chou chu-shan chiao-jan chuan*, [Biography of Chiao-jan of Chu-shan mountain in Hu-chou region] is a short biography of a monk Ch'ing-hua, who appears to have been a well-known writer of *stupa* inscriptions. Many *stupa* inscriptions he composed were used by Tsan-ning as sources for his *Sung kao-seng chuan*. I have so far been unable to determine the status of this document. Since it does not use the standard terms for designating a *stupa* inscription in its title, we cannot conclude that this short text was in fact a *stupa* inscription. Tsan-ning, however, treats it in exactly the same manner as he handles *stupa* inscriptions, and his biography is a word for word copy of this text.[19]

Since these four examples of biographical sources appear to have been treated as equivalent to *stupa* inscriptions by Tsan-ning, and their content is very similar to *stupa* inscriptions, I believe it is appropriate at least initially to take this material into consideration in our examination of *stupa* inscriptions. Later, I will return to one of these four examples, the miracle inscription associated with Yüan-kuei and examine it in some detail. I shall pay special attention to the complex question of the relationship between *stupa* inscriptions and miracle stories in my later discussion.

If we include these four examples, our sample expands to 25 cases. Instead of examining each of these inscriptions individually, I will here comment generally on the form of *stupa* inscriptions and the use made of them by the biographer Tsan-ning.

Stupa inscriptions normally follow a conventional form. They begin with a highly rhetorical passage that uses symbolic expressions, sometimes obviously Buddhist, but sometimes not[20], and locate the life of the deceased monk within a broad context of cosmic processes described by these symbols. This is followed by an narrative of the life of the deceased monk, culminating with the description of his death and funeral, and then usually a verse ("*tsan*"), glorifying his life in highly rhetorical and symbolic language. Very often, either at the beginning or the end, one finds a passage describing the circumstances of the composition of the inscription.[21]

In most of these 25 cases, the text of the biography follows the text of the inscription virtually word for word through the main, historically informative sections. When other information is available, the biography occasionally expands the narrative in the inscription[22]. What is most striking in comparing the text of the biography with the inscription is the fact that the rhetorical and symbolic passages at the beginning and end of the inscription are usually not copied in the biography. Generally speaking, the compilers appear to use inscriptional sources for historical facts and events.

The compilers of the "Biographies of Eminent Monks" also wrote rhetorical passages, using highly symbolic language. Each of the ten categories in which compilers classified their biographies ends with a section designated as "*lun yüeh*" ("The critical estimate says"[23]). These sections describe the significance of the categories of accomplishments under examination and comment on and evaluate the biographies collected in the respective categories. These passages, therefore, correspond in function to the rhetorical passages in the inscriptions, and what the compilers did in fact was to separate the historical and rhetorical passages more clearly and systematically. Whereas the rhetorical introductions in *stupa* inscriptions tended to be highly eclectic, sometimes using expressions that come from Confucian or Taoist scriptures, the "*lun yüeh*" passages describe the broad religious significance of the collected biographies in a unified, orthodox, and clearly Buddhist language.

4. References to *stupa* inscriptions in the collected biographies

Many of the biographies in the three collections mention explicitly the *stupa* inscriptions composed and erected for their subjects.[24] Circumstances of the construction of inscriptions probably varied from case to case, and, moreover, different, often highly rhetorical expressions are used in describing this process. This makes the comparison of related cases and generalizing about the practice of erecting inscriptions difficult. In most cases, it appears that it was the disciples of the deceased monk who took the initiative and prepared a document listing relevant facts in their master's life *(hsing chuang:* Account of Conduct). In many cases, the passage mentions the name(s) of well-known literary figures as authors of the *stupa* inscriptions. The disciples of the deceased monk must have approached these well-known figures and requested them to compose the *stupa* inscriptions. Sometimes, a name of a monk particularly known for his literary accomplishments is mentioned. In some cases, the name of the calligrapher is also mentioned.[25] The text was then carved on stone and placed at the site of the deceased monk's *stupa*.

As I noted above, this use of famous secular writers for composing monks' inscriptions was a well-established secular convention adopted by Chinese Buddhists for their *stupa* inscriptions. As in the case of tomb inscriptions in general, the names of well-known authors must have enhanced the value of these inscriptions. Since such writers would not necessarily have agreed to compose a *stupa* inscription for just any monk, a *stupa* inscription by a well-known writer points to the social importance of the deceased monk. Moreover, as an example of a famous personage's literary composition the text of the inscription must have acquired greater visibility and its chance of preservation over a long period must have improved considerably. The same consideration must have motivated the practice of having a well-known calligrapher draft the copy of the inscription to be carved on stone.

The compilers of the biographical collections either saw the *stupa* inscriptions themselves or at least had a copy of these inscriptions as their source. The compilers must have paid attention to the names of the authors of these inscriptions. It is probably safe to assume that they mentioned the names of the authors in cases where these names were widely recognized and likely to enhance the prestige of the subjects.[26]

It was a natural consequence of the convention of having a well-known and highly placed literary figure compose tomb inscriptions that the evaluation of the worth of the subject of a tomb inscription was linked to the status of its author. This consequence introduced a peculiar distortion in the Buddhist context. In the final analysis, it implies that secular criteria, that is, the official status and literary fame of the authors of the inscriptions, entered the evaluation of the worth of monks' lives.

We may be able to explore this development further by examining systematically the references to the authors of inscriptions in the three collections of "Biographies of Eminent Monks". As a first step in such an exploration, I counted the number of these references in each of the ten categories of biographies. The most striking fact that emerged was the concentration of biographies that mention the names of authors of *stupa* inscriptions in certain categories. In Hui-chiao's first collection, these biographies are mostly found in the category of "exegetes" (19 of the total of 25 inscriptions mentioned); in Tao-hsüan's collection, they are again found in greatest number in the category of "exegetes" (41 out of the total of 69), but both the categories of "meditation masters" (15) and "*vinaya* masters" (6) also contain a significant number; in Tsan-ning's collection, it is the category of "meditation masters" (45 out of the total of 112) that contains by far the largest number of these biographies, that of "*vinaya* masters" (20) follows it, and categories such as "exegetes" (11), "miracle workers" (11), and "promoters of works of merits" (9) contain a significant number of them.[27]

It is probably safe to conclude that the categories with the largest numbers of biographies that mention the authors of the inscriptions represent the most respected and important classes of Buddhist monks in the eyes of the secular leaders during the period of time covered by each of the three collections. The changes in the categories from collection to collection represent the shift in the secular leaders' views of Buddhism, which must have indirectly and at least partially reflected the changes in the nature of Chinese Buddhism itself. The interests of Chinese Buddhists, both monastic and lay, were initially, at least in the South where Hui-chiao collected his sources, directed toward philosophical exegesis; this emphasis continued, but other forms of orthodox Buddhist practices, such as meditation and strict observances of monastic rules, also became important during the period that Tao-hsüan's collection covers. In the subsequent period covered by Tsan-ning's collection, the rise and dramatic expansion of *ch'an* Buddhism changed the emphases and it was then the meditation masters who attracted the most attention.

A systematic investigation of the backgrounds of the authors of these *stupa* inscriptions would probably throw considerable light on the nature of the *stupa* inscriptions which served as sources for biographies. As an initial step toward such an investigation, the following observation may be helpful.[28] Hui-chiao's collection contains 25 references to *stupa* inscriptions that mention their authors. One author[29] wrote three of them. Tao-hsüan's collection has 69 references. To list those who are mentioned as authors of tomb inscriptions on multiple occasions, one author, a layman,[30] wrote five; another author, also a layman,[31] wrote four; five authors, two layman[32] and three monks,[33] wrote three each; and five authors, two monks[34] and three laymen,[35] wrote two each. Tsan-ning's collection contains 112 references. Again to list those who are mentioned on more than two occasions, three authors, two laymen[36] and one monk,[37] wrote 4; two authors, one layman[38] and one monk,[39] wrote three each; and five authors, three laymen[40] and two monks,[41] wrote two each. These figures suggest that there was a significant concentration of authorship on a limited number of writers. There was probably only a small number of writers who were known as being particularly competent and willing to draft *stupa* inscriptions.[42] The majority of these, and especially those who were prominent among them, were secular figures, perhaps, lay followers of Buddhism. But some monks, not particularly known for their spiritual accomplishments,[43] also wrote a significant number of inscriptions. This fact suggests that certain monks, known mainly for their literary gifts, began to write *stupa* inscriptions, most probably following the model of those written by secular authors.

5. References to death and funerals in the collected biographies

The next question I should like to address is the problem of how universal the reliance on *stupa* inscriptions written by lay admirers or monks really was. A closer examination of the biographical collections reveals that not all biographies contained in them are based on *stupa* inscriptions.

In all three collections, by far the largest number of biographies mention the death of the subjects and often describe the circumstances of their death and funeral in considerable detail. In many cases, as those examined above, the description of the funeral includes a reference to *stupa* inscriptions. One can assume that in most of these cases, the compiler had at least the rubbings of *stupa* inscriptions at his disposal and that the biographies were based on the inscriptions.

All three collections, however, also contain a considerable number of biographies which do not mention the death of their subjects, and in some cases it is clear that the subjects were still alive at the time of the composition of the biographies.[44] These biographies obviously could not have been based on *stupa* inscriptions. Even more importantly, a significant number of biographies in all three collections end with a brief statement to the effect that the circumstances of the subjects' death are unknown. Since *stupa* inscriptions usually describe the circumstances of the subjects' death and funeral in considerable detail, we must assume that all these biographies which explicitly state that such facts were unknown must have been based on sources other than *stupa* inscriptions.[45] As we shall examine further below, one such source may have been records of miracles.

In order to explore this question further, I prepared a list giving the number of the biographies in question according to the ten categories used by the compilers of these biographical collections. Focusing our attention on the number of biographies which explicitly state that the circumstances of the subjects' death were unknown, the findings of this work may be summarized as follows. In Hui-chiao's collection the categories of "translators" (10=28.6% of all biographies in this category) and "miracle workers" (8=40%) are particularly notable for the number of biographies which explicitly state that the circumstances of the subjects' death were unknown.[46] In Tao-hsüan's collection the category of "miracle workers" (24=20%) is particularly notable.[47] In Tsan-ning's collection, we note the categories of "translators" (10=31%), "miracle workers" (16=17.9%), and "reciters of scriptures" (8=19%).[48] Finally, if we take the total numbers of these biographies, we note that in Hui-chiao's collection the number is 30 (out of 257; 11.7%), in Tao-hsüan's collection it is 40 (out of 485; 8%)[49] and in Tsan-ning's collection it is 53 (out of 531; 9.98%).[50]

My interpretation of the significance of these figures is as follows.
(1) In all three collections the category of "miracle workers" is characterized by the notable number of these biographies in which it is stated that the circumstances of the subject's death are unknown. This suggests that there is something particular about miracle stories and the way they shape a biography. In fact, I shall later contend that many of the biographies in the miracle workers sections may be based on sources originally written as miracle stories and lack information concerning the death of the monks involved.
(2) In Hui-chiao's and Tsan-ning's collections, the category of "translators" contains a notable number of the biographies which explicitly state that it is unknown how the monks concerned ended their lives.[51]
(3) None of the three central categories of monks, i.e., "exegetes", "meditation masters", and "*vinaya* masters" contains notable numbers of this type of biographies. This probably indicates that monks known for their accomplishments in these areas were probably widely known and that their biographies were mostly based on *stupa* inscriptions written by prominent literary figures.
(4) The categories, "reciters of scriptures", contain biographies that often tell stories of miracles. Thus, the large number of biographies that acknowledge the absence of information about the subjects' deaths in these categories may be explained in the same way as in the case of miracle workers.[52]
(5) The fact that the ratio of these biographies remains substantial and stable in the later collections by Tao-hsüan and Tsan-ning may be significant. It suggests

that Chinese Buddhist biographies were never based exclusively on *stupa* inscriptions and that compilers of these biographies always used other materials, such as miracle stories, as an important though clearly secondary source.

It should be clear from all of the above that miracle stories are of particular interest in an investigation of the nature and sources of Chinese Buddhist biographies. Chinese Buddhist biographies contain a large number of miracle stories. They are found not only in biographies in the miracle workers section but also in all other sections. Thus, the prevalence of miracle stories is an important major characteristic of Chinese biographies of monks. Some accounts of miracles are found in *stupa* inscriptions: a good example here may be the *stupa* inscription for the monk Tuan-fu composed by P'ei Hsiu[53] which reports a number of miracles associated with relics. Other accounts of miracles in monks' biographies were based on independent miracle stories. It is these independent miracle stories that will occupy my attention in this paper as I explore the sources of Chinese Buddhist biographies other than *stupa* inscriptions. I shall be concerned with answering the question of how this material came to be incorporated into the biographies of monks in the *Kao-seng chuan* collections, and I shall proceed by discussing a few specific examples of biographies in the light of their miracle story sources.

5. Miracle stories as a source for Hui-chiao's "Biographies of Eminent Monks".

As we noted above (footnote 4), in his preface to the "Biographies of Eminent Monks", Hui-chiao lists diverse sources he used for his collection. Wang Man-ying's letter provides further information on sources.[54] Some of these sources are collections of miracle stories (for example, *Hsüan yen chi* and *Yu ming lu* both by Liu I-ch'ing, Prince K'ang of Lin-ch'uan (403-444); *Ming hsiang chi* by Wang Yen; Wang Yen-hsiu's *Kan ying chuan*; Chu Chün-t'ai's [572-640] *Cheng ying chi; Sou shen lu*, which is said to be by T'ao Yüan-ming [365?-427], though this attribution is questionable).[55] Though most of these sources are no longer extant in a complete form, a medieval Chinese Buddhist encyclopedia *Fa-yüan chu-lin* (completed by Tao-shih [dates unknown] in 668) preserves in fragments a large part of the miracle collection called "*Ming hsiang chi*" compiled by Wang Yen sometime after 479.[56] These fragments contain materials on monks whose biographies are found in Hui-chiao's collections. Some existing fragments from *Yu ming chi, Hsüan yen chi*, also contain similar materials.[57] Though not mentioned explicitly by Hui-chiao or by Wang Man-ying, three collections of Avalokitesvara miracles rediscovered in Japan, Fu Liang's (374-426) *Kuang-hsi-yin ying-yen-chi, Hsü kuang-shih-yin ying-yen-chi* by Chang Yen (first half of the fifth century), Lu Kao's (459-532) *Hsi kuan-shih-yin ying-yen-chi*[58] likewise contain materials that are closely related to Hui-chiao's biographies. A comparison of the *Ming hsiang chi* and other miracle stories with Hui-chiao's biographies provides us with some clues as to the role of miracle stories in the development of Chinese Buddhist biographies.

In addition to the miracle stories, there are also two earlier collections of biographical materials that throw light on a number of Hui-chiao's *Kao-seng chuan* biographies. Pao-ch'ang's *Ming-seng chuan*, a large compilation of biographies of Buddhist monks completed in 514/15, some years earlier than Hui-chiao's collection (c. 531), was used extensively by Hui-chiao as a source, though Hui-chiao appears to have been highly critical of this work and it is not mentioned explicitly in his preface. This work too is now preserved only in fragments.[59] Hui-chiao also made extensive use of the biographies in the *Ch'u san-tsang chi chi* compiled by Seng-yu (445-518).[60] In a small number of cases where parallel materials are preserved in these sources we can partially trace the process through which miracle stories were reshaped or incorporated into later biographies.

I have so far identified 26 cases of monks whose stories are found in the *Ming hsiang chi* and whose biographies in the *Kao-seng chuan* bear some relationship with the *Ming hsiang chi* stories. I have also identified a smaller number of parallels between *Kao-seng chuan* biographies and miracle stories in other existing miracle story collections or fragments from such collections. There are five cases for Lu Kao's *Hsi kuan-shih-yin-ying-yen-chi;* three for the *Yu ming lu*; two for Fu Liang's *Kuang-shih-yin ying-yen-chi*; one for the *Hsüan yen chi*. In three cases (Tao-chiung, Chu Fa-ch'un, and Seng hung) both the *Ming hsiang chi* fragments and Lu Kao's *Hsi kuan-shih-yin ying-yen-chi* contain parallels to the same *Kao-seng chuan* biographies. In one case (Chu Fa-yi) the parallel material is found both in the *Ming hsiang chi* and Fu Liang's *Kuang-shi-yin ying-yen-chi*. In all cases where biographies in the *Kao-seng chuan* have parallels in earlier miracle story collections, I have found that Pao-ch'ang's *Ming-seng chuan* also contained biographies on the same subjects. Though the majority of these corresponding *Ming-seng chuan* biographies have now been lost, a comparison of the few *Ming-seng chuan* biographies preserved in the *Meisodensho* (Chu Fa-yi, Tao-wang, Chu Fa-ch'un, and Seng-hung) and the corresponding *Kao-seng chuan* biographies indicates that Hui-chiao must have relied heavily on Pao-ch'ang's biographies. Since by far the largest number of parallels between the *Kao-seng chuan* biographies and miracle stories in earlier collections are found in the *Ming hsiang chi*, here I will focus on the parallels between the *Ming hsiang chi* and the *Kao-seng chuan*. Where other parallel biographies or miracle stories are preserved, I will also take them into consideration. Finally I shall comment briefly on related parallel versions found in miracle story collections other than the *Ming hsiang chi*, but not in the *Ming hsiang chi* itself.

A comparison of the materials in the *Kao-seng chuan* and the *Ming hsiang chi* shows that there are three distinct modes of relationship between these two texts.

(I) Hui-chiao simply rewrote the material in the *Ming hsiang chi* (seven cases: Fa-an from the exegetes section; Chu Fa-tiao and Chien-t'uo-le from the miracle workers section; Seng-ch'un and Seng-yü from the self-immolators section; Fa-hsiang, and Hui-chin from the reciters of scriptures section). Stories about monks in the *Ming hsiang chi* are written in the form of biographies, but in each case the biography contains a story or stories about miraculous feats and/or events. Though written in the form of biographies, Wang Yen obviously collected these materials as records of miracles. My hypothesis is that these materials were originally transmitted as records of miracles, the biographical format appearing clearly only when they were written down, or at some later stage of rewriting and editing, as a matter of convenience. From the very beginning what was important in these materials was the descriptions of the miracles, and references to person, place and time were included because these details served an important function. In records of miracles stories written as biographies such information as the secular surname of the monk and his place of origin, even when not specifically relevant to the miraculous events themselves, would nevertheless enhance the verisimilitude of the accounts. In these cases the distinction between miracle stories and biographies becomes blurred. Hui-chiao sometimes took these miracle stories written as biographies and incorporated them into relevant sections of his collection.

(II) Hui-chiao's biographies parallel for the most part the *Ming hsiang chi's* story, but also contain additional information (eleven cases: Chu Shih-hsing, K'ang Fa-lang, Yü Fa-lan, Chu Fa-yi, Chu Seng-lang from the exegetes section; Shan Tao-k'ai, Shih-yü from the miracle workers section; Chu Fa-ch'un, Tao-chiung and Hui-ch'ing from the reciters of scriptures section; Seng-hung from the promoters of meritorious works section). In these examples the *Kao-seng chuan* biographies generally report the same miracles as the *Ming hsiang chi* stories. In some cases it adds further miracles (Yü Fa-lan, Shih-Yü, Hui-ch'ing), and in some cases details of the same events are different (e.g., Yü Fa-lan, Shih-Yü, Chu Shih-hsing, Chu Fa-yi).

Several of these biographies have parallels in other existing sources, giving us a glimpse into the history behind the miracles stories and biographies in question. The clues here to unraveling the complex relationships between the various accounts and understanding the development of the biography are the unmistakable relationships in matters of content and the relative dates of the works. The *Kuang-shih-yin ying-yen-chi* is a reconstruction of materials that were first collected before 399;[61] the *Ming hsiang chi* was completed shortly after 479; the *Hsi kuan-yin ying-yen-chi* was completed in 501;[62] the *Ming-seng chuan* in 513;[63] the *Chu san-tsang chi chi* between 510 and 518, and the *Kao-seng chuan* around 530. Thus, for example, where the contents of the biographies in the *Ming hsiang chi*, the *Ming-seng chuan*, and the *Kao-seng chuan* show unmistakable mutual dependence, we must understand that the account of the *Ming hsiang chi* must have been the earliest account, which was known at least to Pao-ch'ang and possibly to Hui-chiao as well.

I will here examine six cases that are of particular interest.

(a) Chu Shih-hsing
To begin with an example from the "translators" section, Chu Shih-hsing's biography is found in Seng-yu's *Ch'u san-tsang chi chi* and as in other cases of the *Ch'u san-tsang chi chi* biograhies, Hui-chiao's *Kao-seng chuan* biography is based directly on Seng-yu's biography. Though there are frequent minor differences in the choice of characters and phraseology, the relationship between these two biographies is unmistakable. The miracle story in the *Ming hsiang chi* also is quite similar to those in the two biographies. In the *Ming hsiang chi* version, however, the circumstances that explain why Chu Shih-hsing embarked on the trip to obtain the original text of the Perfection of Wisdom scripture, given in virtually the same words in Seng-yu's *Ch'u san-tsang chi chi* biography and Hui-chiao's *Kao-seng chuan* biography, are not mentioned, and there are some differences in the account of the central miracle. There may have been a general tradition about the miracle performed by this Chinese monk who died in Central Asia, and the accounts in the *Ming hsiang chi* and the *Ch'u san-tsang chi chi* may represent two different versions that come from this tradition. Seng-yu, in that case, might not have known the *Ming hsiang chi*'s story. It is also possible that Seng-yu knew the *Ming hsiang chi* version of the miracle story and that he revised it, perhaps on the basis of another account known to him.

(b) Chu Fa-yi

In the second example, Chu Fa-yi from the "exegetes" section, the material in the *Ming hsiang chi* story (as found in the *Fa-yüan chu-lin, chüan* 17) tells a story in which "a man of the Way", probably Avalokitesvara, appears in a dream and cures Chu Fa-yi's disease by taking out his inner organs and washing them. This material was incorporated into the *Ming-seng chuan* biography, which in turn formed the basis of the *Kao-seng chuan* biography. There is a significant difference in the number of disciples listed: over 100 according to the *Ming hsiang chi* story and the *Kao-seng chuan* biography, but over 40 according to the *Ming-seng chuan* biography. There is also a quotation attributed to Fu Liang in the *Ming hsiang chi* story ("My father had contacts with Chu Fa-yi. Every time Chu Fa-yi told him the story, he felt frightened and renewed his respect for him") and the *kao-seng chuan* biography (the quotation is slightly modified here). The quotation is absent in the *Ming-seng chuan* biography. These observations confirm that Hui-chiao also had access to the *Ming hsiang chi* and revised the account of the *Ming-seng chuan* biography using this source.

In this example there is another source of the same story preserved in the *Fa-yüan chu-lin, chüan* 95[64] where the origin of this version of the story is attributed to a work called the *Shu yi chi.*[65] In this section of the *Fa-yüan chu-lin* a story virtually identical with that in the *Ming hsiang chi* is told in different words, with a different date of death, and with a differently worded quotation of Fu Liang's words. Makita Tairyo showed that this passage is in fact a quotation from the *Kuang-shih-yin ying-yen-chi* and not the *Shu yi chi* as claimed by the *Fa-yüan chu-lin*.[66] According to the preface of the *Kuang-shih-yin ying-yen-chi*, the seven stories recorded there are based on what its editor Fu Liang (374-426) remembered of an earlier collection. Hsieh Fu of the Eastern Chin dynasty compiled a work of the same name consisting of over ten stories and sent it to Fu Liang's father, but due to the confusion caused by Sun Yen's rebellion (399) the work was lost; failing to find the work anywhere, Fu Liang wrote down the seven stories that he remembered.[67]

If we accept this account of the origin of Fu Liang's text given in this preface, the oldest existing source of the story about Chu Fa-yi (307-380)[68] describing a miracle that occurred in the year 372 according to the *Kao-seng chuan*[69] would be Hsieh Fu's *Kuang-shih-yin ying-yen-chi*, to be dated some time earlier than 399. We must then assume that Fu Liang's comment about his father's contact with Chu Fa-yi was added to what he remembered of Hsieh Fu's version by Fu Liang himself; he added this information as the compiler's comment, using the first person pronoun "*yü*." This statement was preserved as a rather abruptly introduced quotation from a statement of a famous person in the *Ming hsiang chi*. There is, however, nothing in the *Ming hsiang chi* account that explains the relationship between this famous person Fu Liang and the content of the story. This obscure quotation was then dropped in the *Ming-seng chuan* biography, but Hui-chiao, who probably knew both the *Kuang-shih-yin ying-yen-chi* and *Ming hsiang chi* stories, restored it with some changes in wording in his *Kao-seng chuan* biography. In this case of Chu Fa-yi we are thus able to trace the miracle story preserved in the *Ming hsiang chi* to an earlier source (ie., the *Kuang-shih-yin ying-yen-chi)*, though the precise relationship between the two is still largely obscure.

(c) Chu Seng-lang

The biography of another "exegete", Chu Seng-lang, in the *Kao-seng chuan* appears to be based on the *Ming hsiang chi* material (T. Vol.53, 428bc; 592f.). The wording of the two stories reporting Seng-lang's extraordinary ability to know things happening at distant places is very similar. Yet, other incidents in his life are reported in both sources in different words (eg., the account of how Seng-lang's temple was spared at the time of the persecution of Buddhism under Fu-chien [338-385] of the Former Ch'in dynasty). There also is a fair amount of information in the *Kao-seng chuan* biography which is not found in the *Ming hsiang chi*. The *Ming hsiang chi* fragment in the *Fa-yüan chu-lin* may be itself an abbreviated version of the original story in this collection, or we must surmise that Hui-chiao had before him another rather extensive source.

(d) Chu Fa-ch'un

A rich body of material has survived around the three "reciters of scriptures" biographies, ie., those of Chu Fa-ch'un, Tao-chiung, and Hui-ch'ing.

Thus, the same central story is told in the *Ming hsiang chi*, *Hsi kuan-yin ying-yen-chi*, [70]*Ming seng chuan*, and *Kao-seng chuan*. Chu Fa-ch'un runs into a storm on his trip to buy materials for repairing temple walls; when he recites the *Kuan-shih-yin ching*, a large boat appears and he is able to board it and reach the other side of the river safely. In all four versions the same description of the geographical and chronological setting appears; we are given the same name of his temple Hsien-yi-ssu[71] and the same period during which the incident occurred, namely "during the Yüan-hsing period of the Chin dynasty (402-404)". This common description of the setting points to a close relationship among these accounts. In the *Ming hsiang chi* and *Hsi kuan-yin ying-yen chi* Chu Fa-ch'un is explicitly said to have been the head of the temple *(ssu chu)*. In the *Ming-seng chuan* he is said to have been diligent in ascetic practice and accomplished in meditation and therefore was asked to become the head of the temple. The *Kao-seng chuan* account mentions Chu Fa-ch'un's ascetic practice and virtue but not the fact that he was the head of the temple. The *Kao-seng chuan* story contains certain key expressions[72] that are also found in the *Ming-seng chuan* but not in the other two earlier sources, suggesting that here as elsewhere Hui-chiao depended heavily on the *Ming-seng chuan*. Two expressions[73] are shared in the *Kao-seng chuan*, *Ming-seng chuan*, and *Ming hsiang chi* versions of the story, indicating that at least Pao-ch'ang, and possibly both Pao-ch'ang and Hui-chiao, were acquainted with the *Ming hsiang chi* story, and that they relied less on the *Hsi kuan-yin ying-yen-chi* version of the story. One obscure phrase that appears only in the *Ming hsiang chi* (*"ch' i ssu hsing chiang"*) and *Hsi kuan-yin ying-yen-chi* (*"ch' i ssu hsing lu"*) in slightly different forms due probably to textual corruption, suggests that these two earlier accounts were probably both based on a common source. Only the *Kao-seng chuan* biography mentions that Ch'u Fa-ch'un was good at reciting the "old *wei-mo* (Vimalakirti)"[74] scripture. Perhaps Hui-chiao had another source for this information.

The above analysis suggests the following relationship between the four available versions of Chu Fa-ch'un's story. There was a common tradition of this story on which all four versions are based, though the two earlier versions, ie., those of the *Hsi kuan-yin ying-yen-chi* (possibly the earliest) and *Ming hsiang chi*, show significant differences in phraseology. These differences make it clear that both the *Ming-seng chuan* and the *Kao-seng chuan* versions are based on the *Ming hsiang chi* account. The compiler of the *Kao-seng chuan*, Hui-chiao, based his biography of Chu Fa-ch'un on Pao-ch'ang's *Ming-seng chuan* biography. He was possibly also acquainted with the *Ming hsiang chi* story about Chu Fa-ch'un. Hui-chiao seems to have had another source of information about Chu Fa-ch'un's recitation of the Vimalakirti scripture.

This framework enables us to interpret two interesting features of the four available versions of Chu Fa-ch'un's story in a manner that might throw some light on the process in which compilers of biographical collections used miracle stories and also on the development of miracle stories themselves.

Perhaps the most important difference between the *Ming hsiang chi* and *Hsi kuan-yin ying-yen-chi* versions of this story is the reference in the *Ming hsiang chi* to the building material as belonging to a woman. We learn that Chu Fa-ch'un was crossing the lake on a small boat with the woman who owned the materials when the storm arose. The *Hsi kuan-yin ying-yen-chi* does not mention this fact. The *Ming-seng chuan* biography elaborates on the fact that Chu Fa-ch'un was in the same boat with a woman, and states explicitly that he was particularly fearful that if the boat sank his body would be found beside that of a woman. The seriousness of this embarrassment, or the suspiciousness of the fact that a monk should be sharing a small boat with a woman, is reflected in the care that both the *Ming hsiang chi* and *Ming-seng chuan* take to explain her presence by saying that she was the owner of building materials that Chu Fa-ch'un was purchasing. This detail is no doubt inserted in order to make it clear that Chu Fa-ch'un was not guilty of any misconduct. This twist to Chu Fa-ch'un's story, namely that he was not only afraid of perishing in storm, but was doubly threatened since he was with a woman, is probably an elaboration that was introduced to increase the story's dramatic effect at some point in the course of its development. The *Kao-seng chuan* biography does not mention the fact that Chu Fa-ch'un was in the same boat with a woman. Hui-chiao eliminated this twist from his biography, perhaps mindful of the fact that there are other versions which do not mention it (he was possibly acquainted with the *Hsi kuan-yin ying-yen-chi* version itself) or perhaps because he considered this reference to a woman distasteful.

Another interesting feature of Chu Fa-ch'un's biography is the comments on the nature of the large boat that saved him. The *Ming hsiang chi* version says that since it was night time and no one else was travelling, such a boat could not have just happened to be on the lake, and that Chu Fa-ch'un suspected it to be miraculous in nature ("*shen li*": "supernatural power"). The story ends simply by saying that they reached the other shore quickly on this boat. The *Hsi kuan-yin ying-yen-chi* version reports that Chu Fa-ch'un later showed the large boat which saved him to many people, but no one turned turn up claiming to be its owner (*wu chu*). The *Ming-seng chuan* version says that although he looked for the owner (*chu*) of the new boat, he could not find him. The boat is said to have been the result of the cosmic response to his sincere recitation/meditation. The *Kao-seng chuan* biography says that he sought but could not find the owner (*chu*), that the boat disappeared in a short while, and that both monks and lay people admired the miraculous results of this monk's effort. The miraculous nature of the event is suggested and highlighted through two different devices in the earlier accounts: the reference to the unlikelihood that such a boat would appear at night, as in the *Ming hsiang chi*, and the story that no one turned up to claim it, as in the *Hsi kuan-yin ying-yen-chi*. In this case the two biographers, Pao-ch'ang and Hui-chiao, both preferred the second explanation: in their retelling of the story, the miraculous nature of the event is emphasized not only by stating this fact explicitly but also by devising further details.

(e) Tao-chiung

As shown in detail in the list in my Appendix II, the *Fa-yüan chu-lin* preserves two fragments about Tao-chiung from the *Ming hsiang chi*. The *Hsi kuan-shih-yin ying-yen-chi* also preserves two fragments about Tao-chiung. The relationship between these fragments and the *Kao-seng chuan* biography is rather complex. I will first summarize the contents of each fragment and then compare them with the content of the *Kao-seng chuan* biography.

The *Ming hsiang chi* fragment in the *Fa-yüan chu-lin, chüan* 17, contains three stories:

(i) In the ninth month of the second year of the Yüan-chia period (425) while the monk was performing the Samantabhadra ceremony *(p'u-hsien chai)*, a man riding a horse appeared and later disappeared, and a bright red light was seen all over the sky.

(ii) In the twelfth month of the third year of the same period (427) Tao-chiung was performing the Samantabhadra ceremony in a layman's house. Two ordinary looking monks came to worship. People did not pay attention to them, but a layman, Chang Tao, noted something unusual about them and followed them when they left the ceremony. After walking a short distance they flew up in the sky and disappeared.

(iii) In the seventh year of the same period (430), Tao-chiung went to the capital with his fellow students. While he was staying at the Nan-chien-ching-she residence, four people appeared at night riding in a new carriage and took him to the Shen-ch'iao bridge. There he saw a nobleman, surrounded by hundreds of assistants and guards, all wearing yellow robes. The nobleman was surprised and said that he only wanted to know where the man of the Way who practiced the *pan-chou* meditation, that is, Tao-chiung, lived. He asked his attendants why they had brought Tao-chiung over, and ordered them to take him back. When they came back to Tao-chiung's residence, the guards disappeared leaving him outside the building. He knocked on the door, and the monks inside, frightened, opened the door to let him in. The door of Tao-chiung's room was also still locked as usual.

The second *Ming hsiang chi* fragment from the *Fa-yüan chu-lin* tells the following stories:

(i) In the 18th year of the Hung-shih period of Ch'in (416)[75] Tao-chiung's teacher Tao-yi sent him and his fellow student Tao-lang and two others to gather stalactites at the Huo-shan mountain in He-nan. They went into the grotto with torches in their hands. Three miles into the grotto, they ran into a deep body of flowing water. They used a piece of wood to cross it. Tao-chiung went first and safely crossed the water, but when the three others tried to cross, the piece of wood sank and they all died. The torch also went out. Tao-chiung recited the

Kuan-shih-yin (Avalokitesvara)[76] scripture and vowed to hold a ceremony for 100 monks (*po jen hui*). At the close of the night, a bright light that looked like a firefly appeared, and suddenly the grotto was lit up. Tao-chiung saw the path and came out from under a huge rock.

(ii) In the 19th year of the Yüan-chia period (442) Prince K'ang of Lin-ch'uan, based in Kuang-ling, asked Tao-chiung to perform certain ceremonies. In the ninth month Tao-chiung was performing a ten day Avalokitesvara ceremony. After they had completed nine days of the ceremony, at three o'clock in the morning all the monks were asleep. Tao-chiung rose to worship and as he returned to his seat to meditate, the heads and top torsos of numerous monks emerged from the four walls. Tao-chiung also saw a Buddha clearly. An awesome looking elder, wearing a hair dress and riding pants, and holding a long sword in his hand, picked up some incense and gave it to Tao-chiung. Tao-chiung first did not accept it, but the monks in the wall told him to accept the incense as a protection for his patron (? *chu-jen*). Suddenly everything disappeared.

The first fragment in the *Hsi kuan-shih-yin ying-yen-chi* (no. 6) reports an incident in the seventh year of the Yüan-chia period of the Sung dynasty (430). Tao-chiung was travelling with four fellow students crossing the Yellow River on ice at Meng-chin. The ice broke and first one student fell and died, and shortly after that three more fell. Tao-chiung was a diligent practitioner of the Buddhist path and recited the Kuan-shih-yin scripture. Thereupon, he felt something under his feet that supported him, and he was able to avoid falling into the water. He made a vow saying that if he could cross the river he would perform a ceremony for fifty monks. He then saw a red light in front of him, and following it in a straight line, he was able to reach the other shore.

The second fragment in the *Hsi kuan-shih-yin ying-yen-chi* (no.60) reports the incident that took place in a stalactite grotto during the 18th year of the Hung-shih period of Ch'i (416).[77] The story told here is virtually identical in form to the one in the *Ming hsiang chi*, though with a number of differences in phraseology.

The *Kao-seng chuan* biography of Tao-chiung consists largely of the following stories:

(i) The stalactite grotto incident, told in a similar manner as in the *Ming hsiang chi* and the *Hsi kuan-shih-yin ying-yen-chi*, but, as in the case of all the following stories, Hui-chiao omits the reference to the date of the incident (416). Tao-chiung's promise to perform the ceremony for 100 monks is not mentioned. This version mentions that the light that guided him out of the grotto looked like a firefly. This comparison is mentioned in the *Ming hsiang chi* version, but not in the *Hsi kuan-shih-yin ying-yen-chi*. The explicit statement that the torch light went out that appears immediately following the drowning of the three fellow students in the *Kao-seng chuan* retelling of the story, on the other hand, is also found in the same context, though phrased in different words, in the *Hsi kuan-*

shih-yin ying-yen-chi. This statement is not found in the *Ming hsiang chi* version.

(ii) Miracles that occurred during the Samantabhadra ceremonies, involving a foreign monk or a man riding on a horse. Here Hui-chiao may be summarizing the two Samantabhadra stories in the first *Ming hsiang chi* fragment summarized above, though the themes in these stories, ie., the red light and flying into the sky are not mentioned. These incidents are given the dates of 425 and 427 in the *Ming hsiang chi*, but again no dates are mentioned in the *Kao-seng chuan* biography.

(iii) The story of Tao-chiung's crossing the Yellow River on ice. Here the story (dated 430) in the first *Hsi kuan-shih-yin ying-yen-chi*, not paralleled in the *Ming hsiang chi* fragment, is summarized.

(iv) The story in which Tao-chiung is taken to a man sitting at the Shen-ch'iao bridge in a carriage. Here Hui-chiao is retelling the story found in the first *Ming hsiang chi* fragment in a manner that closely parallels that version. The *Ming hsiang chi* gives the date of 430 to this incident, but no date is mentioned in the *Kao-seng chuan*.

v) There is a reference to the fact that Prince K'ang of Lin-ch'uan took Tao-chiung to Kuang-ling in the 20th year of the Yung-chia era of the Sung dynasty (443). We saw above the reference to the service that Tao-chiung provided Prince K'ang in the second *Ming hsiang chi* fragment. Hui-chiao's statement may be related to this reference in the *Ming hsiang chi*, but the date given in the *Ming hsiang chi* is the 19th year of the Yung-chia period, which would indirectly contradict the information given here. This statement is followed by a comment that Tao-chiung ended his life there in Kuang-ling.

A few observations may be made on the basis of the above comparison of the content of the three sources on Tao-chiung:

(1) The close relationship between the stories (i), (ii), and (iv) in the *Kao-seng chuan* summary above and the corresponding materials in the *Ming hsiang chi*, second fragment (i), first fragment (i), (ii), and (iii), shows that Hui-chiao, or possibly Pao-ch'ang, if Hui-chiao was copying from Pao-ch'ang, relied heavily on the *Ming hsiang chi* in writing the biography of Tao-chiung.

(2) The story about crossing the Yellow River on ice, which is story (iii) in the above summary of the *Kao-seng chuan* biography of Tao-chiung, has a parallel in the *Hsi kuan-shih-yin ying-yen-chi*, but not in the *Ming hsiang chi*. This fact indicates that Hui-chiao, or again possibly Pao-ch'ang, was familiar with the story in the first *Hsi kuan-shih-yin ying-yen-chi* fragment. The parallel between the story (i) in the *Kao-seng chuan* biography and the second *Hsi kuan-shih-yin ying-yen-chi* fragment, both stating explicitly that Tao-chiung's torch went out, may also be significant in this context.

(3) It is striking, as we noted above, that the *Kao-seng chuan* biography omits the references to the year and month attached to the incidents recorded there, except in the case of the item (v) which speaks about Tao-chiung's relationship

to Prince K'ang of Lin-ch'uan in Kuang-ling and then concludes by stating that Tao-chiung died in Kuang-ling. All the miracle story fragments examined here give the dates of the incidents with meticulous care. If we restore these dates to the stories adopted in the *Kao-seng chuan* biography, however, it becomes clear that these stories are in fact arranged in the proper chronological sequence. Hui-chiao, or again perhaps Pao-ch'ang, must have known these stories in versions that gave the dates of the incidents and so was able to arrange them in chronological order, yet at the same time removing all chronological references except for one. The one date given in connection with the comment that Tao-chiung went to Kuang-ling and ended his life there may have an important function as a part of the overall framework of the biography. As we have seen above, Chinese biographies of monks often emphasize details of the circumstances of the subject's death. Since the date of Tao-chiung's death appears not to have been known to Hui-chiao, the date of Tao-chiung's move to Kuang-ling may have been given as the last known date that approximates the date of his death. We have also noted above that the date given here conflicts with the one given in one of the miracle stories in the *ming hsiang chi*.

This analysis of Tao-chiung's biography has shown how the compiler of biographical collections used two different sources (or sources based on or related to them) and organized a number of stories into a coherent biography.

(f) Hui-ch'ing

In the case of Hui-ch'ing, a short story describing how his boat escaped a storm when he recited and meditated on the *Kuan-shih-yin ching* scripture is told in different words but in the same sequence and with the same details in the *Ming hsiang chi* and the *Ming-seng chuan* (23-19, p.12a). The *Ming-seng chuan*, however, also contains other information concerning his study of scriptures (Fa-hua, Shih-ti, Wei-mo, and Ssu-yi scriptures). The brief *Kao-seng chuan* biography mentions both the story of the storm and his study of scriptures, adding an interesting detail to the latter, that when he recited the scriptures at night the snapping of fingers and voices of praise were heard in the darkness. These details must have been included because they were regarded as being quite extraordinary: they probably were meant to indicate that the gods were praising the monk. What we see here may be an example of the development of a biographical detail into a miracle story: a reference to the reciting of a scripture leads to a story of an intensive study of scriptures, which in turn occasions a story describing how well he recited scriptures.

(g) Seng-hung

The case of the "promoter of meritorious works", Seng-hung, is rather unusual. In other cases where the sources for the *Kao-seng chuan* biographies are preserved in both the *Ming hsiang chi* and the *Hsi kuan-shih-yin ying-yen-chi* (Chu Fa-yi, Chu Fa-ch'un, and Tao-chiung) the comparison of biographies and miracle stories indicates that the *Ming-seng chuan* and/or *Kao-seng chuan* biographies draw more directly from the *Ming hsiang chi* than from the *Hsi kuan-*

shih-yin ying-yen-chi. But in the case of Seng-hung, the comparison of the texts of the two miracle story versions, the *Ming hsiang chi* and the *Hsi kuan-shih-yin ying-yen-chi*, with the *Ming-seng chuan* biography shows that though the two miracle story versions tell the same story with little difference in content, Pao-ch'ang's biography is more closely related in phraseology to the *Hsi kuan-shih-yin ying-yen-chi* version, while Hui-chiao's *Kao-seng chuan* biography is clearly based on the *Ming-seng chuan* biography.[78]

With this we conclude our investigation of those cases in which Hui-chiao based his biography primarily on the *Ming hsiang chi*, but also used other material. We move now to a consideration of the third way in which he seems to have used materials in the *Ming hsiang chi* in writing his *Kao-seng chuan* biographies.

(III) In some cases Hui-chiao based his biography on a source other than the *Ming hsiang chi*, but the *Ming hsiang chi* miracle story was incorporated into this larger framework (eight cases: Chu T'an-mo-lo-ch'a [Dharmaraksa; Fa Hu], T'an Wu-chieh [Dharmodgata; Fa-yüng] and Ch'iu-na-pa-mo [Gunavarman] from the translators section; Chih Tao-lin, Hui-yüan, and Hui-yen, Tao-wen from the exegetes section; and Hui-ta from the promoters of meritorious works section). In general (with the exception of Hui-ta's biography to be examined in some detail below and perhaps also of the Ch'iu-na-pa-mo biography), the biographies here were not originally written as records of miracles. The subjects were well known as translators or exegetes, and the *Kao-seng chuan* biographies often quote directly from their writings. In the case of the translators, the biography takes the form of a record of the subject's travel to the West.

Let me again discuss the relationship between the *Kao-seng chuan* and the *Ming hsiang chi* biographies with a few examples from this group. The three *Kao-seng chuan* biographies of the "translators" in the above list are based on the *Ch'u san-tsang chi chi* biographies compiled by Seng-yu. In the two cases of Chu T'an-mo-ch'a (Fa-hu) and T'an Wu-chieh, the relationship among these three sources is relatively straightforward: the *Kao-seng chuan* parallels the *Ch'u san-tsang chi chi* biographies closely with only minor differences in phraseology and the miracle story in the *Ming hsiang chi* is already found in the *Ch'u san-tsang chi chi* biography.[79]

The Ch'iu-na-pa-mo (Gunavarman) biography presents a more complex situation. Although the broad outline of the biography in the *Kao-seng chuan* parallels that of the *Ch'u san-tsang chi chi*, suggesting that the former is ultimately based on the latter, the *Kao-seng chuan* biography is a great deal longer and contains many stories of miracles associated with different places that Gunavarman visited in his travels. The *Ch'u san-tsang chi chi* biography only mentions his taming of wild animals and the miraculous occurrences at the time of his death. When he died he looked as if he were in meditation and an extraordinary fragrance pervaded the air; everyone saw a dragon-like creature go up to heaven. The story about Ch'iu-na-pa-mo's death is found in more or less the same form in the quotation from the *Ming hsiang chi* in the *Fa-yüan chu-lin*, but that is the only miracle reported in that fragment. It is possible, however, that the original entry on miracles associated with this monk in the *Ming hsiang chi* included accounts of other miracles. The *Kao-seng chuan* repeats the same story and also tells the story about taming wild animals differently and with vivid details ("when he met the tiger, he patted its head with his stick and played with it before parting" 340c). This biography also contains many other stories of miracles which must come from sources other than the *Ch'u san-tsang chi chi* and probably also other than the *Ming hsiang chi.*[80]

The *Kao-seng chuan* biography of Hui-yüan ("exegetes" section), tells two miracle stories associated with a spring in the Lu-shan mountain[81] where this important scholar monk lived a secluded life. The outline of Hui-yüan's biography in the *Kao-seng chuan* is based on the biography in the *Ch'u san-tsang chi chi*, but the biography in the *Ch'u san-tsang chi chi* lacks any story of the spring in Mt. Lu-shan. Perhaps its compiler, Seng-yu, was not familiar with such stories, or possibly he was acquainted with them but did not consider them trustworthy or worthy of inclusion into his biography. The same two stories associated with the spring in the Lu-shan mountain are also told in a fragment from the *Ming hsiang chi* preserved in the *Fa-yüan chu-lin.*

In the existing summary of Hui-yüan's biography in the *Ming-seng chuan* there is a reference to the first and perhaps the more important of these two stories about the spring in the Lu-shan mountain.[82] At least the first story about this spring then was already present in Pao-ch'ang's biography. Pao-ch'ang, the compiler of the *Ming-seng chuan*, may have taken the reference to the spring (one or two stories) either from the *Ming hsiang chi* or from another source[83] and incorporated it into the biography of Hui-yüan. Hui-chiao, the compiler of the *Kao-seng chuan* biography, might then have followed Pao-ch'ang and included the two stories about this spring in his biography of Hui-yüan. If the *Ming-seng chuan* biography told only one story about the spring, Hui-chiao could have expanded it to the full two story version using the *Ming hsiang chi* or another source. As we noted earlier, there is also the possibility that the miracle stories of the spring existed in a common source that lay behind the *Ch'u san-tsang chi chi* biography and was also accessible to the compilers of the *Ming hsiang chi*, the *Ming-seng chuan* and *Kao-seng chuan.* We would then have to assume that they are missing in the *Ch'u san-tsang chi chi* because its compiler Seng-yu had intentionally suppressed them. Even if this happens to be the case, the complex relationship between these sources would highlight the fact that the miracle story as a compact unit was highly portable, and could make its way in and out of biographies with remarkable ease. I suspect it to be in fact an interloper in the biography of Hui-yüan.

Up to this point in my discussion I have been concentrating on the relationship between the *Kao-seng chuan* biographies and the *Ming hsiang chi* miracle stories. I will, however, conclude this analysis by commenting briefly on the same *Kao-seng chuan* biographies which have parallels not in the *Ming hsiang chi* but in other miracle story collections.

Fu Liang's *Kuang-shih-yin ying-yen-chi* contains a story about Po Fa-ch'iao which appears to have been the main source for Hui-chiao's biography (perhaps mediated through Pao-ch'ang's *Ming-seng chuan* biography).[84] The *Kao-seng chuan* biography centers around the story of Avalokitesvara's miraculous gift of a strong voice to Po Fa-ch'iao, and though the *Kuang-shih-yin ying-yen-chi* story is extensively rewritten, parallels in details between the two versions point to a close relationship between them.

The *Hsi kuan-shih-yin ying-yen-chi* materials on Seng-pao and Tao-wang tell one story in each case that is incorporated as a part of the more extensive *Kao-seng chuan* biographies. Tao-wang's case is of interest because Lu Kao's *Hsi kuan-shih-yin ying-yen-chi* story ends with an explanation that Lu Kao heard the story from Tao-wang's disciple Tao-hsien. This authenticates the story in a manner found frequently in Chinese records of miracle stories,[85] enabling us to trace the source of one anecdote in a *Kao-seng chuan* biography to its origin in oral transmission.

In the three parallel cases from the *Yu ming lu*, the stories in the miracle story collection again parallel portions of the longer *Kao-seng chuan* biographies. An Ch'ing [Shih-kao]'s biography is worthy of special attention. The main portion of the *Kao-seng chuan* biography, based closely on the *Ch'u san-tsang chi-chi* biography, tells the story of An Ch'ing that is known from the *Yu ming lu*, but in greater detail, showing several close parallels to the *Yu ming lu* in phraseology. Since Liu I-ch'ing, who compiled the *Yu ming chi*, lived between 403 and 444, the *Yu ming chi* version of the story must have existed by the time the *Ch'u san-tsang chi chi* version was composed (early sixth century). The parallel in the case of Chu Fa-lan is close in content but brief; that of Fo-t'u-teng is a minor, almost negligible one.

The *Hsüan yen chi* tells two stories involving K'ang Seng-hui. These stories are found both in the *Ch'u san-tsang chi chi* and *Kao seng chuan* biographies. These parallels between the *Kao-seng chuan* biographies and miracle collections other than the *Ming hsiang chi* are significant, but the small number of parallel cases makes it difficult to draw broader conclusions from them concerning the relationship between biographical and miracle collections.

To return to the parallels between the *Kao-seng chuan* biographies and the *Ming hsiang chi* miracle stories, our analysis indicates that miracle stories were an important source of Chinese Buddhist biographies. In roughly two thirds of the parallel cases, the *Kao-seng chuan* biography is based primarily on the miracle story in the *Ming hsiang chi*. In other cases, the *Kao-seng chuan* biography is primarily based on a source not particularly oriented to recording miracles, but even in these cases Hui-chiao shows a strong tendency to expand the biography by borrowing miracle stories from other sources such as the *Ming hsiang chi*.[86] It appears that Hui-chiao had little hesitation in using available accounts of miracles associated with Buddhist monks as a source for his biographical collection.[87]

The different patterns of relationships between the *Kao-seng chuan* biographies and miracle stories suggest that the *Kao-seng chuan* collection contains different types of "biographies". Some of the biographies (illustrated in the present discussion by the examples in the category III, but certainly numerous other examples exist in the *Kao-seng chuan* as a whole) are of well-known and clearly important Buddhist leaders. Rich biographical traditions existed around these figures, and Hui-chiao composed his biographies using a number of sources available to him. Other biographies (especially those illustrated by the examples in category I and in some cases those in category II; again there must be other examples of this type in the *Kao-seng chuan* as a whole) are different in nature. The subjects of the biographies based exclusively on miracle stories in the *Ming hsiang chi* must have been monks who were known only or primarily from their connection to these miracle stories. In these cases the stories were probably better known than the monks. When these stories associated with specific monks were adopted into collections of biographies, the relative emphasis on monks and stories was reversed and, reading biographical collections without the knowledge of this background, we are left with the impression that these monks were also well-known leaders in their own right.[88]

The detailed analysis of the parallels above also throws some light on the manner in which compilers of biographical collections used miracle stories. In one case (Tao-chiung) we saw how the biographer (Pao-ch'ang or Hui-chiao) constructed a biography by collecting several isolated miracles from different sources, stories associated with the subject, and arranging them in chronological order. In the case of Hui-ch'ing we saw details of a miracle story develop as the story was incorporated in the biographies written by Pao-ch'ang and Hui-chiao. Chu Fa-ch'un's miracle stories and biographies showed how different ideas were developed and also dropped in the course of the repeated retelling of the story (the device for highlighting the miraculous nature of the large boat and the female companion theme). The examples of Chu T'an-mo-lo-ch'a, T'an Wu-chieh, and Chu Shih-hsing in which the *Ming hsiang chi* miracle stories were seen to have been incorporated into the *Ch'u san-tsang chi chi* biographies, either directly from the *Ming hsiang chi* itself or from other parallel sources, reveal the compiler Seng-yu's openness to miracle stories as sources for biographies. The biography of Ch'iu-na-pa-mo and that of Hui-yüan in particular showed how Pao-ch'ang and Hui-chiao shared the same openness and expanded the *Ch'u san-tsang chi chi* biographies with further miracle stories.[89]

Earlier, noting that some of the biographies in the *Kao-seng chuan* collections state explicitly that the circumstances of the subjects' death are unknown, I suggested that some of these biographies must have been based on miracle stories. This question might be explored further by examining the references to death in the *Kao-seng chuan* biographies that we can be relatively certain are ultimately based on the *Ming hsiang chi*. Of the seven biographies in Hui-chiao's collection, which appear not to have sources other than the *Ming hsiang chi* miracle stories (category I in the discussion above), two (the biography of Fa-an in the "exegetes" section and one of Chien-t'uo-le in the "miracle workers" section) end with a note that the we do not know how the subject ended his life. The other biography from the "miracle workers" section (Ch'u Fo-tiao) contains a reference to his apparent death, but that reference is a part of the miracle story which says that he was seen later by eight lay disciples and that when his grave was dug out it was discovered that his corpse had disappeared (388a). This then is a story that tells that the subject in fact did not die. Two others (Seng-ch'un and Seng-yü) are from the "self-immolators" section, and again the stories of the death of the subjects are an integral part of the miraculous events. Only two biographies, both from the "reciters of scriptures" section (Fa-hsiang and Hui-chin) describe the death of the subjects in a brief but conventional manner.

Of the eleven biographies that appear to be primarily based on *Ming hsiang chi* stories (category II in the discussion above), three state explicitly that the circumstances of the death are unknown (K'ang Fa-lang, Shih-yü, Chu Fa-ch'un). The other eight biographies contain some reference to the subject's death, though the reference is sometimes very brief--only the place of death (of Tao-chiung) or that he died of ascetic practices (Seng-hung).[90] The significant fact in this group of biographies is that only three of the original *Ming hsiang chi* biographies mention the circumstances of death (Chu Shih-hsing, Chu Fa-yi, and Shan Tao-k'ai). In five cases (Yü Fa-lan, Chu Seng-lang, Tao-chiung, Hui-ch'ing, Seng-hung), the *Kao-seng chuan* biographies supply some information about the death of the subject where that information is missing in the *Ming hsiang chi* story. In the case of Hui-ch'ing, Pao-ch'ang's *Ming-seng chuan* biography is preserved in the *Mesodensho*, and this biography gives the same information as the *Kao-seng chuan* about the subject's death. Furthermore, in the three cases where the *Kao-seng chuan* biographies state explicitly that the circumstances of the subject's death are unknown, the *Ming hsiang chi* stories simply fail to mention the subject of death. This pattern seems to suggest that the compilers of biographical collections were particularly interested in the information about the subject's death and added this information to miracle stories where such information was available.[91] Otherwise, they stated explicitly that such information was not available.[92]

Out of the eighteen cases where miracle stories from the *Ming hsiang chi* sources constitute the main source of the *Kao-seng chuan* biography (ie., categories I and II reviewed above), in five cases the *Ming hsiang chi* accounts already contain some references to the circumstances of the subject's death (Fa-hsiang, Hui-chin, Chu shih-hsing, Chu Fa-yi, and Shan Tao-k'ai). This fact may indicate that the tendency for including some information about the subject's death goes back further than the compilers of biographical collections. It suggests that miracle stories often used the conventional form of biographies. Thus the miracle stories in almost all fragments from the *Ming hsiang chi*[93] begin by stating the name of the subject to whom the miracle occurred, in most cases capped with the name of the dynasty under which he lived and generally followed by a short description of his personal names and place of origin. Sometimes, in the case of secular subjects, some information about their ancestors are provided. This emphasis on the subject to whom the miracle happened and the way in which details about him are given appears to be derived from the conventions of Chinese biography. Here, then, the process analyzed above that transforms accounts of miracles into biographical records may be said to have already started in the manner in which the author of the *Ming hsiang chi* recorded his material.

Although it is difficult to reconstruct this process from available fragments of miracle story collections, I might point out that some miracle story fragments from other collections do not begin in the same manner,[94] a fact indicating that the format of the *Ming hsiang chi* fragments is not necessarily inherent in the *genre* of Chinese miracle stories. We must therefore ask why miracle stories came to be recorded using the format of biography. The answer has also been suggested above: it may be that this important form of historical writing was chosen because it tended to enhance the verisimilitude of the account by providing factual details about the subjects who experienced the miracles.

The relationship between biographies and miracle stories was as we have seen a very complex one. As noted earlier, some accounts of miracles were given in the *stupa* inscriptions that appear to have determined the basic format of monks' biographies in China. On the other hand, some miracle stories were recorded using the well-established literary form of biographical writing. The distinction between biographies of monks and miracle stories must have become blurred in some cases.[95]

I have so far determined that *stupa* inscriptions constitute probably the most important source of Chinese Buddhist biographies and that the form of these biographies is to a great extent determined by that of *stupa* inscriptions. I have also shown, however, that the biographies could not have been based exclusively on *stupa* inscriptions, and there can be no doubt that miracle stories generated biographies. Miracle stories were often written in the form of biographies, as was the case sometimes with the *Ming hsiang chi*, and Hui-chiao, the first compiler of the standard biographies of Chinese monks, used this source extensively. I have also shown that miracle stories were fluid and were often elaborated in the course of rewriting. They were easily incorporated into the framework of existing biographies. Miracle stories thus may have been a more dynamic force in the development of biographies than the *stupa* inscriptions that tended to be more fixed in form and content. I will explore this question further by examining in some detail two concrete cases that we have already encountered in the more general discussion above.

6. The cases of Yüan-kuei and Hui-ta

A. Yüan-kuei's miracle inscription and biography

At the conclusion of this paper I present a list of 25 inscriptions (Appendix I). These inscriptions are found in collections of T'ang writings and clearly constitute the source of Tsan-ning's biographies collected in his "Sung Biographies of Eminent Monks". I noted above that one text written for the image hall of Yüan-kuei, *Sung-yüeh kuei ch' an-shih ying-t' ang chi* (no. B, 3), tells a miracle story. This material is of particular interest here since it may be taken as an example in which a miracle story (in this case associated with a *stupa)* is incorporated into an inscription and eventually becomes a part of an official biographical collection.

The inscription in question[96] begins with a passage describing how the author Hsü Ch'ou, a Presented Scholar (*chin-shih*), visited the sacred mountain Sung-shan and was shown a memorial building (*yin t' ang*: "image hall") of master Yüan-kuei. On this occasion Hsü Ch'ou was told that Yüan-kuei miraculously moved cedar trees to the eastern part of the mountain where his *stupa* was later built, but that this feat was not mentioned in his *stupa* inscription. For this reason Hsü Ch'ou was requested to write another inscription describing this event. Later he obtains a document (a *hsing chuang*) from two lay people, Yü Ying-chen and Ch'en Wei-fu, describing the miracle in detail. This brief introduction is followed by a short biographical passage. The passage gives Yüan-kuei's monastic name, his secular surname ("Li"), place of origin ("Yi-chüeh district"), dates of birth (644), conferring of complete precepts (663) and death (716), and the age at death (73 years old). This in turn is followed by references to his earlier study of meditation and *vinaya* at the Hsien-chü temple, practice of meditation at the Shao-lin temple, and later residence at the P'ang-wu village; finally, it is explained how shortly before his death Yüan-kuei ordered his disciple Jen-su to build his *stupa* in the eastern mountain that stood near the Hsien-chü-ssu temple ("*hsien chü ssu tung ling*"), explaining how he began his monk's career in that temple. In the eleventh year of K'ai-yüan (723) Jen-su realized his master's wish by building the *stupa*. This passage is then followed by the miracle story reported by Yü Ying-chen and Ch'en Wei-fu.

Yüan-kuei encountered the mountain deity of the Sung-shan mountain and instructed him in Buddhist teaching. He conferred on him the five precepts and explained their meaning, using such concepts as "no mind", "no precepts", and "no self". He also discussed the differences between the mountain god's ten supernatural powers and the Buddha's ten supernatural powers, again using the Buddhist logic of negation. The mountain deity was impressed, recognizing that he had not understood the teaching of emptiness and, expressing gratitude for having received the five precepts, he offered to help Yüan-kuei by using his superhuman powers. Yüan-kuei first declined by saying that there was nothing he wanted, but after a short exchange mentioned the request to have the forest of large trees on the northern peak moved to the eastern part of the mountain *(tung ling*: referring to the mountain where Yüan-kuei's *stupa* was to be built as explained earlier). The eastern mountain served as the wind barrier to the temple, but there were no trees on it at that time. The mountain god agreed and warned Yüan-kuei that there would be wind and lightening at night. The mountain god then took his leave, and when Yüan-kuei followed him to the gate he saw that he was accompanied by a long line of guards as if he were a king. "Blue smoke, red mist, purple wind, and white air" mixed and spread all over. Flags of different shapes filled the sky. There was a huge storm that night and the monks at the temple were frightened. Master Yüan-kuei calmed the monks, explaining the agreement he had made with the mountain god to have the forest moved. In the morning they saw that the forest on the northern peak had been moved to the eastern part of the mountain. The master said, "If someone builds a *stupa* and erects an inscription after my death, and fails to mention this event, he will cause magical harm to me".

A brief *stupa* inscription by Jen-su is also preserved.[97] This inscription gives the monk's posthumous name ("Yüan-kuei"), and place of origin ("Yi-chüeh in Henan) and explains that in the second year of Shang-yüan (675) he was ordained on the occasion of the death of the Emperor Hsiao-ching (ie., Crown Prince Hung who was killed by his mother, Dowager Empress Wu). Later he achieved enlightenment without a teacher. After receiving further instruction at the Shao-lin temple (by the "*shao lin ts'un che*"), the subject spent his later years in P'ang-wu village where he instructed numerous monks and laymen. He died on the tenth day of the eighth month in the fourth year of K'ai-yüan (717) in P'ang-wu. He was 73 years old. On the thirteenth day Yüan-kuei's remains were buried temporarily at the eastern side of the northern hill. Then in the eleventh year of K'ai-yüan (723) a *stupa* was built on the eastern side of the mountain. The text says that the master was attached (? *wei ching*) to this place and there were cedar trees there. There is no reference to the miracle described above.

This example illustrates how a biography might develop in connection with a miracle story. Precise details of this process cannot be reconstructed from the limited sources available to us now, but the difference between the two inscriptions is striking and suggests certain possibilities. We might speculate, for example, that the miracle story of moving the cedar trees might have developed some time after the death of Yüan-kuei, perhaps in relationship to his *stupa*, which had been built in the eastern part of the sacred mountain which boasted a magnificent cedar forest. The original motive behind the story could have been to illustrate the greatness of Yüan-kuei by linking him to the unusually beautiful cedar forest at the site of his *stupa*. It is even possible that he had loved this forest and requested his *stupa* to be built there as Jen-su's inscription suggests. The miracle story then would have developed as a colorful and dramatic way of explaining the special relationship between Yüan-kuei and this beautiful forest. Another rather speculative possibility is that some story about the origin of the forest had existed before Yüan-kuei's *stupa* was built, and that the story developed later into the present miracle story associated with Yüan-kuei after his *stupa* became a prominent feature of this part of the mountain. Whatever the origin of the miracle story may have been, it was authenticated as a story of miracle that happened to Yüan-kuei and his followers in the temple in a stone inscription by a highly respected secular writer. Thus, Hsü Ch'ou's inscription is a miracle inscription, designed to publicize and preserve for posterity the account of a miraculous event associated with a specific location and specific monk.

It is noteworthy that the compiler, Tsan-ning, in producing his biography of Yuan-kuei, a "miracle worker", chose to use this miracle inscription by Hsü Ch'ou, rather than the shorter *stupa* inscription by Jen-su, which we may assume was also available to him.[98] Jen-su's stupa inscription does not mention any specific accomplishment of this monk, and the brief biographical passage in Hsü Ch'ou's inscription mentions only in passing that Yüan-kuei studied the *vinaya* and meditation. Clearly, it was the importance of the miracle associated with him that motivated Tsan-ning to include his "biography" in his collection and place it in the miracle workers section. Here, then, we have another example illustrating how a miracle story is preserved as a biography and a biography of a rather insignificant monk ends up in a collection of "eminent monks". As we noted above (footnote 95), compilers were often aware of the relative importance of the biography proper and miracle stories associated with the figure and treated the material accordingly, usually assigning this type of material to the category of biographies of "miracle workers".

B. Hui-ta's biographies

The biography of the monk Hui-ta (secular name: Liu Sa-he)[99] appeared earlier in our discussion above of Hui-chiao's biographies in the *Kao-seng chuan* and corresponding preserved fragments of the miracle story collection *Ming hsiang chi*.[100] In that context we treated Hui-chiao's biography of Hui-ta as an example of the third categories of biographies: Hui-chiao based his biographies on sources other than the *Ming hsiang chi*, but also included the miracle story taken from this miracle story collection in his biography. I should like to consider Hui-ta's biography here in some detail, because in one respect it is quite unusual. His biography is also found in Tao-hsüan's *Hsü kao-seng chuan* collection.[101] Tao-hsüan mentions Hui-chiao's earlier biography explicitly and then produces some new materials that constitute the main part of his biography. Thus we can reconstruct a chain of developing biographies for this monk. (i) The earliest datable material is the miracle story about Hui-ta in the

Ming hsiang chi. Later summaries of this story contains details that are slightly different from the *Ming hsiang chi* version, suggesting that the story existed in more than one version. (ii) Hui-chiao seems to have been aware of this story and presented a brief summary of a story similar but not identical to this *Ming hsiang chi* version in the biography he produced for this monk.[102] Hui-chiao's biography centering around stories about Asoka *stupas* and images, however, is primarily based on other sources.[103] (iii) Tao-hsüan's biography of this monk in *Hsü kao-seng chuan* mentions both (a) the miracle story, similar but not identical to the miracle story in the *Ming hsiang chi*[104] and the *Kao-seng chuan* summary of that story, and (b) Hui-chiao's earlier biography.[105] The main part of Tao-hsüan's biography of Hui-ta, however, is based on materials taken from other sources.

The story about Liu Sa-he/Hui-ta seems to have been widely known in connection with the legend of Asoka *stupas*,[106] and other summaries of it and references to it have also survived. The *Liang shu*, the official history of the Liang dynasty, completed by Yao Ssu-lien in 629, who had continued the work that had been begun by his father Yao Ch'a, also records stories about Hui-ta and his discovery of the locations and relics of Asoka *stupas*. These stories parallel certain themes in the accounts in the *Ming hsiang chi* story and the *Kao-seng chuan* biography.[107] In Tao-hsüan's collection of miracle stories, called *Chi shen-chou san-pao kan-t'ung-lu* (664), a number of miracle stories associated with Asoka *stupas* and images of the Buddha are collected, and the stories about the Asoka *stupas* and the Buddha images included in Hui-ta's biographical tradition appear among them.[108] This work also contains an important passage on Liu Sa-he/Hui-ta in its section on miracle-working monks (*shen seng*).[109] Tao-hsüan's autobiographical account of his own encounter with gods toward the end of his life also includes passages on the *stupas* and images associated with Hui-ta.[110] A reference to the Asoka *stupa* in Mao-hsien in the Ssu-ming mountain discovered by Liu Sa-he is also found in the *Sung kao-seng chuan* biography of Wei-tse.[111] A detailed comparison of all these sources enables us to reconstruct partially the process through which the biography of Liu Sa-he/Hui-ta developed in connection with the development of local miracle stories.

(i) The Miracle Story in the *Ming hsiang chi*

The story in the *Ming hsiang chi* describes an unusual experience of the layman Liu Sa-he, which is as follows.[112]

When this man of the Li-shih district of the Hsi-he Commandary was young he travelled extensively on military duties, did not follow the Buddhist teaching, and was fond of hunting. At age 31 he died of sickness, but was revived after seven days and told the following story. When his life was about to expire, two people appeared to him. They bound him with a rope and took him in the northwestern direction. There were trees on both sides of the road, and a man holding a bow in his hand and wearing a sword on his body was standing in the middle of the road. He told them to go in the western direction. Then Liu Sa-he saw many houses with white walls and red pillars. When he entered one of these houses, he saw a woman wearing beautiful clothes. Liu Sa-he asked for food, but a voice was heard from the sky: "Do not give him food". A man jumped out of the ground and tried to hit him with an iron hammer. Liu Sa-he fled and went to another house. But the same thing happened there again. He went through more than ten houses, but he could not get any food in the end. Going further in the northwestern direction, Liu Sa-he saw an old woman riding in a carriage; she gave him a book in one *chüan*. Going further west, he reached a beautifully decorated house. An old woman who had tiger's teeth in her mouth was sitting outside the house. The house was also beautifully decorated inside with curtains, carpets, bamboo seats and tables. Again a woman was there and asked Liu Sa-he whether he had brought the book. When he offered her the book, the woman took it and compared it with other books. Suddenly Liu Sa-he saw two monks who asked whether he knew them. Liu Sa-he said no, and the monks said, "You should now take refuge in the Shakyamuni Buddha", and Liu Sa-he decided to obey their words and seek salvation through the Buddha. He therefore followed the monks and they all walked off together. He then saw a large city at a distance. The city looked like the earthly city of Ch'ang-an but its colour was black. It was an iron city. He saw that the people there were very tall, their skin was black, and that they dragged their long hair on the ground. The monks said that they were the creatures (*kuei*) of hell. The place was very cold and pieces of ice flew around cutting the heads and limbs off people. The two monks said this was the hell of cold ice. Liu Sa-he then suddenly remembered that he knew these monks in his previous life. They were his teachers in the past at the time of the Wei-wei-fo (Vipasyin) Buddha. In that birth he had committed offenses as a novice and could not receive the precepts. Even though there was a Buddha in the world, he could not get to see him. Later he twice attained rebirth as a human being, once among non-Chinese people and now he was reborn among Chinese people. Liu Sa-he also saw his uncle in this hell. The uncle said, "When I was in the city of Yeh, I failed to serve the Buddha. I saw a man pouring water over a Buddha's image and tried it myself a bit. But I did not become a Buddhist myself. So, I am receiving punishment here. I will later draw the merit of pouring water over an image and be reborn in heaven". Liu Sa-he then saw the sword hell, and one by one he saw many hells peopled with numerous sinners just as they are described in scriptures.

When he had finished seeing the hells, he suddenly saw a man, two *chang* tall, whose golden body was beautifully decorated. There was a crowd of people on either side of this man; they said that the man was the great being Kuan-shih (Avalokitesvara). Everyone rose and paid respect to him. There were two monks who looked just like each other. They went eastward together. After Liu Sa-he finished paying his respects to the bodhisattva, the bodhisattva preached a sermon of over one thousand words for him. This sermon ended with a number of instructions; on how to relieve his relatives of their punishments in hell;[113] how to remove the karmic consequences of misconducts; on how great were the merits of building *stupas* and temple buildings; and how failing to remove weeds and other unsightly objects that a person sees around *stupas* and temple buildings results in annihilating the merits acquired by worship. The bodhisattva also commented on the merits of the Perfection of Wisdom and *Shou leng yen* scriptures. When Liu Sa-he took his leave, the bodhisattva said, "You ought to receive numerous punishments through the period of many *kalpas*. But because you have once listened to the teaching of the scripture and experienced the feeling of joy, you will now be punished only lightly and then released. When you are revived you should become a monk. In each of the five places, ie., Lo-yang, Lin-tzu, Chieh-yeh, Mou-yin, and Ch'eng-tu, there is a *stupa* built by King Asoka. In addition, in the Wu* area there are two stone images which were built by supernatural beings *(kuei shen)* sent by King Asoka. These images are really perfect and those who go there and worship them will not fall into hell". Having said these words, the bodhisattva went away towards the east. Liu Sa-he worshipped him and left.

He came out to the main road going south. The road was more than ten paces wide and there were numerous people walking on it. At the road side there was a high seat, more than ten *chang* above the ground. A monk was sitting there. And there were numerous other monks lined up on either side of him. A man stood up facing north and holding a pen. He asked Liu Sa-he, "Why did you kill a deer when you were in Hsiang-yang?" Liu Sa-he knelt down and answered, "Other people shot the deer. I only injured it. Moreover, I did not eat its meat. Why should I be punished for it?" Thereupon, the place where he had killed the deer appeared. Grasses, trees, mountains, and creeks filled the horizon, and the black horses on which hunters rode all spoke, all testifying that on such and such a month and day Liu Sa-he had killed the deer. Liu Sa-he was frightened and had no reply. Shortly afterward a man picked him up with a spear and threw him into a cauldron of boiling water. Liu Sa-he saw his limbs crumble and fall apart. A wind blew gathering pieces of his body together at the edge of the cauldron, and suddenly his body was restored to its original form. The man with a pen spoke again, "You shot a pheasant and also killed a goose". As soon as he finished speaking, Liu Sa-he was again thrown into the boiling cauldron with a spear. He was cooked in the same manner again. After these punishments Liu Sa-he was let go. He entered a large city. There was a man sitting there who said to Liu Sa-he, "You received light punishments and are also brought back to life. This is because the force of merits assisted you. Do not commit sins any more". He then ordered a man to take Liu Sa-he back. Liu Sa-he saw his old body from a distance and he did not wish to go back, but the man who was accompanying him gave him a push and pull. After a long while Liu Sa-he was again attached to his old body and he was revived.

The *Ming hsiang chi* story ends by briefly noting that Liu Sa-he served the Buddhist teaching diligently, and renouncing the householder's life became a monk called Hui-ta. He lived in the capital city at the end of the T'ai-yüan period (376-396). Later he went to Hsü-ch'ang. It was not known how he ended his life.

The story of Liu Sa-he in the *Ming hsiang chi*, thus, is a story about karmic consequences. The story obviously was told to teach that the evil deeds a person commits in this world will be punished in hell after his death, and that good deeds, such as worshipping *stupas* and images, will be rewarded. This lesson is taught through reporting the experience of a man who died once and was miraculously revived after seeing how sinners were punished in the many hells after their death. This basic plot is found in many existing examples of medieval Chinese Buddhist miracle stories, in most cases teaching the lesson of karmic consequences. Thus, the *Ming hsiang chi's* story about Liu Sa-he is best characterized as an example from this familiar group of medieval Chinese Buddhist miracle stories.

This story of Liu Sa-he's experiences in hell appears in a shorter form in other sources. The passage on Liu Sa-he in the official history *Liang shu* begins in a manner that parallels closely the beginning of the *Ming hsiang chi* version, saying that Liu Sa-he's body was warm for seven days after his death, when he woke up again. It also mentions the two officials who came to fetch him and his travel in the north-west direction. It then states that Liu Sa-he saw the punishments in the eighteen hells, and heard Avalokitesvara's words telling him to go and worship the Asoka *stupas* in Lo-hsia, Ch'i-ch'eng, Tan-yang, and K'uai-chi. Though the locations are identified by different names from those used in the *Ming hsiang chi* story, they are in fact identical with the first four locations mentioned in that list: Lo-hsia is a different name for Lo-yang, Ch'i-ch'eng for Lin-tzu, Tan-yang for Chien-yeh, and K'uai-chi for Mao-yin. The last location in the *Ming hsiang chi list*, Ch'eng-tu, is not mentioned in the *Liang shu* list. The stone images that floated on the Ch'ang-chiang river mentioned in the *Ming hsiang chi* passage (920a18f.) are also not mentioned in the *Liang shu* passage.

In the *Chi shen-chou san-pao kan-t'ung-lu* on the Asoka *stupa* in the Mao-hsien district (also found in the *Fa-yüan chu-lin*) Liu Sa-he's experience is described by quoting an earlier biography (? "*ch'ien chuan*", 404b14). Here it is said that he was born in a family that lived by hunting and fishing; he died and saw a "foreign monk", who told him that his sins were grave enough to send him to hell, but since Liu Sa-he was unaware of the graveness of those sins he would take pity on him and would release him temporarily; the monk then told him that if he found and worshipped in Lo-hsia (Lo-yang), Ch'i-ch'eng (Lin-tzu), Tan-yang (Chien-yeh), and K'uai-chi (Mao-yin) the old *stupas* and the stone images that came floating on the Ch'ang-chiang river, all built and produced by the order of King Asoka, he would be able to avoid punishment in hell. Though this list identifies these places with different names, the places mentioned here in fact match those in the *Ming hsiang chi* list (except for the reference to Ch'eng-tu in the latter). The list of the location of the Asoka *stupas* here is identical to that in the *Liang shu* passage, but the *Chi shen-chou san-pao kan-t'ung-lu* passage also mentions the two stone images that floated on the Ch'ang-chiang river.

The *Chi shen-chou san-pao kan-t'ung-lu* passage on Liu Sa-he (also found in the *Fa-yüan chu-lin, chüan* 31) summarizes the background of Liu Sa-he, specifying his place of origin differently, as the Wen-ch'eng Commandary and not as Li-shih in Hsi-he or Ping-chou region, which is given in all the sources reviewed above. In the account of Liu Sa-he's death and his experiences in the netherworld, this passage mentions Avalokitesvara and the Asoka *stupas* in Lo-hsia, Ch'i-ch'eng, Tan-yang, and K'uai-chi. The floating stone images are not mentioned here.

The summary of Liu Sa-he's background and his experience in hell in Hui-chiao's *Kao-seng chuan* biography, to be described below, gives a shorter list of locations of the Asoka *stupas*. The brief summary of Liu Sa-he's background in the *Hsü kao-seng chuan* gives "south east of Hsien-yang" as his place of origin and later mentions the Wen-ch'eng Commandary as his place of birth. Though this biography mentions Liu Sa-he's experience in hell, it does not give a list of Asoka *stupas* and refers the reader to a source called "*pieh chuan*" (a separate and independent biography) for details.

These parallel accounts of Liu Sa-he's story indicate that the story was widely known among medieval Chinese Buddhists and many versions existed side by side, mentioning essentially the same list of Asoka *stupas*' locations in different forms. The stability of the list points to the existence of firmly established and widely known local traditions about Asoka *stupas* in the Wu-yüeh region.

(ii) The *Kao-seng chuan* Biography

Hui-chiao's biography of Hui-ta in the *Kao-seng chuan (chüan* 13, 409b-410a) begins by summarizing the story of Liu Sa-he's visit to hell. The outline of the story is quite similar to the long story in the *Ming hsiang chi* and shorter summaries in other sources reviewed above, but there are also some differences. The bodhisattva Avalokitesvara is here called simply a "man of the Way" *(tao jen)* and the list of Asoka's *stupas* and image(s) in his instructions to Liu-Sa-he mentions Tan-yang, K'uai-chi, and Wu* Commandary.

The main part of Hui-chiao's biography consists of a series of miracle stories involving the *stupas* and images. We read there of the rebuilding of the Asoka *stupa* at the Ch'ang-kan-ssu temple in the capital city Chien-k'ang during the Ning-k'ang period (393-375); of the image in the same temple originally produced by Asoka's fourth daughter, but discovered during the Hsien-he period (326-334) by the governor of Tan-yang, Kao Li; and of the stone images that came floating down the Ch'ang-chiang river in the first year of Chien-hsing (313). There is also an undated story of the rebuilding of the Asoka *stupa* in K'uai-chi.

The first two stories involving the Ch'ang-kan-ssu temple probably were meant to correspond to the first location, Tan-yang, in the list given by the "Man of the Way" at the beginning of the biography, and the last two stories are associated with the two other locations mentioned in the list, Wu* Commandary and K'uai-chi. The order of the two locations, however, is reversed in the telling of miracle stories. This may be because the biography describes the miracles as events that took place as Hui-ta travelled from one place to another, and the three locations of Tan-yang, Wu* Commandary, and Mao-hsien district in K'uai-chi stand in that order in a line that runs in the southwestern direction.

The first three miracle stories mention the dates of the incidents, perhaps reflecting the common preoccupation with such details in the telling of miracle stories. Earlier, in examining Tao-chiung's biography, we noted that Hui-chiao seemed to have constructed that biography by arranging known miracle stories associated with the figure according to their dates in the miracle story collection, and at the same time dropping the references to the dates of the individual miracles that existed in his sources. In the case of Hui-ta's biography under examination here, the miracle stories were not arranged according to chronological order and perhaps for that reason the dates of the miracles were kept in the biography.

Each of these miracle stories is independent of each other in content, and the examination of their parallel sources shows that they existed as independent miracle stories outside of the *Kao-seng chuan*. We shall therefore examine them separately, focusing on one miracle story at a time and comparing it with its parallels in other sources.

(a) The Ch'ang-kan-ssu *Stupa*.

During the Ning-k'ang period (373-375) of the Eastern Chin dynasty, Hui-ta went to the capital, Chien-k'ang. Earlier Emperor Chien-wen (reign: 371-372) had constructed a three story *stupa* at the Ch'ang-kan temple. After the *stupa* was completed light appeared from it every night. Going up to the place called Yüeh-ch'eng, Hui-ta saw from a distance an extraordinary colour at the tip of this *stupa* and worshipped it frequently by going there day and night. At night he saw a light appearing at the base of the *stupa* and told men to help him dig there. When they dug about three *chang* (about 7 meters) deep they obtained three stone inscriptions. The middle piece covered an iron box. Inside the iron box was a silver box, and inside the silver box was a golden box. The golden box contained three pieces of relics, one finger nail and one piece of hair. The hair was several *ch'ih* (about 2 meters) long and curled like the Buddha's hairs. All these pieces were shining brightly. During the reign of King Ching (520-477 B.C., or King Hsüan who reigned 827-782 B.C., according to a variant reading) of the Chou dynasty, King Asoka had built 84,000 *stupa*s. The relics and other objects obtained by Hui-ta had come from one of them. Both monks and laymen were filled with wonder and built a *stupa* to the west of the older *stupa* and placed the relics there. On the sixteenth year of the T'ai-yüan period (391), Emperor Hsiao-wu (rule: 372-396) expanded the *stupa* to a three story *stupa*.

In the *Liang shu* passage on Hui-ta, the story of Hui-ta's discovery of the Asoka *stupa* in Tan-yang, that is, Chien-k'ang, is placed in a larger context that begins by describing the legend of the Asoka *stupa* ("After the death of the Buddha, King Asoka used supernatural beings and produced 84,000 *stupa*s in one day and one night"), and focuses on the rebuilding of the *stupa* later by Emperor Wu, the founder of the Liang dynasty, during the Ta-t'ung period. The early history of the Tan-yang *stupa* is described as follows. During the period in which the area was ruled by the Wu* Kingdom, a nun lived at the site of the Asoka *stupa* and there was a small temple (*hsiao ching she*) there. After the *stupa* was destroyed by Sun Ch'en of the Wu* Kingdom, some monks rebuilt the *stupa* at the original spot. Emperor Yüan (reign: 317-322), who reestablished the Chin dynasty in the South, repaired this *stupa*. During the Hsien-an period (371-372), Emperor Chien-wen ordered the monk An Ch'eng to build a small *stupa*, but the monk died before completing the task, and his disciple Seng-hsien continued the work and finished the *stupa*. In the ninth year of the T'ai-yüan period (384), Emperor Hsiao-wu placed the golden rings on top of the *stupa*. Liu Sa-he/Hui-ta's story appears at this point, summarizing his experiences in hell and the instructions he received from Avalokitesvara.

The story of Hui-ta's discovery of the Asoka *stupa* is told in this text in a manner similar to what we have seen from the *Kao-seng chuan* passage. One important difference is that at the beginning of this *Liang shu* passage which describes the incident, there is no direct reference to an existing temple or a *stupa*. Hui-ta went to Tan-yang, following Avalokitesvara's instructions, but he did not know the location of the Asoka *stupa*. He climbed to Yüeh-ch'eng and looked around in the four directions. He saw that there was an extraordinary atmosphere (? "*yu yi ch' i se*") in the Ch'ang-kan-li area, and therefore he went there to worship. This was the location of the Asoka *stupa*. He saw light shining forth from the spot from time to time, and so he knew that there must be relics buried in that place. He gathered people and dug at the spot and found the three stone tablets and the relics. The passage then says that Hui-ta moved the relics northward, and built a one story *stupa* to the west of the *stupa* built by Chien-wen. In the 16th year of Ta-yüan (391), Monk Seng-shang-chia expanded this structure into a three-story *stupa*.

The main theme of the *Liang shu* passage is Emperor Wu's rebuilding of this *stupa*, an event which is described in some detail. The date is given as the eighth month of the third year of the Ta-t'ung period (537). The contents of the relic container are described in detail, along with the three major ceremonies performed to honour the relics. We learn that on the 27th day of the eighth month the Emperor went to the temple; on the fifth day of the ninth month one relic was brought to the palace, and on the 15th day of the ninth month, the relics were placed under the two newly built *stupas*. The *Liang shu* passage also mentions that in the second year of the Ta-t'ung period (536), the Emperor had opened the *stupa* in the Mao-hsien district in K'uai-chi and brought its relics to the palace. We will return to this information later.

Tao-hsüan wrote a long discussion of this *stupa* in his *Chi shen-chou san-pao kan-t'ung-lu* later (664).[114] The location of the *stupa* is given in detail as "in the precinct of the now defunct Ch'ang-kan-ssu temple in the old Yüeh-ch'eng, which in turn was situated to the south east of the Chu-ch'iao gate of the old city Yang in the Chiang-ning-hsien district of the Jui-chou region". Tao-hsüan then says that in the old village of Ch'ang-kan-li was the site of one of the ancient *stupas* built by King Asoka. It may be significant that Tao-hsüan refers to "the Ch'ang-kan-ssu temple" in specifying the location of the *stupa* in Tao-hsüan's time, but uses the expression the "old village of Ch'ang-kan-li" in reference to the original site of the Asoka *stupa*. This distinction, perhaps deliberately, communicates the impression that at the time when the original Asoka *stupa* existed (and for some time after that) no temple existed in the village Ch'ang-kan-li, but that later a temple called Ch'ang-kan-ssu was established there. By Tao-hsüan's time this temple had become defunct and the site returned to its original primitive state. In the *Liang shu* version only the expression "Ch'ang-kan-li village" is used, and we have noted earlier that Hui-ta's discovery of the relics is described there without any reference to an existing *stupa* nearby.[115]

Tao-hsüan's account continues. During the Wu-feng period (254-256) the *stupa* was destroyed by Sun Ch'en[116] and its relics disappeared underground. After the Wu* Kingdom was conquered, monks resided in the place which they thought incorrectly was the site of the original Asoka *stupa*.[117] There they built a three-story *stupa*, but they did not find the foundation of the old *stupa*. By that time nothing remained of the old *stupa* and nobody knew anything about it. The statement that the monks did not find the foundation should probably be interpreted as another way of saying emphatically that the location at which the monks built their three-story *stupa* was not the original site of the Asoka *stupa*. In the second year of the Hsien-an period (372), Emperor Chien-wen constructed a three-story *stupa*. Emperor Hsiao-wu (reign: 372-396) placed the golden rings at the top of the *stupa*. At this point Tao-hsüan introduces a quotation from the *Ming hsiang chi*[118] which says that Emperor Chien-wen planned to build a *stupa* but died before he could accomplish the task. Thus, Tao-hsüan says, the three-story *stupa* that existed when Hui-ta arrived was not the *stupa* built by Emperor Chien-wen, but the *stupa* built earlier by the monks who did not find the foundation of the original Asoka *stupa*.

The parallels between the *Liang shu* passage and Tao-hsüan's account suggest that Tao-hsüan may have been familiar with the *Liang shu* passage written earlier, but the differences in detail also suggest that Tao-hsüan had other sources at his disposal. The *Liang shu* passage, for example, gives the date of Chien-wen's building of the *stupa* only as "during the Hsien-an period"; Tao-hsüan gives a more precise date "the second year of Hsien-an", and at the same time he introduces doubt about this whole story, suggesting that Emperor Chien-wen did not actually build the *stupa* at all. The *Liang shu* story that the monk An Ch'eng, whom Emperor Chien-wen ordered to build a small *stupa*, died before he completed the work is probably related to Tao-hsüan's story based on the *Ming hsiang chi* that the Emperor himself died before he could build the three-story *stupa* generally attributed to him. It is also important to note that, though the stories may be related, the implications of the two stories are entirely different. According to the *Liang shu* the Chien-wen *stupa* was in the end completed; according to Tao-hsüan, the *stupa* was never built.

Tao-hsüan's comment on Emperor Chien-wen's *stupa* serves an important purpose in his overall story. We should recall that, while the *Liang shu* passage simply says that monks rebuilt the *stupa* at the original site after it had been destroyed during Sun Ch'en's persecution, Tao-hsüan's account states that they could not identify the original site of the *stupa*. If the three-story *stupa* generally attributed to Emperor Chien-wen was in fact not built by the Emperor, then it must have been the *stupa* built by the monks who could not identify the original site. Thus when Liu Sa-he arrived, nobody knew the original site of the Asoka *stupa*. In introducing this detail, Tao-hsüan therefore is skillfully preparing the setting for the dramatic story that follows about Liu Sa-he's miraculous discovery of the foundation of the original Asoka *stupa* and its relics.

Resuming our story, then, toward the end of the T'ai-yüan period (376-396) of Emperor Hsiao-wu, the monk Liu Hui-ta from the Hsi-he area of the Ping-chou region, whose original personal name was Sa-he, arrived looking for the ancient *stupa*. For details on this monk, Tao-hsüan refers to a source called "biographies of monks" ("*seng chuan*"), probably meaning Hui-chiao's *Kao-seng chuan*. From this we can assume that Tao-hsüan's account of Hui-ta's discovery of the Ch'ang-kan-ssu Asoka *stupa* in his miracle story collection *Chi shen-chou san-pao kan-t'ung-lu* that we are examining here must have at least in part been based on Hui-chiao's biography. The date of Liu Sa-he's visit given here is, however, different from that in the *Kao-seng chuan* biography. This new date, roughly 25 years later than the date in Hui-chiao's *Kao-seng chuan* biography ("during the Ning-k'ang period [373-375]), still places Liu Sa-he's visit during the reign of Emperor Hsiao-wu, but it conflicts with the information in the *Kao-seng chuan* biography that Emperor Hsiao-wu expanded Liu Sa-he's *stupa* to a three-story *stupa* in the 16th year of T'ai-yüan (392), and the reference to this date is dropped in Tao-hsüan's account.

We saw earlier that in the *Liang shu* account the name of Ch'ang-kan-li village was not mentioned in connection with the *stupa* built by monks at the original site of the Asoka *stupa*, nor with Chien-wen's *stupa*. Similarly, now in Tao-hsüan's account the name Ch'ang-kan does not appear in the discussion of the *stupa* built by the monks who could not locate its original foundation. In both these accounts the name is introduced as an essential part of the story of Hui-ta's miraculous discovery. Perhaps the name is introduced at this later point in order to suggest indirectly that the site of the original Asoka *stupa* discovered by Hui-ta was at some distance from that of the existing *stupa* rebuilt by the monks. There is also a passing note, both in the *Liang shu* and Tao-hsüan's miracle story account, which appears to indicate that the new *stupa* built after Hui-ta's discovery was located to the north of the original spot of the Asoka *stupa* and to the west of the existing *stupa*, which would be the Chien-wen *stupa* in the case of the *Liang shu* story and the Asoka *stupa* rebuilt by the monks in the case of Tao-hsüan's story. Tao-hsüan states at this point that this *stupa* was expanded into a three-story *stupa* by Emperor Hsiao-wu, repeating the information that is found both in the *Kao-seng chuan* and the *Liang shu* accounts, both of which give the date for this event as the sixteenth year of T'ai-yüan (391). We have speculated above about a possible reason why this date does not appear in Tao-hsüan's miracle story. Tao-hsüan concludes this section of his account by saying that there were thus two *stupas* in the temple, and that the western *stupa* was the ancient Asoka *stupa*. Here he is probably describing the Ch'ang-kan-ssu temple that was established some time later, and the ancient Asoka *stupa* in this case must simply mean the *stupa* containing the relics discovered by Hui-ta at its original site somewhere to the south of the temple.

It is noteworthy that both the *Liang shu* and the *Chi shen-chou san-pao kan-t'ung-lu* stories appear to suggest that Hui-ta discovered the original site of Asoka's *stupa* in the Ch'ang-kan-li village, which stood at some distance from the site of what was then believed to be the rebuilt Asoka *stupa*. The impression is that at the time of Hui-ta's discovery Ch'ang-kan-li was an ordinary village without any special religious significance. This impression contrasts rather strikingly with Hui-chiao's earlier account in the *Kao-seng chuan*. Hui-chiao talked only about the Ch'ang-kan-ssu temple and mentioned the light that was seen after the Chien-wen *stupa* was completed there. This earlier account also suggests that the relics were found right at the bottom of this Chien-wen *stupa*.

Tao-hsüan continues his account of the Ch'ang-kan *stupa* with a series of later stories. The governor of Tan-yang Wang Ya was a follower of the Five Peck of Rice Taoism, and Taoist priests were constantly telling him that he should persecute Buddhism and destroy *stupa*s. An imperial edict was issued ordering the Taoist follower Wang to visit the Ch'ang-kan-ssu temple and observe the relics. When monks brought out the relics in front of Wang Ya, miracles occurred. The monks held the relic container upside down in mid-air and hit it repeatedly, but the relics stuck to the container and did not fall; Wang Ya, stating that he did not believe in Buddhism, challenged the spirit of the

Buddha to perform some miracle, and immediately the relics sent forth light. These miracles persuaded Wang Ya not to speak ill of Buddhism again.

During the Ta-t'ung period (535-546) of the Liang dynasty, an astrological pattern ("*yüeh fan wu ch'e lao jen hsin chien*"; "the Moon entered the Five Vehicle Stars configuration and the South Polar Star was seen"?) led to the rebuilding of the Asoka *stupa* in the Ch'ang-kan-ssu temple. The relics, hair and nail were brought out. The Emperor issued an edict celebrating this event and arranged a large religious feast. The text of the Emperor's edict is given, but other details of this event recorded carefully in the *Liang shu* passage are not found in Tao-hsüan's account.[119]

Tao-hsüan reports that at the time he was writing, in the old site in the Chiang-ning-hsien district in the Jui-chou region only the foundation (of the three-stories *stupa*?) and the Buddha hall remained. The place was overgrown with small trees and bushes, and tigers (*ta ch'ung*) lived there. Those who tried to excavate the foundation of the *stupa* often died unnaturally.[120] This description of the old site appears to have been based on what Tao-hsüan saw himself, since he then tells us how he brought the relics from the base of the Ch'ang-kan-ssu *stupa* to the Jih-yen-ssu temple in the capital city, Ch'ang-an. The relics were buried under the *stupa* in this temple with an inscription placed on top. Tao-hsüan at this point mentions the charge of "over fifty great monks in the south" that the relics under the *stupa* in the capital were not from the Asoka *stupa*, suggesting that there was a controversy about the reliability of this story about the transfer of relics. In the seventh year of the Wu-te period (625), the Jih-yen-ssu temple was closed down, and its relic *stupa* was left unprotected. Tao-hsüan and ten of his students were transferred to the Ch'ung-yi temple. They dug under the Jih-yen-ssu *stupa* and found three relics, one nail, dozens of hairs and other treasures. The hairs were not curled as in the Buddha image ("*luo fa*") and the nails were yellow and small like human nails and not like the Buddha's nails, which were believed to be bigger and of red copper colour. The description of the hair here contrasts with that of the hair discovered by Hui-ta, which was said earlier to have been curled, matching the conventional description of the Buddha's hair. Tao-hsüan and his students placed the objects they found at the Jih-yen-ssu *stupa* in a large copper box and lowered it under the *stupa* southwest of the Buddha hall of the Ch'ung-yi temple. Old monks told Tao-hsüan that the nail and hairs were those of Emperor Wu of the Liang dynasty, but they did not know about the relics.

This story, together with the emphasis on Emperor Wu's rebuilding of the Ch'ang-kan-ssu *stupa* in some of our accounts, points to a symbolic process in which the image of this Chinese Emperor is gradually overlaid on top of the image of the Indian King Asoka in this cycle of relic *stupa* stories. Though the relics were mostly transferred to the capital city, miracles continued to occur in the site of the original *stupa*, and thus Tao-hsüan recorded materials regarding both these sites. This last story about the transfer of the relics is of particular interest since it shows Tao-hsüan's personal interest in and direct connection with the Ch'ang-kan-ssu miracle stories.

We have noted earlier that the parallels between the *Liang shu* passage on the Tan-yang *stupa* and Tao-hsüan's discussion of this *stupa* in his miracle story collection suggest that Tao-hsüan may have known the earlier *Liang shu* passage. We also noted that the differences in detail even in parallel passages from these two sources suggest that Tao-hsüan must have had other sources at his disposal. Many stories about the later history of this *stupa* suggest further that a growing tradition of stories about this *stupa* circulated within the monastic community. It is possible that the *Liang shu* passage, probably based in part on the *Kao-seng chuan* biography, also made use of records preserved at the central government and the palace library. Tao-hsüan's sources may have supplemented this *Liang shu* passage with other monastic records. At any rate the existence of stories about the Ch'ang-kan-ssu *stupa* which describe events that took place after Hui-ta's discovery of the relics there suggests that the story of Hui-ta's (or Liu Sa-he's) discovery of the Asoka *stupa* relics in the *Kao-seng chuan* biography may itself have been part of a larger local tradition, and that this tradition continued to develop after Hui-chiao.

(b) Kao Li's Image.

The *Kao-seng chuan*'s second miracle story is about an image and not a *stupa*. During the Hsien-he period of the Eastern Chin dynasty (326-334), the Governor of Tan-yang, Kao-li, obtained a golden image at the beach near the Chang-hou-ch'iao. It lacked the decorative halo and base *(kuang fu)* but the craftsmanship was of a very high quality. According to an earlier Sanskrit source, this image was created by the fourth daughter of King Asoka.[121] Kao Li carried this image to the street in front of the Ch'ang-kan temple. At this point the ox stopped and could not be controlled by the men. When they let the ox go as it wished, it went to the Ch'ang-kan temple. A year or so later, a fisherman called Chang Hsi-shih, who lived in Lin-hai, found a copper image base decorated with lotus flower petals *(t'ung lien-hua fu)* that was floating on the ocean. He presented it to the district office, which sent it to the higher office. When the base was placed under the golden image discovered earlier, the base and image matched perfectly. Later five Central Asian monks told Kao Li, "We obtained an image made under King Asoka in India, but when we brought it to Yeh, we encountered political disorder. So we hid it near a river. After the road became passable again, we went back, but could not find the image any more. Recently we had a dream in which we were told that the image had reappeared and was in the possession of Kao Li in the Chiang-tung area. So we have come across mountains and ocean hoping to see the image and worship it again". Kao Li then took them to the Ch'ang-kan temple. The five monks cried aloud and shed tears when they saw the image, and light appeared from the image illuminating the whole hall. The five monks said, "Originally there was a round decorative halo (*yüan kuang*). It is somewhere far away now. But it will reappear soon." In the first year of Hsien-an (371) of the Eastern Chin dynasty Tung Tsung-chih, a man who dived for pearls at the He-p'u district of Chiao-chou region, found one decorative halo of a Buddha's image (*fo kuang*) at the bottom of the sea. The Regional Inspector reported this discovery, and Emperor Chien-wen of the Chin dynasty ordered the halo to be fitted to the golden image. The image and the decorative halo fit together perfectly. Thus all the pieces of this Buddha image were brought together through various miracles in the course of over forty years.

This story of Kao Li's image is also told in the *Liang shu*, immediately following the story of the Tan-yang and Mao-hsien *stupas*.[122] Though the name Liu Sa-he is mentioned explicitly in the preceding two stories of these *stupas*, his name does not appear in the *Liang shu*'s story of Kao Li's image. The story of the discovery of the image itself, its base, and its halo at different places over a period of "more than thirty years" is told in a manner that closely parallels the *Kao-seng chuan* account, but in the *Liang shu* passage, two new details are introduced.

Monk Hui-sui of the Wa-kuan-ssu temple wanted to copy this image, but the head monk of the Ch'ang-kan-ssu temple, Seng-shang, feared that Hui-sui might damage the golden colour of the image, and said that if Hui-sui could make the image send forth light and turn toward the west he would give him the necessary permission. Hui-sui prayed to the image, earnestly requesting this miracle, and in the following night the image sent forth light and turned toward the west. The next morning he received his permission and copied the image.

The second detail is an elaboration on one passage in Hui-chiao's account. Hui-chiao's account mentions at one point that the image had a Sanskrit inscription saying that it was made by Asoka's fourth daughter. The *Liang shu* states that the base of the image had an inscription in foreign letters, which nobody could decipher. Later Tripitaka Gunavarman deciphered it as saying that King Asoka made it for his fourth daughter.

Tao-hsüan also records the story of the image discovered by Kao Li in the image miracle section of the *Chi shen-chou san-pao kan-t'ung-lu*.[123] This story appears to have been based on both the *Kao seng chuan* biography and the *Liang shu* passage. Tao-hsüan includes in his account the two new stories introduced in the *Liang shu* passage, about Gunavarman and Hui-sui respectively. Interestingly the text of the old Sanskrit inscription on the "flower base" ("*hua t'ai*") of the image is here given as "the image was made by Asoka's fourth daughter" as it was in Hui-chiao's biography. This version also conforms to the new legend of Asoka's daughter introduced by Tao-hsüan elsewhere in his writing.

As in the case of the Ch'ang-kan-ssu *stupa*, Tao-hsüan's account of the origin of this image, which is based on Hui-chiao's biography as well as the *Liang shu* passage, is followed by a long account of other miracles that occurred later. During the reign period of Emperor Wu of the Liang dynasty (502-549), images of seven deities performing music and two bodhisattvas were added above the halo. In the second year of Yung-ting of the Ch'en dynasty (558), Wang Lin encamped his soldiers at the beach of the Ch'ang-chiang river facing the capital city of Chin-ling. Emperor Wu ordered his generals to attack them. When the soldiers were about to leave, the image moved and could not be stabilized. This strange development was reported to the court and the Emperor examined the image himself and found the report to be true. Suddenly, before the soldiers crossed swords, Wang Lin's army scattered, and Wang Lin fled northward by himself. Emperor Wu's army followed him upstream and pacified the whole region. During the T'ien-chia period (560-566) there was a rebellion in the Southeastern region. When the emperor prayed in front of the image, requesting that the rebels be rejected, the image shone and illumined the hall. Shortly after that the difficulties in the region were removed. Monk Hui-hsiao rebuilt the building and in the beginning of the Chih-te period (583-587) built a square base for the image. The rulers of five dynasties, from the Chin dynasty to the Ch'en dynasty, all paid respect to this image, and in times of drought the image with oil poured over it was brought to the palace on the Emperor's carriage. While the image was *en route* to the palace, rain would fall. In the second year of the Chen-ming period (588), the image turned westward and even after people made it face in the correct direction, it again turned westward by itself. The Emperor took a jeweled hat and placed it on the head of the image, and then placed a silk hat on top of the jewelled one. In the morning the jeweled hat was hanging from the hand of the image, although the silk hat was still on its head. The Emperor burned incense and prayed, saying, "If inauspicious things are to happen to the state, let the image take the jewelled hat again to indicate this unhappy state of affairs". He then placed the jewelled hat again on the head of the image. In the morning the jewelled hat was again hanging from the image's hand as before. Both the ruler and ministers were frightened. Shortly after that the state of Ch'en was conquered by the state of Sui. The Emperor Wen of the Sui dynasty brought the image to the palace. Since the image was a standing image, the Emperor also stood and paid respect to it. Saying that he was old and could not stand for a long time, the Emperor ordered officials to prepare a sitting image with the same features, and sent the original standing image to the Ta-hsing-shan temple. The image was placed facing north, but in the morning it was found facing the south. People were amazed and moved it back again to the first location facing north. But the next morning it was again found facing south. People were amazed and realized that they had failed to pay proper respect to the image; they should have treated it as if it were the ruler, who always sat facing south. Tao-hsüan concludes this section by saying that he collected these stories of miracles from a variety of sources and that some stories were recorded briefly because he did not want to invent elaborate details for them.

As in the case of the first story of the Ch'ang-kan-ssu *stupa*, the record of miracles that happened later around this image found by Kao Li point to the existence of a flexible and living local tradition. The absence of the reference to Liu Sa-he/Hui-ta in the *Liang shu* and *Chi shen-chou san-pao kan-t'ung-lu* makes us wonder why this story was included at all in Hui-chiao's *Kao seng chuan* biography of Hui-ta. The fact that the image was located in the Ch'ang-kan-ssu temple, which is the location of the Asoka *stupa* discussed earlier, does not fully explain this anomaly. Perhaps the reference to King Asoka was the crucial reason why this story became closely associated with Hui-ta's *stupa* stories and eventually entered his biography. Perhaps the *stupa* and the image were known as two objects associated with King Asoka in the Ch'ang-kan-ssu temple. The story about Kao Li's image was thus always told locally in close association with that of the Asoka *stupa*. Hui-chiao may then have followed this local tradition in including the story about Kao Li's image in his biography of Hui-ta.[124] Thus, the accidental character of the relationship between the two stories suggests that these stories had a long history behind them before they became part of Hui-chiao's biography.[125]

(c) The Two Floating Stone Images in the Wu* Commandary.

To return to the *Kao-seng chuan* biography, we learn that Hui-ta, encouraged by these miracles associated with a *stupa* and an image of the Buddha, then went to the Wu* district. When the Western Chin dynasty (265-316) was about to end, in the first year of Chien-hsing (313), a stone image came down floating to the point where the Hutu, down-stream of the Sung-chiang river of the Wu* area, enters the ocean. Fishermen mistook it for the ocean god and sent a female medium to welcome it. Thereupon strong winds began to blow and waves rose high, and the medium returned, frightened by the change. A man who worshiped Huang-lao said that the image was the god of Heavenly Masters' Taoism.[126] They took him to welcome the image, but again he encountered wind and waves. Later a man in the Wu* district[127] called Chu-ying, who worshipped the Buddha as a lay Buddhist, heard about this and said, "Couldn't this be a miraculous intervention of the Great Awakened One (the Buddha)?". He purified himself and together with the nun Po-ni (?) of the Tung-yün-ssu temple and several lay Buddhists came to the point where the Hu down-stream entered the ocean. Bowing their heads and expressing utmost reverence, they chanted Buddhist verses praising great virtues. Then the wind and tide calmed down, and at a great distance they saw two human shapes come floating towards them. These were the stone images. On the back of the images were inscriptions saying that one was called Wei-wei (the past Buddha Vipasyin) and the other Chia-yeh (the past Buddha Kasyapa). Welcoming these images, they took them to the T'ung-hsüan-ssu temple. Many people in the Wu area, both high-born and low-born, were impressed by this miracle and numerous people were converted. Hui-ta stayed at the T'ung-hsüan-ssu temple for three years altogether, and diligently performed reverent rites.

Avalokitesvara's instruction to Hui-ta in the *Ming hsiang chi*[128] had mentioned "the two stone images in the Wu* area", which were said to have been "created by Asoka, using supernatural beings (*kuei shen*)". The corresponding passage in the parallel account in the *Chi shen-chou san-pao kan-t'ung-lu* (404b18) and the *Fa-yüan chu-lin* (585b1) mentions "the stone images that floated on the Ch'ang-chiang river", which were again said to have been made by King Asoka. Although Hui-ta's biography does not mention King Asoka in connection with these stone images, the reference to Asoka in the earlier *Ming hsiang chi* indicates that the story of these stone images and their connection with King Asoka must have been quite well-established by the time of Hui-chiao.[129]

The discussion of these two stone images in the parallel passages in *Chi shen-chou san-pao kan-t'ung-lu* and *Fa-yüan chu- lin* consists of two stories. The first and longer story parallels the *Kao-seng chuan* story summarized above closely except for a few new details. The images were very heavy, and when people tried to lift them, a storm arose again. Later several tens of people could not move them, but when they requested the images politely to move, people suddenly could move them. A central Asian monk called Fa-yüan (or Fa-k'ai according to the *Fa-yüan chu-lin* version) said that there was a scripture that spoke of two images and Asoka *stupas* in the east that free those who worshipped them from sins committed during many previous world ages.[130]

The second story states that eleven Indian monks brought the images to the Commandary. The images then stood on water, not sinking and not going any further. When this incident was reported to the court, permission was granted to let the images stay in the Commandary. The entry on these images in Tao-hsüan's *Chi shen-chou san-pao kan-t'ung-lu* is accompanied by a note saying that these stories come from Hui-chiao's *Kao-seng chuan* and Hou Po's *Ching-i chi*.[131] Since the first of the two stories does indeed correspond closely with the *Kao-seng chuan* version, my suspicion is that the second story only briefly summarized here is based on a story in the *Ching-i chi*.[132]

In this case of the two stone images in the Wu* Commandary later parallels to the *Kao-seng chuan* story and other references including the earlier one in the *Ming hsiang chi* point to a well-established local tradition, precisely as we have seen in the other miracle stories about Hui-ta that we have examined thus far.

(d) The Mao-hsien *stupa*.

The last miracle story in the *Kao-seng chuan* biography is again about a *stupa*. After a while Hui-ta went to K'uai-chi and paid respect to the *stupa* at the place called Mao.[133] This *stupa* also had been built by King Asoka. The place had been deserted for many years and the foundation of the *stupa* had been covered over. Hui-ta meditated with concentration and saw a flame of miraculous light there. Therefore he built a stone *stupa (k'an ch'i)* at the place from which the light emanated. Birds did not dare to nest in it. Those who hunted and fished near the *stupa* were never successful. Monks and laymen spread stories about the miracles here and everyone believed in its power. Later, Commandary Governor Meng Yi cleared and populated the area to a greater extent. Wherever Hui-ta went (and found relics from the Asoka *stupas*),[134] there were frequently miracles. He was diligent in Buddhist practice all his life. It is not known where he went after these events.

The story of the Mao-hsien *stupa* in K'uai-chi is assigned to the Western Chin (265-316) period and appears at the beginning of the *stupa* miracle section of Tao-hsüan's *Chi shen-chou san-pao kan-t'ung-lu* (404b-405b)[135] and the corresponding section in the *Fa-yüan chu-lin* (585a-586a).[136] In these texts the accounts of Liu Sa-he's experiences in hell, the instructions to him by the "foreign monk" to worship the *stupas* and stone images built by King Asoka, and Liu Sa-he's renunciation of the householder's life, which are said to be based on an "earlier tradition or biography" ("*ch'ien chuan*"), are immediately followed by the story of Hui-ta's quest for the Mao-hsien *stupa*. Hui-ta went to K'uai-chi and looked for the *stupa* everywhere in the mountains and rivers there but could not find it. When filled with sorrow and distressed he threw himself on the ground, he heard the sound of bells from under the ground. He immediately marked the place and placed a piece of wood (?) as the symbol of a temple ("*ch'a*"). Three days later a jewelled *stupa* and relics appeared from the ground. The colour of the *stupa* was dark green (*ch'ing*: "blue"), and though it looked as if it was made of stone that was not the case. Its height was one *ch'ih* and four *ts'un* (c 40 cm) and each side was seven *ts'un* (c. 20 cm) long. It had a five layered rings on top. The *stupa* looked like those built in the Central Asian kingdom Yü-t'ien. The open windows on each of its sides were decorated with heavenly bells and in the middle of the *stupa* hung a copper *ch'ing** bell. Hui-ta suspected that the sound of the temple bell that he had heard earlier must have been the sound of this *ch'ing** bell. All around the *stupa* images of Buddhas, bodhisattvas, guardians holding *vajra*, and holy monks were carved in fine detail. When you looked at the *stupa* closely, hundreds of thousands images immediately appeared in your field of vision. The details of each of the images were perfectly executed, a feat that was clearly beyond the reach of men, and must certainly have been accomplished by gods. During Tao-hsüan's time this *stupa* was kept within a larger wooden *stupa* building and on the eight days of seasonal changes ("*pa wang jih*") it was carried around the villages. The relics were kept at the base of the wooden *stupa*. To the eastern side of this *stupa* were many ancient sites of miracles (? *ku chi*).[137]

This account of the Mao-hsien *stupa* is followed by a long entry, based on local gazetteers, of miracles and other notable incidents in the general region around the *stupa*. The details of this account are too long to be summarized here, but the following entry is particularly notable for our purposes here. The old city of Mao-hsien, located over 300 *li* (over 150 m) to the east of Chü-chang, was the capital of the Min and Yüeh kingdoms in the past. The miraculous *stupa* ("*ling t'a*") is located at the district border in the Hsiao-yi-hsiang village. According to the Local Gazetteer ("*ti chih*"), this *stupa* is one of the 84,000 *stupas* King Asoka built. Meng Yi, the administrator for K'uai-chi under the Sung dynasty, repaired this *stupa*. There is a rock cave in the mountain, three *ch'ih* (c 75 cm) in height and width. The water there is pure, and warm in winter and cool in summer. Another Gazetteer (? "*yü ti chih*") says the following. King Asoka was a disciple of Sakyamuni, and was capable of controlling supernatural beings *(kuei shen)*. In one night he created 84,000 treasure *stupas* of the Buddha's bones in the Realm under Heaven. These *stupa*s all appeared from the ground. According to monk Hui-ta of the Chin dynasty, there are two Asoka *stupa*s in Eastern China; one *stupa* is here and the other is in P'eng-ch'eng. The *stupa* that is now located in the Ch'ang-kan temple in Mo-ling (ie., Tan-yang) is also an Asoka *stupa*. Thus, there are three *stupa*s altogether (in the Eastern China?). After an obscure passage, the account of Asoka *stupa*s continues, quoting from a document called the K'uai-chi Gazetteer. According to Wang Tao, prime minister of the Eastern Chin dynasty, when he was crossing the Ch'ang-chiang river, he met an ordinary looking monk ("*tao jen*") who said that he had come from across the ocean, and that in the past he had travelled to Mao-hsien with King Asoka and lowered authentic relics of the Buddha in the ground and built a *stupa* to protect it. An obscure story concerning King Asoka and an island of man-shaped stones follows this. Returning to the discussion of the Mao-hsien *stupa*, this long and somewhat confusing account then mentions the rebuilding of the *stupa* in the third year of P'u-t'ung (523) by the Emperor Wu, the founder of the Liang dynasty. We have noted that this incident was mentioned briefly in the *Liang shu* passage on Hui-ta's *stupa*s earlier, where the date of the second year of Ta-t'ung (536) and the names of monk Ch'ing-t'uo of the Kuang-chai-ssu temple and Houseman (*she jen*) Sun-chao were mentioned.[138]

As in the case of the Ch'ang-kan-ssu *stupa* discussed above, Tao-hsüan's account of this incident and the description of the same incident in the *Liang shu* passage are significantly different. In the *Chi shen-chou san-pao kan-t'ung-lu* passage, the beauty of the temple, renamed as the Asoka temple ("A-yü-wang-ssu temple"), is emphasized. This account also mentions an inscription by Editorial Director Ku Yin-tsu, the miraculous appearance of the Buddha's footprints at places miles apart from each other, a miraculous pond to the north of the temple where an eel, called the "Boddhisattva Eel" lived and performed extraordinary deeds, and other miracles associated with the *stupa*.

In Tao-hsüan's account of his own miraculous encounter with supernatural beings found in a text called *Tao-hsüan lü-shih kan-t'ung-lu*, the story of the Mao-hsien *stupa* appears again.[139] In a rather obscure passage, the god explained that the relic of the Mao-hsien *stupa* was the arm bone of the past

Buddha Kasyapa of the Age of the Wise, but that no human being has ever seen it. The god said further that the *stupa* appeared from the ground to bring fortune to the ordinary people, that the two fish in the well were gods protecting the *stupa,* that the marks of the Buddha on the rock were made by three earlier Buddhas, and that many people had lived in the area during the Chou period in the past and that is why the *stupa* had been built there. The stories told by gods to Tao-hsüan in this extraordinary text are of particular interest to us. The circumstances of the exchange implies that Tao-hsüan must have asked questions about things that he himself was familiar with, and perhaps these things that he asked were similarly known to his fellow Buddhists in medieval China as well. By contrast the stories that the supernatural beings told Tao-hsüan, must have been unknown to the great historian Tao-hsüan, and by implication to everyone else, until they were revealed to him through this miracle. Thus, we see in this text how new details of some relatively well-known stories evolved in the tradition. Tao-hsüan's reference to the Mao-hsien *stupa* implies that the *stupa* was known to the readers of this text; more importantly it also indicates that Tao-hsüan himself was keenly interested in this *stupa* to the point that he attempted to introduce new details of legends associated with the *stupa.*

The Mao-hsien *stupa* must also have enjoyed a wide-spread reputation later on. In the biography of Wei-tse in the *Sung kaoseng chuan*, there is a note that Wei-tse heard about this *stupa* and visited it to worship it. He then made a small model of the *stupa*, which he later brought back to his home temple Tz'u-ssu, built earlier during the Yüan-he period (808-820).[140] The story of Mao-shan relic *stupa* and miracles is told in the later Buddhist history, the *Fo tsu t'ung chi* compiled by Chih-p'an over the twelve year period between 1258-1269. The passage found in the 53rd *chüan* of this work (T. Vol. 49, p. 461ab) mentions events around this *stupa* that occurred after Tao-hsüan's life time, indicating that the tradition continued to develop well into the Sung period.

Let us briefly comment on the significance of the above investigation of the miracle stories for interpreting the *Kao-seng chuan* biography of Hui-ta. I will begin with a few comments on the text of the *Kao-seng chuan* biography itself.

The *Ming hsiang chi's* account of the layman Liu Sa-he's extraordinary experience and the *Kao-seng chuan*'s account of *stupa*s and images that the monk Hui-ta visited are bound together by Avalokitesvara's instruction to Liu Sa-he to worship King Asoka's *stupa*s and the two stone images. These instructions are given toward the end of the *Ming hsiang chi*'s story. Our accounts are also tied together by references to King Asoka and his daughter in three of the *Kao-seng chuan's* stories. Without the story of Avlokitesvara's instructions (or the instructions from the "man of the Way" as in the *Kao-seng chuan)*, the string of miracle stories associated with *stupa*s and images that constitute the substance of the *Kao-seng chuan* biography would not at all constitute a coherent whole, at least in the form in which they are presented in this biography. In fact, Hui-ta's role in these stories about *stupas* and images is rather limited: in the first and last stories about *stupas*, he plays an important role as the person who identified the site of King Asoka's *stupa*, but in the second and third stories about images Hui-ta in fact plays no role at all. The story about Kao Li's golden image is embedded in the middle of Hui-ta's biography without any explicit statement about its relationship with Hui-ta until the very end of this passage, where a comment that Hui-ta was greatly encouraged by the image and its miracle appears. The location Tan-yang is mentioned in the brief summary of Liu Sa-he's story, but Hui-chiao's biography contains two stories from this location, the story of the Ch'ang-kan-ssu *stupa* and that of Kao Li's image also at the Ch'ang-kan-ssu temple. The second image story, the story about the stone images in Wu* Commandary, is integrated into Hui-ta's biography by the presumed fact that these are the images in the temple where Hui-ta stayed for three years. Hui-ta, however, again plays no role in the miracles associated with these images. It should also be noted that there are no internal relationships between the four stories about *stupas* and images in this biography. If we limit our attention to the text of the *Kao-seng chuan* biography itself, these stories appear to be bound together rather artificially only by the force of the earlier reference to King Asoka's *stupas* and images in Liu Sa-he's story.

The phenomenon that binds the *Kao-seng chuan* miracle stories together, perhaps more closely than the text of this biography makes explicit, appears to have been the cult of King Asoka's *stupas* and Buddha images in China. The story about Kao Li's golden image may have been inserted in Hui-ta's biography because this image was believed to have been made by Asoka's fourth daughter. As an image that was made by Asoka's daughter this image may have been treated as a part of the group of *stupas* and images associated with King Asoka. The *Kao-seng chuan* does not mention King Asoka in connection with the two stone images in the Wu* Commandary, but we have seen that the brief reference to these images in Avalokitesvara's instructions in the earlier *Ming hsiang chi* explicitly states that these images were made by King Asoka using supernatural beings. Perhaps by Hui-chiao's time (early sixth century) in south China a number of *stupas* and Buddha images were widely known to have originated with this famous Indian King. Liu Sa-he must have been widely known as an actor in this legend, as the person who rediscovered Asoka's *stupas* in Tan-yang and Mao-hsien. The two stories of images associated with Asoka may have become a part of Liu Sa-he/Hui-ta's biography because the stories of *stupas* and images made by Asoka were remembered together, and Liu Sa-he occupied a prominent place in the collection of these stories as a whole. The fact that the list of the stories about Asoka *stupas* and images mentioned in the instructions given by Avalokitesvara/ "a man of the Way"/ "a foreign monk" in the sources examined above appears to be basically stable, though containing minor variations including different ways in which the same places are named, tends to support this interpretation. Not only the cycle of legends but the locations of the *stupas* and images may also have been relatively well established by the time the stories in the sources we have been discussing took shape.

Since existing parallel sources on these *stupa* and image miracle stories examined above come from a period later than the *Kao-seng chuan* and generally appear to be dependant on the *Kao-seng chuan* biography of Hui-ta, it is difficult at this point to reconstruct the development behind the *Kao-seng chuan* biography more precisely. But several relevant observations can be drawn from the review of these sources above.

(a) The *Liang shu* passage tells the story of the Liang Emperor Wu's rebuilding of the Ch'ang-kan-ssu *stupa* in Tan-yang in detail and then adds a brief note that the Mao-hsien *stupa* had also been rebuilt by Emperor Wu earlier. Liu Sa-he's name is mentioned explicitly in connection with these *stupas*. These discussions of the Asoka *stupas* are then followed immediately in the *Liang shu* by the story of Kao Li's golden image. The passage explicitly quotes the words of the five foreign monks to the effect that this golden image had been made by Asoka in India, but was lost while it was being transported to China by them and was rediscovered by Kao Li. The story, on the other hand, does not mention Liu Sa-he's name. A brief note at the end of this story describes the expansion of the Ch'ang-kan-ssu temple during the Ta-t'ung period, thus giving the impression that the whole passage is first about Emperor Wu's rebuilding of the Asoka *stupas* and secondly about the Ch'ang-kan-ssu temple. The story of Kao Li's golden image thus appears to have been included here as an explanation of another important object associated with King Asoka in the Ch'ang-kan-ssu temple.

Tao-hsüan's miracle story collection, *Chi shen-chou san-pao kan-t'ung-lu*, begins the discussion of *stupa* miracles with the stories of the Mao-hsien *stupa* and of the Ch'ang-kan-ssu *stupa*, and these stories mention Liu Sa-he's name explicitly. The stories of the two stone images in the Wu* Commandary and of Kao Li's image are placed separated in the subsequent section on image miracles, and there is no reference to Liu Sa-he's name in these stories given there.

The treatment of the four miracle stories in the *Kao-seng chuan* biography of Hui-ta in these two later sources shows that at least by the seventh century Liu Sa-he's name was associated only with the Asoka *stupa* stories, and that the Asoka image stories circulated without any reference to this monk.

(b) It is perhaps also significant that in the two *Liang shu* passages describing the Asoka *stupas*, the name of the person who miraculously located the *stupas* is first given as Liu Sa-he. In the story about the Ch'ang-kan-ssu *stupa*, it is then said that Liu Sa-he became a monk and changed his name to Hui-ta. In the shorter reference to the Mao-hsien *stupa* the name Hui-ta is not mentioned at all. In Tao-hsüan's miracle story collection, the story of the Mao-hsien *stupa* again first identifies the man by the name Liu Sa-he and then says that he became a monk and changed his name to Hui-ta. The Ch'ang-kan-ssu *stupa* story briefly mentions the rediscovery of the original site of the *stupa* by "Liu Hui-ta, whose original personal name was Hsieh(Sa)-he". The emphasis on the complete secular name of the person in these stories may indicate that these stories circulated primarily as the stories of layman Liu Sa-he and only secondarily as those of monk Hui-ta. The monk's name Hui-ta may have been introduced somewhat later, though the fact that the *Ming hsiang chi* story ends with mentioning Liu Sa-he's renunciation of householder's life and the monk's name Hui-ta indicates that this theme must also have been introduced relatively early at least in some circles.

Without the story of his renunciation and the monk's name Hui-ta, Liu Sa-he's stories could not have entered the corpus of the biographies of monks. Thus it should be entirely natural that in our sources, which were after all mostly collected by compilers of biographies of monks, considerable emphasis would be placed on the name Hui-ta. Hui-chiao explicitly states in his biography that Liu Sa-he became a monk and changed his name to Hui-ta and then travelled to the sites of Asoka *stupa*s and images. Thus, according to this account the person who identified the Asoka *stupa*s must have appeared at the sites as monk Hui-ta. But perhaps the stories as they were retold in the sites where the *stupa*s were rediscovered were still better known as the stories of layman Liu Sa-he in the seventh century. This may explain why the later miracle stories examined above continued to emphasize the layman's name in the these stories. If the stories of Liu Sa-he's rediscovery of the Asoka *stupa*s, going back beyond Hui-chiao in origin, were preserved at the sites of these *stupa*s independently of Hui-chiao's biography, and if later historians knew these local stories of layman Liu Sa-he, it would have been natural for them to keep emphasizing the layman's name as a way of calling the readers' attention to these local sources, while at the same time identifying the subject of these local traditions as the same as that of Hui-chiao's biography of Hui-ta.

(c) The *Liang shu* stories of the Liang Emperor Wu's rebuilding of the Ch'ang-kan-ssu and Mao-hsien *stupa*s and its record of a later miracle associated with Kao Li's golden image suggest that a rich tradition of miracle stories existed in each of these sites by the beginning of the seventh century, and thus before Tao-hsüan wrote his collection of miracle stories. Frequent references to local gazetteers in Tao-hsüan's account of later miracles at the Mao-hsien *stupa* also indicate that these later stories were recorded and preserved at the site of this *stupa*. Similar local traditions not included in our sources may also have existed at the other sites under examination here. Together this evidence suggests that by the seventh century, independent local traditions of *stupa* and image miracles existed at the sites mentioned in Hui-chiao's *Kao-seng chuan* biography of Hui-ta. We have also seen evidence that at least some of these stories were well known before Hui-chiao's time, and that Hui-chiao used the earlier records of these traditions in composing Hui-ta's biography. We have noted above, for example, that Hui-chiao's reference to Kao Li's image in his biography of Hui-ta appears to be rather out of place until we focus on the fact that the image existed in the Ch'ang-kan-ssu temple and must have belonged to the cycle of stories associated with King Asoka's *stupa*s and images. There appears to have been a local tradition at the Ch'ang-kan-ssu temple about King Asoka's *stupa* and image, and Hui-chiao in writing Hui-ta's biography drew from this source without rigorously distinguishing from others the part involving Hui-ta directly. The fact that an earlier source, the *Ming hsiang chi*, mentions the floating images in the Wu* Commandary as images made by Asoka helps to explain why this story was also included in the same biography. Again the main reason why Hui-chiao included this story in Hui-ta's biography must have been the connection between the images and King Asoka. This connection must have been firmly established in the local tradition along with the accompanying miracle stories. We have also commented above that the frequent use of the layman's name Liu Sa-he may mean that the stories going back beyond Hui-chiao's *Kao-seng chuan* biography existed at the sites of the *stupa*s in connection with the lay devotee.

(d) A very large part of the later materials on the Ch'ang-kan-ssu and Mao-hsien *stupa*s and the Kao Li and Wu* Commandary images appears to have survived through the effort of Tao-hsüan. Thus, we may conclude that Tao-hsüan must have been extremely interested in the story of Hui-ta. In writing his biography of this monk, Tao-hsüan did not make use of the main part of the materials he collected that are directly related to Hui-ta's biographical tradition, perhaps because these materials were primarily about the stories found in the earlier *Kao-seng chuan* biography. I shall show below that for his *Hsü kao-seng chuan* biography of Hui-ta Tao-hsüan used other materials that were nevertheless similar in character to the miracle stories in the *Kao-seng chuan* biography.

(iii) The *Hsü kao seng chuan* biography

This biography begins by giving Hui-ta's secular name as Liu Su(?)-he. His place of origin is also given differently as "Ting-yang, northeast of Hsien-yang (644c16)". He is explicitly said to have been a foreigner of the Chi group (*chi hu*).[141] He originally did not follow the Buddhist teaching and was illiterate. His personality was violent. He was strong and enjoyed hunting. He served as an elite cavalry man *(t'u ch'i)* at the city of Liang-ch'eng and defended the city of Hsiang-yang. His parents and brother were all alive. His family was wealthy and his family members conducted themselves selfishly without regard to reason. Because of his drinking Liu Su-he became sick. After his life ended, he saw in detail the different ways in which sinners suffer in various hells. Tao-hsüan notes at this point that details of this story are found in the *pieh chuan* (a separate and independent biography). Since this source is mentioned in connection with Liu Su-he's experiences in hell, the content of *pieh chuan* probably centered around the story of hell similar to the story we have seen in the *Ming hsiang chi.*

Tao-hsüan's biography continues by stating that the subject renounced the householder's life and lived in his birth place in the Wen-ch'eng Commandary located in the plateau southeast of Tz'u-chou. At the time Tao-hsüan was writing this biography, there was an image and shrine of Hui-ta worshipped by both Chinese and non-Chinese people. The image and the shrine were located in the precinct of the An-min-ssu temple in the city where the local government was situated.

Hui-ta's trips to Wu* and Yüeh regions are mentioned with a note that the details of this trip are found in the "earlier biography" (*ch'ien chuan*). It is probably safe to assume that this refers to Hui-ta's biography in Hui-chiao's *Kao-seng chuan.* In the first year of Tai-yen (435) of the Emperor T'ai-wu of Northern Wei dynasty (rule: 423-452), Hui-ta returned to the West. When he arrived at a place northeast of the Fan-he Commandary in Liang-chou region, he looked toward the valley and bowed down toward it from a distance. People did not understood the meaning of this conduct, and asked for an explanation. Hui-ta said, "An image of the Buddha will appear at this cliff. If the image is complete, then the world will be at peace. If something is missing, there will be disorder and people will suffer."

Hui-ta reached the rocky stream seven *li* to the west of the city of the Chiu-ch'üan district in the Su-chou region. His bones splintered into fragments the size of Sunflower seeds. It was possible to drill holes in them (to string them together?) and these bone fragments are now placed on the hand of a clay image at an old temple in the western part of the city. There is an inscription in the temple which says "I am not a great sage; I made wandering and teaching my profession". Tao-süan comments on this inscription that "the text is not detailed" *(wen pu chü yi),* without making it clear whether the inscription contained only the quotation given here or other information about Hui-ta's life was also given, though briefly.

Eighty-seven years later, at the beginning of the Cheng-kuang period (520-525), there was a sudden great storm and the mountain surface was split by thunder and lightening, exposing a stone image, eight *chang* (c. 20 m) tall. The body features of this image were handsome and awesome, but the image was headless. People selected an appropriate piece of rock, made a stone mason carve a separate head and placed it on top of the body, but the head would always fall. Finally they let the image stand without the head. In the course of the Northern Wei period Buddhism declined slowly. The appearance of this image confirmed Hui-ta's earlier predictions. On the first year of Northern Chou rule (557) in a creek seven *li* to the east of the city of Liang-chou, a light appeared illuminating the darkness around it. Those who saw it all found it extraordinary.

The source of the light was the head of a Buddha image. When they placed it on the image at the cliff, the head and body matched perfectly. The image had stood without the head for over 40 years and the head and body were found over 200 *li* apart. The image was restored to its wholeness and peace reigned in the world. In the first year of Pao-ting (561) a temple called Jui-hsiang-ssu ("Temple of Auspicious Image") was officially established at this site. A light, like the light from a lamp, floated in the sky, illuminating the area, and the sound of bells was heard. This continued for a while ceaselessly, and people had no idea where the light and sound came from. On the first year of Chien-te (572), the head of the image fell many times. Prime minister (*ta-chung-tsai*)[142] who was also Prince of Ch'i went to observe this phenomenon himself. He ordered the head to be replaced securely, but the head fell at night. This was repeated dozens of times. He also employed other objects to replace the original head, but the objects always fell in the end. Later, the Chou dynasty persecuted Buddhism and within four years a neighboring state (Ch'i) was conquered by the Chou. Learned people understood the predictive power of the image. Although Buddhism was persecuted (in the conquered state of Ch'i as well), the image was left standing as a special exception. At the beginning of the K'ai-huang period (581-600, of the new Sui dynasty) Buddhist scriptures and images were promoted again. The stone image was redecorated and the temple was honored again. In the fifth year of Ta-yeh (611), the Emperor Yang-ti came to the site of the image and worshiped it. Offering many gifts, he changed the name of the temple to Kan-t'ung-ssu ("Temple of Supernatural Occurrences"). Copies of the stone image were made but the exact size of the image could never be determined.[143]

Tao-hsüan concludes his biography of Hui-ta by stating that in the beginning of the Chen-kuan period (627-649) he travelled in the west (*kuan piao*: "outside of the [Han-k'u] gate) and visited Hui-ta's main shrine (*pen miao*). He saw that the drawing of the image *(t' u hsiang)* of Hui-ta was worshipped daily. In Shih-chou, Hsi-chou, Tz'u-chou, Tan-chou, Yen-chou, Sui-chou, Wei-chou, Lan-chou, and others, there were drawings of Hui-ta's image and these drawings were worshipped as "the Master Liu's Buddha" (*liu shih fo*). Tao-hsüan notes that because of these drawings many non-Chinese people overcame their barbaric nature and followed the Buddhist precepts. The biography ends with a statement that Tao-hsüan saw an inscription on the rock image composed by a sixth century monk Yao Tao-an.[144]

Hui-ta's shrine that Tao-hsüan visited appears to have been the shrine around the An-min-ssu (or An-jen-ssu) temple in Tz'u-chou region.[145] The last section of Tao-hsüan's collection, *Chi shen-chou san-pao kan-t'ung-lu,* is devoted to the records of "miracle working monks" (*shen-seng*) and the last item in this section is an extremely interesting passage on Liu Sa-he (434c2-435a9).[146] This story contains materials that parallel some sections in Tao-hsüan's *Hsü kao-seng chuan* biography of Hui-ta, but the stories are told in the *Chi shen-chou san-pao kan-t' ung-lu* passage in greater detail and in such a manner that suggests that the corresponding parts of the *Hsü kao-seng chuan* biography must have been based on this material.[147] The passage begins by describing the location of the Liu Sa-he's shrine ("*miao*"), suggesting that at least some of the materials included in this passage may have come from a source intended as an explanation of the special virtues of this shrine.[148] The location of the shrine is described as follows. The shrine existed to the west of the An-jen-ssu temple, which was located in the outside section of the city of Tz'u-chou. The village where the temple and shrine were found was originally called the Wen-ch'eng Commandary, and was located in a high plateau not very far to the southeast of the city of Tz'u-chou. These details closely parallel the corresponding passage at the beginning section of the *Hsü kao-seng chuan* with the single exception that the name of the temple is given here as the An-jen-ssu, and not as the An-min-ssu temple as in the *Hsü kao-seng chuan* account. There is, however, little doubt that the two names refer to the same temple.

At this point the name of Liu Sa-he is mentioned again, specifying that Liu was his surname and Sa-he his personal name. His shrine there is said to have been very impressive and beautifully decorated. A brief account of Liu Sa-he's background and his experience in the netherworld is given. As a lay person there was nothing extraordinary about him. He frequently conceived the sinful thought of killing and did not honour the Buddhist teaching. Liu Sa-he died because of an illness but came back to life and told the following story. He saw Avalokitesvara in the netherworld, who said to him, "Your sins were grave and you should be punished severely, but because you were ignorant about the gravity of these sins I will let you be revived. In Lo-hsia, Ch'i-ch'eng, Tan-yang, and K'uai-chi there are Asoka *stupas*. Go there and worship the *stupas*, and then you can escape from punishment for sins committed earlier." Liu Sa-he came back to life and changed his earlier way of life. There were no Buddhists in the area, and hearing that there were some in the outer city of Tz'u-chou, he went there and questioned them in detail. These foreigners of the Chi group believed the story that Liu Sa-he told them. A passage describing the religious celebration held in this foreign Buddhist community on the eighth day of the fourth month follows. It is then said that Liu Sa-he renounced the householder's life and took the monk's name Hui-ta. People looked up to him and respected him as if he were a Buddha, and he performed many miracles. During the day he preached from a tall tower (*t'a*: a *stupa*?) and at night he withdrew into a cocoon. In the morning he came out of the cocoon again. Thus, at first he did not live in a monk's residence. Thus, he was called the holy man of *su-he*. The word *su-he* means cocoon among the foreign Chi people. In the Buddha halls in the villages in the region there was always an image[149] called the "Teacher-of-Foreigners Buddha" ("*hu shih fo*").[150] At the time when the passage was written there was an extremely awe-inspiring image of this "*hu shih fo*" in the An-jen-ssu temple. Local people frequently offered flowers and incense to this image, and every year during the new year's celebration it was taken around neighboring villages on a carriage. It decided where to go by itself without any help from men. If the image wished to go to a certain village, two people could lift it. The wrinkles on the image's forehead (*e-wen*) disappeared and the face looked happy and friendly. This would mean that only a few people would die in that village during the coming year. If the image did not wish to go to a certain village, ten people could not move it. Deep wrinkles would form on the forehead of the image and the face would look gloomy and miserable. Then disastrous catastrophes always occurred in that village during the coming year. Thus, local people had always relied on the image to foretell the future. Local people also believed that Avalokitesvara had come down among the people, temporarily incarnated as the monk Hui-ta, and that was why his name was called "*hui-ta*", a phrase which may be read as "wisdom reaches" or as "compassion reaches", with a common variant writing for "*hui*" using the character meaning compassion.[151] There is a one *chüan* scripture, describing this act on the part of Avalokitesvara, and it is popular among the local people. It is written in a foreign language. But it is written simply, so that anyone who reads it can understand it without any other help. Tao-hsüan at this point introduces an autobiographical comment saying that he has heard the scripture recited himself. He says further that two years earlier (?*wang erh nien*) he travelled around the area extensively and investigated the cult of Hui-ta there exhaustively.[152] In the eight regions of Tz'u-chou, Hsi-chou, Lan-chou, Shih-chou, Tan-chou, Yen-chou, Sui-chou, and Yin-chou, on both the eastern and western sides of the Yellow river, everyone worships this form of Avalokitesvara as Hui-ta and performs the rites described in that scripture. At the time when this record was written there was in every field in this area a earthen mound *stupa (t' u t' a)* with a cedar stick (*po ch' a*) planted on top of it. A Cocoon of silkworm is attached to this cedar stick, to symbolize the place where Hui-ta lived. After spreading the Buddhist teaching in his place of birth, Liu Sa-he traveled eastward to Tan-yang. After worshiping several *stupa*s there, he then went westward to the Fan-he (Commandary) in the Liang-chou region and, worshiping a mountain across the valley, brought an image out (on the surface of the mountain). Liu Sa-he then went to the desert ("*sha-ch' i*") to the west of the town of Chiu-ch'üan in the Su-chou region and died there. His bones were small and fine, and looked like sunflower seeds. Each small piece had a hole in the middle and could be threaded through with a string. Even at the time this record was written local people who suffered from illnesses and other troubles went to the desert and looked for these small pieces of bones. If a person found a piece, his difficulty would disappear; if he did not, even the good fortunes that he possessed were lost. Once a man looked for a piece of Hui-ta's bones and found nothing. He then stole a fragment from the image of Avalokitesvara on the east side of the temple (where Liu Sa-he's tomb was located and the bones were kept on the hand of an image?). When night came the piece he had stolen disappeared. When he went back to the temple in the morning he found that the piece he had stolen had gone back to the image's hand.

Local people honored the image and the bone pieces even more greatly because of this incident.

In this story Liu Sa-he is described an ordinary Chinese person, who after the experience of receiving instruction in hell, went to a foreign community seeking instruction in Buddhism and became a legendary religious figure there. Aside from Avalokitesvara's instruction in hell, given here in a form very similar to that in the *Liang shu* version of Liu Sa-he's experience, and a passing comment later that Liu Sa-he went to Tan-yang to worship *stupas*, there is no other reference to the *stupas* and images built by Asoka in this story. The other references to Avalokitesvara here appear in very different contexts. The first reference identifies Hui-ta with Avalokitesvara, and the second makes the image of Avalokitesvara the guardian of Liu Sa-he/Hui-ta's bone fragments, perhaps again hinting that Liu Sa-he/Hui-ta was an incarnation of Avalokitesvara.

The frequent references to local practices and legends in this material are particularly noteworthy. We have noted earlier that Tao-hsüan in his *Hsü kao-seng chuan* biography of Hui-ta states that he visited the main shrine of Hui-ta on his trip at the beginning of the Chen-kuan period. In the Hui-ta passage in the *Chi shen-chou san-pao kan-t'ung-lu* Tao-hsüan again states that he visited the area himself two years earlier. These two passages must refer to the same visit.[153] Thus, if the phrase "the end of the Chen-kuan period" means the last year of Chen-kuan period (649), and if my reading of the autobiographical comment in the *Chi shen-chou san-pao kan-t'ung-lu* is correct, then the document was probably written around the year 651. At any rate, we may assume that these stories about local practices and legends must have been collected on that occasion by Tao-hsüan himself. Repeated references to local beliefs and practices throughout the text may indicate that the compiler of the present text was an outsider who wrote the text using a variety of local sources. This compiler may well have been Tao-hsüan himself.

The material was then used by Tao-hsüan to compose his biography of Hui-ta. Tao-hsüan appears to have been rather selective in using the information found in this material. He excised the story about the cocoon, which was probably based on some local foreign rite or custom. The name "*hu shih fo*" for Liu Sa-he's image was changed to "*liu shih fo*" in Tao-hsüan's biography, perhaps to emphasize the point that the subject of this image was Liu Su(Sa)-he. The miracle story about the image in the Hui-ta shrine and another about Hui-ta's bone pieces as well as the description of the celebration on the eighth day of the fourth month were also not included in the biography. The biography, by contrast, contains the material on the inscription on Hui-ta at the temple in the Chiu-ch'üan district which is not mentioned in the *Chi shen-chou san-pao kan-t'ung-lu* material. As I noted earlier, while Liu Sa-he is treated as a Chinese who became a saint among the Chi foreigners in the *Chi shen-chou san-pao kan-t'ung-lu*, the *Hsü kao seng chuan* treats him as a foreigner himself.

It was noted above that Tao-hsüan at the end of his *Hsü kao-seng chuan* biography mentions an inscription on the image by Yao Tao-an.[154] This explicit reference suggests that Tao-hsüan was familiar with the text of this inscription and that the substance of Tao-hsüan's story about the rock image in the Liang-chou region was based on this inscription. In addition to the material summarized above, Tao-hsüan's miracle story collection, *Chi shen-chou san-pao kan-t'ung-lu,* also contains a story of the image that appeared from the mountain in Liang-chou.[155] This story parallels closely the story of the same image in the *Hsü kao-seng chuan* biography of Hui-ta and mentions also the inscription by Tao-an ("Details are found in Tao-an's inscription", 417c21/387a22f.). This explicit reference to the inscription again suggests that the miracle story of the rock image in Liang-chou in this collection was also based on Tao-an's inscription. Perhaps the parallel accounts of the rock image in Liang-chou in the *Hsü kao-seng chuan* biography and the *Chi shen-chou san-pao kan-t'ung-lu* miracle story were both directly based on Tao-an's inscription. One interesting fact about the *Chi shen-chou san-pao kan-t'ung-lu* version of this story is that only the name Liu Sa-he is mentioned. In one place where the text mentions the name Liu Sa-he explicitly ("*he yüh*", 417c10) the corresponding passage in the *hsü-kao-seng chuan* changes the name to Hui-ta ("*ta yüeh*", 645a2). This fact seems to strengthen our suspicion mentioned earlier that the miracle stories were originally known as stories of layman Liu Sa-he.[156]

In Tao-hsüan's autobiographical account of his own encounter with supernatural beings, *Tao-hsüan-lü-shih kan-t'ung-lu,* Tao-hsüan had asked when the rock image that appeared from the mountain was originally made.[157] He was then told the following story. During the time of Kasyapa Buddha, there was a bodhisattva called Li-pin, who saw that the people who lived in this mountain did not believe in the teaching of karmic retributions and made their living by killing living beings. At that time there were several tens of thousands of households there, but none of them honored the Buddhist teaching. The bodhisattva Li-pin tried to bring salvation to them, and built a large temple. The god Brahma himself made the image for this temple. After the temple was completed bodhisattva Li-pin used his supernatural power and transformed this image into the Buddha himself, who travelled around teaching people. Yet the people still did not accept the Buddhist teaching. Thereupon, bodhisattva Li-pin held a large rock and threatened to drop it on people if they did not accept the teaching. People then were converted and worshipped the Buddha. All their instruments used for killing turned into lotus flowers. Bodhisattva Li-pin also ordered the people to build seven temples, covering the mountain and surrounding valleys with monks' residences and Buddha halls. The temple buildings were completed after thirteen years and 20,000 people renounced the householder's life to become monks and nuns who lived in these temples. After 300 years these people accumulated powerful good karma. The effects of the past evil karma took effect only lightly in their lives and after death they did not go to hell. The creatures who had been harmed by them earlier lived in inferior realms of existence and made an evil vow, saying that they must take revenge on those who had harmed them earlier before those people achieved salvation. They spat fire, burning down the temple buildings that the residents of the mountain built as well as their villages, and killed all the survivors from this fire with a flood. At that time the god of this mountain took the image out of the temple before the temple was destroyed and held it in space. After the temple was destroyed, the mountain god placed the image inside a rock cave and worshipped it there. After a very long period the cave disappeared. As for Liu Sa-he, the man who brought the image back to light by worshiping the mountain, he was the bodhisattva Li-pin in his earlier life. The passage ends by noting that there is another story, not told here, that explains why the head and body were discovered apart from each other. As we noted earlier in commenting on the reference to the Mao-hsien *stupa*, the stories in Tao-hsüan's *Tao-hsün lü-shih kan-t' ung-lu* are of particular interest to us because these stories show that Tao-hsüan was passionately interested in these miracle stories and illustrate how new legends were added to relatively well-known story cycles.

Both in Tao-hsüan's description of the Liang-chou rock image in the *Chi shen-chou san-pao kan-t' ung-lu* and in his newly introduced legendary account of its origin, there is no reference to King Asoka and the legends concerning his *stupa*s and images. As we have seen above in examining the miracle stories Tao-hsüan collected concerning the Asoka *stupa*s and images mentioned in the *Kao-seng chuan* biography, Tao-hsüan was very well informed about the connection between Liu Sa-he and Asoka *stupa*s and miracles. But his *Hsü-kao-seng chuan* biography is written on the basis of materials that hardly mention this connection. Perhaps by the time of Tao-hsüan, the stories about Liu Sa-he/Hui-ta had spread more widely, going beyond the narrower circle of miracle stories associated with the Asoka *stupa*s and images in the South, and they now included new stories that were set in different geographical contexts with little connection to Asoka *stupa*s and images. This new situation may explain the fact that Tao-hsüan's biography consists primarily of stories about images and miracles in Northern China and the Northwestern frontier region that do not mention the Asoka legend.

Tao-hsüan's reference to the circumstances of Hui-ta's death gives his biography a more complete form--earlier accounts in the *Ming hsiang chi* and *Kao-seng chuan* both ended with a note saying that these circumstances were unknown. We must, however, also note that Tao-hsüan's account of Hui-ta's death is itself a story of a minor miracle, describing the splitting of his bones into small fragments that could be threaded together. In the parallel account in the *Chi shen-chou san-pao kan-t' ung-lu,* the miraculous character of Hui-ta's bone fragments is described in greater detail. Tao-hsüan in the *Hsü kao-seng chuan* biography mentions a brief inscription that existed in the temple where Hui-ta's bone fragments were kept. This inscription is mentioned right after the account of Hui-ta's death, giving the impression to the reader that it was in fact Hui-ta's *stupa* inscription. And, if the ambiguous phrase "*wen pu chü yi*" ("the text is not detailed") explaining the text of this inscription does not mean that all that was written on the inscription was the quoted line, but rather that the inscription does not mention many of the important details about the life of Hui-ta well-known to Tao-hsüan, the account of Hui-ta's death in Tao-hsüan's *Hsü kao-seng chuan* biography and the paralleling passage in the *Chi shen-chou san-pao kan-t'ung-lu* may have been based on this inscription.

I believe, however, that this inscription was probably not the *stupa* inscription for Hui-ta. The story of Hui-ta's bones told in different ways in the *Hsü kao-seng chuan* biography and the *Chi shen-chou san-pao kan-t'ung-lu* passage reads more like another example of a miracle story associated with a specially venerated image. It explains where the fragments of bones that are found on the hand of the image came from and why they were believed to have supernatural powers. Aside from the fact that the inscription describes Hui-ta very generally as a wandering monk, there is little in this miracle story that compels us to believe that its subject must have been the Liu Sa-he/Hui-ta whose biographical tradition we have been studying. Perhaps the story was another example of the miracle story associated with the widely-known Liu Sa-he, and because the miracle was connected with Liu Sa-he's own relics, the location of the image was said to be the site of Liu Sa-he's death and an inscription possibly in the style of a *stupa* inscription came into being. If this interpretation is correct, then we have here an example in which an essential feature of a biography developed in the form of a miracle story.

The biographies of Hui-ta are of particular interest to us since a good deal of parallel material happens to have been preserved in miracle story collections and other sources.[158] Tao-hsüan appears to have been keenly interested in this figure and the miracle stories associated with him, and perhaps a good part of the surviving materials was first collected by him. At any rate, the existing parallel materials enable us to trace how a biographical tradition developed along with local traditions of miracle stories and how the two types of traditions interacted with each other. The miracle story, now preserved in the fullest form in the *Ming hsiang chi*, lies behind the *Kao-seng chuan* biography. Tao-hsüan clearly knows and depends on the miracle stories about Asoka *stupas* and images in the *Kao-seng chuan* biography in his own discussion of the same *stupas* and images in his miracle story collection, *Chi shen-chou san-pao kan-t'ung-lu*. Tao-hsüan's treatment in this miracle story collection as well as other parallel sources indicates that the stories of miracles associated with these *stupas* and images developed as local traditions at their respective sites. Finally, in Tao-hsüan's *Hsü kao-seng chuan* biography, we saw how other miracle stories from entirely different regions were incorporated into the tradition of Hui-ta's biography. We also saw in connection with the Asoka *stupas* in the Ch'ang-kan-ssu temple and the Mao-hsien district as well as the rock image in the Liang-chou region how Tao-hsüan himself attempted to introduce new legends through an account of his own miraculous experiences.

Two rather different types of miracle stories appear to have contributed to the development of the biographical tradition of Liu Sa-he/Hui-ta. As we have noted earlier, the *Ming hsiang chi* story belongs to a recognizable type of medieval Chinese *karma* story. The miracle stories that constitute the substance of both the *Kao-seng chuan* and the *Hsü kao-seng chuan* on the other hand were stories about specific objects, *stupas* and images. These stories enhance the sanctity of the object in question by explaining its ancient and extraordinary origin and also by recording the miracles that occurred around the object in the past. The most natural context for the development and preservation of these stories would have been the actual sites of these objects. Unlike the *karma* stories, these stories about specific objects do not teach any specific religious doctrine. At the present moment I am not prepared to enter into the difficult question of the relationship between these two different types of miracle stories as sources of Chinese Buddhist biographies. Perhaps the references to ghosts and hell in the *karma* story have some symbolic connection to the fact that the Asoka *stupas* and images that are the centerpiece of that other group of miracle stories were said to have been made by this king miraculously in one day and one night using supernatural beings (*kuei shen*: "ghosts and gods"). It may be significant that in the case of Liu Sa-he/Hui-ta's biography, the oldest existing material is a *karma* story, and with its broader range the other type of miracle stories appears to have developed later.

Hui-ta's biographies raise many as yet unanswerable questions. If a fictitious biography of this monk developed in connection with one sentence describing Avalokitesvara's instruction in the miracle story, as our analysis seems to suggest, was this process a unique development? Where did this sentence in the *karma* story come from? Was the story of Asoka *stupas* and images well-known in South China before the stories about Liu Sa-he/Hui-ta developed? Or did the story about Liu Sa-he/Hui-ta develop initially as an aspect of the Asoka *stupa* and image legends? What are the broader social and cultural developments that lie behind the expanding geography of Liu Sa-he/Hui-ta's biography? Hui-ta is described as a wandering monk ("pilgrim"?). Can this analysis of Liu Sa-he/Hui-ta's biography throw any light on the stories and biographies of other wandering monks?

The analysis of two concrete examples of Yüan-kuei and Hui-ta indicates that though the form of monk's biographies may have been determined by the form of *stupa* inscriptions, these biographies often developed over time by incorporating miracle stories. In the case of Yüan-kuei the appeal of miracle stories was such that compiler of his standard biography chose to base his biographies on miracle story inscriptions rather than on *stupa* inscriptions. We may note further that the miracle story in question here belongs to a now familiar type: a story of a miracle associated with a specific object and location. In the other case of Hui-ta, a miracle story teaching the lesson of karmic retributions provided the framework around which miracle stories of a different type, stories about specific objects such as *stupas* and images, could be collected to constitute a biography. Furthermore, we also noted in this case that the miracle stories and biographies developed side by side over a long period of time and that each of these developing traditions drew freely from the other. Perhaps the two examples examined here constitute rather exceptional cases. But it would probably be safe to assume that miracle stories affected the development of biographies in a similar, but less extreme manner in a very large number of cases. Miracle stories were an important dynamic force in the development of Chinese Buddhist biographies.

7. Concluding remarks

The discussion in this paper began with an observation concerning the richness of Chinese biographies of Buddhist monks. I suggested that a study of sources for these biographies might contribute to the discussion of the reason why Chinese Buddhism produced this large body of biographical literature. As a modest contribution to this discussion I examined in this paper two examples of these sources. I indicated that the well- established Chinese convention of erecting tomb inscriptions appears to have stimulated the production of *stupa* inscriptions and that this material constituted one, and perhaps the most important, source for the compilation of biographies of Buddhist monks. I have also shown that *stupa* inscriptions could not have been the only source of these biographies, and in examining one other important source, miracle stories, I called attention to the fact that miracle stories may have constituted an important dynamic force in the development of Chinese Buddhist biographies. It may be appropriate to conclude this discussion by calling attention again to the tentative character of my discussion. I am interested in certain general characteristics of Chinese Buddhist biographies. I have proposed a number of hypothetical generalizations, and I must stress the speculative nature of these generalizations. I believe, nevertheless, that an enterprise of this nature is necessary. Specific studies of individual biographies that have been done to date need to be interpreted and evaluated within a broader framework which treats the study of monks' biographies as a distinctive form of Chinese religious literature and an important religious phenomenon in its own right. I will conclude my preliminary discussion by mentioning a few possible directions of further investigation.

At different points in my discussion of *stupa* inscriptions as an important source of Chinese Buddhist biographies I pointed out different directions in which further and more systematic analysis of this material may proceed. The investigation of *stupa* inscriptions should be conducted within a broader context of a discussion of traditional Chinese tomb inscriptions in general. It also requires a fuller exposition and analysis of the nature of lay Buddhist religiosity among the literate elites of traditional Chinese society. A fuller analysis of the social and political situation of these elites and the content of the *stupa* inscriptions might throw important light on the nature of Chinese Buddhist biographies in general.[159] An analysis of the symbolic dynamics of *stupa* inscriptions, perhaps in the form of a detailed and in-depth study of the often difficult rhetorical passages, may lead to a more substantial analysis of the complex relationship between the basic orientation of *stupa* inscriptions and that of biographical collections compiled by monks.[160]

The analysis in this paper points to the importance of miracle stories as a dynamic force in the development of Chinese Buddhist biographies. This analysis needs to be supplemented by a fuller discussion of the nature of Chinese Buddhist miracle stories. We need to investigate, for example, how these stories developed, and how they were recorded and disseminated--perhaps these miracles were preserved in relation to specific locations where stone inscriptions were later established. The analysis of miracle stories thus may have to be based on an examination of temple records and other sources on local legends.

The relationship between biographies and miracle stories needs to be examined in greater detail using extensive biographical materials that developed around a large number of important Buddhist figures.[161] Our analysis indicated that the historical segment of *stupa* inscriptions tended to be copied with only minor revision into biographies in standard collections. Typical information recorded in *stupa* inscriptions may have been a rather static element in the biographical tradition. This hypothesis again needs to be examined in more detail using examples of multiple biographies on the same subjects.[162]

Appendix I

A.Existing inscriptions and similar materials on which the *Sung kao-seng chuan* biographies are directly based:

1. Tao-yin (T. Vol. 50, p. 716c)

Li Yen, *Yi-chou to-pao-ssu tao-yin fa-shih pei-wen ping hsü*(CTW, *chüan* 201).

The inscription mentioned in the biography. Category: *pei wen.*

2. Shan-wu-wei (714b)

Li Hua, *Tung-tu sheng-shan-ssu wu-wei san-tsang pei* (*chüan* 319).

The inscription not mentioned in the biography. Category: *pei.*

3. Hui-jih (Chen Fa-shih, 890c)

Wang Sui, Ta-t' ang k' uei-chi chün yüyao hsien ( ) ssu chu chen-fa-shih hsing-yeh tsan ping hsü (chüan 363).

The inscription mentioned in the biography. Category: *tsan ping hsü.*

4. Fa-ch'in (764b)

Li Chi-fu, *Hang-chou ching-shan-ssu ta-chüeh ch' an-shih pei-ming (chüan* 512).

The inscription mentioned in the biography. Category: *pei-ming.*

5. Shang-heng (806c)

Po Chü-yi, *T' ang fu-chou ching-yün-ssu ku lüta-te shang- hung he-shang shih-t' a pei-ming ping hsü (chüan* 678).

The inscription mentioned in the biography. Category: *shih-t' a pei-ming ping hsü.*

6. Shen-ts'ou (807ab)

Po Chü-yi, *T'ang chiang-chou hsing-kuo-ssu lü-ta-te ts'ou-kung t'a chieh-ming ping hsü* chüan 678).

The inscription mentioned in the biography. Category: *t'a pei-ming ping hsü*

7. Ta-kuang (866abc)

Li Shen, *Mo-chao ch'ih-ching ta-te shen-yi pei-ming (chüan* 694).

The inscription is mentioned in the biography. Category: *pei-ming.*

8. Ch'i-a (776b)

Lu Chien-ch'iu, *Hang-chou yen-kuan-hsien hai-ch'ang-yüan ch'an-men ta-shih t'a pei (chüan* 733).

The inscription mentioned in the biography. Category: *t'a pei.*

9. Tsung-mi (741c)

P'ei Hsiu, *Kuei-feng ch'an-shih pei-ming ping hsü(chüan* 743).

The inscription not mentioned in the biography. Category: *pei-ming ping hsü*

10. Tuan-fu (741a)

P'ei Hsiu, *T'ang ku tso-chieh seng-lu nei-kung-feng san-chiao t'an-lun yin-chia ta-te an-kuo-ssu shang-tso szu-tzu fang-p'ao ta-ta fa-shih yüan-mi-t'a pei-ming ping hsü (chüan* 743).

The inscription is mentioned in the biography. Category: *t'a pei ming ping hsü*

11. Tsang-huan (778c)

Ts'ui Ch'i, *Hsin-ching ta-shih pei (chüan* 804).

The inscription mentioned in the biography. Category: *pei.*

12. Yi-ts'un (781c)

Huang T'ao, *Fu-chou hsüh-feng-shan ku chen-chüeh ta-shih pei-ming (chüan* 826).

The inscription not mentioned in the biography. Category: *pei-ming.*

13. Ch'u-chin (864c)

Fei-hsi, *Ch' u-chin ch' an-shih pei (chüan* 916).

The inscription mentioned in the biography. Category: *pei.*

Ref. Ts'en Hsü, *Ta-t' ang ch' ien-fu-ssu to-pao-fo-t' a kang-ying pei-wen (chüan* 379).

14. Tao-kuang (797a)

Ch'ing-hua, *T' ang hang-chou hua-yen-ssu ta-lü-shih t' a ming ping hsü(chüan* 917).

The inscription not mentioned in the biography. Category: *t' a ming ping hsü.*

15. Shen-wu (814a)

Ch'ing-hua, *T' ang shih-yi-shan ku ta-ch' an-shih t' a ming ping hsü (chüan* 917).

The inscription not mentioned in the biography. Category: *t' a ming ping hsü.*

16. Ch'i-han (799c)

Ch'ing-hua, *T' ang su-chou tung-wu ch' iu-ssu lüshih t' a ming ping hsü(chüan* 918).

The inscription not mentioned in the biography. Category*: t' a ming ping hsü*

17. Fa-shen (736a)

Ch'ing-hua, *T' ang hang-chou ling-yin-shan t' ien-ch' u-ssu ta-te shen fa-shih t' a ming ping hsü(chüan* 918).

The inscription mentioned in the biography. Category: *t' a ming ping hsü*

18. Pien-hsiu (800c)

Ch'ing-hua, *T'ang su-chou k'ai-yüan-ssu lü he-shang fen-ming ping hsü (chüan* 918).

The inscription mentioned in the biography. Category: *fen-ming ping hsü.*

19. Tao-tsun (879a)

Ch'ing-hua, *Su-chou chih-yen-shan pao-yen-ssu ta-he-shang pei (chüan* 918).

The inscription not mentioned in the biography. Category: *pei.*

20. Shen-hao (802c)

Ch'ing-hua, *T'ang tung-t'ing-shan fu-yüan-ssu lü he-shang fen t'a ming ping hsü(chüan* 918).

The inscription not mentioned in the biography. Category: *fen t'a ming ping hsü.*

21. Chen-shu (770b)

Chih-hsien, *Yang-ch'i-shan chen-shu ta-shih pei ming (chüan* 919).

The inscription mentioned in the biography. Category: *pei-ming.*

B. Inscriptions about buildings:

1. Hsüan-yen (795a)

Wan Ch'i-ju, *Fa hua ssu chieh t'an yüan pei (chüan,* 335).

The inscription mentioned in the biography. Category: *pei* for a building.

2. Wei-k'uan (768ab)

Po Chü-yi, *Hsi-ching hsing-shan-ssu ch'uan-fa-t'ang pei-ming (chüan* 678).

The inscription not mentioned in the biography. Category: *pei-ming* for a building.

3. Yüan-kuei (828b)

Hsü Ch'ou, *Sung-yüeh kuei ch'an-shih ying t'ang-chi (chüan* 790).

The inscription mentioned in the biography. Category: *ying t'ang chi*, a record for a building. May not have been an inscription.

C.A biography in a similar style but not an inscription:

1. Chiao-jan (891c)

Fu-lin, *T'ang hu-chou chu-shan chiao-jan chuan (chüan* 919).

This source not mentioned in the biography. Category: *chuan*. This biography comes from the collected works of Ch'ing-hua (*Chiao jan chi)* and most probably not an inscription.

Appendix II

Parallels between the *Kao-seng chuan* and miracle story collections:

TRANSLATORS SECTION:

She-mo-t'eng

Kao-seng chuan (KSC): 322c-323a
Ming hsiang chi (MHC): 375/565 *(Fa yüan chu lin* [FYCL]:12, 379b)

Relationship between the KSC and the MHC unclear.

Chu Fa-lan

KSC: 323a
Yu ming lu (YML): 277/433f.

The KSC parallel is found in 323a19-23.

An Ch'ing (Shih-kao)

KSC: 323a-324b
YML: 274/430f. *(T'ai p'ing kuang chi* [TPKC]: 295)

The KSC biography is based on the *Ch'u san-tsang chi chi* [CSTCC] biography in T. Vol. 55, p. 95abc. The YML story parallels CSTCC: 95a28-c15;KSC: 323b14-323c29.

K'ang Seng-hui

KSC: 325a-326b
Hsüan yen chi: 367/554-6

The KSC biography is based on the CSTCC biography in 96a-97a. The *Hsüan yen chi* stories parallel KSC: 325b14-c5; 326a17; CSTCC: 96b13-29; c21-a9.

Chu T'an-mo-lo-ch'a (Chu Fa-hu) (III)

KSC: 326c-327a
MHC: /576f.(FYCL: 63, 764c-765a)

The MHC fragment forms a part of the story about Yü Fa-lan. The KSC biography parallels the account of the fragment closely, 326c16-22. The KSC biography is based on the CSTCC biography in 97c-98b. Not marked in Makita's list.

T'an Wu-chieh (III)
KSC: 338b-339c
MHC: 424/614 (FYCL: 65, 786a)

The KSC biography is based on CSTCC biography, 113c-114a.

Ch'iu-na-pa-mo (Gunavarman, III)
KSC: 340a-342b
MHC: 416/606f.(FYCL: 42, 616c-617a)

The outline of the KSC biography is based on the CSTCC biography, 104abc.

EXEGETES:

Chu Shih-hsing (II)
KSC: 346ab
MHC: 376/566(FYCL: 28, 491ab)

The KSC biography based on the CSTCC biography, 97ab.

K'ang Fa-lang (II)
KSC: 347ab
MHC: 385/575 (FYCL: 96, 988a)

Chih Tao-lin (III)
KSC: 348b-349c
MHC: 402/592 (FYCL: 72, 833c)

Yü Fa-lan (II)
KSC: 349c-350a
MHC: (384?)/576f.(FYCL: 63, 764c-765a)

Mismarked in Makita's list? Makita's list gives the page number 384 for MHC for Yü Fa-k'ai that appears in the next line. There is no material on Yü Fa-k'ai in the existing MHC fragments.

Ref., *T'ai-p'ing kuang chi, chüan* 87.

Just a reference to the monk in another place in the MHC, 574 (FYCL: 28, 492a).

Chu Fa-yi (II)

KSC: 350c-351a

MHC: FYCL: 17, 409 (398/588f.)

KSYYYC: 18 (no. 7)

The *Ming-seng chuan* biography is in *Meisodensho*, 7B. The FYCL, 988b, gives a quote from the "*Shu yi chi*". Lu Hsün tentatively reconstructed the MHC story from the two FYCL passages. Makita identified the second FYCL quote in the *Kuang-shih-yin ying-yen chi*, p. 18 and showed that the reference to the *Shu yi chi* in the FYCL and later in the *T'ai p'ing kuang chi* that accompany this quote was in fact a mistake. This may indicate that the passage in the FYCL, *chüan* 17, reproduces the MHC story as the attribution there indicates.

Chu Seng-lang (II)

KSC: 354b

MHC: 402/592f.(FYCL: 19, 428bc)

Mismarked in Makita's list which gives the page number 402 for Chu Fa-t'ai that appears in the next line; there is no material on Chu Fa-t'ai in the MHC.

Hui-yüan (III)

KSC: 357c-361b

MHC: ?/576 (FYCL: 63,764c)

The parallel passage is found in KSC 358a23-28. This parallel is not marked in Makita's list.

Fa-an (I)

KSC: 362bc

MHC: 412/602 (FYCL: 19, 428c)

Hui-yen (III)
KSC: 367b-368b
MHC: 452/642f.(FYCL: 18,418c)

Hui-yi
KSC: 368c-369a
MHC: 416/611 (FYCL: 83,901a)

No common theme between the KSC biography and the MHC story. The two materials may not be about the same monk. Makita's page number does not seem to match the location of the reference to the Hui-yi in the *Lu Hsün ch' üan chi* version (possibly a typographical mistake?).

Seng-pao
KSC: 369bc
HKSYYYC: 39 (no. 31)

Seng-han
KSC: 370bc
MHC:428/617f. (FYCL: 6,314bc)

No common theme between the KSC biography and the MHC story. The two materials may not be about the same monk.

Tao-wang
KSC: 371c-372a
HKSYYYC: 48f. (no. 53)

The *Ming-seng chuan* biography is preserved in the *Meisodensho*, 11B.

Tao-wen (III)
KSC: 372b-373a
MHC: 443/633f. (FYCL: 17, 408c)

MIRACLE WORKERS SECTION:

Fo-t'u-teng
KSC: 383b-387a
YML: 378 *(T' ai p' ing yü lan*, 370)

Only a loose parallel between one passage in the KSC (384b12) and the YML material. The KSC sentence (384b12) paralleling the YML story is only a passing remark in a longer story that describes the same incident in a very different manner.

Shan Tao-k'ai (II)
KSC: 387bc
MHC: 415/605 (FYCL: 27, 485a)

Chu Fo-tiao (I)
KSC: 387c-388a
MHC: 383/573f.(FYCL: 28, 491c-492a)

Shih-yü (II)
KSC: 388abc
MHC: 381/571f.(FYCL: 28,491bc)

Chien-t'uo-le (I)
KSC: 388c-389a
MHC: 384/574 (FYCL: 28,492a)

SELF-IMMOLATORS SECTION:

Seng-ch'un (I)
KSC: 404a
MHC: 381/571 (FYCL: 63, 764c)

Seng-yü (I)
KSC: 405ab
MHC: 434/624 (FYCL: 63, 770ab)

RECITERS OF SCRIPTURES SECTION:

Fa-hsiang (I)
KSC: 406c
MHC: 403/593 (FYCL: 19, 428c)

C'u Fa-ch'un (II)
KSC: 406c
MHC: 409/599 (FYCL: 17, 409c)
KSYYYC: 29
The *Ming-seng chuan* biography in *Meisodensho*, 12A.

Tao-chiung (II)
KSC: 407ab
MHC: 425/615 (FYCL: 17, 408c-409a);
437/627f.(FYCL: 65, 784c-785a)
HKSYYYC: 28 (no. 6); 52 (no.60)

The entry on this monk appears twice in the MHC fragments preserved in the FYCL. The first entry in *chüan* 17 is not found in the Taisho edition of the FYCL.

Hui-ch'ing (II)
KSC: 407b
MHC: /622 (FYCL: 65, 785c-786a)

Not marked in Makita's list.
The *Ming-seng chuan* biography in *Meisodensho*, 12A.

Hui-chin(I)
KSC: 407c-408a
MHC: 456/646f.(FYCL: 95,989ab)

PROMOTERS OF MERITORIOUS WORKS SECTION:

Hui-ta (III)
KSC: 409b-410a
MHC: 406/596-598
(FYCL: 86,919b-920b)

A biography also found in the *Hsü kao-seng chuan* 644c (33).

Seng-hung (II)
KSC: 410c-411a
MHC: 457/647f.
KSYYYC: 35 (no.22)

The MHC story is also found in the *Pien cheng lun* (T. Vol. 52, p. 537c). The *Ming-seng chuan* biography in *Meisodensho*, 13B.

Po Fa-ch'iao
KSC: 413bc
KSYYYC: 14f. (no. 2)

Notes

1. Arthur Wright, commenting on Hui-chiao's use of inscriptions, stated, "We are perhaps safe in assuming that as a general rule, when he mentions the existence of a memorial inscription as a biographical fact, he had access to the data it contained". The quotation is found in p. 427 of the classic study, "Biography and Hagiography: Hui-chiao's Lives of Eminent Monks", *Silver Jubilee Volume of the Jimbun Kagaku Kenkyusyo, Kyoto University*, Kyoto, 1954, p. 383-432. The same assumption may also be made with regard to the later collections.

I would like to take this opportunity to thank Prof. James R. Hightower, Harvard University for reading this paper carefully and giving me many valuable suggestions.

2. Compilers of biographical collections often mention other sources. As we shall show in some detail below, a systematic examination of the biographies themselves also indicates that some biographies could not have come from *stupa* inscriptions.

3. Hui-chiao's preface mentions, for example, temple records *(Yi-pu ssu chi, Ching-shih ssu chi)* and biographical collections associated with certain geographical areas *(Tung-shan seng chuan* and *Lu-shan seng chuan).*

4. In the preface to the first collection of Chinese biographies of Buddhist monks, its compiler Hui-chiao comments on several earlier collections of biographies and briefly describes the types of sources he used in producing his collection. A letter of Hui-chiao's lay friend, Wang Mang-ying, provides further information on sources (the text of the letter is found appended to the Taisho edition of the *Kao-seng chuan* [Vol. 50, p.422bc]; it is also included in Tao-hsüan's *Kuang hung ming chi*, T. Vol. 52, p. 275ab; in both these places the text of Wang Mang-ying's letter is followed by Hui-chiao's reply). One prominent type of source among those that appear there is collections of miracle stories. Arthur Wright in the article mentioned earlier discussed the nature of Hui-chiao's collection by analyzing this preface in detail and supplementing the information given there with evidence from the collected biographies themselves. More recently, Makita Tairyo discussed this collection with a similar emphasis on the examination of earlier collections mentioned by Hui-chiao and the significance of Hui-chiao's classification of biographies (Makita Tairyo, "*Kosoden no seiritsu (jo.)*", *Tohogakuho (Kyoto)*, 44 (1973), pp. 101-125; "*Kodosen no seiritsu (ge)*", *ibid.*, 48(1975), pp. 229-259).

These two detailed studies of the sources of Hui-chiao's collection, however, have very little to say about inscriptional sources, while recognizing that inscriptions were an important category of sources for Hui-chiao's work. Both

Wright and Makita focused their study on determining the distinctive features of Hui-chiao's work. For such a study it suffices to examine the text in its immediate historical context by comparing it with other earlier compilations of biographical materials, without asking where the biographical materials in earlier collections themselves ultimately came from. The investigation in this paper has a broader scope. When we turn to Hui-chiao's work later, we shall be interested in it as an example illustrating a general pattern which compilers of biographical collections followed. Thus, it is important to note that even in Hui-chiao's collection, a large number of biographies mention *stupa* inscriptions, suggesting that these biographies are based on *stupa* inscriptions. If that is the case, the nature of these biographies must have been determined to a large extent by this origin. Even in examining the earlier biographical collections and other sources explicitly mentioned in the preface, we would still need to take into account the possibility that they too may have been based on *stupa* inscriptions, and that the biographies taken from these sources may have been conditioned indirectly by this ultimate origin. On the other hand, some biographies in Hui-chiao's collection appear to have had different origins. Some of the biographies, for example, come from collections of miracle stories. These biographies would then be expected to have a different nature from those that come from *stupa* inscriptions.

5. For a more recent discussion of the date of this work, see Makita Tairyo, "*Kosoden no seiritsu (jo)*", *ibid.*, pp.103-104. Following the observation of Yamanouchi that the generally accepted date 519 refers to the date of the latest material in the collection and not to the date of compilation, Makita dates the completion of the work around 531. Wright gives the date "about 530", *ibid.*, p.400. A French translation of the first three *chüans* of this work containing the biographies of "translators" is found in Robert Shih, *Biographies des moines éminents (kao seng tchouan) de Houei-kiao* (Louvain, 1968).

6. Tao-hsüan actively collected new biographies in the last years of his life and the existing versions of the *Hsü kao-seng chuan* contains a large number of these new biographies. According to Maekawa Takashi, Tao-hsüan had compiled a second collection of biographies of monks, the *Hou-chi kao-seng chuan* by 664, but his disciples incorporated the materials in this second collection in the *Hsü kao-seng chuan* shortly after Tao-hsüan's death. See Maekawa Takashi, "*Dosen no koshu kosoden ni tsuite: zoku ko so den to no kanren*", *Ryukoku shidan*, 46 (1960), pp. 20-37. Yanagida Seizan, also discusses this question briefly in his monumental *Shoki zenshu shisho no kenkyu* (Kyoto, 1967), pp.3-11.

7. The nature of traditional Chinese biographies is discussed in D.C. Twitchett, "Chinese Biographical Writing", in W.G. Beasley and E.G. Pulleyblank, *Historians of China and Japan*, 1961; D.C. Twitchett, "Problems of Chinese Biography" in Arthur F. Wright and Denis Twichett, *Confucian Personalities*, 1962; D.S. Nivenson, "Traditional Chinese Biography", *Journal of Asian Studies*, 21 (1962); P. Olbricht, "Die Biographie in China", *Saeculum* 8 (1957).

8. For details, see, Twichett, "Chinese Biographical Writing", *ibid.*, pp.103-107.

9. In theory the Account of Conduct was an official government document to be prepared by the Department of Merit Assessments (*K'ao-kung-ssu*) for members of the bureaucracy. Twitchett shows how the practice appears to have departed from theory and Accounts of Conduct were produced by family members, disciples, former subordinates, and local officials. Such Accounts of Conduct were prepared even for persons without office and of low status. The Account of Conduct became in effect a more "private" document whose composition was closely connected with the family cult and funerary rites. For details see, Twitchett, *ibid.*, pp. 103-106.

10. The Taisho edition of the *Sung kao-seng chuan* contains Tsan-ning's memorial (*piao*) presented to the court accompanying the newly completed collection and the court's reply indicating that the order to include this collection was given to the Central Buddhist Registry. T. Vol. 50, p. 709ab. The *K'ai-yüan shih-chiao-lu* compiled by Chih-sheng in 730, *chüan* 13, T. Vol. 55, p. 625a mentions the *Kao-seng chuan* and the *Hsü kao-seng chuan*. Here the note on the *Kao-seng chuan* states that the work is mentioned earlier in Fei Ch'ang-fang's *Li-tai san-pao chi* (597) and that it was recently included in the canon *(hsin pien ju tsang)*. The note on the *Hsü kao-seng chuan* similarly mentions that the work was earlier mentioned in Tao-hsüan's *Ta-t'ang nei-tien lu* (664) and that it was recently included in the canon. The *Li-tai san-pao chi* mentions the *Kao-seng chuan* in *chüan* 11 (T. Vol. 49, 100a). The *Ta-t'ang nei-tien lu* mentions both the *Kao-seng chuan* and the *Hsü kao-seng chuan*: the *Kao-seng chuan in chüan* 4 (267a) and *chüan* 10 (331c); the *Hsü kao-seng chuan* in *chüan* 5 (282b) and *chüan* 10 (333a).

11. For a more detailed discussion of the ten categories used by Hui-chiao, see Wright, *ibid*, pp. 390-392, 405-407; Makita, "*Kosoden no seiritsu (ge), ibid*, pp. 230-244. Hui-chiao used the ten categories of (1) *yi ching* (translators), (2) *yi chieh* (exegetes), (3) *shen yi* (miracle workers or theurgists), (4) *hsi ch'an* (meditation masters or meditators), (5) *ming lü* (vinaya masters or disciplinarians), (6) *yi shen* (self-immolators), (7) *sung ching* (reciters of scriptures or

cantors), (8) *hsing fu* (promoters of works of merits), (9) *ching shih* (hymnodist), (10) *ch'ang tao* (sermonists). Tao-hsüan revised this list of categories as follows: (1) *yi ching* (translators), (2) *yi chieh* (exegetes), (3) *hsi ch'an* (meditation masters), (4) *ming lü* (vinaya masters), (5) *hu fa* (protectors of dharma), (6) *kan t'ung* (miracle workers), (7) *yi shen* (self-immolators), (8) *tu sung* (reciters), (9), *hsing fu* (promoters of meritorious works), (10) *tsa-k'e sheng-te p'ien* (miscellaneous sermonists). Tsan-ning used Tao-hsüan's categories without modification. For studies of biographies contained in the category of "self-immolators" and that of "scriptural teachers (ie., hymnodists)" and "reciters", see the two articles by Jan Yün-hua: "Buddhist Self-immolation in Medieval China", *History of Religions*, Vol. 4 (1965), 243-268 and "The Power of Recitation: An Unstudied Aspect of Chinese Buddhism", *Studi Stoirico Religiosi*, Vol. I, no. 2 (1977).

12. Hui-chiao's comment in his preface explaining why he chose to title the work biographies of "eminent" monks rather than "famous" monks may be interpreted as an expression of this basic attitude. Hui-chiao here is criticizing another monk's work, Pao-ch'ang's *Ming seng chuan* ("Biographies of Famous Monks") without mentioning the work itself explicitly. Yet, his criticism appears to express a specifically monastic point of view. The text of this criticism is found in T. Vol. 50, p.419a. For an English translation of this passage, see, Arthur Wright, "Biography and hagiography: Hui-chiao's Lives of Eminent Monks", *ibid.*, p.406. The relationship between Pao-ch'ang's *Ming seng chuan* and Hui-chiao's *Kao seng chuan* is discussed in Wright, *ibid*, 408-412 and Makita, *"Kosoden no seiritsu (jo)"*, pp. 113-115.

13. A few years ago I saw the rubbings of Li Yen's inscription for Tao-yin (no.1 in the list in appendix I), titled *Yi-chou to-pao-ssu tao-yin fa-shih pei-wen ping hsü*, and P'ei Hsiu's inscription on Tuan-fu (no. 10), titled *T'ang ku tso-chieh seng-lu nei-kung-feng san-chiao t'an-lun yin-chia ta-te an-kuo-ssu shang-tso szu-tzu fang-p'ao ta-ta yüan-mi-t'a pei-ming ping hsü*, at the Freer Gallery of Art, Smithsonian Institution, Washington, D.C. Dr. Shen Fu, Curator of Chinese Art of the Freer Gallery kindly informed me that these rubbings were given to the Gallery in 1936 and 37 by The University of Peking and that the original stone stelae are still extant at Pei-lin in Hsi-an. I also saw a rubbing of an interesting inscription by Ts'en Hsü (in the calligraphy of Yen Chen-ch'ing) entitled *Ta-t'ang hsi-ching ch'ien-fu-ssu to-pao-fo-t'a kang-ying pei-wen* (also a part of the gift from The University of Peking). This inscription, dated in the eleventh year of T'ien-pao (753), describes miracles associated with the To-pao *stupa* of the Ch'ien-fu temple in Ch'ang-an and includes a biographical passage on the monk Ch'u-chin. Ch'u-chin's biography (T. Vol. 50, p. 864c) based on Fei-hsi's *stupa* inscription for this monk (no. 12 in our list) is included in Tsan-ning's collection

and mentions the miracles associated with the To-pao *stupa*. Since Ch'u-chin died in the second year of Ch'ien-yüan (759) according to the biography, Ts'en Hsü's miracle inscription was erected in Ch'u-chin's life time. Parallels between the two inscriptions, therefore, suggest that Fei-hsi used Ts'en Hsü's inscription as a source in composing the *stupa* inscription.

14. I have selected biographical inscriptions about monks with titles that end with such terms as *pei, pei-wen, pei-ming, pei-ming ping hsü, tsan ping hsü, t'a, t'a ming, t'a ming ping hsü, fen ming ping hsü, fen t'a ming ping hsü.* These terms at the end of the title indicate clearly that the inscriptions were placed at the sites of the *stupas* of the monks concerned. Ch'en Yüan, *Shih-shih yi-nien lu* (n. d.), gives valuable information on many monks; Kasuga Reichi, *"Zentobun bukkyo kankei senjutsu mokuroku"*, *Nikka bukkyo kenkyukai nenpo* 1 (1936), pp. 20-55 is helpful in identifying the texts of *stupa* inscriptions contained in the *Ch'üan t'ang wen (Collected T'ang Writings* compiled by Tung Kao and other in 1814).

15. The details of these 25 cases are in the list appended below (Appendix I). Tao-hsüan's *Kuang hung ming chi, chüan* 23, preserves the texts of several inscriptions on very early monks, including Seng-chao's inscription for Kumarajiva (264b-265b), Hsieh Ling-yün's inscription on Hui-yüan (T. Vol. 52, p. 267ab; mentioned in Hui-yüan's *Kao-seng chuan* biography, 361b8f.), Hui-lin's inscription for Tao-sheng (265c-266b). Except for a loose parallel in the beginning of Hui-lin's inscription, I found little evidence that the texts of the *Kao-seng chuan* biographies were based directly on these inscriptions. I have not located some of the inscriptions on *Kao-seng chuan* monks mentioned in Ch'en Yüan's work (eg., P'eng Pin's inscription for Buddhabhadra [Ch'en Yüan, *ibid.*, 10] and the Ch'i-hsia-ssu inscription containing information for Fa-tu [*ibid.*, 29f.]). Liu Yü-hsi's inscription for Fa-jung (*Ch'üan t'ang wen, chüan* 606, p. 629f.) has significant parallels in content with the beginning section of the *Hsü kao-seng chuan* biography (603c-605b), but I found little concrete evidence indicating that the biography was in fact based on this inscription. Again there are several relevant inscriptions mentioned in Ch'en Yüan that I have not yet seen, including those for T'an-hsün (*ibid.*, 50), Hui-yüan of Ching-yin-ssu temple (*ibid.*, 50f.), Hsin-hsing (*ibid.*, 62), Seng-yung (*ibid.*, 66). A large number of inscriptions on monks whose biographies are included in the *Sung kao-seng chuan* has survived. Many of these, including some which are explicitly mentioned in the *Sung kao-seng chuan* biographies (which often mentions more than one inscriptions, but seems to have chosen one as its primary source), do not show significant parallels with Tsan-ning's biographies. I have tried to isolate those inscriptions which I can be sure actually did serve as the basis of the corresponding *Sung kao-seng chuan* biographies. My list here remains provisional, though it is useful for the limited purpose of discerning a broad pattern of relationship between the inscriptions and *Sung kao-seng chuan*

broad pattern of relationship between the inscriptions and *Sung kao-seng chuan* biographies.

16. These cases involve biographies of Shan-wu-wei, Tsung-mi, Yi-ts'un, Tao-kuang, Shen-wu, Ch'i-han (which mentions the name Chiao-jan, but not explicitly as the author of the inscription), Tao-tsun, and Shen-hao.

17. I discussed this inscription by a famous T'ang poet Po Chü-yi (772-846) in a paper entitled, "'Structure' and 'Communitas' in Po Chü-yi's tomb inscriptions" to be published in a volume edited by Prof. Hock-Tung Cheu of the National University of Malaysia.

18. This inscription is found in the *Ch'üan t'ang wen, chüan* 790, pp. 8267-8269 in the 1983 Beijing Zhong-hua-shu-ju reprint edition.

19. Fu-lin's biography, reproduced word for word by Tsan-ning, begins by stating that Ch'ing-hua was the tenth generation descendant of the famous poet Hsieh Lin-yün, and mentions that there was a ten *chüan* collection of his writings. Ch'ing-hua obviously had a reputation for being a literary figure and was a typical example of what appears to have been a rather small group of monks who wrote *stupa* inscriptions. We shall return to this topic briefly later in our survey of authors of *stupa* inscriptions mentioned in the three "biographies of eminent monks" collections. Fu-lin's own biography appears as a subsidiary biography (*fu chuan*) attached to Ch'ing-hua's biography in Tsan-ning's collection.

20. See, for example, the beginning lines of the preparatory remark in Tao-yin's inscription. Buddhist themes are introduced at a later point in this preparatory passage.

21. See, for example, the first several lines of Po Chü-yi's inscription on Shang-heng. These lines states that after the death of this monk, his disciples and other admirers, both monks and lay people, came with a text of *hsing chuang* and a large sum of money and requested him to write the inscription for the deceased teacher. He turned down the request twice, but when they returned for the third time, after the stone *stupa* had been completed, he produced the text, and the inscription was erected in the following year.

22. For an example of this elaboration, compare Fa-ch'in's inscription in the *Ch'üan t'ang wen, chüan* 512, with the biography in the Sung collection, *chüan* 9 (764b-765a).

23. This is Arthur Wright's translation of the term. See, Wright, *ibid.*, p. 391.

24. The biographies' descriptions of the circumstances around the erection of the *stupa* inscriptions were in most cases based on the description in the inscriptions themselves.

25. For example, the calligrapher of Hui-yüan's (Ching-yin-ssu) inscription was Yü Shih-chi (491c1); that of Seng-yung's inscription, Ou-yang Hsün (584a23); that of Tao-yin's inscription, Ou-yang T'ung (717b21,22); that of Ling-yu's inscription, Li Shang-yin (777c11: "*t'i-e*"); that of Tsang-huan's inscription, Shao Lang (779a25: "*t'i-e*"); that of Tsang-yi's inscription Wu Ch'ung-yü (780b16); that of Tai-chia's inscription, Yü T'i (834c8); that of Huai-tao's inscription, Ch'u Ch'ang-wen (834c20); that of Ta-kuang's inscription, Yang K'uei (866c4); that of Hui-jih's inscription, Hung Yüan-shen (890c15), and that of Chi-jan's inscription, Liu Yü-hsi (880a19).

26. The review of cases in which Tsan-ning's biographies were based on inscriptions preserved in the *Ch'üan t'ang wen* summarized above indicates that a large part of the biographies which do not mention *stupa* inscriptions explicitly must also have been based on them. It also indicates that in many cases the decision to mention the inscriptions and their authors must have been made rather arbitrarily. The same author, for example Po Chü-yi, was frequently mentioned explicitly, but sometimes not. His inscriptions for Shang-heng (A, 5 in the Appendix I) and Shen-ts'ou (A, 6) are explicitly mentioned in Tsan-ning's biography, but his inscription for Wei-k'uan (B, 2: *Ch'uan fa t'ang pei ming)* is not.

27. The complexity of terminology that appears in the biographies makes it difficult to determine whether the references in some cases are to *stupa* inscriptions or to other kinds of writings. The term *tsan* for example may mean a verse in praise of the monk written at the end of a *stupa* inscription or a verse written without any direct connection with a *stupa*. Here I am assuming that Sun Ch'o's *tsan* mentioned frequently (eg., 326b5ff, 346c25ff., 347b17ff.,350a25ff., 354a12ff., 355a11ff., 357b17ff.) were not from *stupa* inscriptions, and thus I did not count these references as indicating the existence of *stupa* inscriptions. When the term appears in connection with the term *chuan* (biography), I took it as referring to *stupa* inscriptions (eg., 357a7, 370a13, 387c3). I included references to *chuan* mentioned with the name of the author in the numbers of *stupa* inscriptions (eg.,349c7,367a18), but excluded references to *hsiang* ("image") (eg., 316b4, 326c20f., 350a8, 382a21f.). There are also references to inscriptions at places other than a *stupa* (eg., outside of a city gate, 326c23, or at the temple, 382a21, 402c1). I have also excluded these references from the numbers given below, since these inscriptions do not appear

the main entries, and not for supplementary biographies. Where more than one *stupa* inscription was mentioned, I counted each of them separately (eg., 381b20f., 382a19ff., 382b17ff.). Since the references were often unclear as to whether they meant *stupa* inscriptions or some other kinds of writings, the figures given here remain highly tentative. Nevertheless, they are useful in describing a general tendency. I have counted the following instances of references to *stupa* inscriptions. *Kao-seng chuan* (total: 25): exegetes (19); miracle workers (*shen yi*)(1); meditation masters (1); vinaya masters (1); cantors *(sung ching)*(1); promoters of meritorious works (*hsing fu)*(2). *Hsü kao-seng chuan* (total: 69): translators (1); exegetes (41); meditations masters (15); vinaya masters (6); protectors of the teaching (1); miracle workers *(kan t'ung)* (1); reciters of scriptures *(tu-sung)* (1); promoters of meritorious works (2); miscellaneous sermonists *(tsa-k'e sheng-te)*(1). *Sung kao-seng chuan* (total: 112): translators (4); exegetes (11); meditations masters (45); vinaya masters (20); protectors of the teaching (3); miracle workers (11); self-immolators (4); reciters of scriptures (2); promoters of meritorious works (9); miscellaneous sermonists (3).

28. References to authors of inscriptions are, as we noted earlier, often given in a flowery language, and since these inscriptions are for the most part no longer extant, in some cases I had to guess as to the relationship between the names mentioned and the inscriptions they wrote. The figures given below are, therefore, tentative. These figures are nevertheless useful for our purposes here in indicating the general pattern of practice.

29. Liu Hsieh (?-473) wrote inscriptions for Seng-jou (378c27), Seng-yu (402c29), and Ch'ao-pien (408b22). Liu Hsieh's case is rather unusual. According to his biography in the *Liang shu, chüan* 50, Zhung-hua shu-ju edition, p. 710-713, Liu Hsieh lived with the famous monk Seng-yu for over ten years. Toward the end of Liu Hsieh's life he renounced the householder's life, acquiring the monk's name Hui-ti. Liu Hsieh's biography is also found in the *Nan shih, chüan* 72, Zhung-hua shu-ju edition, p. 1781f.

30. Prince Yi of Hsiang-tung wrote inscriptions for Seng-min (463b1,2), Fa-yün (464c26), Chih-tsang (467b12, "*ming*"), Hui-ch'ao (468b19), Seng-fu (550c6). There is also a reference to an inscription by this author in Hui-ch'eng's biography (557b28), but this inscription is said to have been erected inside the palace (*kung nei*) and therefore it was not a tomb inscription.

31. Yü Shih-nan wrote inscriptions for Chih-t'uo (499c1,2), Chih-chü (503b14), Hui-chüeh (516c16,17), and Chu-li (695b24).

32. Li Po-yao wrote inscriptions for Fa-ch'ang (541b23), Seng-yung (584a22), and Hsüan-wan (617b24). I took the expression "*chih pei*" here to mean that he wrote the text of the inscription). Yü Chih-ning wrote inscriptions for T'an-tsang (526a9,10), K'ung-tsang (689c19), and Te-mei (697c1).

33. Ming-tse wrote tomb inscriptions for Hui-tsang (498b28), Ching-hsüan (502b12), and T'an-hsün (559c1,2). Ming-tse's name is also mentioned as the author of the *hsing chuang* in the biography of T'an-ch'ien (574b5). I have interpreted this as a reference to a separate and independent biography of T'an-ch'ien that was written by Ming-tse. The reference to T'an-ch'ien's tomb inscription appears earlier (574a17) ,without naming the author of the text. Fa-hsüan wrote tomb inscriptions for Hui-K'uang (503c17), Hui-lung (515c5), and Kuan-ting (585b10,11). Hsing-yu wrote the tomb inscription for Tao-ch'ien (533c10), and "biographies" for Hai-shun (525c5,6: "*chuan*") and Chih-t'ung (577c20: "*pen chuan*"). The biography for Hai-shun probably was an inscription; the nature of the biography for Chih-t'ung seems less clear, but I have included it in my calculation.

34. Fa-lun wrote tomb inscriptions for Chih-wen (609c28,29) and Fa-ch'eng (701c11: "*mu chih*"). From the contexts I interpreted the "*hsing chuang*" for Ching-sung (501a23) and Chih-nien (509b16,17,18,), written by Tao-chi, as tomb inscriptions and included them in the present calculation.

35. Wang Yün wrote the tomb inscriptions ("*ming chih*") for Fa-yün (464c24) and Hui-yüeh (470a12); Ts'en Wen-pen, for Lo-yün (493b26:"*chih pei*") and Fa-kung (536b1: "*chih hsü*"); Hsiao Chün, for Hui-yin (522b25) and Hsüan-wan (617b23,24: "*chih ming*").

36. Liu K'e wrote tomb inscriptions for Hsi-ch'ien (764a21), Ju-hui (773b14,15), T'ien-jan (773c5,6) and P'u-yüan (775b4,5: no explicit reference to an inscription, but the expression "*chui te sung mei*" appears to indicate that he wrote an inscription); Po Chü-yi wrote tomb inscriptions for Ch'ung-kuei (765c21,22), Shang-heng (806c27), Shen-ts'ou (807b14,15), and Chi-jan (880a18: "*wéi chi*").

37. Ch'ing-hua wrote tomb inscriptions for Shou-chih (798a6), Pien-hsiu (801a14), Shen-hao (803a13) and Hui-ming (876c4,5).

38. Li Yung wrote tomb inscriptions for Hsüan-chüeh (758b14,15), Tao-hsüan (791b13,14,15), and Wen-kang (792b18).

39. Hsüan-t'ai of Nan-yüeh wrote tomb inscriptions for Yüan-chih (776a11,12), Pen-chi (786c2,3), and Ch'üan-huo (856c25,6).

40. Wan Ch'i-ju wrote tomb inscriptions for Tao-liang (757c28: "*ming chi*") and Hsüan-yen (796a11: "*shu sung te pei*"); Lu Chien-ch'iu, for Ling-yu (777c9) and Ch'i-an (777a5: the expression "*chien t'a*" may not mean that he wrote the inscription himself; I have included this case into my calculation nevertheless); Li Hsüan, for Chih-lang (885a13) and Chih-chiang (885c1).

41. Hui-cheng wrote tomb inscriptions for Tao-fu (787b3,4) and Ch'üan-fu (787c12); Tsan-ning, for Te-shao (789b5) and Wang Lo-han (852b8: "*tso pei chi*").

42. It might also mean that inscriptions written by well-known authors had a better chance of survival and eventual inclusion in the "Biographies of Eminent Monks" collections, as we noted earlier. Thus these figures may be interpreted as clues for determining the nature of our collections of the biographies of "eminent monks". They indicate that these well-known and willing writers played an important role in determining the choice of biographies to be included in them.

43. Of the five monks whose names are mentioned more than once as authors of inscriptions in Tao-hsüan's collection, only one, Tao-chi, has a biography (exegete section, 532bc) in the same collection. Neither Tao-hsüan's collection nor Tsan-ning's collection contains any biography of the other four monks. Compilers' comments on some monks who were known as writers of inscriptions are found in 502b (Tao-hsüan [and Hsieh Tao-heng] on Ming-tse) and 721c (Tsan-ning on Ch'ing-hua and Fei-hsi).

44. For example, biographies of Hui-ching ("currently he is 83 years old", 446b22); Hui-hsiu ("At the present time in the 19th year of Chen-kuan, he is 98 years old... and as healthy as ever", 545a12f.); Tao-cho ("Cho is 84 years old this year", 594a29); Tao-liang ("Now in the 19th year of Chen-kuan, he is 77 years old", 619b27); Ming-tao ("In the present year, he is over 60 years old", 624a22); T'an-kuang ("At present in the second year of Lin-te [665], he is preaching and guiding disciples in the Eastern Capital...", 624b8f.); and Fa-ch'ung ("At present in the Lin-te period, he is 79 years old", 666c23f.)

45. As we have noted earlier, compilers often mention a variety of sources other than *stupa* inscriptions. Except for the case of Hui-chiao's preface, this information is found in the biographies themselves. These sources included *pieh chuan* biographies, records of miracles, and local traditions about a temple.

46. These biographies are distributed as follows: 10 biographies in the "translators" section; 4 biographies in the "exegetes" section; 8 biographies in the "miracle workers" section; one biography in the "vinaya masters" section;

one biography in the "self-immolators" section; 3 biographies in the "reciters of scriptures" section; 3 biographies in the "promoters of meritorious works" section.

47. The biographies that explicitly state that it is not known how the subject ended his life are distributed in this collection as follows: 2 biographies in the "translators" section (out of the total of 15 biographies); 3 biographies in the "exegetes" section (161 biographies); 5 biographies in the "meditation masters" section (95 biographies); 3 biographies in the "protectors of the teaching" section (18 biographies); 24 biographies in the "miracle workers" section (118 biographies); one biography in the "self-immolators" section (12 biographies); one biography in the "reciters of scriptures" section (14 biographies); two biographies in the "miscellaneous sermonists" section (12 biographies).

48. The figures for this collection are as follows: 10 biographies stating explicitly that the circumstances of the death of the subject are unknown in the "translators" section (out of the 32 biographies in this section); 7 in the "exegetes" section (72); 4 in "vinaya masters" section (58); one in the "protectors of the teaching" section (18); 16 in the "miracle workers" section (89); 8 in the "reciters of scripture" section (42); 4 in the "promoters of meritorious works" section (50); 3 in the "miscellaneous sermonists" section (45).

49. Tao-hsüan's preface mentions the figure of 340 biographies (T. Vol. 50, p. 425b) as the total number of biographies included in his collection. However, as we noted above, Tao-hsüan continued to add further materials to his collection after its completion and the present work contains a considerably larger number of biographies.

50. Tsan-ning's preface mentions the figure 533 as the total number of biographies in the collection (T. Vol. 50, p. 710a). The figures given at the beginning of each *chüan* corresponding to the number of biographies included in the *chüan* add up to 531.

51. There may have been a more or less distinct *genre* of writing that recorded pilgrims' travels to the West in search of scriptures. Hui-chiao mentions a work by Seng-pao* which contained biographies of pilgrims *(yu fang)* exclusively (418b26), but no further information is available about this work (ref., Wright, *ibid*, 416; Makita, "*Kosoden no seiritsu (jo), ibid*., 106). Yi-ching's *Ta-t'ang hsi-yü ch'iu-fa kao-seng chuan* (T. no. 2066, Vol. 51, pp. 1-12) compiled between 689 and 691 was a collection of 60 biographies of pilgrims. Biographies of translators sometimes take the form of an extended account of their travels to the West (for example, the biography of T'an Wu-chieh which ends with a

comment that it is not known how he ended his life). Some of these biographies may have come from pilgrims' travel stories. Suwa Gijyo, "*Chino narabini hoyu no guho gyoki ni tsuite*", *Otani gakuho*, Vol. 38 (1958), pp. 28-33 examines the biographies of Chih-meng and T'an Wu-chieh (Chinese name Fa-yung) and suggests that their biographies in the *Ch'u san-tsang chi chi* (T. Vol. 55, p. 113 bc and p. 113c-114a) and the *Kao-seng chuan* (T. Vol. 50, p. 343bc and 338b-339a) may have been based on their own records of the travels. Suwa traces the source for Chih-meng's biography to a text written by Chih-meng himself called *Yu wai-kuo chuan* mentioned in the *Ch'u san-tsang chi chi, chüan* 8, p. 60b. The quotation from this work given in this passage in the *Ch'u san-tsang chi chi* (p. 60b14-22) roughly parallels a passage in Chih-meng's biography (*Ch'u san-tsang chi chi, chüan* 15, p. 113c4-10; the *Kao-seng chuan*, p. 343b26-c2). The source for T'an Wu-chieh's biography is identified as the work called *Wai-kuo chuan* mentioned in Fei Ch'ang-fang's *Li-tai san-pao chi, chüan* 10, T. Vol. 49, p. 92c. The note on this title states that T'an Wu-chieh described his experiences in the West in this work and the summary of its content given here matches the content of his biography in the *Ch'u san-tsang chi chi* and the *Kao-seng chuan*. The biography also explicitly states that there existed a separate record of T'an Wu-chieh's travels.

52. One of the two cases of this type listed in the "miscellaneous" section in Tao-hsüan's collection (ie., Tao-chi*'s biography, 701b24) and all the eight cases in the "reciters" section of Tsan-ning's collection centre around miracle stories.

53. *Ch'üan t'ang wen, chüan* 743 (pp. 7694-7695).

54. On the sources mentioned by Wang Man-ying, see Makita, *Kosoden no seiritsu (jo), ibid.*, p. 112.

55. For a discussion of Chinese Buddhist miracle stories, see, Donald E. Gjertson, "The Early Chinese Buddhist Miracle Tale", *Journal of the American Oriental Society*, Vol. 101, No. 3 (July-September, 1981), pp. 287-301. See also Karl S.Y. Kao (ed.), *Classical Chinese Tales of the Supernatural and the Fantastic: Selections from the Third to the Tenth Century*, Bloomington: Indiana University Press, 1985.

56. See the preface to this work preserved in the *Fa-yüan chu-lin, chüan* 14 (T. Vol. 53, p.388c). See also Makita's comment on this work, *ibid.*, p. 108 and note 14 (p.124). Gjertson states, "The date of the collection's compilation is not certain, but tales attributed to is contain internal dates as late as 485, and it is known to have been in circulation before 501", *ibid.*, 293-294.

57. These materials from *Ming hsiang chi, Hsüan yen chi*, and *Yu ming lu* are collected in Lu Hsün's *Ku hsiao-shuo kou-ch'en* (It is now included in the *Lu hsün ch'üan chi*, vol. 8, pp. 129-657, Beijing: 1973). A comprehensive list at the end of Mikita's "*Kosoden no seiritsu (jo)*" *(ibid.*, 115-123) lists the parallels between Hui-chiao's collection and other sources. I am heavily indebted to Makita's work in the discussion here, though where appropriate I supplemented Makita's information with my own findings (commented on in the list given as Appendix II below).

58. These three related collections of Avalokitesvara miracles, were rediscovered in the Seirenin in Kyoto, Japan. The edited text of these works with notes are found in Makita Tairyo, *Kanzenon ogenki no kenkyu*, Kyoto: Heirakusha, 1970. The texts were first discussed in Tsukamoto Zenryu, "*Koitsu rikucho kanzenon ogenki no shutsugen--shin shafu, so furyo, no kosenon ogenki*", *Kyoto jimbungagaku kenkyusho soritsu nijugoshunen kinen ronbunshu*, Kyoto, 1954.

59. The outline and fragments of the contents of this work is preserved in a copy, *Meisodensho*, prepared by a 13th century Japanese monk Sosho, Zukuzokyo, series 2, part 2 Z, case 7, vol. 1 (Taiwan reprint, vol. 134, pp. 1-17B). This copy is discussed in Kasuga Reichi, "*Jodokyo shiryo to shiteno mesodenshijisho, meisoden yobunsho narabini miroku nyorai kano sho daishi sho yin no meisoden ni tsuite*", *Shugakukenkyu*, 12 (1936) 53-118. The *Ming seng chuan* is discussed in Wright, *ibid*, 408-412; Makita, *Kosoden no seiritsu (ge), ibid.*, 113-115, 233-235.

60. Arthur Wright, *ibid.*, 421, dates the work as "between 510 and 518".

61. The preface to Fu Liang's collection states that he wrote down what he remembered of an earlier collection by Hsieh Fu which had been lost during the confusion caused by Sun Yen's rebellion in 399. This suggests that the substance of the stories goes back earlier than 399.

62. Lu Kao's preface states that the *Hsi kuan-shih-yin ying-yen-chi* was completed in the year 501. See Makita, *ibid.*, 26.

63. In some cases one sentence summaries of biograhies in the *Meisodensho* are also relevant. In the case of Yü Fa-lan's biography, the summary is quite different from the stories preserved in the *Ming hsiang chi* and the *Kao-seng chuan*; in another (Hui-chin), the summary is different from the *Ming hsiang chi* and *Kao-seng chuan* versions in one important regard. Wright, *ibid.*, 411, points

out that none of the fragments from the *meisoden* "can be certainly identified as a complete biography from the *Ming-seng chuan*".

64. T. Vol. 53, 988b.

65. For a complex history of this work, see the *Ssu k'u ch'üan shu tsung mu t'i yao, chüan* 142 (Taiwan Shang wu Yin shu kuan ed., p. 2961f.).

66. *T'ai p'ing kuang chi, chüan* 110, Hsin hsing shu chü ed. (Taipei: 1979), p. 766 also attributes the passage to the *Shu yi chi*, perhaps following the *Fa-yüan chu-lin*.

67. Toward the end of the *Fa-yüan chu-lin* passage, there is a statement saying that the six stories starting with that of Chu Ch'ang-shu ending with that of Chu Fa-yi were compiled by Fu Liang. Fu Liang's *Kuang-shih-yin ying-yen-chi* begins with a story about Chu Ch'ang-shu and ends with that of Chu Fa-yi. Though this work contains seven rather than six stories, this reference to Fu Liang's compilation and the close parallel in wording between the *Kuang-shih-yin ying-yen-chi* and the *Fa-yüan chu-lin* passages prove beyond reasonable doubt that the *Fa-yüan chu-lin* passage is based on the *Kuang-shih-yin ying-yen-chi*.

68. These dates are based on the *Kao-seng chuan*. The *Fa-yüan chu-lin* passage attributed to the *Shu yi chi* gives the date of death 382, but this date is not found in the *Kuang-shih-yin ying-yen-chi* passage.

69. 350c22,23.

70. The *Hsi kuan-shih-yin ying-yen-chi* by Lu Kao was completed in 501, makes use of other works such as the *Hsüan-yen-chi* and the *Ming-hsiang-chi* (ref., Makita, *ibid.*, p. 8). Chu Fa-ch'un's story in this collection ends with a statement which says that other stories about storms are also ("*yu*") found in the *Hsüan yen chi* by Prince K'ang of Lin-ch'uan (420-478). This suggests that the story recorded here is based on the *Hsüan yen chi*, a relatively early work from which only a small number of fragments is preserved. If the story in fact comes from the *Hsüan yen chi*, this version may represent its earliest form. The text of the story unfortunately appears to be somewhat corrupt in part and we cannot compare there parts in detail with other versions.

71. The same name of the place where he went to obtain building materials (or "building materials of an old building" [*ku wu ts'ai*] in the *Ming seng chuan*, or simply "an old building" [*ku wu*] in the *Kao-seng chuan*), Lan-shang, appears

in the *Kao seng chuan* (where the order of the two characters are reversed as *shang lan), Ming seng chuan*, and *Ming hsiang chi* versions.

72. In addition to the expression "old house" and the reference to the "ascetic practice" mentioned above, both of the texts describe the time when Chu Fa-ch'un set out into the late as *mu*, ie., "evening".

73. "*ch' uan hsiao*": "the boat was small" referring to the first boat on which Chu Fa-ch'un wanted to cross the lake and "*e*": "suddenly" in describing the manner in which the large boat appeared.

74. This probably refers to the oldest Chinese translation of the scripture, "*Ku wei-mo-chieh ching*", 2 *chüan*-s, by Yen Fo-tiao in the fifth year of Chung-p'ing (188). This work is now lost.

75. The ruler of the Later Ch'in, Yao Hsing died in the first month of this year, and his heir Hung-ssu change the name of the period to Yung-he. Thus, if the date given here is correct, the incident must have happened in the first month of this year, which falls to February and March of the year 416 according to the Western calendar. The 18th year of the Later Ch'in period corresponds to the 12th year of the Yi-hsi period of the Eastern Chin dynasty.

76. Identical with the Avalokitesvara chapter in Chu Fa-hu's *Cheng fa hua ching, chüan* 10, T. Vol. 9, pp. 128f.; Kumarajiva's *Miao fa lien hua ching, chüan* 7, pp. 56-57; the *T' ien p' in fa hua ching* by Jnanagupta and Dharmagupta, *chüan* 7, pp. 191-193. On Avalokitesvara worship during the Six Dynasties period, see Sato Taishun, "*Rikucho jidai no kannon shinko*", *Neiraku*, 13 (1930), pp. 30-45; Kobayashi Taichiro, "*Shinto no kannon*", *Bukkyo geijutsu/ Arts Buddhica*, 10 (1950), pp. 3-46.

77. This date is here restated as the "tenth year of the Yi-hsi period of the Chin dynasty", using the chronology of the Eastern Chin dynasty. This latter date translates into 414 and since the first designation "the 18th year in the Hung-shih period" translates into 416 there appears to be a slight discrepancy between the two dates given here.

78. The last line in the *Ming-seng chuan* biography (13Bb12), differently phrased in the *Hsi kuan-shih-yin ying yen-chi*, is repeated with only minor difference in the *Kao-seng chuan* biography (410b29-411a1).

79. Chu Tan-mo-ch'a's *Kao-seng chuan* biography quotes Chih Tao-lin's verse referring to the miracle. This verse is not mentioned in the *Ch' u san-tsang chi chi;* it is mentioned in a shorter form in the *Ming hsiang chi*, which also describes

the miracle itself in an abbreviated form. This relationship seems to indicate that Hui-chiao, or Pao-ch'ang if the *Kao-seng chuan* biography was copied from the *Ming-seng chuan* biography, had direct access to the *Ming hsiang chi* story as well as to the fuller text of Chih Tao-lin's verse.

80. The *Kao-seng chuan* biography of Gunavarman was translated by Ed. Chavannes: "Gunavarman (369-431 p.C.)", *T'oung-pao* (1904), pp. 193-206.

81. The story is about the origin of the Lung-ch'üan ching-she, the Dragon Spring Temple, which was established by the monk Hui-yüan. When Hui-yüan first came to the south he liked the area and wanted to build a temple. Before he decided on a site he dispatched his disciples to look for a suitable place in a forest or a valley. When they came to the spot of where he later built the Dragon Spring Temple, they stopped and rested. The monks were all thirsty, so Hui-yüan made a vow saying, "If this is the place to build the temple let the supernatural power produce an auspicious spring here". He then dug into the ground with a stick. A pure spring welled up and water accumulated to form a pond. That is why he built the temple building there. Later there was a drought. Hui-yüan led monks and recited the *Lung wang ching* ("The Scripture of Dragon King"; possibly the *Lung wang hsiung ti ching* translated by Chih Ch'ien, T. no. 597, Vol. 15, p. 131.?) and prayed for rain for the sake of the people. When the recitation ended, a creature that looked like a large dragon (or snake according to the *Kao-seng chuan* version) emerged from the spring and went up to the sky. Suddenly, from heaven rain poured down four times. The temple was named Dragon Spring Temple because of this miracle.

82. The summary, found in the appendix to the *Meisodensho*, called *Meisoden setsusho*, p. 15A, HTC, vol. 134, reads as follows: "Hui-yüan struck the ground with his monk's tin staff (*hsi chang*) and clear water flowed. He built a temple building and called it the Dragon Spring Temple". It may be significant that this summary does not include any reference to the second miraculous incident associated with the reciting of the *Lung wang ching* scripture and rising of a dragon to heaven. The name of the temple is given here as "*Lung chung ('many') ching she*". I emended this awkward phrase, assuming that the character "*chung*" resulted from a scribal mistake for the character "*ch'üan*" in the original text.

83. The stories in these sources are told in different words. Thus it is not possible to determine whether Pao-ch'ang/Hui-chiao rephrased the *Ming hsiang chi* version rather freely or the *Kao-seng chuan* version was based on a different parallel account of the two miracles.

84. The list of summaries for the *chüan* 23 of the *Ming-seng chuan* in the *Meisodensho*, 16Ba, includes the following item: "the story about Avalokitesvara answering the requests of beings in this world". This item may at least in part refer to the story of Po Fa-ch'iao.

85. There are numerous examples of such notations in the sources. For a few random examples, see *Fa-yüan chu-lin*, T. Vol. 53, pp.315a11f., 316b9-11, 331a23f.(written origin), 332c18-20; *Hua-yen ching chuan chi*, T. Vol. 51, p. 166b7-9, 167a15-17, 28-29, 177b23f.

86. The comparison of parallel accounts of miracles, often divergent in details, also suggests that rich traditions of miracles associated with certain monks existed in medieval China. These traditions must have given rise to a number of different stories of the same miracles. The divergent accounts found in the preserved fragments probably originated in this way.

87. This finding somewhat contradicts Arthur Wright's suggestions that stories of miracles played only a minor role in Hui-chiao's biography, *ibid.*, 385f. Wright comments, "He (Hui-chiao) was less concerned to awe the simple with accounts of miracles than to persuade the nobles and literati that Buddhism was intellectually respectable and that its clergy had led useful, creative, and well disciplined lives". The difficulty with this analysis lies in the assumption that "the simple" and "the nobles and literati" had two entirely different religiosities. Perhaps, "the nobles and literati" were equally interested in miracles as the "simple", and our analysis suggests that Hui-chiao was fully aware of the interests in miracles on the part of the "nobles and literati". See Peter Brown, *Society and the Holy in Late Antiquity* (London, 1982), pp. 3-21 on the distinction between popular and elite religiosities.

88. This does not mean, however, that miracle stories about monks were all mechanically turned into biographies by compilers of biographical collections. The comparison of the existing fragmentary materials from the *Ming hsiang chi* with the *Kao-seng chuan* biographies reveals that many stories involving monks in the *Ming hsiang chi* were in fact not adopted by Hui-chiao.

89. Our discussion also threw light on the manner in which the miracle stories were transmitted and developed. Thus, for example, Lu Kao's comment on Tao-wang's story called our attention to the fact that these stories were transmitted orally through personal contact before they were written down. Fu Liang's preface mentioning that the original compiler Hsieh Fu sent his collection to Fu Liang's father and Fu Liang's comment in the Chu Fa-yi story about his father's contact with him illustrate how miracle stories, even in their written transmission, depended on personal contacts. The materials reviewed here also illustrate

another significant fact concerning the preservation and transmission of miracle stories, and this is their association with special locations. One obvious example is the miracle story that was incorporated in Hui-yüan's biography, which describes a legend associated with the Dragon Spring Temple on the western side of Mt. Lu-shan. But many of the miracle stories reviewed in analyzing the parallels between the *Kao-seng chuan* biographies and *Ming hsiang chi* miracle stories also specify their geographical setting carefully. To give a few examples to illustrate this point, the location of Seng-lang's temple is said to be known as "Master Lang's valley" at the time of the recording of his miraculous abilities. Chu Fo-tiao's biography describes miraculous events that occurred in the Ch'ang-shan mountain. Seng-ch'un's story about a spring of immortality is precisely set in the Huo-shan mountain. The story of Seng-yü's self-immolation is associated with the Chao-yin temple in the same mountain. Chu Fa-ch'un's experience took place in a lake around a place called Lan-shang. Each of Tao-ch'iung's stories mentions its geographical setting meticulously: these miracles occurred at the Meng-chin crossing over the Yellow River, the stalactite grotto at the Huo-shan mountain, Lo-yang, the Nan-chien residence in the capital, and Kuang-ling. It is probably true that miracle stories often specified the places where the miracles happened as a device to increase their credibility. We have noted earlier that miracle stories often specified the names of the persons to whom the miracles occurred for the same reason, and that this practice explains the close relationship between miracle stories and biographies to some extent. The emphasis on the location may have had a different effect, however; in some cases the stories must have been preserved at the site of the miracle. People must have repeated the story of a miracle most frequently at the site at which it is said to have occurred. Thus, miracle stories must have been best known at these sites and in time inscriptions describing these miracles may have been erected in these places. We shall examine one local miracle inscription from a later period below. In an informal conversation Professor J. R. Hightower called my attention to an "Inscription for the Temple at Lo-ch'ih in Liu-chou" by Han Yü. In this inscription Han Yü describes miracles associated with Liu Tsung-yüan, who was believed to have become a god and for whom a temple was built at Lo-ch'ih in Liu-chou. The story described here, though not Buddhist, may illustrate a general process in which miracle stories associated with a particular figure and a particular place were recorded in a stone inscription. For an English translation and a short discussion of this work, see James R. Hightower, "Han Yü as Humorist", *Harvard Journal of Asiatic Studies*, Vol. 44: No. 1 (June, 1984), pp.24-27.

90. The *Ming-seng chuan* biography of Seng-hung ends with a statement that the subject "gave up his life" (*she-ming*). Hui-chiao, who, as we have shown above, based his biography of Seng-hung on the *Ming-seng chuan* biography,

rephrased this statement and ended his biography by saying that Seng-hung died of ascetic practices.

91. The example of Tao-chiung's biography examined above where the *Kao-seng chuan* biography omits information on the year in which the miracle occurred and gives one date at the end, most probably as a substitute for the missing date of the subject's death, may be significant in this context.

92. Hui-chiao did not always explicitly state that the circumstances of the subject's death were unknown even in cases where he did not know. Ref., biographies of She-mo-t'eng (322c-323a), An Ch'ing (Shih-kao) (323a-324b), Chih-lou-chia-ch'en (324b), Wei Chih-nan (326b), An Hui-tse (389b), Pei-tu (390b-392b), Hui-t'ung (393c-394a), Hui-li (410ab), Hui-shou (410b), Seng-hui (410bc), Seng-liang (411a), Seng-hu (412ab), Fa-yüeh (412b-413a).

93. The only exceptions are the fragment on Seng-ch'un (Lu Hsün, *ibid.*, p. 571, and the short fragment from the *T'ai p'ing yü lan, ibid.*, p. 647.

94. See for example the fragments from the *Yu ming lu*, Lu Hsün, *ibid.*, 353-436.

95. How sensitive was the tradition to this distinction? I have touched on this question in an earlier study of the miracles that appeared in connection with Jen-shou relic *stupas*. On three occasions during the Jen-shou era (601-604), the Emperor Wen of the Sui dynasty distributed relics throughout the empire and built relic *stupas* (*she li t'a*; not to be confused with the use of the term *stupa* simply in the sense of a monk's tomb as it is in the expression *t'a ming*, or "*stupa* inscription" above) in each district to which relics were brought. The building of these *stupas* and the installation of the relics were accompanied by a variety of miracles. These miracles were reported to the government and records of these miracles associated with at least the two earlier occasions of the distribution of relics were eventually compiled and submitted to the court. Thus, the miracles on the first occasion of relic *stupa* building [601] are recorded in the *She-li kan-ying chi* (Records of the Relic Miracles) by Wang Shao, the Sui court historian. This work was probably presented to the court during the Jen-shou era (601-604). The miracles on the second occasion, in the second year of Jen-shou (602), are recorded in the *Ch'ing she-li kan-ying piao* (Memorials Celebrating the Relic Miracles) by An-te-wang [Yang] Hsiung of Sui and other officials. This work appears to have been presented sometime between the second year of Jen-shou (602) and the fifth year of Ta-yeh [609]. Both of these texts are now preserved in the *Kuang hung ming chi* (dated 664), T. Vol. 52, pp. 213-221. Two other summaries of miracles, in a large part corresponding in content to these official records by Wang Shao and Yang Hsiung, are found in Tao-hsüan's *Chi shen-chou san pao kan t'ung lu* (dated 665), T. Vol. 52, pp. 411-412 and Tao-

shih's *Fa-yüan chu-lin* (completed 668 after ten years of preparation), *chüan* 40, pp. 601-605.

Tao-hsüan's *Hsü kao-seng chuan* (Further Biographies of Eminent Monks, completed in 645 according to Tao-hsüan's preface but containing additional materials that may be as late as 667, the year of Tao-hsüan's death), on the other hand, contains numerous biographies of monks who took the relics to each district by imperial order and experienced these miracles. These biographies are found in the "miracle workers", "exegetes", and "vinaya masters" sections. Most notably, one major part of the "miracle workers" section (*chüan* 26) is devoted to the biographies of these monks. The same miracles are described in these biographies as appear in the official reports, but interestingly the two descriptions often show significant differences. These differences between the descriptions of the same miracles may be interpreted as reflecting the changes that these miracle stories underwent over the period that separated the two types of sources. The descriptions in the two official reports are relatively early (between 601 and 609), while the accounts in the biographies are later. The material in the miracle workers section may come from later additional materials as suggested by one scholar (Yamazaki Hiroshi,"*To no dosen no kantsu ni tsuite*", *Tsukamoto hakushi shoju kinen bukkyoshigaku ronshu*, 1961, p. 896). This would mean that they were collected between 645 and 667. The biographies also often make explicit references to other sources, presumably later than the official memorials presented shortly after the occurrence of miracles. Obviously, miracle stories and biographies are closely related to each other in Chinese Buddhist literature and sometimes miracle stories were preserved and developed in their rewriting in biographies.

Tao-hsüan's treatment of the biographies of the monks chosen to take relics to designated districts appears to throw some light on the question raised above. These monks were mostly learned scholars not known for any supernatural feats of their own. Yet, some of the biographies of the monks who served on the first two occasions of the distribution of relics were gathered together in the section on miracle workers by Tao-hsüan. He obviously thought that these biographies were worthy of collection because of the importance of the Jen-shou *stupa* miracles. Thus, Tao-hsüan, in fact, treated these biographies as miracle stories. On the other hand, a number of biographies in the "exegetes" and "vinaya masters" sections of Tao-hsüan's collection mention that the subjects took relics to designated districts on one or two of the three occasions of the distribution of relics and record the miracles that occurred at that time. In these cases, Tao-hsüan treated the material as biographies of monks known in their own right as great scholars and thinkers. The *stupa* miracle stories in these cases, though given in comparable detail, are less emphasized in the total context of each of these biographies. Thus, essentially similar types of materials were used in two different ways by Tao-hsüan, one as an equivalent of miracle stories and the other as biographies. Tao-hsüan seems to have known how to distinguish between the "biographies" that were no more than miracle stories written in the form of biographies (ie., "miracle workers" biographies centered around Jen-shou relic *stupa* miracles) and the more authentic biographies, which also happened to contain stories of miracles (biographies in other parts of his collection mentioning Jen-shou relic *stupa* miracles as matters of secondary importance). I presented a brief summary of my analysis of the Jen-shou relic *stupa* miracles in an earlier paper ("Miracle stories in Chinese Buddhist Biographies: Three Preparatory Investigations") presented to the Eastern Region meeting of the American Academy of Religion held at McMaster University, spring, 1984 and am currently preparing a more extended treatment of this subject for publication.

96. The text of this inscription, entitled "*Sung yüeh kuei ch'an shih ying t'ang chi* (Record for the Image Hall of the meditation master Kuei of Mt. Sung)" is found in the "Collected T'ang Writings", *chüan* 790).

97. This inscription is found in "Collected T'ang Writings", *chüan* 19.

98. Tsan-ning's biography of Yüan-kuei is found in *chüan* 19 of his collection (828b-829b). *Chüan* 19 contains part two of his collection of "miracle workers'" biographies.

99. The name Liu Sa-he is written slightly differently in many of the sources to be examined below. I have chosen to use the *Kao-seng chuan* version of the name as the standard form of this name in this paper unless the variant forms used in a given source is particularly relevant. I will give the variant forms of the name used in the sources examined in footnotes.

100. The name Liu Sa-he is written in this source as Liu Sa-he*.

101. The name Liu Sa-he is written in this source as Liu Su-he.

102. 409b.

103. The summary of the *Ming-seng chuan* biography of Hui-ta (*chüan* 28) in the *meisoden* (17b17) states: "there were indeed relics under the *stupa* built by King Asoka". This short summary probably refers to the story of the Ch'ang-kan-ssu *stupa*, the first story in the list of four miracle stories that constitute the substance of the *Kao-seng chuan* biography of Hui-ta. Pao-ch'ang's *Ming-seng chuan* biography of Hui-ta may have consisted of this first story, or it may have included all the four stories told in the *Kao-seng chuan* biography. In the latter case Soshu, the Japanese monk who summarized the *Ming-seng chuan* biography, simply ignored the other stories.

104. The biography says, "The details of these activities are found in the *pieh chuan" (kuang yu pieh chuan, chü hsiang sheng chi)*, 644c21. The use of the term *pieh chuan* might indicate that Tao-hsüan had access to a separate and independent biography of Hui-ta that described his experience in a manner similar to the description in the *Ming hsiang chi* story of Hui-ta.

105. The biography says "Details are given in the earlier biography" (*pei ju ch'ien chuan*), 644c24. This probably refers to Hui-chiao's *Kao-seng chuan* biography.

106. For a study of the Asoka *stupas* in India, Central Asia, China, and Japan, see Ishizaki Tatsuzo, "*Aikuoto ni kansuru kenkyu,(ichi, ni)*", *Otanigakuho*, Vol. 9 (1928), pp. 291-318; 731-772.

107. This passage in the *Liang shu, chüan* 54, pp. 790-793, is also reproduced in the *chüan* 68 (*Fu-nan chuan*), pp. 1954-1956 of the *Nan-shih*, the official history of the Sung, Ch'i, Liang, and Ch'en dynasties, compiled by Li Yen-shou of the T'ang period (completed in 659). The *Nan-shih* passage on the Asoka *stupa* in Tan-yang is discussed with special attention to the architectural features of the *stupas* mentioned in Kosugi Kazuo, "*Rikucho jidai no butto niokeru busshari no anchi ni tsuite*", *Toyo gakuho*, Vol. 21 (1933), no. 3, pp. 115-118. Kosugi considers this account as an historically reliable one, and believes that it describes a *stupa* that actually existed. In these sources the name Liu Sa-he is written as Liu Sa-he**.

108. This material in Tao-hsüan's collection is reproduced in the *Fa-yüan chu-lin* (completed in 668), where *stupa* miracles are collected in *chüan* 38 and image miracles in *chüan* 13. The *Fa-yüan chu-lin, chüan* 38 discussion of *stupas* as it is found in the Taisho edition (Vol. 53, 584c-587b) is rather confused: the table of contents given at the beginning does not seem to correspond to the contents of the miracle stories that follow. The corresponding *Chi shen-chou san-pao kan-t'ung-lu* version (404a28-410a21) also begins with a table of contents which is virtually identical with that of the *Fa-yüan chu-lin, chüan* 38 section on *stupa* miracles. Except for the widely diverging final section, the *Chi shen-chou san-pao kan-t'ung-lu* version parallels the *Fa-yüan chu-lin* version word for word for the most part, but it also contains other materials inserted at different points in the main body of the text. In this longer version of the text, the list of stories given in the table of contents corresponds perfectly with the miracle stories told in the main body of the text. Since both the *Fa-yüan chu-lin* and *Chi shen-chou san-pao kan-t'ung-lu* versions of the text are accompanied with a virtually identical table of contents, and this table of content corresponds neatly with the *Chi shen-chou san-pao kan-t'ung-lu* version but not with the *Fa-yüan chu-lin* version, it is probably safe to conclude that the *Fa-yüan chu-lin* (completed 668) version

is an awkwardly abbreviated copy of the corresponding passage in the *Chi shen-chou san-pao kan-t'ung-lu* (compiled 664). The image miracle stories are found in the *Fa-yüan chu-lin, chüan*-s 13 and 14, pp. 383-397. Again the first part of this material roughly parallels the section on image miracles in Tao-hsüan's *Chi san-chou san-pao kan-t'ung-lu*, 413a-423a, and is probably based on this latter work. At the very end of the *Chi shen-chou san-pao kan-t'ung-lu* a comment by Tao-hsüan states that he compiled this work on the 20th day of the 6th month in the summer of the first year of Lin-te (664). Here Tao-hsüan also mentions "the *Fa-yüan chu-lin* recently compiled by the Vinaya master Tao of the Hsi-ming-ssu temple" and refers the reader to this work for materials not included in his collection. Since Tao-hsüan died in 667 and the preface of the *Fa-yüan chu-lin* (269b10f) states explicitly that this work was completed on the 30th day of the third month of the first year of the Ts'ung-chang period (668), Tao-hsüan here must be referring to a nearly final version of the *Fa-yüan chu-lin* that was available to him. There appears to have been a close relationship between Tao-hsüan (596-667) and the compiler of the *Fa-yüan chu-lin*, Tao-shih. Both Tao-hsüán and Tao-shih specialized in the vinaya, and the *Sung kao-seng chuan*'s biography of Tao-shih describes Tao-shih's work as that of assisting and spreading widely the authority of Tao-hsüan (726c16f.). When the Hsi-ming-ssu temple was built in the capital city Ch'ang-an in 658, Tao-hsüan was moved there and appointed as the head monk ("*shang tso*"). Tao-shih was also invited and moved to this same temple. There was a large collection of Buddhist literature in this temple. The *Hsi ming ssu lu* listed in the *Fa-yüan chu-lin, chüan* 100, 1023c may refer to a catalogue, now lost, of works contained in that collection. Tao-hsüan's catalogue of Buddhist works, *Ta-t'ang nei-tien lu*, appears to have been based on the collection at the Hsi-ming-ssu temple (ref., Kamata Shigeo, ed., *Chugoku bukkyoshi jiten*, Tokyo, 1981, p. 238; Mizuno Kogen, *Kyoten: sono seiritsu to tenkai*, Tokyo, 1980, p. 224. The specification of the location of works in the library of canonical works given in the third section of this catalogue by Tao-hsüan, T. Vol. 55, pp. 302b-312c, is based on the Hsi-ming-ssu library). Since the two monks lived in the same temple, they may well have had access to each other's materials, and they may possibly have shared a certain body of common source materials. It is tempting to speculate further that there may have been some important connection between the emphasis on miracle stories in the *Fa-yüan chu-lin* on the one hand and Tao-hsüan's growing interest in miracle stories toward the end of his life. Yamazaki Hiroshi discussed Tao-hsüan's interests in miracles: "*To seimeiji dosenrisshiko*", *Fukui hakushi soju kinen toyobunka ronshu*, 1960, pp. 694-707; "*To no dosen no kantsu nitsuite*", *Tsukamoto hakushi soju kinen bukkyoshigaku ronshu*, pp. 895-906. See also Takao Giken, "*Kantsu setsuwashu to shite mitaru sampokantsuroku*", *Ryukoku shidan*, 26 (1940), pp. 1-12.

109. 434c2-435a9. This material is reproduced in the *Fa-yüan chu-lin, chüan* 31, 516c22-517a29. The name Liu Sa-he is written in these passages as Liu Sa-he**.

110. The autobiographical account of Tao-hsüan's miraculous encounter with gods and the exchanges between them are found in the *Tao-hsüan lü-shih kan-t'ung-lu*, T. no. 2107, a work which is also known as the *Lü hsing kan-t'ung-lu*, T. 1898. The *Fa-yüan chu-lin* contains several long quotations from the account of Tao-hsüan's encounter with gods, but interestingly these quotations are attributed to a work or works with slightly different titles from the existing works mentioned above and the content of these quotations does not always parallel the account in the *Tao-hsüan lü-shih kan-t'ung-lu/Lü hsiang kan-t'ung-chuan.* So far I have identified the following quotations: 353c22-355b18 (no title); 376a25ff.("*Tao-hsüan lü-shih kan-ying-chi*"); 393b17-397b6 (title mentioned for the second half of this long quotation: "*Hsüan-shih kan-t'ung-chi*, 394a2); 560a24-563b29? (no title, but the first line includes the two expressions "*chu-ch'ih*" and "*kan-ying*" that appear frequently in titles given for other quotations); 568a18-24 ("*Tao-hsüan lü-shih kan-t'ung-chi*"); 589b14-591a5 ("*Hsüan-shih chu-ch'ih kan-ying*"); 597c28-598b13 ("*Tao-hsüan lü-shih kan-ying-chi*"); 1008a16-1009a9 ("*Tao-hsüan lü-shih chu-ch'ih kan-ying*"). The complex relationship between the *Fa-yüan chu-lin* quotations and the existing version of the record of this incident suggests that at one time the story about Tao-hsüan's miraculous experience existed in more than one version. The quotations in the *Fa-yüan chu-lin* may represent a relatively early version of this story. The event is said to have taken place in 667 ("in the second month of the second year of the Ch'ien-feng period", 353c26) several months before Tao-hsüan's death in the same year ("the third day of the tenth month of the second year of Ch'ien-feng", *Sung kao-seng chuan* biography of Tao-hsüan, 791a20); the *Fa-yüan chu-lin* according to its preface was completed in 668. I will postpone the detailed discussion of this interesting material to another occasion, and here comment briefly on the case of two quotations closely related to the other *Fa-yüan chu-lin* materials mentioned earlier. The last part of the *Fa-yüan chu-lin* discussion of the *stupa* miracles in *chüan* 38 (589b14-591a5) is a quotation from the record of Tao-hsüan's miraculous experience. The source of this quotation is given as "*Hsüan-shih chu-ch'ih kan-ying*", 589b14. The second half of this quotation parallels roughly the *Tao-hsüan lü-shih kan-t'ung-lu*, 438c19-439a29 and *Lü hsiang kan-t'ung-chuan*, 878c1-879a8. No passage paralleling the first of half of the quotation (589b14-590b10) is found in the *Tao-hsüan lü-shih kan-t'ung-lu/Lü hsiang kan-t'ung-chuan.* The last part of the *Fa-yüan chu-lin, chüan* 13 and 14 section on image miracles (394a-397b) is also based on Tao-hsüan's autobiographical account of his miraculous conversation with supernatural beings. Here the name of the source of this section given as "*Hsüan-shih kan-t'ung-chi*", 394a2. The content of this section roughly corresponds to the *Tao-*

hsüan lü-shih kan-t'ung-lu, 436a9-439c9; *Lü hsiang kan-t'ung-chuan*, 875b1-879b16.

111. 880c16f. The name Liu Sa-he is written here as Liu Sa-he***.

112. The *Ming hsiang chi* fragment on Liu Sa-he/Hui-ta is preserved in the *Fa-yüan chu-lin, chüan* 86 ("repentance section"), pp. 919b20-920b8. It is collected by Lu Hsün, *Ku hsiao-shuo kou-ch'en*, Lu-hsün ch'üan-chi edition, pp.596-598.

113. This instruction is quoted with a summary of Liu Sa-he's temporary death and encounter with Avalokitesvara but without mentioning the source *Ming hsiang chi* in *Shih-shih yao-lan, chüan hsia* (3), 304b compiled by Tao-ch'eng of the Sung dynasty (completed in 1019).

114. The text is found in T. Vol. 52, p. 405b-406a. The name Liu Sa-he is given in the edition used by Taisho collection as Liu Hsieh-he.

115. The *Liang shu* passages gives the impression that the Chien-wen *stupa* mentioned both before and after the story of Hui-ta's discovery of Asoka relics (p. 791, l.1; l. 9) stood at some distance from the site of discovery in the Ch'ang-kan-li village. In the first paragraph giving the background of the Asoka *stupa*, there is no indication that the Chien-wen's *stupa* existed in Ch'ang-kan village. Later, it is explicitly said that the relics discovered by Hui-ta were moved north to the place of the new *stupa* standing to the west of the Chien-wen *stupa*.

116. Written mistakenly as Sun Lin in the Taisho edition, 405b15.

117. This is my interpretation of the somewhat obscure passage "*Chu seng p'o yi ku ch'u erh chü*" (405b16). I have taken the crucial word "*p'o*" to mean "incorrectly".

118. This information is not found among the preserved fragments of the *Ming hsiang chi*.

119. The complete text of the edict is found in Tao-hsüan's collection of historical documents, *Kuang hung ming chi, chüan* 15 (T. Vol. 52, p. 203c).

120. This information is also given in a passage in Tao-hsüan's *Kuang hung-ming chi, chüan* 15 (T. Vol. 52, p. 201c-202a).

121. The story of Asoka's fourth daughter is summarized in Tao-hsüan's *Tao-hsüan lü-shih kan-t'ung-lu*, T. Vol.52, 439b9-22; *Lü hsiang kan-t'ung-chuan*, Vol. 45, 879a16-29. The same passage is quoted in the *Fa-yüan chu-lin, chüan*

14, T. Vol. 53, p. 397a13-27. According to this passage, the fourth daughter of King Asoka was ugly and was always troubled by this fact. She made an image of the Buddha, whose physical features were not like those of the Buddha but rather were like those of herself. After the image was completed she uttered these words which were like a vow: "The Buddha's physical features are superior to and different from those of human beings. How could the Buddha look like me?" The logic of this vow appears to be this. She has made the features of the Buddha look like her own, but it is a given that the Buddha cannot be ugly. Therefore, if the Buddha is to look like her and still be a Buddha, he must make her beautiful. She performed ascetic practices and waited for a long time. Suddenly the Buddha caused a miracle to happen, and her features were transformed. Her father, King Asoka, asked her about this, and she told him about the vow she had made earlier. The passage then states that the images in the Yü-hua temple in Pei-shan, the Ch'ang-sha temple in the Ching-chou region, the image discovered by Kao Li of the capital city of the Yang-chou region (ie., Chien-k'ang) as well as the image in the present day Ch'ung-ching-ssu temple (in the capital city Ch'ang-an) are all (copies of?) this image. Someone wrote an inscription on the decorative halo and base (*kuang fu*). The inscription is written in a foreign language and very few Chinese people can decipher it. King Asoka used this image to cause supernatural beings to realize the truth of the Buddha's teaching. (This last sentence phrased differently in sources is obscure and my translation tentative). The images listed above all have female features. As we shall point out again below, the setting of Tao-hsüan's autobiographical miracle stories in the *Tao-hsüan lü-shih kan-t'ung-lu/Lü hsiang kan-t'ung-chuan* is such that the stories told in the text must have been unknown until they were introduced in this text for the first time. What we see here then is likely to be a process of developing legends concerning the images attributed to Asoka's fourth daughter. See also Vol.52, p. 438a8/ Vol. 53, p. 396a22.

122. The passage is found in the *Liang shu, chüan* 54, pp. 792-793. It is also found in the *Nan shih, chüan* 78, pp. 1956-1957.

123. 414a26-c18. This same passage is also found in the *Fa yüan chu lin, chüan* 13, 383c-384b. The Taisho index volume, volume 30, page 127, gives the term Kao Li mistakenly as a name of a temple. Tao-hsüan's *Kuang hung-ming chi, chüan* 15 (T.Vol. 52, p. 202b) also contains a summary of the story of Kao Li's image. The story of this image is also included in Tao-hsüan's discussion of miraculous images attached to the biography of Seng-ming in the *Hsü kao-seng chuan, chüan* 29, T. Vol. 50, p. 693a28-b21.

124. The treatment of this story in the *Liang shu* where it is told immediately following the two stories associated with Liu Sa-he/ Hui-ta and with a conclud-

ing section commenting on the later renovation of the Ch'ang-kan-ssu may also reflect this local situation.

125. Tao-hsüan's biography of Hui-ts'ui in his *Hsü kao-seng chuan* (507bc) contains a story about a Buddha image that closely parallels the story of Kao Li's Buddha image under examination here. The story reports that this monk took the relics to the Lung-ch'ien tao-chang hall of the Ta-hsing-kuo-ssu temple in the Ching-chou region and later to the Fa-meng-ssu temple in the Chi-chou region as the imperial emissary during the Jen-shou period. The text gives some details about the miraculous events that occurred on these occasions and then tells a story about a Buddha image that existed in the Fa-meng-ssu temple. In the fifth year of the Ta-ming period of the Sung dynasty (461), monk Fa-chün dreamt of an extraordinary golden image and heard the pure voice of the Buddha coming from somewhere off in the distance. He went to the San-ch'ü-chiang river and saw a Buddha image at the deep bottom of the river. The light from the image illuminated the surface of the water . He brought the image out of the river with the help of Governor Chou Chan. The image weighed 1,000 *chin* (about 20 to 60 kg) on a scale but (when it was carried) it was as light as several *liang* (about 70 to 200 g). It was six *ch'ih* and four *ts'un* tall (about 160 cm) and was made of gold- plated copper. Later a halo and a base of a Buddha image were sent from the Ch'ang-sha Commandary to the capital city (of Ch'ien-k'ang?). The Emperor Wen-ti ordered them to be sent to the location of the image, and the halo, the base, and the image fitted each other perfectly. Altogether the height of the image was over nine *ch'ih*. More than ten Sanskrit letters were written below the hem of the Buddha's clothing. People could not decipher them at the beginning. Later a monk from the Western regions read the inscription as saying "The fourth daughter of King Asoka of the state of Chia-wei-lo-wei (Kapilavastu) made this". After reading the inscription, the monk suddenly disappeared.

Later toward the end of the T'ien-chien period of the Liang dynasty (502-519), the image send out light and illumined the room in which it was placed. Emperor Wu requested that the image be brought to the capital, but circumstances prevented this transfer. In the seventh year of Ta-t'ung (541) the body of the image sweated. In that year Liu Ching-hsüan became a rebel and burnt down the Commandary. The fire reached the temple and everything in the temple was burnt down except the Buddha Hall. This "Commandary" mentioned here probably refers to the Lu-ling Commandary which was an old centre established by Sun Ts'e during the Three Kingdoms period (220-280) in the area where the Chi-chou region was established later during the Sui dynasty. According to the *Liang-shu* (Beijing: Chung-hua shu-chü, 1973), *chüan* three, p. 87, a citizen of the An-ch'eng* Commandary, Liu Ching-kung rebelled as a leader of a heretical teaching (*tso-tao*) in the first month of the eighth year of the Ta-t'ung period (542) and attacked Lu-ling, proceeding further toward the Yü-chang Commandary. The name of the rebel leader is given as Liu Ching-kung* in the biography of Chang Wan in the *Liang-shu, chüan* 34, p. 504 and the *Nan shih* (Beijing: Chung-hua shu-chü, 1975), *chüan* 56, p. 1389. See also the *Tz'u-chih t'ung-chien* (Beijing: Chung-hua shu-chü, 1956), *chüan* 158, *liang chi*, 14. The rebellion of "Liu Ching-hsüan" mentioned in the story of the golden image in the Fa-meng-ssu in the *Hsü kao-seng chuan* must refer to the incident mentioned in these secular historical sources.

In the tenth year of the same period (544) the Prince of Hsiang-tung brought the image to Chiang-ling and prayed for good fortune and the image sent forth light. The title Prince of Hsiang-tung here must refer to Hsiao Yi, the seventh son of the Emperor Wu who later ruled as Emperor Yüan during 552-554). In the twelfth year of the same period the image was brought back to the Fa-meng-ssu temple. When it reached the temple the image sent forth light and continued to do so for three days. In the sixth year of the T'ien-chia period of the Ch'en dynasty (565) further decorations were added to the image. Because of many stories of miracles that have been transmitted, the image was copied in many places. Since this appears to be the only other existing example of the story about the golden image made by King Asoka's fourth daughter and since there are some remarkable parallels between the story of Kao Li's image and this story of the Fa-meng-ssu image, it would be appropriate to infer that the two stories must have been somehow directly related with each other. The Fa-meng-ssu image is here said to have been discovered in the year 461. According to the *Kao-seng chuan* the pieces of Kao Li's image had been brought together by 371. I am inclined to believe that the author(s) of the Fa-meng-ssu image story was familiar with the story of Kao Li's image, which by then had become fairly widely known. The records of later incidents associated with this image in the Fa-meng-ssu temple suggests that once this story about the origin of the image was firmly established, further stories of miracles about the image evolved in this location in a manner similar to the case of the later stories associated with Kao Li's image. It may be significant that these later stories were associated with an obviously widely known event and with a very important figure.

126. In the *Chi shen-chou san-pao kan-t'ung lu* text, to be examined below, the Taoist is described as "the follower of the Huang-lao of the Way of the Five Peck of Rice" (413c26; *Fa yüan chu lin* version: 383a1). M. Strickman in "The Mao Shan Revelations: Taoism and Aristocracy", *T'oung Pao*, Vol. LXIII, 1, pp.6-8 describes the relationship between the ecstatic cults of the exorcists *wu* renowned for displays of possession and the Way of Heavenly Masters that arrived after 311 from the North. The relationship between the local medium cult and Heavenly Masters Taoism in this story appears to correspond closely to the relationship described by Strickman.

127. The *Chi shen-chou san-pao kan-t' ung-lu* gives the location as the Hua-li village in the Wu* Commandary.

128. *Fa-yüan chu-lin*, 920a18f.

129. There is also the remote possibility that the reference was interpolated into the existing *Ming hsiang chi* fragment by the compiler of the *Fa yüan chu lin*, who, as we noted, makes this connection explicit in the other reference which parallels a section in Tao-hsüan's collection of miracle stories.

130. A summary of the story of the two stone images also appear in Tao-hsüan's *Kuang hung-ming chi, chüan* 15 (T. Vol. 52, p. 202b).

131. For a brief comment on this collection completed under the Emperor Wen (reign: 581-604) of the Sui dynasty, see Gjertson, *ibid.*, 294. Lu Hsün's collection of the existing fragments from this collection reproduces from the *Fa-yüan chu-lin, chüan* 13 the whole section on the two stone images consisting of the two stories summarized above. I am inclined to believe that not all of this material was based on the *Chih-i chi*. No other independent fragment on these images from the *Ching-i chi* is found in Lu Hsün's collection.

132. The *Fa-yüan chu-lin* generally mentions the sources for materials reproduced in it, while Tao-hsüan's *Chi shen-chou san-pao kan-t' ung-lu* generally does not mention its sources. The reference to the sources in a note embedded in the texts of both the *Fa-yüan chu-lin* and the *Chi shen-chou san-pao kan-t' ung-lu* accounts of the two stone images of the Wu* Commandary thus follows a format that is typical of the *Fa-yüan chu-lin* entries but quite unusual for the *Chi shen-chou san-pao kan-t' ung-lu*. This fact gives rise to the suspicion that in this case, perhaps as an exception, the *Fa-yüan chu-lin* version of the story may have been written first and that Tao-hsüan may have copied this *Fa-yüan chu-lin* version into his miracle collection later. As we noted earlier, the *Fa-yüan chu-lin* entries generally appear to be based on Tao-hsüan's account.

133. An obscure character is used for the place name in the *Kao-seng chuan* account (410a1). But the place is explicitly said to be in K'uai-chi and the comparison with the *Ming hsiang chi* list (920a17f.) and the *Fa-yüan chu-lin/ Chi shen-chou san-pao kan-t' ung-lu* version (584c29, 585a24; 404a28, b12) shows that the character should have been Mao as indicated here.

134. The meaning of the original expression *chin li* here is obscure. Here I tentatively took the implicit object of this verb to be Asoka relics.

135. The name Liu Sa-he is given in the edition adopted for the Taisho collection as Liu Sa-he*. A variant reading from the Sung edition gives the name as Liu Hsieh-he.

136. The name Liu Sa-he in the edition adopted for the Taisho collection is given as Liu Sa-he**, a form identical to that given in the *Chi shen-chou san-pao kan-t'ung lu* version of this story. A variant reading in the Ming edition gives the name as Liu Sa-he***.

137. The story of the Mao-shan *stupa* is also found in a summary form in Tao-hsüan's *Kuang hung-ming chi, chüan* 15 (T. Vol. 52, p. 201b).

138. The original passage is found in the *Liang shu*, p. 792.

139. T. Vol. 52, p. 439a1-12. The name Liu Sa-he is given here as Liu Sa-he**. In the *Lü hsiang kan-t'ung-lu*, the passage is found in 878c11-23, and the name is given as Liu Sa-he***. The *Fa-yüan chu-lin* reproduction of this passage, giving the name as Liu Sa-he**, is found in Vol. 53, p.590b22-c2. This passage also mentions the Ch'ang-kan-ssu *stupa* and explains the meaning of the word "*kan*" in the name of the temple Ch'ang-kan-ssu as the local expression for a hill. There are some differences between the *Tao-hsüan lü-shih kan-t'ung-lu* and *Fa-yüan chu-lin* versions, and the passage is somewhat obscure.

140. T.Vol.50, p. 880c.

141. The meaning of the term *chi hu* is unclear. As we shall see later this reference appears to be based on the story about this group in the story of Liu Sa-he in the *Chi shen-chou san-pao kan-t'ung-lu*, 434c11f.,18 (*Fa-yüan chu-lin, chüan* 31, 517a2,9). I read this as a story of an ordinary Chinese man, with a typical Chinese surname Liu, who had an extraordinary experience of returning from death and who after returning from death went to the community of Chi barbarian's and became a saint among them. Tao-hsüan appears to have read the story differently, if my hypothesis that Tao-hsüan's *Hsü kao-seng chuan* biography is partly based on the *Chi shen-chou san-pao kan-t'ung-lu* story is correct, and concluded that Liu Sa-he was a foreigner. Tao-hsüan did not call Liu Hsieh(Sa)-he a foreigner in other passages where he mentions the name of this monk (see, 404b15 [*Fa-yüan chu-lin*, 585a26], 405b22, 417c7 [387a7], 437c4 [395c17], 439a2 [590b23]). The *Liang shu* story of Hui-ta's discovery of the Asoka *stupa* in Tan-yang also says that Liu Sa-he was a foreigner ("*hu jen*"). The *Ming hsiang chi* and the *Kao-seng chuan* do not say explicitly that Liu Sa-he was a foreigner and appear to take it for granted that he was a Chinese with the Chinese surname Liu.

142. Prince Hsien, whose biography appears in the 12th fascicle of the *Chou shu*, had been given the title of the Duke of Ch'i and later became the *ta-chung-tsai*. In the miracle story version, emperor Wu, presumably of the Northern Chou dynasty (reign: 560-578), is said to have sent him to confirm the miracle.

143. This passage (645a23f.) is obscure. The present tentative summary is proposed in the light of the parallel passage in the miracle story version (T. Vol. 42, p. 417c25f./387a25f.)

144. The author of the *Erh chiao lun* ("A Treatise on Two Teachings" now preserved in Tao-hsüan's *Kuang hung ming chi*, T. Vol. 52, pp. 136-143). His biography is found in the *Hsü kao- seng chuan*, pp. 628a-630b. The exact dates of the birth and death of this monk are unknown, but the biography says that he died "during the (Northern) Chou period (557-581)" (629b24). The *Chugoku bukkyoshi jiten*, ed. by Kamata Shigeo (Tokyo, 1981) infers from this reference that he must have died around the second year of Ta-hsiang (580)(p. 271).

145. In the story of the rock image Fan-he Commandary found in Tao-hsüan's *Shih-chia fang-chih*, 972ab, the sentence in the *Hsü kao-seng chuan* biography referring to Tao-hsüan's travel in the west at the beginning of the Chen-kuan period is mentioned with a phrase "which is located in a temple in Tz'u-chou region" attached to the expression "original shrine" (*pen miao*). T. Vol. 51, p. 972b16.

146. This material is also preserved in the "recluse" ("*ch' ien tun*") section of the *Fa-yüan chu-lin* (*chüan* 31, pp. 516c22-517a29). Whereas the table of contents for the section on miracle-working monks in the *Chi shen-chou san-pao kan-t' ung-lu* refers to the passage in question as "Shih Hui-ta", the table of contents for the recluse section of the *Fa-yüan chu-lin* refers to the passage containing the same material as "the monk Liu Sa-he of the Western Chin". A variant reading recorded in T. Vol. 53, 520a18 attributes this material to the *Liang kao-seng chuan*, that is to Hui-chiao's *Kao-seng chuan*. This attribution is also found in the Ssu-pu-ts'ung-kan edition of the *Fa-yüan chu-lin* (volume 115, *Fa-yüan chu-lin*, no. 3, *chüan*, 41, 486a13). This material, however, is not found in Hui-chiao's work.

147. Though the close relationship between these sources appears to be unmistakable, there are also some significant differences between them. I noted above that while Tao-hsüan calls Liu Su(Sa)-he a foreigner of the Chi group (*chi hu*) himself, the *Chi shen-chou san-pao kan-t' ung-lu* story sees him as a Chinese who went to the Chi group and became a saint there. Other differences between these two sources will be commented upon briefly below.

148. It is also possible that some of the materials in this passage may come from the "*pieh chuan*" (a separate and independent biography) mentioned at the beginning of Tao-hsüan's biography (644c21).

149. *hsiang*, 434c20 (*Fa-yüan chu-lin*, 517a11). This "image" is called "*tu hsiang*" ["drawing"] in Tao-hsüan's biography, 645a27.

150. The meaning of this phrase is somewhat obscure. I took it to mean the saint who achieved Buddhahood and taught among foreigners. The phrase may also mean "Foreign Master Buddha", that is, the foreign saint who achieved the Buddhahood, or "Master Hu Buddha", the master called Hu who has achieved the Buddhahood.

151. The name is written with the character that means compassion in the *Chi shen-chou san-pao kan-t'ung lu* version (434c26) printed in the Taisho volume 52, with a note that the character wisdom is used in Sung, Yüan, and Ming editions. In the Taisho edition of the *Fa-yüan chu-lin*, the character wisdom appears.

152. This autobiographical comment in 434c27,28 is eliminated in the *Fa-yüan chu-lin* version.

153. The reference to Tz'u-chou region in the sentence in Tao-hsüan's *Shih-chia fang-chih* passage on Liu Sa-he, which is virtually identical to the corresponding sentence in the *Hsü kao-seng chuan* biography describing Tao-hsüan's visit to Liu Sa-he's shrine in this trip, and the reference to Tz'u-chou region in the initial sentence of the *Chi shen-chou san-pao kan-t'ung lu* passage specifying the location of Liu Sa-he's shrine indicate that the two passages must refer to the same incident.

154. On the basis of the parallel comment in Tao-hsüan's miracle story about the rock image in Liang-chou, I interpreted this comment as referring to the rock image and not the image called the "Master Liu Buddha", which is the subject mentioned immediately before the comment on Tao-an's inscription.

155. 417c7-26. The name Liu Sa-he is given here as Liu Sa-he*** with a variant reading Liu Sa-he** in the Yüan and Ming editions. This same passage is also found in the *Fa-yüan chu-lin, chüan* 13, p. 387a6-26. Here the edition adopted for the Taisho collection gives the name as Liu Sa-he**, but the variant reading Liu Sa-he*** is found in the Sung, Yüan, and Ming editions. Tao-hsüan's *Kuang hung-ming chi* also contains a passage summarizing the story of the rock image in Liang-chou. T.Vol. 52, p. 202c. In this passage the Taisho edition gives the name as Liu Sa-he with a variant reading Liu Sa-he***. The story of the rock

image in the Fan-he Commandary is also found in another work by Tao-hsüan, *Shih-chia Fang-chih*, which was composed in the year 650. The passage (T. Vol. 51, p. 972abc) parallels the account in the *Hsü kao-seng chuan* and also contains the brief description of Tao-hsüan's death, a reference to an inscription at a temple, and the story of "Master Liu's Buddha" worshipped in Shih-chou, Hsi-chou, Tz'u-chou, Lan-chou, Yen-chou, Tan-chou, Sui-chou, Yin-chou. These items, again given in virtually the same words as in the *Hsü kao-seng chuan* are then followed by a miracle story Sun Ching-te and his image of Avalokitesvara. The name Liu Sa-he is given here as Liu Sa-he**.

156. Both the *Kao-seng chuan* and the *Hsü kao-seng chuan*, as collections of monks' biographies, had an obvious reason to use the monk's name Hui-ta; the miracle story collection *Chi shen-chou san-pao kan-t'ung-lu*, did not have any reason to prefer either the monk's name or the layman's name. The use of the layman's name Liu Sa-he in the miracle story version thus suggests that this version may have preserved the usage of the original Tao-an's inscription more faithfully. The date of Tao-hsüan's trip mentioned in the *Hsü kao-seng chuan* biography is "at the beginning of the Chen-kuan period" (627-649). Since both *Hsü kao-seng chuan* and *Chi shen-chou san-pao kan-t'ung-lu* were written by the same author, Tao-hsüan, who probably collected a copy of Tao-an's inscription during this trip, the dates of the miracle collection (completed in 664) and of the *Hsü kao-seng chuan* (first draft, which may or may not have contained Hui-ta's biography, was produced in 645) are not particularly relevant in the present context.

The miracle story also states at the beginning that Liu Sa-he went to worship the Mao-hsien *stupa* in the area south of the Ch'ang-chiang river and then excavated the relics distributed by King Asoka in Chin-ling (ie., Chien-k'ang/ Tan-yang). The order of Liu Sa-he/Hui-ta's travel is here thus reversed from that of Hui-chiao's account in the *Kao-seng chuan* biography. It may be significant that Tao-hsüan begins his miracle story collection, *Chi shen-chou san-pao kan-t'ung lu*, with the story of the Mao-hsien *stupa* followed immediately by that of the Ch'ang-kan-ssu *stupa*. Another tradition may have existed by Tao-hsüan's time concerning Liu Sa-he's itinerary on his visit to the Asoka *stupas*.

157. 437b13-c5. The name Liu Sa-he is given in this passage as Liu Sa-he**. In the *Lü-hsiang kan-t'ung-chuan*, this passage is found in 876c5-27, using the name Liu Sa-he***. In the *Fa-yüan chu-lin* the same passage is found in 395b26-c19. Taisho edition gives the name as Liu Sa-he** with a variant reading Liu Sa-he***.

158. Tanaka Ryosho, *Tonko zenshu bunken no kenkyu* (Tokyo, 1983) mentions some passages in the Tun-huang manuscripts where references to Liu Sa-he appear (pp. 83, 87, 88, 92, 95, 641). Most notably one text titled *Liu sa-he he-*

shang yin-yüan chi is recorded in three manuscripts, P. 2680, P. 3570, P. 3727. This text is particularly interesting to us: a number of familiar stories about Liu Sa-he are told here but often with major differences in details. Liu Sa-he is described as a man of Ting-yang in Tan-chou. The place name Ting-yang is given in the *Hsü kao-seng chuan* biography as his place of origin, but there the location is described as northeast of Hsien-yang, and the location given here as Tan-chou does not match this description in the *Hsü kao-seng chuan* biography. The story of Liu Sa-he's visit to hell is told here in some detail and several themes in the *Ming hsiang chi* version, such as the reference to the shooting of a deer, exchanges with his uncle, and the instruction of the bodhisattva Kuan-shih-yin, also appear here. But the differences in the stories around these themes, and the presence of other themes which have no parallel in the *Ming hsiang chi* version, indicate that this account must have been based on a different tradition from that of the *Ming hsiang chi*. The account of Liu Sa-he's activities after returning to life also includes a few familiar stories but it also refers to some events that are not mentioned in the earlier sources we have reviewed in this paper. There is a reference to Liu Sa-he's image ("the image of the monk"), but the story is told somewhat differently here: it is said that the image could be lifted by one or two people if they had faith, but could not be lifted by over a hundred if they did not have faith. The section on the rock image in Fan-he mentions Tao-an's inscription and though the story is mentioned only briefly here, the phraseology shows similarity to the corresponding passage in the *Hsü kao-seng chuan* biography and the *Chi shen-chou san-pao kan-t'ung lu* story (417c). The story of Liu Sa-he's death is told in a manner similar to the account in the *Chi shen-chou san-pao kan-t'ung lu* passage on Liu Sa-he (435a), mentioning a *stupa* and the miracle of relics that appear to those who seek them with sincere devotion. The text ends with a reference to Liu Sa-he's prediction about the Mo-kao-k'u caves in Tun-huang. Since the Mo-kao-k'u caves are found near Chiu-ch'üan and the caves contained the library which included these three manuscripts were discovered later, this brief reference appears to suggest that the *Liu sa-he yin-yüan chi* story may represent a local tradition that has been transmitted in some site(s) in this areas particularly closely associated with Liu Sa-he. Finally, it is notable that in this text only the name Liu Sa-he is used, though the name is used explicitly as the name of a monk (*he shang*). The name Hui-ta does not appear at all.

159. In fact the we need to investigate the social and political context of the entire process through which Chinese Buddhist biographies came into being. The example of secular biographies indicates that the writing of biographies and compiling official biographical collections was a highly political act. The composition, development, and preservation of monks' biographies similarly must have reflected specific social and political contexts. A study of this material therefore would not be complete without an adequate discussion of this

relationship. For a very insightful analysis of a biography of monks that takes account of the local social-political context, see Yanagida Seizan's biography of Lin-chi I-hsüan: "The Life of Lin-chi I-hsüan", *Eastern Buddhist*, 5 (Oct., 1972), pp. 70-94.

160. My study of Po Chü-yi's tomb inscriptions mentioned earlier is a modest and limited attempt to place the analysis of *stupa* inscription within a broader framework and examine its symbolic dynamics from the viewpoint proposed here.

161. Albert Welter's paper in this volume analyzes such materials that developed around Yung-ming Yen-shou.

162. After I completed this paper, I learned from my colleague Dr. Jan Yün-hua that Prof. Jao Tsung-yi (Rao Zong-yi) of Hong Kong Chinese University had presented a paper on Liu Sa-he at the International Conference on Dunhuang Grottoes in the fall of 1987. The summary of this paper, entitled "*Liu Sa-he shih-chi yü jui-hsiang t'u*" (English translation: "Liu Sa-ke's Deeds and Portrait of Buddha") is found in *International Conference on Dunhuang Grottoes: Summary ofPapers, 1987* (Dunghuang Research Institute, 1987), pp. 34-37 (Chinese original) and pp. 48-52 (English translation). The summary contains a number of points that are relevant to my discussion; Professor Jao refers to the "East Pagoda Yard" (*tung t'a yüan*) in the "Asoka Guangli Temple" in Ningbo which is said to have been the place where the relic that Liu Sa-he worshipped appeared (*Ningpo-fu chih, chüan* 33)(*ibid.*, pp. 36f., 52); Prof. Jao also comments on the possible relationship between the painting describing Liu Sa-he's miracles in Wu* and Yüeh area in the Tunhuang cave no. 323 and the paintings by Chang Yu, a native of Wu*" mentioned in the *Liang shu* (p.793). I look forward to the publication of a fuller version of Prof. Jao's article.

CHARACTERS

Aikuoto ni kansuru kenkyu (ichi, ni) 阿育王塔に関する研究

An Ch'ing (Shih-kao) 安清(世高)

An Hui-tse 安慧則

An Ch'eng 安程

An-ch'eng* 安成

An-jen-ssu 安仁寺

An-min-ssu 安民寺

An-te-wang [Yang] Hsiung 安德王[楊]雄

A-yü-wang-ssu 阿育王寺

Bukkyo geijutsu 仏教藝術

ch'a 刹

ch'an 禅

ch'ang tao 唱導

Ch'ang-an 長安

Ch'ang-chiang 長江

Ch'ang-kan-li 長干里

Ch'ang-kan-ssu 長干寺

Ch'ang-sha 長沙

Ch'ang-shan 常山

Ch'ao-pien 超辯

Ch'en Wei-fu 陳惟復

Ch'en Yüan 陳垣

Ch'en 陳

Ch'eng-tu 成都

ch'i ssu hsing chiang 起寺行牆

ch'i ssu hsing lu 起寺行爐

Ch'i 齊

Ch'i-an 齊安

Ch'i-han 齊翰

Ch'i-hsia-ssu 棲霞寺

ch'ien chuan 前傳

Ch'ien-feng 乾封

Ch'ien-fu 千福

Ch'ien-yüan 乾元

ch'ih 尺

Ch'in 秦

Ch'ing she-li kan-ying piao 慶舍利感應表

ch'ing 青

Ch'ing-hua 清畫

Ching-t'uo 敬脫

ch'ing* 磬

Ch'iu-na-pa-mo 求那跋摩

Ch'u Ch'ang-wen 褚長文

Ch'u Fa-hu 竺法護

Ch'u Seng-lang 竺僧朗

Ch'u T'an-mo-lo-ch'a 竺曇摩羅刹

Ch'u Fo-tiao 竺佛調

Ch'u Fa-yi 竺法義

Ch'u Fa-lan 竺法蘭

Ch'u Ch'ang-shu 竺長舒

Ch'u Fa-hu 竺法護

Ch'u san-tsang chi chi 出三藏記集

Ch'u Fa-t'ai 竺法汰

Ch'u Fa-ch'un 竺法純

Ch'u-chin 楚金

Ch'u-chin ch'an-shih pei 楚金禪師碑

Ch'üan t'ang wen 全唐文

Ch'uan fa t'ang pei ming 傳法堂碑銘

ch'üan 泉

Ch'üan-fu 全怤

Ch'üan-huo 全豁

Ch'ung-ching-ssu 崇敬寺

Ch'ung-kui 崇珪

Ch'ung-yi 崇義

Chang Yen 張演

Chang Wan 張綰

chang 丈

Chang Yu 張繇

Chang Tao 張道

Chang Hsi-shih 張希世

Chang-hou-ch iao 張候橋

Chao-yin 招隱

Chen Fa-shih 真法師

Chen-kuan 貞觀

Chen-ming 禎明

Chen-shu 甄叔

Cheng fa hua ching 正法華經

Cheng-kuang 正光

Cheng-ying-chi 徵應記

chi hu 稽胡

Chi shen-chou san pao kan t'ung lu 集神州三寶感通錄

Chi 稽

Chi-chou 吉州

Chi-jan 寂然

Chia-wei-lo-wei 迦維羅衛

Chia-yeh 迦葉

Chiang-ling 江陵

Chiang-ning-hsien 江寧縣

Chiao jan chi 皎然集

Chiao-chou 交州

Chiao-jan 皎然

Chien-yeh 建業

chien t'a 建塔

Chien-hsing 建興

Chien-k'ang 建康

Chien-t'uo-le 揵陀勒

Chien-te 建德

Chien-wen 簡文

Chih Ch'ien 支謙

chih ming 制銘

chih pei 製碑

chih hsü 制序

Chih Tao-lin 支道林

Chih-chiang 智江

Chih-chü 智聚

Chih-hsien 至賢

Chih-lang 智朗

Chih-lou-chia-ch'en 支樓迦讖

Chih-meng 智猛

Chih-nien 志念

Chih-p'an 志盤

Chih-sheng 智昇

Chih-t'ung 智通

Chih-t'uo 智脫

Chih-te 至德

Chih-tsang 智藏

Chih-wen 智文

chin 斤

Chin 晉

chin li 覲禮

Chin-ling 金陵

ching shih 經師

Ching 敬

Ching-chou 荊州

Ching-hsüan 靖玄

Ching-i chi 旌異記

Ching-shih ssu chi 京師寺志

Ching-sung 靖嵩

Ching-yin-ssu 淨影寺

Chimo narabini hoyu no guho gyoki ni tsuite 智猛並に法勇の求法行記について

Chiu-ch'üan 酒泉

Chou 周

Chou Chan 周湛

chu 主

Chu seng p'o yi ku ch'u erh chü 諸僧頗依故處而居

Chu Chün-t'ai 朱君台

Chu Shih-hsing 朱士行

Chu-ch'iao 朱雀

chu-ch'ih 住持

Chü-chang 句章

chu-jen 主人

Chu-li 住力

Chu-ying 朱應

chuan 傳

chüan 卷

Chugoku bukkyoshi jiten 中國仏教史辞典

chui te sung mei 追德頌美

chung 衆

Chung-p'ing 中平

Dosen no koshu kosoden ni tsuite: zoku kosoden to no kanren 道宣の後集高僧伝について―續高僧伝との関連

e 俄

e-wen 額文

Erh chiao lun 二教論

Fa hua ssu chieh t'an yüan pei 法華寺戒壇院碑

Fa Hu 法護

Fa-an 法安

Fa-ch'ang 法常

Fa-ch'eng 法稱

Fa-ch'in 法欽

Fa-ch'ung 法沖

Fa-chün 法均

Fa-hsiang 法相

Fa-hua chieh-t'an-yüan pei 法華戒壇院碑

Fa-hua 法華

Fa-jung 法融

Fa-k'ai 法開

Fa-kung 法恭

Fa-lun 法輪

Fa-meng-ssu 發蒙寺

Fa-shen 法詵

Fa-tu 法度

Fa-yüan 法淵

Fa-yüan chu-lin 法苑珠林

Fa-yüeh 法悅

Fa-yün 法雲

Fa-yung 法勇

Fan-he 番禾

Fei Ch'ang-fang 費長房

Fei-hsi 飛錫

fen ming ping hsü 墳銘并序

fen t'a ming ping hsü 墳塔銘并序

Fo tsu t'ung chi 佛祖統記

fo kuang 佛光

Fo-t'u-teng 佛圖澄

Fu Liang 傅亮

Fu-chien 苻堅

Fu-chou hsüeh-feng-shan ku chen-chüeh ta-shih pei-ming 福州雪峯山故真覺大師碑銘

Fu-lin 福琳

Fu-nan chuan 扶南傳

Fukui hakushi soju kinen toyobunka ronshu 福井博士頌壽記念東洋文化論集

Hai-shun 海順

Han Yü 韓愈

Han-k'u 函谷

Hang-chou Ching-shan-ssu ta-chüeh ch'an-shih pei-ming 杭州徑山寺大覺禪師碑銘

ming

Hang-chou yen-kuan-hsien hai-ch'ang-yüan ch'an-men ta-shih t'a ming 杭州鹽官縣海昌院禪門大師塔銘

he shang 和尚

he yüeh 訶曰

He-nan 河南

He-p'u 合浦

Heirakusha 平樂社

Hou Po 侯白

Hou-chi kao-seng chuan 後集高僧傳

Hsi ming ssu lu 西明寺錄

hsi ch'an 習禪

Hsi kuan-shih-yin ying-yen-chi 繫觀世音應驗記

hsi chang 錫杖

Hsi-ch'ien 希遷

Hsi-ching hsing-shan-ssu ch'uan-fa-t'ang pei-ming 西京興善寺傳法堂碑銘

Hsi-chou 隰州

Hsi-he 西河

Hsi-ming-ssu 西明寺

hsiang 像

Hsiang-tung 湘東

Hsiang-yang 襄陽

Hsiao Yi 蕭繹

hsiao ching she 小精舍

Hsiao Chün note 35 34 蕭鈞

Hsiao-ching 孝敬

Hsiao-wu 孝武

Hsiao-yi-hsiang 孝義鄉

Hsieh Tao-heng 薛道衡

Hsieh Ling-yün 謝靈運

Hsieh Fu 謝敷

hsien chü ssu tung ling 閑居寺東林

Hsien-an 咸安

Hsien-chü 閑居

Hsien-chü-ssu 閑居寺

Hsien-he 咸和

Hsien-yang 咸陽

Hsien-yi-ssu 顯義寺

hsin pien ju tsang 新編入藏

Hsin shing shu chü 新興書局

Hsin-ching ta-shih pei 心鏡大師碑

Hsin-hsing 信行

hsing fu 興福

hsing chuang 行狀

Hsing-yu 行友

Hsü kuang-shih-yin ying-yen-chi 續光世音應驗記

Hsü kao-seng chuan 續高僧傳

Hsü Ch'ou 許筹

Hsü-ch'ang page 87 92 許昌

Hsü ch'ang 許昌

Hsüan yen chi 宣驗記

Hsüan-chüeh 玄覚

Hsüan-shih kan-t'ung-chi 宣師感通記

Hsüan-shih chu-ch'ih kan-ying 宣師住持感應

Hsüan-t'ai 玄泰

Hsüan-wan 玄琬

Hsüan-yen 玄儼

hu shih fo 胡師佛

hu fa 護法

Hu 滬

hu jen 胡人

hua t'ai 花臺

Hua-li 華里

Hua-yen ching chuan chi 華嚴經傳記

Huai-tao 懷道

Huang T'ao 黃滔

Huang-lao 黃老

hui 惠

Hui-ch'ao 慧超

Hui-ch'eng 惠成

Hui-ch'ing 慧慶

Hui-chiao 慧皎

Hui-chin 慧進

Hui-ching 慧淨

Hui-chüeh 慧覺

Hui-hsiao 慧曉

Hui-hsiu 慧休

Hui-jih 慧日

Hui-K'uang 慧曠

Hui-li 慧力

Hui-lin 慧琳

Hui-lung 慧隆

Hui-ming 慧明

Hui-shou 慧受

Hui-sui 慧邃

Hui-t'ung 慧通

Hui-ta 慧達

hui-ta 慧達, 惠達

Hui-ts'ui 慧最

Hui-tsang 慧藏

Hui-yen 慧嚴

Hui-yi 慧義

Hui-yin 慧因

Hui-yüan 慧遠

Hung 弘

Hung Yüan-shen 洪元

Hung-shih 弘始

Hung-ssu 泓嗣

Huo-shan 霍山

Ishizaki Tatsuzo 石崎達三

Jao Tsung-yi (Rao Zong-yi) 饒宗頤

Jen-shou 仁寿

Jen-su 仁素

Jih-yen-ssu 日嚴寺

Jodokyo shiryo to shiteno mesodenshijisho meisoyobunsho narabini
浄土教資料としての名僧傳指示抄名僧要文抄並に弥勒如来感應
mirokujyorai kanosho dai shi shoyin no meisoden ni tsuite
抄第四所引の名僧傳について

Ju-hui 如會

Jui-chou 潤州

Jui-hsiang-ssu 瑞像寺

K'ai-huang 開皇

K'ai-yüan 開元

K'ai-yüan shih-chiao-lu 開元釋教錄

k'an ch'i 龕砌

K'ang Fa-lang 康法朗

K'ang 康

K'ang Seng-hui 康僧會

K'ao-kung-ssu 考功司

K'ung-tsang 空藏

Kamata Shigeo 鎌田茂雄

kan t'ung 感通

Kan ying chüan 感應傳

kan 干

Kan-t'ung-ssu 感通寺

kan-ying 感應

Kantsu setsuwashu to shite mitaru sampokantsuroku
感通説話集として見たる三宝感通録

Kanzenon ogenki no kenkyu 觀世音應驗記の研究

Kao Li 高悝

Kao-seng chuan 高僧傳

Kasuga Reichi 春日禮智

Kobayashi Taichiro 小林太市郎

Koitsu rikucho kanzenon ogenki no shutsugen 古逸六朝觀世音應驗記の出現

Kosoden no seiritsu (jo, ge) 高僧傳の成立(上, 下)

Kosugi Kazuo 小杉一雄

Ku wei-mo-chieh ching 古維摩詰經

ku chi 古迹

ku wu ts'ai 故屋材

ku wu 故屋

Ku hsiao-shuo kou-ch'en 古小說鉤沉

Ku Yin-tsu 顧胤祖

kuan piao 關表

Kuan-shih 觀世

Kuan-shih-yin 觀世音

Kuan-shih-yin ching 觀世音經

Kuan-ting 灌頂

kuang yu pieh chuan, chü hsiang sheng chi 廣有別傳具詳聖迹

kuang fu 光趺

Kuang hung ming chi 廣弘明記

Kuang-chai-ssu 光宅寺

Kuang-hsi-yin ying-yen-chi 光世音應驗記

Kuang-ling 廣陵

Kuei 珪

kuei 鬼

kuei shen 鬼神

Kui-feng ch'an-shih pei-ming ping hsü 圭峯禪師碑銘并序

kung nei 宮內

Kyoten: sono seiritsu to tenkai 経典—その成立と展開

Kyoto Jimbungagaku kenkyusho soritsu nijugoshunen kinen ronbun-shu 京都人文科學研究所創立二十五周年紀念論文集

Lan-chou 嵐州

Lan-shang 蘭上

Li 李

Li Chi-fu 李吉甫

Li Shen 李紳

Li Shang-yin 李商隱

Li Yung 李邕

Li Yen-shou 李延壽

Li Po-yao 李百藥

Li Hua 李華

Li Hsüan 李鉉

Li Yen 李儼

Li-pin 利賓

Li-shih 離石

Li-tai san-pao chi 歷代三寶記

Liang note 104 82 梁

Liang shu 梁書

liang 兩

Liang kao-seng chuan 梁高僧傳

Liang-ch'eng 梁城

Liang-chou 涼州

Lin-ch'uan 臨川

Lin-hai 臨海

Lin-te 麟德

Lin-tzu 臨淄

ling t'a 靈塔

Ling-yu 靈祐

Liu Ching-kung 劉敬躬

Liu Su-he 劉窣和

Liu Yü-hsi 劉禹錫

Liu Sa-he*** 劉薩訶

Liu K'e 劉訶

Liu Sa-he** 劉薩何

Liu Sa-he* 劉薩荷

Liu Sa-he 劉薩河

Liu Ching-hsüan 劉敬宣

Liu Tsung-yüan 柳宗元

Liu I-ch'ing 劉義慶

liu shih fo 劉師佛

Liu Sa-he shih-chi yü jui-hsiang t'u 劉薩訶事迹與瑞像圖

Liu sa-he he-shang yin-yüan chi 劉薩訶和尚因緣記

Liu Hsieh-he 劉屑荷

Liu Hsieh 劉勰

Liu-chou 柳州

Lo-ch'ih 羅池

Lo-hsia 洛下

Lo-yang 洛陽

Lo-yÜn 羅雲

Lü hsing kan-t'ung-lu 律師感通錄

Lu Hsün 魯迅

Lu hsün ch'üan chi 魯迅全集

Lu Kao 陸杲

Lu Chien-ch'iu 盧簡求

Lu-ling 廬陵

Lu-shan seng chuan 廬山僧傳

Lu-shan 廬山

lun yüeh 論曰

Lung wang ching 龍王經

Lung wang hsiung ti ching 龍王兄弟經

lung chung ching she 龍衆精舍

Lung-ch'ien tao-chang 龍潛道場

Lung-ch'üan ching-she 龍泉精舍

luo fa 螺髮

Maekawa Takashi 前川隆司

Makita Tairyo 牧田諦亮

Mao-hsien 鄮縣

Mao-yin 鄮陰

Meisoden setsusho 名僧傳說抄

Meisodensho 名僧傳抄

Meng Yi 孟顗

Meng-chin 孟津

Miao fa lien hua ching 妙法蓮華经

Min 閩

ming 銘

Ming hsiang chi 冥詳記

ming lü 明律

Ming seng chuan 名僧傳

ming chih 銘誌.

ming chi 銘紀

Ming-tao 明導

Ming-tse 明則

Mizuno Kogen 水野弘元

Mo-chao ch'ih-ching ta-te shen-yi pei-ming 墨詔持经大德神異碑銘

Mo-kao-k'u 莫高窟

Mo-ling 秣陵

mu 墓

mu chih ming 墓誌銘

mu chih 墓誌

Nan shih 南史

Nan-chien 南澗

Nan-chien-ching-she 南澗精舍

Nan-yüeh 南嶽

Neiraku 寧樂

Nikka bukkyo kenkyukai nenpo 日華佛教研究會年報

Ning-k'ang 寧康

Ningpo-fu chih 寧波府志

Otanigakuho 大谷學報

Ou-yang T'ung 歐陽通

P'ang-wu 龐塢

P'ei Hsiu 裴休

P'eng Pin 彭濱

P'eng-ch'eng 彭城

p'o 頗

p'u-hsien chai 普賢齋

P'u-t'ung 普通

P'u-yüan 普願

pa wang jih 八王日

pan-chou 般舟

Pao-ch'ang 寶唱

Pao-ting 保定

pei ju ch'ien chuan 備如前傳

pei 碑

pei wen 碑文

pei ming 碑銘

Pei-lin 碑林

pei-ming ping hsü 碑銘并序

Pei-shan 北山

Pei-tu 杯度

pen chuang 本傳

pen miao 本廟

Pen-chi 本寂

piao 表

pieh chuan 別傳

Pien-hsiu 辯秀

Pien cheng lun 辯正論

Ping-chou 并州

po jen hui 百人會

po ch'a 柏刹

Po Fa-ch'iao 帛法橋

Po Chü-yi 白居易

Po-ni 帛尼

Rikucho jidai no butto niokeru busshari no anchi ni tsuite
六朝時代の仏塔に於ける仏舎利の安置に就いて

Rikucho jidai no kannon shinko 六朝時代の観音信仰

Ryukoku shidan 龍谷史壇

San-ch'ü-chiang 三曲江

Sato Taishun 佐藤泰舜

seng chuan 僧傳

Seng-ch'un 僧群

Seng-chao 僧肇

Seng-fu 僧副

Seng-han 僧含

Seng-hsien 僧顯

Seng-hu 僧護

Seng-hui 僧慧

Seng-hung 僧洪

Seng-jou 僧柔

Seng-lang 僧朗

Seng-liang 僧亮

Seng-min 僧旻

Seng-ming 僧明

Seng-pao 僧苞

Seng-pao* 僧寶

Seng-shang 僧尚

Seng-shang-chia 僧尚伽

Seng-yü 僧瑜

Seng-yu 僧祐

Seng-yung 僧邕

sha-ch'i 沙磧

Shan Tao-k'ai 單道開

Shan-wu-wei 善無畏

shang tso 上座

Shang-heng 上恒

Shang-yüan 上元

Shao Lang 邵朗

shao lin ts'un che 少林尊者

Shao-lin 少林

she li t'a 舍利塔

she jen 舍人

She-li kan-ying chi 舍利感應記

she-ming 捨命

She-mo-t'eng 捨摩騰

shen seng 神僧

shen yi 神異

shen li 神力

Shen-ch'iao 沉橋

Shen-hao 神皓

shen-tao pei 神道碑

Shen-ts'ou 神湊

Shen-wu 神悟

Shih-chou 濕州

Shih-shih yi-nien lu 釋氏疑年錄

shih-t'a pei-ming ping hsü 石塔碑銘并序

Shih-ti 十地

Shih-yü 耆域

Shinto no kannon 晋康の觀音

Shoki zenshu shisho no kenkyu 初期禪宗史書の研究

Shou leng yen 首楞嚴

Shou-chih 守直

Shu yi chi 述異記

shu sung te pei 述頌德碑

Shugakukenkyu 宗學研究

Sosho 宗性

Sou shen lu 搜神錄

Ssu k'u ch'üan shu tsung mu t'i yao 四庫全書總目提要

ssu chu 寺主

Ssu-ming 四明

Ssu-pu-ts'ung-kan 四部叢刊

Ssu-yi 思益

Su-chou 肅州

Su-chou chih-yen-shan pao-yen-ssu ta-he-shang pei 蘇州支硎山報恩寺大和尚碑

su-he 蘇何

Sui 隋

Sui-chou 綏州

Sun Ch'o 孫綽

Sun Ch'en 孫綝

Sun Lin 孫琳

Sun Yen 孫恩

Sun Ts'e 孫策

Sun-chao 孫照

sung ching 誦經

Sung 宋

Sung kao-seng chuan 宋高僧傳

Sung-chiang 松江

Sung-shan 嵩山

Sung-yüeh kui ch'an-shih ying t'ang-chi 嵩嶽珪禪師影堂記

Suwa Gijyo 諏訪義讓

t'a ming 塔銘

t'a ming ping hsü 塔銘并序

t'a 塔

t'a pei ming 塔碑銘

t'a pei-ming ping hsü 塔碑銘并序

T'ai p'ing kuang chi 太平廣記

T'ai-wu 太武

T'ai-yüan 太元

T'an Wu-chieh 曇無竭

T'an-ch'ien 曇遷

T'an-hsün 曇詢

T'an-kuang 曇光

T'an-tsang 曇藏

T'ang 唐

T'ang fu-chou ching-yün-ssu ku lü-ta-te shang-hung he-shang shih-
唐撫州景雲寺故律大德上宏和尚石塔碑銘并序

t'a pei-ming ping hsü

T'ang chiang-chou hsing-kuo-ssu lü-ta-te ts'ou-kung t'a chieh-ming
唐江州興果寺律大德湊公塔碣銘并序
ping hsü

T'ang hang-chou hua-yen-ssu ta-lü-shih t'a ming ping hsü
唐杭州華嚴寺大律師塔銘并序

T'ang hang-chou ling-yin-shan t'ien-ch'u-ssu ta-te shen fa-shih t'a-
唐杭州靈隱山天竺寺大德詵法師塔銘并序
ming ping hsü

T'ang hu-chou chu-shan chiao-jan chuan 唐湖州杼山皎然傳

T'ang ku tso-chieh seng-lu nei-kung-feng san-chiao t'an-lun yin-chia
唐故左街僧錄內供奉三教談論引駕
ta-te an-kuo-ssu shang-tso szu-tzu fang-p'ao ta-ta fa-shih yÜan-mi-
大德安國寺上座賜紫方袍大達法師元秘塔碑銘并序
t'a pei-ming ping hsü

T'ang shih-yi-shan ku ta-ch'an-shih t'a ming ping hsü
唐石圮山故大禪師塔銘并序

T'ang su-chou k'ai-yüan-ssu lü he-shang fen-ming ping hsü
唐蘇州開元寺律和尚墳銘并序

T'ang su-chou tung-wu ch'iu-ssu lü-shih t'a ming ping hsü
唐蘇州東武邱寺律師塔銘并序

T'ang tung-t'ing-shan fu-yüan-ssu lü he-shang fen t'a ming ping hsü
唐洞庭山福願寺律和尚墳塔銘并序

T'ao YÜan-ming 陶淵明

t'i-e 題額

T'ien p'in fa hua ching 添品法華經

T'ien-chia 天嘉

T'ien-chien 天監

T'ien-jan 天然

T'ien-pao 天寶

t'u ch'i 突騎

t'u hsiang 圖像

t'u t'a 土塔

t'ung fu 銅蓮華趺

T'ung-hsÜan-ssu 通玄寺

ta ch'ung 大蟲

ta chung tsai 大冢宰

Tao-hsüan lü-shih kan-t'ung-lu 道宣律師感通錄

Tao-hsüan lü-shih kan-t'ung-chi 道宣律師感通記

Tao-hsüan lü-shih kan-ying-chi 道宣律師感應記

Tao-hsüan lü-shih chu-ch'ih kan-ying 道宣律師住持感應

Tao-hsüan 道宣

Tao-kuang 道光

Tao-lang 道朗

Tao-liang 道亮

Tao-sheng 道生

Tao-shih 道世

Tao-tsun 道遵

Tao-wang 道汪

Tao-wen 道温

Tao-yi 道謚

Tao-yin 道因

ta yüeh 達曰

Ta-hsiang 大像

Ta-hsing-kuo-ssu 大興國寺

Ta-hsing-shan 大興善

Tao-hsüan lü-shih kan-ying-chi 道宣律師感應記

Ta-kuang 大光

Ta-ming 大明

Ta-t'ang nei-tien lu 大唐内典錄

Ta-t'ang hsi-yü ch'iu-fa kao-seng chuan 大唐西域求法高僧傳

Ta-t'ang nei-tien lu

Ta-t'ang k'ui-chi chün yü-yao hsien hua ( ) ssu chu chen-fa-shih 大唐會稽郡餘姚縣化口寺主真法師行業讚並序 hsing-yeh tsan ping hsü

Ta-t'ang (hsi-ching) ch'ien-fu-ssu to-pao-fo-t'a kang-ying pei-wen 大唐西京千福寺多寶佛塔感應碑文

Ta-t'ung 大同

Ta-yeh 大業

Tai-chia 待駕

Tai-yen 大延

Taiwan shang wu yin shu kuan 台灣商務印書館

Takao Giken 高雄義堅

Tan-chou 丹州

Tan-yang 丹陽

Tanaka Ryosho 田中良昭

tao jen 道人

Tao-ch'ien 道謙

Tao-chi 道基

Tao-chi* 道紀

Tao-chiung 道冏

Tao-cho 道綽

Tao-fu 道悠

Tao-hsien 道仙

Te-mei 道美

Te-shao 德韶

ti chih 地誌

Ting-yang 定陽

To seimeiji dosenrisshiko 唐西明寺道宣律師考

To no dosen no kantsu nitsuite 唐の道宣の感通について

To-pao 多寶

Tohogakuho (Kyoto) 東方學報(京都)

Tonko zenshu bunken no kenkyu 敦煌禪宗文献の研究

Toyogakuho 東洋學報

Ts'en Wen-pen 岑文本

Ts'en Hsü 岑勛

Ts'ui Ch'i 崔琪

ts'un 寸

Ts'ung-chang 總章

tsa-k'e sheng-te p'ien 雜科聲德篇

tsan ping hsü 贊并序

tsan 贊

Tsan-ning 贊寧

Tsang-huan 藏奐

Tsang-yi 藏廙

tso pei chi 作碑記

tso-tao 左道

Tsukamoto hakushi shoju kinen bukkyoshigaku ronshu 塚本博士頌壽記念佛教史學論集

Tsukamoto Zenryu 塚本善隆

Tsung-mi 宗密

tu sung 讀誦

tu hsiang 圖像

Tuan-fu 端甫

Tun-huang 敦煌

tung ling 東嶺

Tung Kao 董誥

Tung Tsung-chih 董宗之

tung t'a yüan 東塔院

Tung-shang seng chuan 東山僧傳

Tung-tu sheng-shan-ssu wu-wei san-tsang pei 東都聖善寺無畏三藏碑

Tung-yün-ssu 東雲寺

Tz'u-chih t'ung-chien 資治通鑑

Tz'u-chou 慈州

Tz'u-ssu 慈寺

Wa-kuan-ssu 瓦官寺

Wai-kuo chuan 外國傳

Wan Ch'i-ju 萬齊融

Wang Mang-ying 萬曼穎

Wang Sui 王邃

Wang Lo-han 王羅漢

Wang Yen 王琰

Wang Yen-hsiu 王延秀

Wang Ya 王雅

Wang Lin 王琳

Wang Tao 王導

Wang Shao 王邵

Wang Yün 王筠

wang erh nien 往二年

wei ching 味淨

Wei 魏

wei chi 為記

Wei Chih-nan 維祇難

Wei-chou 威州

Wei-k'uan 唯寬

Wei-mo 維摩

Wei-tse 惟則

Wei-wei 惟衛

Wei-wei-fo 惟衛佛

Wen 文

wen pu chü yi 文不具矣

Wen-ch'eng 文成

Wen-kang 文綱

Wen-ti 文帝

Wu Ch'ung-yü 吳重裕

Wu 武

wu chu 無主

wu ti 武帝

Wu-feng 五鳳

Wu-te 武德

Wu-yüeh 吳越

Wu* 吳

Yamazaki Hiroshi 山崎宏

Yanagida Seizan 柳田聖山

Yang K'uei 楊夔

Yang 楊

Yang-ch'i-shan chen-shu ta-shih pei ming 楊岐山甄叔大師碑銘

Yang-chou 揚州

Yang-ti 煬帝

Yao Ssu-lien 姚思廉

Yao Ch'a 姚察

Yao Hsing 姚興

Yao Tao-an 姚道安

Yeh 鄴

Yen Fo-tiao 嚴佛調

Yen Chen-ch'ing 顏真卿

Yen-chou 延州

yi ching 譯經

yi chieh 義解

yi shen 遺身

Yi 繹

Yi-ching 義淨

Yi-chou to-pao-ssu tao-yin fa-shih pei-wen ping hsü 益州多寶寺道因法師碑文并序

Yi-chüeh 伊闕

Yi-hsi 義熙

Yi-pu ssu chi 益部寺忌

Yi-ts'un 義存

yin t'ang 影堂

Yin-chou 銀州

ying t'ang chi 影堂記

Yü Shih-chi 虞世基

Yü Ying-chen 喻應真

Yü T'i 于頔

yu fang 遊方

Yu wai-kuo chuan 遊外國傳

yu yi ch'i se 有異氣色

Yü Shih-nan 虞世南

Yü Chih-ning 于志寧

yü 余

yu 又

yü ti chih 輿地誌

Yu ming lu 幽明錄

Yü Fa-lan 于法蘭

Yü Fa-k'ai 于法開

Yü-chang 豫章

Yü-hua 玉華

Yü-t'ien 于闐

yüan kuang 圓光

Yüan-chia 元嘉

Yüan-chih 圓智

Yüan-he 元和

Yüan-hsing 元興

Yüan-kuei 元珪

yüeh fan wu ch'e lao jen hsin chien 月犯五車老人星見

Yüeh 越

Yüeh-ch'eng 越城

Yung-he 永和

Yung-ming Yen-shou 永明延壽

Yung-ting 永定

Zentobun bukkyo kankei senjutsu mokuroku 全唐文仏教関係撰述目錄

Zhong-hua-shu-ju 中華書局

Zukuzokyo 續藏經

PORTRAIT AND SELF-PORTRAIT: A CASE STUDY OF BIOGRAPHICAL AND AUTOBIOGRAPHICAL RECORDS OF TSUNG-MI

Yün-hua Jan

THE PROBLEM

Careful examination of sources is the basis of all sound historical research. This maxim is important in the study of Chinese religious history where the problem of sources presents a particularly complex problem. The basic difficulty confronting the student in this field is that despite the large volume of material available, the accounts of the events recorded in these sources are highly stylized. Consequently, these accounts are often repetitive, and sometimes the records are questionable with regard to accuracy. Numerous biographies of eminent Chinese Buddhist monks are contained in large collections; some monks have separate biographies; a few even have left behind autobiographical records. In general, biographies are brief, dry and impersonal. Autobiographical records are personal, but incomplete in most cases. Speaking figuratively, we might compare biographical records to portraits painted by an artist. The modes of expression and certain elements in the picture reflect the painter's own style and understanding of the figure painted. In contrast, the autobiographical account may be compared to a self-portrait. A self-portrait may be less objective or complete, and yet it will include some elements and expressions that no other material can provide.

HTC: *Hsü-tsang-ching* (Taipei: 1976), 150 vols.
T: *Taisho shinshu daizokyo* (Tokyo: 924-1935), 100 vols

Needless to say, both biographical and autobiographical materials are essential for historians in their research and reconstruction. Most historical researchers in fact use all available sources, analyze them and then write a new and 'complete' biography.

In such historical reconstructions, however, a detailed analysis of the limits and the functions of the sources themselves remains a secondary consideration. This latter is the focus of my discussion here. The study of the respective characteristics of biographical and autobiographical sources in Chinese religious history is in its infancy. The subject constitutes a vast field and any comprehensive discussion is naturally beyond the scope of a short paper. In this paper I will examine the respective strengths and limitations of the biographical and autobiographical materials for the study of Tsung-mi (780-841), an eminent thinker in Chinese Buddhism.[1] It is hoped that such an examination will contribute to a larger discussion of biographies and autobiographical records in general as sources for students of Chinese Buddhist history.

Tsung-mi lived a very colorful and controversial life and he changed his religious beliefs and scholarly career several times. From a student of Confucian learning he became a practitioner of Ch'an, and from Ch'an practice he turned to Hua-yen philosophy. Apart from his Buddhist community, Tsung-mi was also associated with some of the leading intellectuals of the time. This association stimulated his philosophical thought and brought him considerable reputation as a scholar. It also brought no small measure of troubles. Because of the complexity of his career, he was variously loved or rejected by later sectarian historians, especially of the *ch'an* school. Reactions to his changing inclinations are also clearly reflected in his biographies, such as the one written by Tsan-ning.

THE SOURCES

The biographies of Tsung-mi written by various historians are found in a number of collections. According to Shigeo Kamata, there are at least ten biographies of the monk that are still extant.[2] The earliest is the text of the inscription of Tsung-mi composed after his death by P'ei Hsiu (ca 797-870) who was a close friend. The latest biography of Tsung-mi in traditional Chinese Buddhist historiography was published in 1680.

It is commonly held that the earlier historical records are closer to the events and therefore more authentic. The text of the inscription in Tsung-mi's honour, written by P'ei, falls into this category of earliest records.[3] Because of P'ei's close association with Tsung-mi, as well as his reputation in the field of Chinese literature and calligraphy, this inscription has always been regarded as the authoritative source on the life and writings of the monk. I do not intend here to dispute the value of this text. Nevertheless, I must point out that a careful examination reveals that P'ei's writing was indeed very much limited by specific circumstances of its composition, ie., at the time of the composition of the text, some persons related to the monk were still alive. P'ei seems to have been unwilling to enter into controversies that surrounded Tsung-mi and, therefore, did not mention certain things about him in his writing. Tsung-mi's involvement in politics is one such example. Tsung-mi was a close friend of Li Hsün (d. 835) and was harassed after Li fell into disgrace. But P'ei did not mention this matter at all in his writings.[4] Another illustration is Tsung-mi's critical remarks on the Confucian theories of the nature of man put forward by Han Yü (768-824) and Liu Yü-hsi (772-842). Their theories were criticized by Tsung-mi in the *Yüan-jen lun (Treatise on the Origin of Man)* and in other works. Again, no mention was made of this matter in the inscription.[5]

The standard, and most important, biography of Tsung-mi is found in the *Sung Kao-seng-chuan* or *The Biographies of the eminent monks compiled in the Sung Period* by Tsan-ning (919-1001).[6] Although Tsan-ning's biography of Tsung-mi borrowed heavily from the inscription, new material was also added to the account of the monk. Tsung-mi's political involvement and his dignified stand throughout the storm of controversy are all clearly noted in this biography. This shows that later biographies often enjoyed a greater degree of freedom than the earlier inscriptions, resulting in a higher level of objectivity. A later biographer would have been free from the pressures under which the earlier writer, who had to consider the effects of his work on the relatives of his subject, composed his inscription.

The *Ching-te ch'uan-teng lu* ("The Record on Transmission of the Lamp compiled during the age of Ching-te") dated 1004,[7] is a sectarian history of the Ch'an school. Tsung-mi was a member of the school during his early career, but later changed his affiliation to the Hua-yen school. Nevertheless, his interest in Ch'an doctrines and practices, and in Ch'an history, remained strong throughout his life. Because of the change of affiliation, Tsung-mi has been denounced by a few sectarian Ch'an Buddhists; yet his contribution to the history and understanding of Ch'an thought earned him high respect from the school, especially from its learned members. This Ch'an record, *Ching-te ch'uan-teng lu*, also notes a few episodes of the monk which had not been recorded in earlier biographies. It also contains an appendix containing short excerpts from Tsung-mi's writings.

Another important biography of Tsung-mi is found in the *Fa-chieh-tsung wu-tsu lüeh-chi* ("An Outline of the Five Patriarchs of Dharmadhatu School").[8] This is a sectarian history of the Hua-yen school of Buddhism, compiled by the monk Hsü-fa sometime around 1680. This work contains the most complete biography of Tsung-mi in all of traditional Buddhist historiography and its date is much later than the other texts mentioned above. A study of this biography indicates that the biographer used some of Tsung-mi's autobiographical materials in addition to the materials found in standard works mentioned earlier. These new autobiographical materials make the biography richer and more authentic.

Apart from the biographies of Tsung-mi found in these four major works, several other important biographical collections also contain records of this monk. Kamata has mentioned six of them, namely, the *Tsu-t'ang chi*, compiled in 952 by Ching and Yün; the *Ch'uan-fa cheng-tsung chi* compiled by Ch'i-sung in 1061, *Lung-hsing fo-chiao pien-nien t'ung-lun* by Tsu-hsiu in 1061, *Shih-men cheng-t'ung* by Tsung-chien in 1237, *Fo-tsu t'ung-chi* by Chih-p'an in 1269, and *Fo-tsu li-tai t'ung-tsai* by Nien-ch'ang in 1341. Other works that contain biography or notes on Tsung-mi do not provide any new information not found in the major sources. For instance, the biography of Tsung-mi in the *Wu-teng hui-yüan* , compiled by P'u-chi in 1252 A.D., was copied from the *Ching-te ch'uan-teng lu* with no new material added.[9]

Unlike most Chinese Buddhist monks, Tsung-mi wrote some autcbiographical notes. As in the case of many other writers, Tsung-mi's autobiographical notes are scattered throughout his various writings, and some of these notes are found repeated in more than one place. Chronologically speaking, the earliest note on himself is the letter he wrote to his teacher, Ch'eng-kuan (737-838), dated October 4, 811 A.D.[10] It was written at the time when Tsung-mi was in difficulty because one of his followers had sacrificed an army as an expression of his devotion to religion. The police took up the case, and Tsung-mi wrote to his future teacher, introducing himself and explaining the difficulties with which he was confronted. Tsung-mi's request was that the teacher should help him by admitting him as a disciple.

The next autobiographical reference is found in a preface to *Yüan-chüeh-ching ta-shu* ("The Great Commentary on the Scripture of Perfect Enlightenment"). In order to explain how he was influenced by the scripture, Tsung-mi wrote a few lines on the evolution of his thought, mentioning his early career as a student of Confucian teaching and as a monk in the Ch'an school. These autobiographical notes were further elaborated when the sub-commentary of the same scripture, *Yüan-chüeh-ching ta-shu ch'ao* was compiled between 823-827. Most of these elaborated references were retained when he abridged the sub-commentary into a shorter version, *Yüan-chüeh-ching lüeh-shu ch'ao*.

The letter and the sub-commentaries of *Yüan-chüeh-ching* are the major sources for Tsung-mi's autobiographical materials. Apart from these, a few other works also contain short remarks useful for understanding the thought and the career of the monk. The well-known historical introduction to the Ch'an doctrine and its relation to Buddhist philosophies at large, the *Ch'an-yüan chu-ch'uan-chi tu-hsü*, is a good example of this kind. The *Yüan-jen lun* mentioned earlier is another example. Some of his writings, such as his commentary to *Yü-lan-p'en-ching*, a work which might appear unimportant for historical research at first glance, also supply autobiographical references not mentioned in any other source. To cite but one example, it is in this commentary that Tsung-mi describes his home-coming after he became well-known in the imperial capital.[11]

THE PORTRAIT

The biographical sources of Tsung-mi draw a portrait of this monk focusing on various facets of his life. The first important event in the life of Tsung-mi was his abandonment of secular learning. All sources agree that he was a student of Confucian learning in his youth, and he excelled in his studies. By pure chance, he met his future master, Reverend Tao-yüan. The manner of the master impressed Tsung-mi greatly, who decided to renounce the householder's life at once, even without "a conversation" with the master.[12] This account of Tsung-mi's renunciation could give readers the impression that he was an impulsive person who acted rather hastily. Was this true? No clarification is given in the biographies.

Another important event in Tsung-mi's life was his switch from Ch'an to the Hua-yen school of Buddhism. The biographies describe Tsung-mi as a brilliant and talented scholar who made a great impression on his teachers and friends. In his home country he was a member of the Ch'an school of Buddhism. But he changed his affiliation to the Hua-yen school of Buddhism as soon as he arrived at the capital of the T'ang empire. This sudden change of mind made him a controversial figure in the history of Ch'an Buddhism and has brought suspicion upon his motives from modern scholars as well. What was going on in his mind? Did he change his affiliation purely for the sake of personal fortune, as suggested by Hu Shih?[13] No sufficient explanation is found in the biographical sources.

According to the biographies Tsung-mi also wrote a large number of books and treatises. Not only is the number of his writings impressive, but their contents are equally outstanding. The subjects that Tsung-mi discussed in his works include the doctrines and practices of Ch'an Buddhism, Buddhist philosophy, Classical Chinese thought, and the history of Ch'an schools. He appears as a man of broad learning, who did not lose himself in the ocean of ideas. He regarded the concept of the Absolute Mind as the source of all human conditions. It is through this central idea that Tsung-mi organized all the philosophies he studied into one system. It is on the basis of this Absolute Mind, which is transcendent in "substance" and adaptable in "functions", that Tsung-mi was able to see a convergence among the Ch'an doctrine, Buddhist philosophies and Classical Chinese traditions and forge a new and great system of his own.

Another facet of Tsung-mi's portrait that can be discerned from the biographies is that he was an active figure. All the biographical materials note that he had the honour of a royal summons to the palace in 828. They carefully note that he discoursed on Buddhism before the throne and received the purple-robe and honorific title from the imperial court. His friendship with the future prime minister, P'ei Hsiu, is universally acknowledged, but his close association with Li Hsün is largely ignored by various biographers with the exception noted above of Tsan-ning. Li was the anti-eunuch leader, who organized a plot against the powerful forces of eunuchs and was killed by his opponent when the plot failed.

Tsung-mi has also been presented by most biographers as a compassionate and able teacher. He earned the respect of his biographers by his eagerness in helping other people. P'ei writes glowingly,[14]

> ... Our master would feel ashamed if the three vehicles of Buddhism were not flourishing and the four Divisions of Discipline were not observed. Our Master would feel ashamed if loyalty and filial piety were not taught together. He would feel that he had failed to fulfil his responsibility in this regard. Our Master would feel ashamed if he avoided fame for the sake of formalities or if he escaped reputation for the sake of pride. He therefore devoted himself fully to helping and saving others, and busily to leading others to the truth.

To summarize, the portrait of Tsung-mi drawn by his biographers focuses on the following themes: Tsung-mi came from a respectable family, was well-trained in Confucianism, ordained as a Ch'an monk but converted to Hua-yen Buddhism; he was a great scholar, writer and thinker who mastered a number of philosophies; he was very active in the imperial court and associated with a number of distinguished ministers and intellectual leaders; he was also an active monk in high society, involved in political struggle and was a compassionate teacher of religion. Tsung-mi is thus represented by his biographers as a monk of great achievement, a philosopher with great distinction, and an active member of the imperial court.

Some of these facets of the portrait are rather controversial. His inconsistency in religious conviction and affiliation and his close association with the imperial court are two of the most controversial points in his biography. How did the biographers handle these controversial problems? The answer is clear, loud and unanimous: they defended the hero.

The criticism of Tsung-mi has been summarized in the *Sung Kao-seng chuan* in these words[15]

> The critics consider that the Master did not observe the practice of Ch'an, but extensively lectured on *sutras* and *sastras*, that he travelled to famous cities and big capitals, and made it his business to construct mo-

> nastic establishments. Does this not show that he was enslaved by over-learning (*bahu-sruta*)? Is it not that he had not yet forgotten fame and profit?

Tsung-mi's biographers defend him from two different angles. One of the defenders, P'ei Hsiu, argued that the central philosophy of Buddhism is the One Mind. The Mind is the source of all religious practices, and meditation is merely one of the practices. Tsung-mi took the concept One Mind as his starting point; naturally Ch'an sectarians could not understand his ways. Another biographer, Tsan-ning, agreed with this reasoning although he used different words to defend the monk:[16]

> Someone asked whether Master Mi was an adept of Ch'an or of *Vinaya* or of the *sutra* and *sastra*. The answer is that Master Mi was like a land disputed by different warring powers, no one being able to claim him under any banner. All well considered, one would say that he was a great, wise, perfect and illuminated Bodhisattva, who had realized the truth himself and worked for the benefit of others.

Did the hero really change his position on doctrine and affiliation because he wanted to help others, or did he do so for his own sake? Did he change his mind because he had achieved enlightenment himself? His biographers would answer all of these questions in a way that is favorable to Tsung-mi. How would they know that this is so? No explanation appears to have been necessary to traditional Buddhists, nor is one given in the biographies.

The relationship between Buddhist clergy and government is another controversial problem in Chinese history. In a traditional sense, when a person has "Gone forth", he is no longer interested in politics. The traditionalist or puritan always looked down on those who were associated with politics and regarded it as a sign of attachment. Attachment is, of course, one of the three poisons that must be eliminated in spiritual progress. In the case of Tsung-mi, he formed close friendships with some politicians and involved himself in a major political conflict. He was, therefore, criticised by some Buddhists for improper association with nobles, officials, and the imperial court. His actions were defended by his biographer in these words:[17]

> The Buddha has entrusted the Dharma to kings and ministers. If one has no connection with kings and ministers, how can the religion be spread and flourish? Is the Buddha's instructions of helping sovereigns and ministers incorrect?

In other words, the biographer defended the hero in terms of a religious purpose; he held this religious purpose, and not personal gains, as the real motive behind Tsung-mi's involvement in politics. He thus saw Tsung-mi's work in this area as a great achievement and praised it, rejecting what he considered to be petty criticisms.

THE SELF-PORTRAIT

We have seen above that biographies of Tsung-mi do not provide satisfactory answers to some important questions that natural arise in the mind of the reader. The absence of satisfactory answers to these and similar questions explains why readers often get the impression of lifelessness from biographies of Chinese Buddhist monks. Luckily, in the case of Tsung-mi and some other monks, some of these unanswered questions are answered in autobiographical materials. To take Tsung-mi's change in religious faith and education as an example, autobiographical materials give some very personal and convincing reasons for his decisions.

As noted previously, Tsung-mi's first change of religious attitude was his abandonment of Confucian studies and his entrance into the Buddhist order. In explaining this change, the biographical sources only state that "Being a man of eminent talent, he was compelled to follow the Inspector-accountant"[18]. He then encountered meditation master Yüan and converted. This passage might give the misleading impression to readers that Tsung-mi's conversion from Confucianism into Buddhism was due exclusively to external reasons, namely, that he was unwilling to submit himself to a government officer. This impression might further be enforced by the comment that the conversion happened so abruptly that he did not even have a conversation with the Buddhist master before it took place.

The autobiographical materials make it clear that long before Tsung-mi met his future guru he had already wavered between Confucian training and Buddhism. The autobiographical source states[19],

> Speaking exactly, I was a student of Confucian learnings between the age of 7 and 17; in the age between 18 and 22, I wore simple clothes and lived at home, listened to and practiced sutra and sastras, as well as studied commentaries and attended lectures. At the age of 23, I again withdrew from Buddhist studies and exclusively concentrated on Confucian learnings. Not until 25 did I have a good opportunity thus to renounce the householders' life.

The passage here describes the basic facts, ie., what actually happened. It does not, however, explain the reasons for which Tsung-mi found Confucian learning unsatisfactory. For such explanations, one has to turn to other autobiographical sources, particularly the letter to master Ch'eng-kuan.

In this letter Tsung-mi reports that the reason for his shift from Confucian learning to Buddhism was that he was "deeply interested in the Tao but was not fond of the skills (*yi*). Even when I was learning the skills of art, the skills had to be rooted in Tao."[20] Although he studied Confucian learning for years and took the *Book of Songs* and the *Book of Historical Documents* as the subject of his study, he confessesd, "I still felt that I had no place to return to. I thereby sought it from Buddhism, and found something to rely on in it, though it was still very vague. When I realised that cause and effect in karmic retribution are matched perfectly ("identical"), just like the relation between form and shadow, or between sound and echo, I stopped eating meat, studied sutras and sastras, associated with Ch'an masters and eminent monks...."[21]

This first association with Buddhism still failed to satisfy Tsung-mi's religious needs. For this reason he returned to Confucian studies in his 23rd year. He became a monk therefore not as a consequence of an abrupt decision, but rather after a long period of internal struggle. He struggled and wavered between Confucianism and Buddhism for years before he came to renounce the householder's life. This renunciation was therefore based on deep religious and philosophical convictions. Confucian learning proved to be unattractive to him because Confucianism, during the time of Tsung-mi, was insufficiently philosophical and personal, being most concerned with the skills which qualified a person to enter government service.

Moreover, his decision to renounce the world was made after a careful deliberation with his future master. In this connection let us recall the account of the biographies: Tsung-mi converted to Buddhism as soon as he met the Ch'an master, even without holding a conversation with him.[22] Tsung-mi himself describes the process very differently.[23]

> Later I met the teacher, monk Yüan of Ta-yün temple of Sui-chou, a religious descendant of the Master of Ho-tse. We became friendly after conversation, the Way of the Master and of the disciple are identical....As I had already known that the karma of the past and the skills of art are originally unrelated I decided to cut off my hair, put on a religious robe and became a disciple....

The autobiographical passage explicitly informs us that Tsung-mi's conversion to Buddhism actually took place after he conversed with the master, or more probably after they shared several conversations. It was through these conversations that Tsung-mi discovered the Way and developed a friendly relationship with his master. It was this friendship, in which the monk and his future disciple achieved mutual understanding, coupled with Tsung-mi's realization of the irrelevance of practical skills in achieving spiritual liberation that finally led him to convert to Buddhism. According to Tsung-mi's own statements, then, all of this happened only after long and serious deliberation; his renunciation of the householder's life was not an impulsive decision, in contrast to the impression that one receives from the account of this event in the biographies.

Tsung-mi also explained why his early association with Buddhism had failed to make of him a convert. It failed because, "what I learned was not the ultimate teaching, and I did not understand the perfect principle. My understanding did not reach the Source which is the Mind, and delusive feelings still remained."[24]

It has been noted previously that Tsung-mi's change from the Ch'an school into the Hua-yen school brought some resentment from the sectarian followers of Ch'an Buddhism. The reason for the sectarian resentment is obvious, and the absence of any explanation in the biographies for this shift in affiliation has implicitly affected many subsequent interpretations of Tsung-mi's behaviour. It seemed unavoidable that some would ask the uncomfortable question: was Tsung-mi an opportunist who ran after personal gains rather than acting on principle? It was probably such a suspicion that led Hu Shih, one of the modern authorities on Ch'an history, to question Tsung-mi's motives.[25] But if the biographies are silent on this point, the autobiographical materials do in fact clearly describe the reasons that led Tsung-mi to switch from Ch'an to Hua-yen Buddhism. They also reveal that Tsung-mi's problems with Ch'an Buddhism had begun long before his change of affiliation. In his letter to Ch'eng-kuan, Tsung-mi reported the difficulty he faced soon after he joined the Ch'an school.[26]

> However, I still find no answer to the questions related to the body and mind, cause and effect. The principles of matter and forms still remain undefined in my mind.

From these words it is clear that Ch'an Buddhism, taught by master Tao-yüan, put more stress on practice than on doctrine. The problems in which Tsung-mi was interested were matters like the relationship between body and mind, cause and effect, and matter (*rupa*) and form (*nama*). These questions are all philosophical in nature. Ch'an Buddhism appears to have helped Tsung-mi to bring his personal problems under self-control, but his philosophical questions still remained unsettled.

With these philosophical questions in mind, Tsung-mi writes in his autobiographical passages, he constantly queried his teachers , and finally received a copy of *Hua-yen Fa-chieh kuan-men* ("Contemplation on the Realm of Reality") by the great master of Chung-nan (i.e., Tu Shun, 557-640).[27] Although, as its title clearly indicates, the work is related first of all to contemplation, it also discusses the philosophical concepts of *li* (noumenon) and *shih* (phenomenon), the concrete and the empty, individual and universal, mutual relations and mutual penetrations. It is on the basis of these philosophical concepts that the Hua-yen school developed its system of doctrines. There is no reason why a Ch'an Buddhist scholar should not be initiated into doctrinal Buddhism. Tsung-mi in a moving passage describes his excitement after he obtained this work. He says,[28]

> The precious treasury of Buddha was at once manifest from this book; we four comrades spent a few years in the study of it. If there was a sentence that penetrated into principle (*li*, another translation: "noumenon"), we discussed it throughout a whole night, and not even a single point was omitted from our discussions.

His excitement over the work, however, soon led to other difficulties. While the ideas seemed clear and important, when he compared them with the ideas explicitly discussed in the scriptures, he could not determine the relationship between them. One has to remember that Tsung-mi was now a monk, and his ideas had to conform to those expressed in Chinese translations of Buddhist scriptures brought from India. Unless his ideas conformed to what was acceptable as orthodox doctrine, his understanding and teaching could not be regarded as authentic. The work attributed to Tu Shun which excited Tsung-mi is a typical example of a Buddhist philosophical text composed in China. Although the problems discussed in the work fall within the framework of Buddhist philosophy, its terminology and style of thinking are more typically Chinese. In Chinese Buddhist philosophical treatises there is less emphasis on analysis and argument, and systems of ideas tend to be presented without detailed justification. Because of these characteristic features, it is often very difficult to connect Chinese concepts with Indian original terms. The terms *shih* and *li*, central concepts in Chinese Hua-yen Buddhist system for which there are no corresponding Indian terms, are two excellent examples which illustrate this difficulty.

The study of *Hua-yen Fa-chieh kuan-men* constituted the second stage in Tsung-mi's religious career, but at this stage the formal change of faith from Ch'an to Hua-yen Buddhism had not yet taken place. That change occurs only when the link between Hua-yen teaching and the scripture is firmly established in Tsung-mi's mind. This link is found in the commentary of *Hua-yen ching*, compiled by Ch'eng-kuan. Tsung-mi obtained a copy of the commentary while he was travelling in Hsiang-yang. The scholarship of the commentator, the relation between textual evidence and religious ideas developed in the text, the clarification it provided of the structural relationships among the translated scriptures, and the organization of commentary and sub-commentary as presented in Ch'eng-kuan's writings all impressed Tsung-mi and removed whatever reservations he had concerning Hua-yen Buddhism. In this work Tsung-mi found a way to read Buddhist literature, to discover the content of its teaching, and fully to assimilate the teaching in his own mind. All doubts disappeared from his mind and he was led to a new stage of religious realization. He explains his progress in the following words: [29]

> I used the sub-commentary to understand the commentary, and penetrated the scripture with the help of the commentary. Too literal an interpretation ("looking for letters") leads one to depart from the essence ("nature"); one transcends ("forget") one's personal feelings if (the passage is) illuminated by the principle (*li*, "noumenon"). I applied this insight to mind, and harmonized this mind with the teaching. I searched the branches through the root, and the principle and the patterns were all clearly manifested as they were. Whatever doubt remained in my mind now went like smoke and clouds. I have now completely penetrated the meaning; the external object and internal mind at once are united without any obstruction.

The above discussion offers an explanation of why and how Tsung-mi gradually shifted his attention from Ch'an to Hua-yen that is based on Tsung-mi's own words. It indicates that Tsung-mi was an honest and earnest student of Buddhism. His shift from Ch'an to Hua-yen was not the result of any impulsiveness nor was it motivated by personal gain; rather, it was based on the progress of his learning and self-understanding. It would seem that lack of careful consideration of Tsung-mi's autobiographical statements such as those cited here, coupled with the fact that the biographies are silent as to his motivations, has led scholars in the past as well as in more recent times to speculate freely about the sources for Tsung-mi's behaviour and possibly paint a portrait that is distorted and unclear.

Tsung-mi was criticized by some Buddhists as a man who was 'over-learned'. They suspected that his interest in learning and in lecturing was merely a consequence of his love of display. In answering this charge his defenders simply stated that this was not the case and that Tsung-mi was a great master whom no one sect could claim exclusively.

The autobiographical materials again present a different picture. Tsung-mi explains that his interest in meditation and doctrinal teachings was inspired by several motives: self-effort, compassion towards others, and a realization that practice and doctrines have both originated with the Buddha, and that therefore there is no difference between them as far as their ultimate religious goal is concerned. Most of these reasons are not fully analyzed and presented in the portrait drawn by Tsung-mi's biographers. Tsung-mi explained his position in one of his important works, explaining how meditation and wisdom are both fundamental to a Buddhist, and why he himself needed both of them:[30]

> Although Buddha said that increasing compassion is the practice, yet I thought that I might not be able to prevent views of attachment from arising; I, therefore, detached myself from my associates, dwelling on a mountain, practiced concentration and harmonized wisdom, and quietly contemplated for a period of ten years in total.

Yet, in another passage he described his compassion for others and his determination to help them in these words,[31]

> I, Tsung-mi do not know what deeds I have done in my previous life, and thus affected the quality of my mind in this life. Although I have not liberated myself, yet I wish to liberate others from bondage. For the sake of religion (*dharma*), I forget my own life; for the sake of compassion toward others I transcend my spirit and emotion of my own.

Compassion in these passages refers above all to teaching the Buddhist truth to others so that they can achieve liberation. This teaching inevitably takes the form of discussing scriptures and doctrines. Tsung-mi regarded the practice of meditation as a matter of seeking one's own liberation and contrasted it with teaching,which he regarded as a matter of compassion toward others. Compassion, then, is one fundamental reason that Tsung-mi himself gives for explaining his interests in doctrines.

In the passage quoted above Tsung-mi also explains his interest in all branches of Buddhist teaching by making a more theoretical point. In his view, it is wrong to conceive of learning and practice as two different things. To the contrary they are actually two aspects of the same thing. He says,[32]

> Sutras are the words spoken by the Buddhas, Ch'an is the intention of the Buddhas. The mouth and the mind of the Buddhas certainly are not different.

Tsung-mi's view was that the words and the intention of Buddhas are never in conflict. It was the narrow sectarian mind and its limited understanding that differentiated them. He says,[33]

> The disciples (of doctrines and Ch'an) of the present age are both confused about the

> Source: those who cultivate the mind consider the scriptures and commentaries as something which belong to another school; those who lecture on scriptures regard *dhyana* practice as a different *dharma* (from their own).

Based on the above reasoning, Tsung-mi chose different means, eg., doctrinal discourse or meditation, under different circumstances involving different problems. It is this free adaptation of means which made him subject to criticism from sectarian opponents. Yet, we should also remember that this broader and non-sectarian attitude earned Tsung-mi a great deal of respect later in the history of Buddhism in Asia.

CONCLUSION

This case study of the biographical "portrait" and autobiographical "self-portrait" of Tsung-mi has revealed some of the strengths and significant limitations of both biographical and autobiographical accounts for the scholar who seeks through them to understand a particular historical figure. The greatest potential strength of the biographical "portrait" is a certain kind of "completeness". Biographers wrote their works long after the death of the monk who was their subject and were in a position to collect all available data to produce a balanced biography. We saw that one biographer, P'ei Hsiu, who was close to Tsung-mi and composed his inscription shortly after his death, appears to have made a self-conscious decision not to mention certain controversial matters in Tsung-mi's life. A later biographer, Tsan-ning, standing at a greater distance from the subject, produced a more balanced portrait that included these controversial matters. Given the desire to do so, then, a biographer could have seen his task as collecting and transmitting all available data about his subject. That this was not the case for those who wrote Buddhist biographies in China is the result of what I would consider the concomitant limitations of Chinese Buddhist biographical writings.

Traditional biographies have obvious limitations. Most of these biographies were composed with the intention of glorifying their subject. The attitude of the biographer towards his subjects' lives was not primarily analytical. The biographers often describe their aim explicitly as creating heroes for monks to esteem; they also hoped to upgrade the social standing of the religion by showing its adherents in a decidedly favorable light. These biographies are, therefore, often highly selective and "subjective" in the sense that they reflect the biased viewpoints of their composers. These biographies are also relatively short. These factors, the "subjective" bias and limitations of space, often made the biographers overlook a number of significant points, detracting from the potential completeness and balance that one might expect from a biography. Chinese Buddhist biographies are in this regard significantly "incomplete" and "unbalanced". One important consequence of these limitations is that these biographies often merely record that an event happened and rarely explain the reasons behind the events they recount. Where explanations are offered, it is impossible to be sure that they are not otherwise motivated. And in some cases, certain events are disregarded altogether.

Tsung-mi's traditional biographies illustrate all of these limitations clearly. Tsung-mi was presented as their hero in an idealized light: he was a great master, had a profound understanding of Buddha's teaching, and had achieved a high degree of religious attainment. We have seen that there were controversial issues in Tsung-mi's life, eg., his repeated changes in religious affiliation. Interestingly biographers did defend him against criticisms and sometimes even provided their own reasons to justify his actions, but these reasons did not always match the reasons Tsung-mi himself gave in his autobiographical comments.

Autobiographical materials have a different function from that of traditional biographies. They are written to convey the author's own understanding of his situation and definitely provide the interpretations he wished others to place on the events of his life. They often give detailed accounts of what has happened and a description of the subject's thoughts and reactions to these situations. Such a psychological narrative should be extremely important for all students of biography, and particularly so for those who study religious biographies.

As is the case with biographies, autobiographical accounts also have their limitations. They are sometimes fragmentary, and are still as "subjective" as biographies, although the viewpoint they represent is that of the writer and not a third party. Nonetheless, they can contribute greatly to an understanding of a given historical figure and his religious development precisely because they provide material that is not elsewhere recorded and that can serve as a corrective to the portrait drawn by others. In the case of Tsung-mi, his biographers produced a portrait which presented the external details of the subject's life, particularly those standard characteristics Buddhist biographers normally highlighted; the autobiographical accounts in contrast have produced a self-portrait presenting the inner world of Tsung-mi's intentions and self-justifications. It is these inner elements that make the subject come alive. Traditional Chinese biography and autobiographical remarks by the subjects themselves throw light on their common subjects from different angles. They are both important sources to historians of religion and must be used with full awareness of their respective strengths and limitations.

Notes

1. For his life, thought and his place in the history of Chinese religion, see the author's "Tsung-mi, His analysis of Ch'an Buddhism", *T'oung Pao* LVIII (1972), pp. 1-54.

2. Kamata, *Shumitsu kyogaku no shishoshiteki kenkyu* (Tokyo: Toyo bunka kenkyuso, University of Tokyo, 1975), pp. 9-101.

3. The inscription on Tsung-mi composed by P'ei is preserved in *Chin-shih Ts'ui-pien*, ed. by Wang Ch'ang (1724-1806), chapter 114. The edition used in this paper is by the Ts'ui-liu t'ang of Shanghai, 1893.

4. See Jan, *loc. cit.*, TP, pp. 16-22.

5. For the background of *Yüan-jen lun*, see Peter N. Gregory, "The Teaching of Man and Gods: The Doctrinal and Social Basis of Lay Buddhist Practice in the Hua-yen tradition", in the *Studies of Ch'an and Hua-yen*, ed. by R. M. Gimello (Hawaii: University of Hawaii Press, 1983), pp. 253ff. For Tsung-mi's critique of Confucianism, see Jan, "Tsung-mi's Questions Regarding the Confucian Absolute", *Philosophy East and West* 30/4 (1980), pp. 495-504.

6. For Tsan-ning and his work mentioned here, see Jan, "Buddhist Historiography in Sung China", *ZDMG* 114 (1964), pp. 360ff., and his work on Tsung-mi is in Chapter 6, 741c-743a.

7. See Jan, *loc. cit.*, ZDMG, pp. 364ff. A selected translation of the work has been published by Chang Chung-yuan, *The Original Teachings of Ch'an Buddhism* (New York: Random House, 1971), though the emphasis is largely on the sectarian development of later ages. Tsung-mi's biography is in Ch. 13 of the original work, which is excluded from the translation by Chang.

8. The work is found in HTC vol 134, p. 277a-278a. A modernized version is found in *Chung-kuo fo-chiao ssu-hsiang tzu-liao hsüen-pien*, vol. II, part 2, ed. by Shih Chun *et al.* (Beijing: Chung-hua shu-chu, 1983), pp. 475-477.

9. The biographies on Tsung-mi are found in *Tsu-t'ang chi*, ch. 6 (Taipei: Kuang-wen shu-chu, 1972), p. 114; *Ch'uan-fa cheng-tsung chi*, T.51, p. 753b; *Lung-hsing fo-chiao pien-nien t'ung-lun*, HTC vol. 130; pp. 336-337; *Shih-men cheng-t'ung*, ch. 8, HTC vol. 130, pp. 456c-457; *Fo-tsu t'ung-chi*, T.49, p. 293c; *Fo-tsu li-tai t'ung-tsai*, T.49, pp. 635b-636a; *Wu-teng hui yüan*, ch. 2, HTC vol. 138, pp. 35c-38b or the modernized edition by Su Yüan-lei (Beijing: Chung-hua shu-chu, 1984), vol. 1, pp. 105-112.

10. The letter is preserved in T.39, pp. 576c-577c, as an appendix to Tsung-mi's *Yüan-chüeh hsiu-to-lo liao-yi-ching lüeh-shu.* For the background and significance of this letter, see Jan, "Tsung-mi chu *Tao-su ch'ou-ta wen-chi* te yen-chiu", *Hwakang Buddhist Journal* (Taiwan), Vol. IV (1980), pp. 132-166, especially, 140-142, 145-153.

11. See Jan Yün-hua, "A Study of *Ta-ch'eng ch'an-men yao-lu*: Its Significance and Problems", *Chinese Studies* 4/2 (1986), pp.533ff., esp. 542f.

12. The inscription says, "*sui-chou wei yü yü*" ; and Tsan-ning says that "*yüan wei yü*". See *Chin-shih ts'ui-pien*, ch. 114, p. 6c and T.50, p. 741c (which is mistakenly punctuated).

13. Hu, "Pa P'ei Hsiu ti T'ang ku Kuei-feng Ting-hui ch'an-shih ch'uan-fa-pei", *Bulletin of the Institute of History and Philology* XXXIV (1962), pp. 5-26. Ref., Jan Yün-hua, "Tsung-mi ch'uan-fa-shih-hsi te tsai-chien-t'ao (A Reexamination of the Lineage of Ch'an Buddhism Given by Tsung-mi)", *Chung-hwa Buddhist Journal* vol. 1 (1987), pp.43-57.

14. This is a new translation from *Chin-shih tsui-pien*, ch. 114, p.7a.

15. My translation, *ibid.*, p. 25; original T. 50, 742c.

16. *Ibid.*, pp. 26-27; original, T. 50, 742b.

17. Translated from T.50, p. 743a.

18. My translation, TP. *loc. cit.*, p. 6; original, T.50, 741c. According to the examination system prevailing during the time of the monk, that candidate in the imperial examination should be led by the accountant-officer from the local Government to the capital for final examination.

19. Translated from the *Yüan-chüeh-ching lüeh-shu ch'ao* in HTC vol. 15, p. 106a.

20. Translated from T.39, p. 576c.

21. *Ibid.*

22. See note 11 above.

23. Translated from T.39, p. 576c.

24. *Ibid.*

25. Hu, *loc. cit.*, note 12.

26. Translated from T.39, p. 576c.

27. *Ibid.* For the philosophy of this treatise, see Thomas Cleary, *Entry into the Inconceivable: An Introduction to Hua-yen Buddhism* (Honolulu: University of Hawaii Press, 1983), pp.24ff. The treatise has been translated into English by Garma C. C. Chang with a discussion of the life of the monk, see *The Buddhist Teaching of Totality: The Philosophy of Hwa Yen Buddhism* (University Park: Pennsylvania State University Press, 1971), 207-223, 231-234.

28. *Ibid.*, p. 576c.

29. *Ibid.*

30. Translated from *Ch'an-yüan chu-chu'an-chi tu-hsü*, ch. 1, as found in Kamata's edition, Zen no goroku 9 (Tokyo: Chikuma shobo, 1971), p. 30.

31. *Ibid.*, p. 29.

32. *Ibid.*, p. 44.

33. *Ibid.*

CHARACTERS

Ch'an-yüan chu-chu'an-chi tu-hsü 禪源諸詮都序

Ch'an/ch'an 禪

Ch'eng-kuan 澄觀

Ch'i-sung 契嵩

Ch'uan-fa cheng-tsung chi 傳法正宗記

Chih-p'an 志磐

Chikuma shobo 筑摩

Chin-shih Ts'ui-pien 金石萃编

Ching 静

Ching-te ch'uan-teng lu 景德傳燈錄

Chung-hua shu-chu 中華書局

Chung-kuo fo-chiao ssu-hsiang tzu-liao hsüen-pien 中國佛教思想資料選编

Chung-nan 終南

Fa-chieh-tsung wu-tsu lüeh-chi 法界宗五祖略記

Fo-tsu li-tai t'ung-tsai 佛祖歷代通載

Fo-tsu t'ung-chi 佛祖统纪

Han Yü 韓愈

Ho-tse 荷澤

Hsiang-yang 襄陽

Hsü-tsang-ching 續藏經

Hu Shih 胡適

Hua-yen Fa-chieh kuan-men 華嚴法界觀門

Hua-yen ching 華嚴經

Hua-yen 華嚴

Li Hsün 李訓

li 理

Liu Yü-hsi

Liu Yü-hsi 劉禹錫

Lung-hsing fo-chiao pien-nien t'ung-lun 隆興佛教編年通論

Nien-ch'ang 念常

P'ei Hsiu 裴休

P'u-chi 普濟

Pa P'ei Hsiu ti T'ang ku Kuei-feng Ting-hui ch'an-shih ch'uan-fa-pei 跋裴休的唐故圭峯定慧禪師傳法碑

Shigeo Kamata 鎌田茂雄

shih 事

Shih Chun 石峻

Shih-men cheng-t'ung 釋門正統

Shumitsu kyogaku no shishoshiteki kenkyu 宗密教学の思想史的研究

Su Yüan-lei 蘇淵雷

Sui-chou 遂州

sui-chou wei yÜ yÜ 遂州未與語

Sung Kao-seng-chuan 宋高僧傳

Ta-yün 大雲

Taisho shinshu daizokyo 大正新修大藏經

Tao-yüan 道圓

Ts'ui-liu t'ang 醉六堂

Tsan-ning 贊寧

Tsu-hsiu 祖琇

Tsu-t'ang chi 祖堂集

Tsung-chien 宗鑑

Tsung-mi ch'uan-fa-shih-hsi te tsai-chien-t'ao 宗密傳法世系的再檢討

Tsung-mi 宗密

Tu Shun 杜順

Wang Ch'ang 王敞

Wu-teng hui-yüan 五燈會元

yi 藝

Yü-lan-p'en-ching 盂蘭盆經

Yüan 圓

yÜan wei yÜ yÜ 圓未與語

Yüan-chüeh-ching 圓覺經

Yüan-chüeh-ching lüeh-shu ch'ao 圓覺經略疏鈔

Yüan-chüeh-ching ta-shu ch'ao 圓覺经大疏鈔

Yüan-chüeh-ching ta-shu 圓覺经大疏

Yüan-jen lun 原人論

Yün 筠

Zen no goroku 禪の語錄

THE CONTEXTUAL STUDY OF CHINESE BUDDHIST BIOGRAPHIES:

THE EXAMPLE OF YUNG-MING YEN-SHOU (904-975)

Albert Welter

A. Introduction

A substantial portion of the source material available to the scholar of the history of Chinese Buddhism consists of biographies of Chinese Buddhist monks. This can largely be attributed to the fact that biography was a major branch of Chinese historical writing.[1] A strong tendency persists in modern scholarship to view these biographical records as containing historically reliable material. As a consequence, the biographies of Chinese Buddhist monks are often read as if they accurately reflect the historical details of monks' lives, without sufficient regard for the very special circumstances in which these particular records were written or the unique forces that motivated them. In the end such an approach does little more than to repeat the idiosyncratic and often imaginative depictions of the monks' lives that the tradition has developed, for some materials recorded in the lives of Chinese monks obviously have no basis in historical fact.

In contrast to this procedure, more critical historians of Chinese Buddhist biography have recognized that the biographical records of Chinese monks are filled with legendary elements that have little relation to actual history. Consequently these scholars have as a rule chosen simply to disregard the legendary elements that are often found in the form of stories. This approach may appear appropriate to those interested only in the "hard" historical facts of monks' lives. To historians of religion, however, this approach is also problematical for two reasons. Firstly, in these traditional accounts of Buddhist monks "fact" and "fiction" are often hard to distinguish. Without proper regard for the circumstances under which the lives of monks were recorded and for the forces motivating their compilation, the investigator who approaches the material with the critical intention to sort out the "facts" from "fiction" nevertheless often ends up overestimating the reliability of details presented as historical "facts" in such accounts. Secondly, by disregarding the obviously legendary materials contained in the biographies, the investigator simply ignores a substantial amount of material recorded in the traditional accounts of Buddhist monks. Much of this material is interesting in its own right even though it has no value in determining historical facts concerning the life of the monk who is the ostensible subject of the biography. Other methods and approaches are necessary in order to interpret such legendary material appropriately.

These issues in the study of Chinese Buddhist biography call for an involved and complex discussion. In this paper I will limit myself to offering some comments on them based on the study of several renditions of the life of Yung-ming Yen-shou (904-975). It is hoped that these comments will throw some light on the nature of Chinese Buddhist biography in general and point to some avenues along which future studies of Chinese Buddhist biography might fruitfully proceed.

There are several factors which make Yen-shou an excellent example on which to focus in discussing the issues of method that arise frequently in the study of Chinese Buddhist biographies.[2] Yen-shou was a guiding figure for many of the developments that came to characterize post-T'ang Buddhism.[3] His importance was widely accepted, and yet he was also long to remain at the centre of lively controversies. Thus, a study of the evolving renditions of Yen-shou's "biographical image"[4] should throw light on the conflicts at the core of post-T'ang Buddhism itself, for Yen-shou's biographies may be seen to reflect clearly these conflicts. It was these conflicts that in fact determined how the biographer came to terms with the data of Yen-shou's life; that is, how he understood just what kind of Buddhist, in essence, Yen-shou was. The two claimants who vied with each other for the right to represent Yen -shou as one of their own were the Ch'an and T'ien-t'ai schools. The debate between them was generally contained within the polite conventions governing Chinese Buddhist historiography, which often served the function of legitimizing the authority of the school whose history was being recounted. It also had the potential to erupt into verbally explicit hostility. In brief this paper will attempt to demonstrate that the biographical images of Yen-shou were often molded by the demands of later chroniclers in an atmosphere where Buddhist historiography was used as a battleground to substantiate the legitimacy of a particular school in competition with other groups .[5]

Existing biographies of Yen-shou describe this monk's life in many different ways. I have elsewhere reviewed the historiographical development of Yen-shou's biography.[6] For the purpose of the discussion here I will compare these highly divergent biographies in terms of two important transitional periods in Yen-shou's life. The first period involves Yen-shou's renunciation of the householder's life, i.e., a shift in his career from that of a government official to that of a Buddhist monk. In some biographies the account of this event in Yen-shou's biographies is designed to describe Yen-shou's remarkable attainments even at this early stage in his career as a Buddhist monk. The second period involves Yen-shou's religious career on Mt. T'ien-t'ai. In some biographies the account of this period in Yen-shou's life is designed to clarify the nature of his Buddhist affiliation. Focusing on divergent accounts of these two crucial periods in Yen-shou's life as examples, I hope to show how legend and history are often confused in Yen-shou's biographies and demonstrate how the particular needs of later Buddhist communities entirely unrelated to the life of Yen-shou himself were instrumental in determining the shape his biographical image took. Before discussing the divergent accounts in Yen-shou's biographies, I would like to review briefly the sources containing Yen-shou's biography and comment on the manner in which I analyze these sources.

B. Sources for the Study of Yen-shou's Biography

The sources for the study of Yen-shou's biography are numerous and varied. Chinese sources which include an account of Yen-shou's life begin shortly after his death, with Tsan-ning's *Sung-kao-seng chuan* in 988, and extend down to the present, with the publication of volume two of *Chung-kuo fo-chiao* by the Chinese Buddhist Association in 1981.[7] Between these two works are frequent and persistent attempts to record the significant events of Yen-shou's life, attesting to his continuing importance. In order to explore the development of Yen-shou's biographical image among these numerous biographies, I first prepared a larger list of available biographical sources on Yen-shou and then chose what I consider to be representative examples and examined them in greater detail. While not completely exhaustive the larger list includes the principal sources available today to students of the biography of Yen-shou. Listed according to period, they are as follows.

Sung (960-1279)

(988) *Sung kao-seng chuan*, ch. 28
(1001) *Ching-te ch'uan-teng lu*, ch. 26
(1029) *T'ien-sheng kuang-teng lu*
(1061) *Ch'uan-fa cheng-tsung chi*, ch. 8
(1123) *Ch'an-lin seng-pao chuan*, ch. 9
(1160) *Lung-shu ching-t'u wen*, ch. 5
(1183) *Lien-teng hui-yao*, ch. 28
(1200) *Lo-pang wen-lei*, ch. 3
(1230) *Jen-t'ien pao-chien*
(1237) *Shih-men cheng-t'ung*, ch. 8

(1252)*Wu-teng hui-yao*, ch. 10
(1269)*Fo-tsu t'ung-chi*, ch. 26
(c.1270)*Hsien-ch'un lin-an chih*, ch. 82

Yüan (1279-1367)
(1305)*Lu-shan lien-tsung pao-chien*, ch. 4
(1341)*Fo-tsu li-tai t'ung-tsai*, ch. 18
(c.1350)*Shih-shih chi-ku lüeh*, ch. 3

Ming (1368-1661)
(c.1420)*Sheng-seng chuan*, ch. 9
(c.1600)*Ling-yin ssu-chih*, ch. 3A
(1606)*Yung-ming tao-chi*
(c.1625)*Ching-tz'u ssu-chih*, ch. 8
(c.1650)*Szu-ming shan-chih*, ch. 2

Ch'ing (1662-1911)
(1669)*Shih-kuo ch'un-ch'iu*, ch. 89
(1681)*Hsüeh-t'ou ssu-chih*, ch. 3
(1744)*Yün-lin ssu-chih*, ch. 4
(c.1790)*Ching-t'u sheng-hsien lu*, ch. 3
Hang-chou fu-chih, ch. 171
Che-chiang t'ung-chih, ch. 198

A brief description of my method in comparing the accounts of Yen-shou's life in these sources may be helpful. I will examine the sources looking for the images or models of Yen-shou that they present; in each case I will show how a particular image is constructed through the selection and arrangement of incidents in Yen-shou's life. Particularly important are the unique developments in some of these sources; as these sources are datable the new developments recorded in them should enable us to chart the evolution of Yen-shou's image.

As will be seen in detail below, some of the existing sources represent significant attempts to produce an image of Yen-shou that is compatible with the aims of a particular biographer and the aspirations of the community that he represents. Others merely reiterate the details and patterns of Yen-shou's life established in earlier sources. It is not my intention to examine the latter. From the discussion it should become clear that because of the marked tendency in all the sources studied to fashion the image of Yen-shou in a likeness that reflects contemporary needs, it is not possible to separate the images of Yen-shou from the historical facts from which these images were most likely originally derived.

In the discussion below we will focus on the following sources: the *Sung kao-seng chuan* (SKSC), the *Ching-te ch'uan-teng lu* (CTCTL), the

Ch'an-lin seng-pao chuan (CLSPC), the *Lung-shu ching-t'u wen* (LSCTW), the *Lo-pang wen-lei* (LPWL), and the *Shih-men cheng-t'ung* (SMCT).

C. Pivotal Transition Periods in Yen-shou's Biographies

In biographical accounts Yen-shou's life is patterned after a generally accepted scheme consisting of certain events.[8] This scheme of more or less fixed events which are said to have occurred in Yen-shou's life emerged over a period of time. Throughout this paper it shall be my contention that the descriptions that we possess of these events are a product of circumstances surrounding the compilation of various biographies of Yen-shou. Consequently these descriptions are much more appropriately interpreted as a reflection of these circumstances than as historical accounts of Yen-shou's life itself. In support of this hypothesis I shall investigate in detail how the various biographical accounts of the two transitional periods in Yen-shou's life developed.

1. Accounts of Yen-shou's Career

Change from Government Official to Buddhist Monk

The standard rendition of events describing Yen-shou's renunciation of the householder's life is arrived at after a considerable passage of time and several recorded attempts. The wide range of different explanations seen in earlier biographies makes it apparent that circumstances surrounding Yen-shou's renunciation of the secular life were not clear to early biographers. As Buddhist biographers they obviously felt a strong need to explain this important change in Yen-shou's career, but they appear to have possessed no information on which to base their accounts. It is also conceivable that earlier biographers felt that what they knew was problematic and not appropriate to be included in their biographies. The fact that Yen-shou had initially embarked on a career as a civil servant made the biographers' task of describing his renunciation of secular life more complicated than usual.

In the earliest account compiled by Tsan-ning in the *Sung kao-seng chuan* (SKSC),[9] it is stated that Yen-shou held a position as a government official in charge of military provisions. At that time the teaching of the Ch'an master Ts'ui-yen Ling-ts'an[10] flourished, and Yen-shou left his wife and child to become Ts'ui-yen's disciple. This reference to abandoning his wife and child reminds one of the description of renunciation in the widely known life of the Buddha, and may have been included here as a device for associating Yen-shou's life with that of the Buddha. We might also note that this reference to Yen-shou's abandoning his wife and child to become a monk is found only in the biography found in the SKSC. Tsan-ning was a contemporary of Yen-shou and must have known of him. He was also familiar with the situation of Wu Yüeh Buddhism personally.[11] It is significant that there appears to be no trace in the SKSC of the conflict associated with Yen-shou's renunciation of an official career to become a monk that characterizes many later biographical accounts.

Towards the end of Yen-shou's biography in the SKSC there is the statement that Yen-shou bought living beings and set them free as an expression of his altruism and compassion. Sometimes, the biography continues, Yen-shou was unreasonable in this connection [original unclear here], (but) his facial expression was unaffected. This account is unclear in the context of the SKSC biography. The assertion that "his facial expression was unaffected," seems curiously out of place in the context of the SKSC biography. We shall see below, however, that this vague description in the SKSC has considerable bearing upon the dramatic descriptions of events regarding Yen-shou's passage from official to monk that developed in later accounts.

The other account of Yen-shou's life compiled by a contemporary is that of Tao-yüan in the *Ching-te ch'uan-teng lu* (CTCTL).[12] According to the events describing Yen-shou's passage from official to monk recorded there, Yen-shou served as a garrison commandant who guarded the southern border town of Hua-t'ing. The Ch'an master Ts'ui-yen propagated his teachings in the region at this time, and eventually came to reside at the Lung-ts'e temple where he spread his teachings far and wide. Prince Wen-mo of Wu Yüeh realized Yen-shou's devotion to Ch'an and sympathized with his strong faith in Buddhism. He therefore released Yen-shou from government service, permitting him to become a monk. Consequently Yen-shou became Ts'ui-yen's disciple.

In the light of other accounts of this transition in Yen-shou's life that appear in later biographies, the most significant development in the CTCTL account is the appearance of the Wu Yüeh Prince Wen-mo and the role that he plays in sanctioning Yen-shou's renunciation of the householder's life. The role of the prince provides the first hint of the conflict that later accounts associated with this transition in Yen-shou's life.

In the *Ch'an-lin seng-pao chuan* (CLSPC),[13] events surrounding Yen-shou's renunciation begin to take a dramatic turn. In the CLSPC, we are informed that when Yen-shou was returning to Ch'ien-t'ang by boat, he saw a fishing boat with numerous fish gasping for air in agony. He bought them and set them free in the river. As a result of this incident, we are told, Yen-shou ripped off his official robe and went to study under Ts'ui-yen. When he moved with Ts'ui-yen to take up residence at Lung-ts'e temple, Prince Wen-mo got wind of the incident. He admired Yen-shou and allowed him to discard his household duties and become a monk. From here the story continues in an already familiar manner.

In addition to the graphic portrayal of Yen-shou's religious awakening, this account of the circumstances surrounding Yen-shou's change from official to monk is of particular interest in our attempts to trace the evolution of Yen-shou's biography because this incident of setting fish free appears for the first time here in connection with Yen-shou's renunciation. From this point on this connection will be a leading feature in the biography of Yen-shou.

There is reason to assert that Yen-shou was widely known in his biographies for this act of compassion in setting fish free, and that the ultimate source of the story of Yen-shou's liberating the dying fish may in fact be Yen-shou's own words. The CTCTL biography also ascribes this practice to Yen-shou, but it is there connected with his activities on Mt. T'ien-t'ai near the end of his life. Yen-shou himself in his own works mentions the act of releasing animals. For example, in Chapter I of the *Wan-shan t'ung-kuei chi*, Yen-shou states:[14]

> The overturning of birds in a cage or fish in
> a sacrificial vessel is called joyful bliss.

Among Yen-shou's non-extant works there was an essay entitled: "On Releasing Living Beings" (*Fang-sheng wen*)[15].

But the most important parallel to this story about Yen-shou setting fish free is to be found in an earlier tradition regarding the life of Chih-i, founder of the T'ien-t'ai school.[16] According to this tradition, Chih-i greatly lamented the suffering caused by those living around him who engaged in fishing for a living. As a consequence, he sold his clothes and with the money bought the captured fish and set them free. He also created ponds for the special purpose of setting fish free (*fang-sheng chih ch'ih*). It is said that associations (*fang-sheng hui*) became widely established to carry out this practice as a result of Chih-i's advocacy of setting fish free.

The CLSPC version of Yen-shou's change from official to monk may be interpreted as connecting the image of Yen-shou with the example of Chih-i. Stories about setting fish free to demonstrate Buddhist compassion have a special meaning in the T'ien-t'ai tradition. A story of this nature may, therefore, have been included in Yen-shou's biography as an affirmation of his association with that tradition. We shall discuss in more detail below the association of Yen-shou with T'ien-t'ai, and how this association influenced later accounts of Yen-shou's life. In the present context I would like to call attention to the following: here a story which seems best interpreted as revealing Yen-shou's connection with the T'ien-t'ai school in the CLSPC is found for the first time in a biographical collection of the Ch'an school. This rather curious situation appears to point to a problem concerning Yen-shou's identity.

Starting with the CTCTL, the Ch'an tradition sought to lay claim to Yen-shou by positing him as the third patriarch in the Fa-yen sect, following Fa-yen Wen-i and T'ien-t'ai Te-chao.[17] From the outset, however, there appear to have been certain difficulties with the Ch'an school's claim. The SKSC, non-sectarian in orientation, had initially categorized Yen-shou as a "Promoter of Works of Merit" (*hsing-fu*) rather than as a "Ch'an Meditator" (*hsi-ch'an*).[18] The difficulty in the Ch'an school's claim to Yen-shou may also explain the fact that Yen-shou's biography does not appear in some later Ch'an collections[19]. This omission is often explained as a consequence of intra-school rivalry within the larger Ch'an school itself. But such rivalry cannot explain the fact that Yen-shou's biography is not included in Li Tsun-hsü's collection entitled the *T'ien-sheng kuang-teng lu*. In this work, the Fa-yen sect is recorded, but Yen-shou is not recognized as a member.[20] Nor is he included among any of the other Ch'an sects recorded there. In this case, his absence suggests much more than intra-group conflict. Yen-shou's identity as a Ch'an master appears to be denied here by a compiler who represents the wider interests of the Ch'an school as a whole and recognizes the legitimacy of the Fa-yen sect.

We have noted above that Tsan-ning classified Yen-shou under the category of "Promoters of Works of Merit" in the SKSC, and that this classification had the effect of undermining the Ch'an school's claim over Yen-shou's identity as a Ch'an master. The Ch'an school's sensitivity to this situation is illustrated, for example, in Hui-hung's critique. In his *Lin-chien lu* (1123) Hui-hung openly challenged Tsan-ning's categorization and wrote,[21]

> Tsan-ning compiled the extensive *Sung kao-seng chuan*, utilizing ten categories for the purpose of classification. He placed Exegetes at the top. This is laughable. Moreover, he presented the Ch'an master Yen-tou Huo as a "Practitioner of Asceticism" and the Ch'an master Chih-chüeh (Yen-)shou as a "Promoter of Works of Merit". The great teacher Yün-men is chief among monks. He is contemporary with these people, but surprisingly (Tsan-ning) does not even mention him.

Furthermore, as if to restore the tarnished image of Yen-shou the Ch'an master, Hui-hung wrote the extensive biography of Yen-shou that appears in the CLSPC that is under examination here.

We noted above that a significant new development in the biographical image of Yen-shou appears in this biography by Hui-hung; this development, moreover, is preserved in the later records of the Ch'an school. We detect here a paradoxical situation that is frequently found in the history of religions: while in the CLSPC Hui-hung intended to restore the image of Yen-shou as a Ch'an master, the materials recorded there reflect new forces at work in the construction of Yen-shou's image. Increasingly, the formation of Yen-shou's image came under the direction of forces associated with Mt. T'ien-t'ai. Ultimately significant among these forces in the case of Yen-shou were those promoting Pure Land practices.

An emphasis on the Pure Land movement is characteristic of many T'ien-t'ai historiographical works of this period. It is in one such biographical collection documenting the strength of Pure Land beliefs, the *Lung-shu ching-*

t'u wen (LSCTW),[22] that the description of events associated with Yen-shou's renunciation of his career of a official to become a monk achieves what may be considered its standard form.

According to this source, Yen-shou, in his capacity as a government official, often took public funds in order to buy and release living things. The penalty for such a crime was death. When he summoned Yen-shou to receive his judgement, the Prince specifically sent his representative to gauge Yen-shou's reaction. If his countenance expressed apprehension, he was to be executed. If he was unaffected, the representative was to return and report this fact to the throne. When his execution was announced, Yen-shou's countenance was unaffected. As a result, the Prince pardoned him, and he became a monk. The incident, as it is related here, has interesting parallels in an earlier biographical account and in the writings of Yen-shou himself. As previously noted, in the SKSC account we encounter an enigmatic statement: "Yen-shou's facial expression did not change." In the LSCTW, this statement is directly tied to the judgement of Yen-shou. If he reacts when his death penalty is announced, this will be interpreted as an indication of guilt, as a sign that Yen-shou is still attached to life and not a true Buddhist.. If he does not react, this will indicate that his intentions were sincere and he was above reproach.

In the LSCTW's account of Yen-shou's renunciation of the career of a secular official, new elements are introduced which expand and alter not only the image of Yen-shou, but also the role of the ruler. The transition here revolves, as in the CLSPC biography, around Yen-shou's practice of buying of living things and setting them free, but in the account of the LSCTW it is in violation of Yen-shou's official capacity that he does so. Subsequently, the proscription of civil law figures prominently in the story. This incident becomes the occasion for depicting the dynamic tension between the compassionate Buddhist in the person of Yen-shou, and the prime arbitrator of secular matters, the Prince.[23]

As mentioned above, Yen-shou's own writings contain vague, yet suggestive, comments that parallel the details included in the account of his transition to becoming a monk in the LSCTW. In the *Wan-shan t'ung-kuei chi*, it is recounted how one may be protected from the misfortunes of burning in hell and may complete the primary cause of the life of wisdom by setting fish and birds free and saving people from the death penalty with a payment.[24] The two acts recommended here loosely parallel Yen-shou's deeds and the Prince's pardon in the LSCTW account. In other places in the *Wan-shan t'ung-kuei chi*, reference is made to facing the death penalty, and pardoning prisoners and rescuing people facing execution are encouraged as meritorious deeds.[25]

It is not clear what exact relation these passages in Yen-shou's *Wan-shan t'ung-kuei chi* have to the biographical account of Yen-shou's renunciation in the LSCTW biography. But the wide range of divergent stories that developed in later biographies indicates that to the authors of these biographies Yen-shou's renunciation of secular life was a mystery in need of a suitable explanation. They developed many stories to explain why Yen-shou gave up his career as a government official, and these stories naturally reflected the different orientations of the biographers. Since there stories were not primarily tied to the bare historical facts of Yen-shou's life itself but were fabricated by the tradition in an attempt to provide a persuasive explanation for his renunciation, it seems plausible to assume nonetheless that in their origin they must somehow be "true" to Yen-shou. I have tried to uncover certain passages in Yen-shou's own writings which might have provided the kernel around which the stories then collected. The parallels between certain details in the LSCTW biographies and the passages in Yen-shou's writings noted above may point to the source for this part of Yen-shou's biographical image.

The final portion of the LSCTW biography provides further evidence for our view that the description of events surrounding Yen-shou's renunciation in this biography reflects the influences of the Pure Land movement.[26] The story related here is about a monk who daily worships the *stupa* of Yen-shou. When asked his reason for doing this, he replies that in a previous life, while dwelling in the underworld, he noticed a painted image of a monk in the corner of the palace of King Yama, the Lord of the Underworld. King Yama himself came and prostrated himself before this image. Upon asking the officer in charge of the palace about the identity of this monk that even King Yama worshipped, he was informed that this is the Ch'an master Yen-shou of Yung-ming temple. The officer in charge further informed him that while common people regularly have to pass through this place, Yen-shou, as an exception, did not pass through the underworld and was able to attain directly a most favorable rebirth in the Pure Land.

This episode is interesting in that it offers an explanation for the process whereby Yen-shou became the object of a cult that centered around the worship of his *stupa*. Earlier in discussing the LSCTW's account of Yen-shou's renunciation, we discussed the story in which Yen-shou, hearing his own death sentence from the secular authorities, remains unaffected. It is possible to understand this story as also asserting that Yen-shou, having become in truth a religious man, was no longer subject to the sphere of the secular; the earthly ruler, who might even decree his death, in reality had no power over him. This theme is here reiterated more forcefully with Yama, the King of Death, actually submitting to Yen-shou. The comment in this story that Yen-shou did not pass through the underworld, the region of death, ought to be interpreted as saying that Yen-shou did not die as do ordinary mortals; he has achieved immortality by his rebirth in the Pure Land. This is the reason why Yama has no power over Yen-shou, who has conquered death utterly and completely. Having achieved this status, Yen-shou is not only honored as an object of worship, but also receives the supplications of others striving for rebirth in the Pure Land. This line of analysis points to another hypothesis: the LSCTW's account of Yen-shou's biography may in part reflect the aspirations of those who worshipped Yen-shou's *stupa*, and such stories about Yen-shou's conquest of death may have been transmitted by worshippers on pilgrimage to his *stupa*. With this second hypothesis our examination of the LSCTW account of Yen-shou's biography has suggested both a source for the stories about Yen-shou's renunciation in his own words and a means for the transmission, spread and growth of those stories in a context of pilgrimage to Yen-shou's *stupa*.

Beyond these more specific theories,this review of representative biographical accounts of Yen-shou's renunciation thus far points to one general conclusion: it is impossible to determine what events actually led to Yen-shou's decision to become a monk. Descriptions of these events in existing records are diverse and reflect the needs of later communities of Buddhist practitioners. Further evidence of the evolving attitudes toward Yen-shou, and the effect that these attitudes had on the way events in his life have been recorded, appears in descriptions of Yen-shou's religious career on Mt. T'ien-t'ai, to which we now turn.

2. *Accounts of Yen-shou's Religious Career on Mt. T'ien-t'ai and the Determination of his Scholastic Affiliation*

Because of its rich spiritual history, Mt. T'ien-t'ai served as an important religious centre in the Wu Yüeh region. Much of the enterprise of Wu Yüeh rulers in rebuilding the physical institutions of Buddhism in the region was aimed at restoring Mt. T'ien-t'ai, which had fallen into decay as a result of neglect and the ravages of war.[27] Because Yen-shou was a Buddhist monk in the Wu Yüeh region at this time, Mt. T'ien-t'ai naturally played a significant role in his career and appears prominently in his biographies. The nature of Yen-shou's activities and training on Mt. T'ien-t'ai, however, varies considerably in different accounts.

In most accounts Yen-shou's association with Mt. T'ien-t'ai commences after the period of his association with the Ch'an master Ts'ui-yen, under whose direction he initially received training as a Buddhist monk. In the earliest record,i.e., the SKSC,[28] Yen-shou's activities on Mt. T'ien-t'ai are only briefly mentioned. When he practiced meditation for ninety days on T'ien-chu peak, birds are said to have built nests in the folds of his robes. When he met Te-chao, Te-chao is said to have confirmed Yen-shou's realization. According to the SKSC, Yen-shou then retreated to Mt. Hsüeh-tou.

The other contemporary source, the CTCTL,[29] follows the SKSC in its outline of Yen-shou's activities, but makes more of Yen-shou's association with Te-chao, reflecting its own specific religious background as a work of the Fa-yen school of Ch'an Buddhism.

The story about Yen-shou's ninety day meditation at Mt. T'ien-t'ai during which birds built nests in his robes appears in the CTCTL virtually unchanged from the SKSC. The meeting with Te-chao, however, is more fully developed in the CTCTL than in the SKSC. It is through Te-chao, we are told, that the essence of Ch'an is transmitted to Yen-shou. Such elaboration here makes sense in terms of its compiler Tao-yüan's intention to verify that the correct line of Ch'an transmission passed from Te-chao to Yen-shou. During this encounter Te-chao predicts that Yen-shou will cause Buddhism to flourish in the future owing to his close relationship with the Wu Yüeh rulers, and secretly predicts that he will attain Buddhahood in the future. Predictions attributing the future success of Buddhism to a warm relationship with political rulers are characteristic of the Fa-yen sect.[30] The inclusion of such a prediction here is a device to strengthen Yen-shou's association with that sect.

On Mt. Hsüeh-tou, we are told, Yen-shou first dwelled as a Ch'an master and attracted many students. At this point the CTCTL biography records the poems and exchanges with students that were supposed to represent the unique character of Yen-shou's Ch'an teaching.

Later sources, particularly those associated with the rising popularity of the Pure Land movement, document a fuller set of activities for Yen-shou on Mt. T'ien-t'ai. It is particularly noteworthy that Yen-shou's activities on Mt. T'ien-t'ai in these accounts reflect different assumptions regarding Yen-shou's character and identity. An important source to document this observation is the *Lo-pang wen-lei* (LPWL).[31]

The identity of Yen-shou as a Ch'an master is not denied in the LPWL biography or in the LSCTW biography, the other Pure Land oriented biography of Yen-shou mentioned above. This indicates that the CTCTL claim was well established by this time. The LPWL accepts, along with the ordinary chronology of events that had naturally accumulated around the life of Yen-shou, his associations with Ts'ui-yen and Te-chao. These Ch'an masters, however, are only briefly mentioned, and the meeting with Te-chao is no longer presented as the culmination of his experience on Mt. T'ien-t'ai. In the LPWL account, Te-chao is no longer credited with affirming Yen-shou's attainments or predicting his extraordinary future. We might note here that these claims of the early accounts in the SKSC and CTCTL continued to be asserted in Ch'an sources. The LPWL biography merely states that through Te-chao, Yen-shou began to awaken to the essentials of the mind (*hsin-yao*). In the LPWL Yen-shou is said to have embarked on his ninety- day period of meditation resulting in birds nesting in his robes after the visit with Te-chao rather than before as in the earlier sources. The place of meditation is also different. In the LPWL it is the cave of Chih-i rather than T'ien-chu peak. These alterations reflect the overall tendency in the LPWL biography to strengthen Yen-shou's association with Mt. T'ien-t'ai and with the leading exponent of the T'ien-t'ai school, Chih-i, in order to demonstrate the precedence of Pure Land practice over *ch'an* contemplation in Yen-shou's life.

In the LPWL biography, the ninety-day meditation constitutes the prelude to the culmination of Yen-shou's experience on Mt. T'ien-t'ai which centers around three episodes involving divine intervention. The stories of these episodes explain Yen-shou's "conversion" to Pure Land practice. In Pure Land inspired biographies Yen-shou's "conversion" to Pure Land practice constitutes a crucial incident in his life, occupying a place similar to that of his achieving enlightenment in Ch'an biographies. The altered emphasis and arrangement of events, as well as the addition of hitherto unrecorded features of Yen-shou's life on Mt. T'ien-t'ai, must be understood with this perspective in mind.

The story of the first episode tells of an incident that supposedly occurred while Yen-shou was performing the Lotus penitential rituals[32] at Kuo-ch'ing temple. During the night, while performing the ritual, Yen-shou is said to have witnessed a god-like man enter clutching a halberd. In surprise, Yen-shou asks the intruder what authority permits him to interrupt Yen-shou's practice. In response, the intruder claims that he has come as a result of Yen-shou's large accumulation of meritorious deeds that lead to rebirth in the Pure Land. The implication seems to be that Yen-shou has practiced *nien-fo*, etc., for a long time and achieved a very high level of accomplishment. The gods, in their concern for Yen-shou's safety, thus have sent a guardian to protect him.[33]

In the story of the second episode, Yen-shou, while circumambulating an image of the bodhisattva P'u-hsien (Samantabhadra) in the middle of the night, suddenly sees a lotus appear in his hand. The lotus had been offered earlier to the image of P'u-hsien. This event makes Yen-shou recall two vows which he had made before: vows to recite the *Lotus Sutra* throughout his life and to devote his life to benefitting all varieties of sentient beings.

After this second episode Yen-shou yearned to carry out the two vows that he has recalled, but he also enjoyed the tranquility of meditation (*ch'an*). He became hesitant, and was unable to decide which course he should follow. In order to resolve his dilemma, Yen-shou is said to have climbed up to the meditation hall of Chih-i (*Chih-che ch'an-yüan*) and written out two divination lots. On one was written: "single-minded practice of *ch'an* meditation (*ch'an-ting*)"; on the other: "solemnly adorn the Pure Land through chanting *sutras* and a myriad of good deeds". Through deep reflection, Yen-shou decided that if one of these two alternatives was the practice to which he should devote his life, he would draw the same lot seven times in succession. After praying to the Buddhas and patriarchs, Yen-shou is said to have drawn the second lot the required seven times. Clearly, this was an indication of divine will. In accordance with the lot, Yen-shou chose the practice of *sutra* recitation and the myriad good deeds that lead to rebirth in the Pure Land. It is significant that a reference to Chih-i appears; Chih-i gives his name to the meditation hall where the resolution of Yen-shou's dilemma takes place. The story might be saying implicitly that Chih-i himself would have approved this resolution in favour of Pure Land practices; perhaps this was the view of the Pure Land movement being sponsored from Mt. T'ien-t'ai at the time of the development of this story. This conclusion is interesting especially if we remember that while both the practice of meditation and Pure Land practices occupy important places in the T'ien-t'ai tradition, meditation along with teaching of doctrines constitute the two basic pillars of the T'ien-t'ai system established by Chih-i.

Following this decisive event, Yen-shou travelled around the Chin-hua and T'ien-chu peaks and recited *sutras* for three years, as if to carry out the letter of his divinely sanctioned vow. At this point in the LPWL, a story about Kuan-yin's annointing Yen-shou's mouth with sweet dew during *ch'an* contemplation (*ch'an-kuan*) appears. Hereafter Yen-shou developed the eloquence of Kuan-yin. A version of this story appeared earlier, in the LSCTW, in a different context.[34] In the LSCTW, the story directly connects Yen-shou's vast scholastic and literary achievement with divine inspiration from Kuan-yin.[35] Perhaps this mythologizing was also in keeping with Yen-shou's new identity as a Pure Land practitioner. In this story the LPWL's biography recognizes that Yen-shou's Buddhist practice included *ch'an* meditation, but at the same time shifts the emphasis in Yen-shou's image from *ch'an* meditation and scholastic writing to the mythological world of the Pure Land movement.[36]

The LPWL biography which promotes the new image of Yen-shou as a Pure Land practitioner mentions Yen-shou's career on Mt. Hsüeh-tou only in passing. This treatment contrasts with that of the Ch'an inspired biographies where, it is to be recalled, this stage of Yen-shou's life figures prominently. Yet, having made the early association with Mt. T'ien-t'ai the focal point for Yen-shou's "conversion" to Pure Land practice, Pure Land biographers were faced with the problem of explaining Yen-shou's career on Mt. Hsüeh-tou adequately. A solution to this problem which is compatible with the new image of Yen-shou is recorded in another work, the *Shih-men cheng-t'ung* (SMCT).

Ch'an biographies describe Yen-shou on Mt. Hsüeh-t'ou as a Ch'an master. In contrast, the SMCT account presents a new image of Yen-shou the Pure Land practitioner on Mt. Hsüeh-tou. At night, it is recorded here, Yen-shou invoked (*nien*) the Buddha Amitabha and circumambulated his image (*hsing-tao*). It is on Mt. Hsüeh-tou, according to the SMCT, that Yen-shou first makes a vow to practice a daily routine of 108 good deeds.[37]

Other parts of the LPWL biography are also in keeping with the new image of Yen-shou as a Pure Land practitioner. Yen-shou's appointment to the Ling-yin ssu, a Ch'an temple, is not mentioned at all. Instead, attention is focused on his activity at the Yung-ming temple, and according to the LPWL, Yen-shou's activity here is quite different from that attributed to him in Ch'an sources.

The LPWL biography's account of Yen-shou's activity at the Yung-ming temple nonetheless still contains some distinctively Ch'an oriented material. In answering a question from a student in his capacity as chief priest of Yung-ming temple, Yen-shou pointed to the mind as the fundamental source (*tsung*) and emphasized enlightenment. Ch'an oriented material, however, is here overshadowed by the emphasis on Yen-shou's Pure Land practices. We are told that in the Yung-ming temple Yen-shou performed his routine of 108 practices everyday. Furthermore, each day at dusk Yen-shou went to an isolated peak to practice ambulatory (*hsing-tao*) *nien-fo*. Those within hearing distance are said to have heard the sound of conch shells and heavenly music on the mountain. Moreover, according to the LPWL, Yen-shou's Pure Land orientated efforts did not escape the attention of earthly authorities. Prince Chung-i admired Yen-shou, saying that since ancient times no one had sought the Pure Land so fervently as did Yen-shou. Consequently, the Prince constructed for Yen-shou a special hall for adoring and worshipping the Pure Land. In this way, secular authority is made to figure prominently in the LPWL biography in confirming the validity of Yen-shou's experience. In the LPWL this religious experience rests ultimately in Yen-shou's Pure Land practice.

D. Conclusions

It has been the underlying assumption of this paper that recorded accounts of the lives of Chinese Buddhist monks were formed and reformed in specific contexts dominated by the interests of different Buddhist communities and are thus more a direct reflection of the larger history of Chinese Buddhism than they are of the specific circumstances of any single monk's life. These communities developed biographical images of monks who were important to them by selecting certain materials from available sources and sometimes generating new stories about these monks. Available sources would, of course, have included a store of historical fact, but would not have placed any particular emphasis on historical fact or distinguished in any obvious way fact from story. Newly developed stories might also, as shown above, exhibit specific links to the subject's life and written works. Collections of these biographies, many of which explicitly profess specific religious points of view, are to be understood, then, as collections of highly selective and clearly manipulated texts. By comparing all the existing biographies of a given monk the modern scholar can study how the Chinese Buddhist tradition has appropriated the life of this monk through complex processes in which the meaning of that life was interpreted and reinterpreted from different points of view. These points of view, often in sharp conflict with each other, were those of a variety of Buddhist communities that emerged in the course of the long history of this tradition. Such a study often reveals the richness of the tradition and its resourcefulness in generating a variety of images of the same monk. These images, however, it must be repeatedly stressed have often little to do with the history of the subject himself.

The case of Yung-ming Yen-shou illustrates this situation in a variety of ways. The nature of the sources for the study of Yen-shou's biography is such that the actual life of Yen-shou remains shrouded in obscurity. There is no satisfactory method to remedy this situation. What has been recorded in biographical collections of Buddhist monks appears to have been produced by later Buddhist communities and is significantly coloured by the aspirations of these communities. My hypothesis for explaining the readiness with which a figure like Yen-shou could be creatively molded by a biographer into an image that suited the biographer's particular religious needs is as follows.In spite of his obvious importance as a major scholar and Buddhist leader, Yen-shou's career was characterized by a multivalence bordering on ambivalence. He lived at a time when the old institutions and practices of T'ang Buddhist life had declined and a new form of Chinese Buddhism that was to emerge later was not yet clearly defined. The rulers of the small Wu-yüeh kingdom in which Yen-shou lived were known for supporting Buddhism, however, and this was an active and creative period in the history of the religion. Given this context, it would not be surprising if Yen-shou's productive life revealed both the old and the seeds of the new. Yen-shou in fact produced a massive doctrinal discussion of the concept of mind more or less in the style of traditional Chinese Buddhist scholarship (*Tsung ching lu*, "Records of [the One Mind], the Source of All Things and the Mirror That Illumines All Things") . At the same time his writings are characterized by a diversity that partly prefigures the tendencies in Chinese Buddhism that were to become more prominent later.[38] This diversity of Yen-shou's intellectual life made the task of writing his biography a more complex task. It was difficult to establish a consensus as to what Yen-shou's important achievements were and more generally what kind of Buddhist monk he was. Different biographers, reflecting the biases of their own communities, saw the meaning of Yen-shou's life differently. This situation explains why his biographical image fluctuates so widely. Attention to the background of the biographers, therefore is essential to help us make sense of the way in which they fashioned Yen-shou's image.

What is the significance of this analysis for the study of Chinese Buddhist biography in general? This analysis teaches us that we should be very cautious in reading Chinese Buddhist biographies as historical records. Historians who read these records simply to learn historical facts in the lives of the subjects must begin by taking account of the inherent biases of these records. Historians of religion, on the other hand, should study Chinese Buddhist biographical records from a viewpoint that encompasses a wider range of questions and at the same time is more open to the religious motives that lie behind their composition. Such a viewpoint will enable us to interpret Chinese Buddhist biographies not primarily as histories of the subjects treated there but as a form of religious literature reflecting larger issues in the development of religion. Legendary materials will also be more meaningfully interpreted as an integral part of the biography as whole.

The legendary materials in Chinese Buddhist biographical records draw attention, with striking vividness, to significant aspects of their subject's lives that the biographer particularly wishes his audience to see. Moreover, as this paper has illustrated, the importance of particular legends in a given biography sometimes becomes clear only after we have examined the views of the Buddhist community that produced the particular version of the biography in which they are found. Sometimes legendary stories represent the arbitration of conflict. In the case of Yen-shou, repeated and highly diverse attempts to define the nature of his life produced a large body of a legendary stories concerning his life. These legendary stories express the issue at hand in a stylized, sometimes abstract, and often symbolic form, but always in a way that stands out within the biography itself. Future research into the lives of Chinese Buddhist monks might pay greater attention to this material and the contexts that produced it. We may then come to a fuller appreciation of the value for the historian of religion of the vast body of existing Chinese Buddhist biographical literature.

Notes

1. For an introduction to the conventions governing Chinese biographical writing, see the article by D. C. Twitchett entitled, "Chinese Biographical Writing", ch. 7 of *Historians of China and Japan*, Beasley and Pulleyblank, eds., pp. 95-114.

2. A recent study of Yen-shou's life in Shih Heng-ching's thesis, *The Ch'an-Pure Land Synthesis in China: With Special Reference to Yung-ming Yen-shou*, pp. 132ff., University of Wisconsin-Madison PhD, 1984, treats Chinese Buddhist biographical records in the naive manner described above. While not entirely undiscriminating, Shih Heng-ching reads the Yen-shou biographies largely as reporting reliable historical facts regarding Yen-shou himself. There is little critical evaluation of the documents as historical sources for reconstructing the life of Yen-shou himself. Consequently, even later embellishments are read as historically dependable descriptions of words and deeds of Yen-shou himself. There is little appreciation of the role that later Buddhist community may have played in shaping the "facts" recorded in these biographies.

3. Yen-shou was awarded status as a patriarch in both the Ch'an and Pure Land schools.

4. For a discussion of the meaning of this term, see Frank E. Reynolds and Donald Capps, eds., *The Biographical Process (Studies in the History and Psychology of Religion)*, The Hague, 1976, "Introduction", pp. 27-30. The following discussion may be of particular use to the reader (from p. 28).

> ...many of those who have studied biographical images have taken some account of the fact that such images have both a mythic and an historical aspect. And many who have concentrated on the study of individual lives have recognized that these lives have been constituted by an intricate interweaving of mythic, paradigmatic, and historical elements. However, without denying that the more sensitive scholars on each side of the division have been concerned with both myth and history, it is clear that those who have been concerned with biographic images have been primarily oriented toward myth, whereas those who have been basically engaged in the study of individual lives have been oriented toward history.

5. The problem of lineage had traditionally been the focus of controversy in the Ch'an school. Works like the *Chuan fa-pao chi*, the *Leng-chia shih-tzu chi*, and the *Li-tai fa-pao chi*, represent the efforts of different factions within Ch'an to

resolve the issue of legitimate lineage in their favour. The sources documenting this controversy are too numerous to mention here. The standard introduction in English is Philip Yampolsky's book, *The Platform Sutra of the Sixth Patriarch*, Columbia, 1967.

6. Chapter II of my PhD dissertation, *The Meaning of Myriad Good Deeds: A Study of Yung-ming Yen-shou and the Wan-shan t'ung-kuei chi ("Treatise on the Common End of Myriad Good Deeds")*, McMaster University, 1987, pp. 38ff.

7. *Chung-kuo fo-chiao*, vol. 2, pp. 237-39.

8. The sequence of events in Yen-shou's life may be divided into six periods: (1) Pre-monastic Period (birth, youth, officialdom); (2) Lung-ts'e Temple Period (study under Ch'an master Ts'ui-yen); (3) Tenure on Mt. T'ien-t'ai (study under Te-chao); (4) Period as Teacher on Mt. Hsüeh-tou; (5) Period as Chief Priest at Ling-yin and Yung-ming Temples; (6) Death on Mt. T'ien-t'ai.

9. *Taisho shinshu daizokyo* (T), vol. 50, p. 887a-b.

10. The biography of Ch'an master Ts'ui-yen is contained in the *Tsu-t'ang chi*, ch. 10, and the CTCTL, ch. 18

11. For a discussion of the special circumstances surrounding the state support of Buddhism in the Wu Yüeh kingdom, see my PhD dissertation, *op. cit.*, pp. 27-37.

Tsan-ning (919-1001) lived on Mt. T'ien-t'ai and had intimate connections with many of the same people as Yen-shou. From this it can be assumed that Tsan-ning had personal knowledge of Yen-shou's activities (see Hatanaka Joen, "Goetsu no bukkyo", *Indogaku bukkyogaku kenkyu*, v. II, no. 1, Sept. 1953, p. 322). On Tsan-ning and his times, see Makita Tairyo, "Sannei to sono jidai", *Chugoku kinseibukkyo shi kenkyu*, pp. 96-133.

12. T 51, pp. 421c-422a. For an English translation, see Chang Chung-yuan, *Original Teachings of Ch'an Buddhism*, New York, 1969, pp. 250-53.

Little is known of Tao-yüan. He is said to have been a fellow student with Yen-shou under Te-chao, which would indicate the likelihood of personal contact between them (see Ishii Shudo, "Eimei enju den", *Komazawa daigaku daigakuin bukkyogaku kenkyugo nenpo*, no. 3, March 15, 1969, p. 78).

13. HTC 137, *Ch'an lin seng pao chuan* section, pp. 239b-41a.

14. T 48, p. 967c.

15. This is according to the list of works attributed to Yen-shou at the end of the *Tzu-hsing lu*, HTC 111, p. 83b-d.

16. See the *Chih-che ta-shih pieh-chuan*, T 50, no. 2050; and the *Kuo-ch'ing pai lu*, ch. 4, T 46, pp. 822b ff.

17. Biographies of Te-chao are contained in SKSC ch. 13 and CTCTL ch. 25. The circumstances surrounding his life have been reviewed by Hatanaka, *op. cit.*, pp. 308-22.

18. The SKSC utilizes ten categories to classify the biographies of eminent Buddhist monks: (1) Translators *(i-ching)*, (2) Exegetes *(i-chieh)*, (3) Meditators *(hsi-ch'an)*, (4) Disciplinarians *(ming-lü)*, (5) Dharma Protectors *(hu-fa)*, (6) Miracle Workers *(kan-t'ung)*, (7) Self Immolators *(i-shen)*, (8) Cantors *(tu-sung)*, (9) Promoters of Works of Merit *(hsing-fu)*, (10) Various Categories of Invokers of Virtue *(sheng-te)*.

19. For example, the *Chien-chung ching-kuo hsü-teng lu*, compiled by Wei-po in 1101 (HTC 136), and the *Chia-t'ai p'u-teng*, compiled by Cheng-shou between 1146 and 1208 (HTC 137).

20. Members of the Fa-yen sect appear in ch. 27, HTC 125, p. 302c.

21. HTC 148, p. 294b.

22. T 47, p. 268b-c.

23. However, the way in which the drama is played out in this case is quite interesting in its deviation from the norm. Here the confrontation is not simply one of secular authority vs. religious authority. Yen-shou, to be sure, is depicted as a paradigmatic Buddhist. He is moved by Buddhist compassion, and in his Buddhist wisdom, death holds no sway over him. In his ability to face death calmly, he is depicted as one who has conquered death. The prince, on the other hand, in serving as the supreme authority in matters where secular as well as religious affairs are concerned, is portrayed not only as one capable of pardoning Yen-shou from his civil offence, but also as one capable of determining the validity of Yen-shou's enlightenment. In performing this latter function, one has the impression that the prince is assuming a role which is traditionally reserved for the enlightened Buddhist master who, in accord with his enlightened state, is able to validate the experience of his students. The role of the prince as arbitrator in affairs secular and religious is a common feature in stories associated with the Wu Yüeh kingdom. These stories are examined in an unpublished study of mine entitled, "Buddhism and the Wu Yüeh Government

in Tenth Century China (as Expressed through Religious Stories in the Lives of Monarchs and Monks)." This served as the basis for a presentation at the Canadian Society for the Study of Religion panel: "Religion and Politics in Chinese History", University of Guelph, June 1984.

24. T 48, p. 981c.

25. T 48, p. 968c and p. 982b.

26. T 47, p. 268b-c.

27. The Buddhist proclivities of Wu Yüeh rulers, including their efforts to restore T'ien-t'ai, are discussed by Abe Choichi, *Chugoku zenshushi no kenkyu*, pp. 81-176; also see Hatanaka, *op. cit.*

28. T 50, p. 887a-b.

29. T 51, pp. 421c-422a.

30. For example, in addition to Te-chao's prediction about Yen-shou, he is also said to have predicted future rulership for Prince Chung-i, at which time the prince would promote the Buddha-Dharma in Wu Yüeh (SKSC ch. 13, T 50, p. 789b).

31. T 47, p. 195a-b.

32. The *Fa-hua ch'an* is a ritual whereby one combines recitation of the *Lotus Sutra (Fa-hua ching)* with the confession of sins. The ritual was developed by Chih-i (see the *Fa-hua san-mei ch'an-i*, T 46, no. 1941) based on the *P'u-hsien kuan ching* and the *Fa-hua ching*.

33. This, at least, is how I tentatively interpret this episode, without knowing more precisely the function of guardian deities in stories such as this and the circumstances through which such a story became associated with Yen-shou.

34. The LSCTW passage is found in T.47, p.268b, l.24f.

35. The role of Kuan-yin (Avalokitesvara) is mysterious here when one considers the fact that another deity Pien-tsai-t'ien (Sarasvati) is more traditionally associated with this role [The literal meaning of the Chinese translation Pien-ts'ai-t'ien is "God of Eloquence"]. Other considerations, however, make Kuan-yin a most appropriate choice in this instance. Kuan-yin appears as an important figures in two main traditions in Chinese Buddhism: one derived from

the Lotus Sutra; the other from the Pure Land Sutra. The appearance of Kuan-yin in Yen-shou's biography serves to strengthen Yen-shou's connection to these two traditions. Forces in Chinese Buddhism at this time were joining the fortunes of the Pure Land movement to the scholastic enterprise of the T'ien-t'ai school . These same forces may have inspired this new development in Yen-shou's biography.

36. HTC 130, pp. 449-50.

37. According to tradition, Yen-shou's propensity for practice manifested itself through 108 deeds. This fact is specifically noted in several of Yen-shou's biographies. In addition, there is a text called the *Tzu hsing lu* ("Record of Practices") purporting to enumerate the details of Yen-shou's 108 deeds, HTC 111, pp. 77-84.

38. I have explored this hypothesis in a more systematic manner in the PhD dissertation cited above.

CHARACTERS

Abe Choichi 阿部肇一

Ch'an 禪

ch'an-kuan 禪觀

Ch'an-lin seng-pao chuan 禪林僧寶傳

ch'an-ting 禪定

Ch'ien-t'ang 錢塘

Ch'ing 清

Ch'uan-fa cheng-tsung chi 傳法正宗記

Che-chiang t'ung-chih 浙江通志

Cheng-shou 正受

Chia-t'ai p'u-teng 嘉泰普燈

Chien-chung ching-kuo hsü-teng lu 建中靖國續燈錄

Chih-che ta-shih pieh-chuan 智者大師別傳

Chih-che ch'an-yüan 智者禪院

Chih-chüeh 智覺

Chih-i 智顗

Chin-hua 金華

Ching-t'u sheng-hsien lu 淨土聖賢錄

Ching-te ch'üan-teng lu 景德傳燈錄

Ching-tz'u ssu-chih 淨慈寺志

Chuan fa-pao chi 傳法寶紀

Chugoku zenshushi no kenkyu 中國禪宗史の研究

Chugoku kinseibukkyo shi kenkyu 中國近世佛教史研究

Chung-i 忠懿

Chung-kuo fo-chiao 中國佛教

Eimei enju den 永明延壽傳

Fa-hua san-mei ch'an-i 法華三昧懺儀

Fa-hua ch'an 法華懺

Fa-hua ching 法華經

Fa-yen Wen-i 法眼文益

Fa-yen 法眼

fang-sheng hui 放生會

fang-sheng chih ch'ih 放生之池

Fang-sheng wen 放生文

Fo-tsu li-tai t'ung-tsai 佛祖歷代通載

Fo-tsu t'ung-chi 佛祖統紀

Goetsu no bukkyo 呉越の佛教

Hang-chou fu-chih 杭州府志

Hatanaka Joen 畑中淨圓

hsi-ch'an 習禪

Hsien-ch'un lin-an chih 咸淳臨安志

hsing-fu 興福

hsing-tao 行道

Hsüeh-t'ou ssu-chih 雪竇寺志

Hsüeh-tou 雪竇

hu-fa 護法

Hua-t'ing 華亭

Hui-hung 慧洪

i-chieh 義解

i-ching 譯經

i-shen 遺身

Indogaku bukkyogaku kenkyu 印度學 教學研究

Ishii Shudo 石井修道

Jen-t'ien pao-chien 人天寶鑑

kan-t'ung 感通

Komazawa daigaku daigakuin bukkyogaku kenkyugo nenpo 駒沢大学仏教學研究所年報

Kuan-yin 觀音

Kuo-ch'ing 國清

Kuo-ch'ing pai lu 國清百錄

Leng-chia shih-tzu chi 楞伽師資記

Li Tsun-hsü 李遵勗

Li-tai fa-pao chi 歷代佛寶記

Lien-teng hui-yao 聯燈會要

Lin-chien lu 林間錄

Ling-yin 靈隱

Ling-yin ssu-chih 靈隱寺志

Lo-pang wen-lei 樂邦文類

Lu-shan lien-tsung pao-chien 廬山蓮宗寶鑑

Lung-shu ching-t'u wen 龍舒淨土文

Lung-ts'e 龍冊

Makita Tairyo 牧田諦亮

Ming 明

ming-lü 明律

nien 念

nien-fo 念佛

P'u-hsien 普賢

P'u-hsien kuan ching 普賢觀經

Sannei to sono jidai 賛寧とその時代

Shen-seng chuan 神僧傳

sheng-te 聲德

Shih-kuo ch'un-ch'iu 十國春秋

Shih-men cheng-t'ung 釋門正統

Shih-shih chi-ku lüeh 釋氏稽古略

Sung 宋

Sung-kao-seng chuan 宋高僧傳

Szu-ming shan-chih 四明山志

T'ang 唐

T'ien-sheng kuang-teng lu 天聖廣燈錄

T'ien-t'ai 天台

T'ien-t'ai Te-chao 天台德韶

Tao-yüan 道原

Te-chao 德韶

Ts'ui-yen Ling-ts'an 翠巖令參

Ts'ui-yen 翠巖

Tsan-ning 贊寧

Tsu-t'ang chi 祖堂集

Tsung ching lu 宗鏡錄

tu-sung 讀誦

Tzu hsing lu 自行錄

Wan-shan t'ung-kuei chi 萬善同歸集

Wei-po 惟白

Wen-mu 文穆

Wu Yüeh 吳越

Wu-teng hui-yao 五燈會要

Yen-shou 延寿

Yüan 元

Yün-lin ssu-chih 雲林寺志

Yün-men 雲門

Yung-ming Yen-shou 永明延寿

Yung-ming tao-chi 永明道蹟